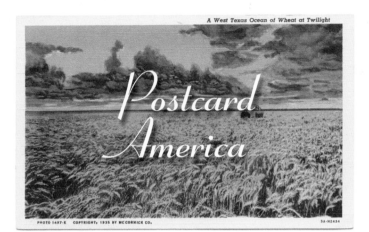

A West Texas Ocean of Wheat at Twilight

Postcard
America

PHOTO 1497-E   COPYRIGHT, 1935 BY MC CORMICK CO.   5A-H2434

POSTCARD AMERICA

Curt Teich AND THE *Imaging* OF A *Nation*

1931–1950

JEFFREY L. MEIKLE

University of Texas Press
AUSTIN

The publication of this book was supported in part by the UT Press Fine Arts Endowment, funded by Frances Dittmer, Michael L. Klein, Christine Mattsson McHale, and Jean Rather. The University of Texas Press and the author also gratefully acknowledge financial assistance provided for the publication of this book from the President's Office at the University of Texas at Austin.

THIS LAND IS YOUR LAND
Words and Music by Woody Guthrie
WGP/TRO-© Copyright 1956, 1958, 1970, 1972, and 1995 (copyrights renewed). Woody Guthrie Publications, Inc. & Ludlow Music, Inc., New York, NY. Administered by Ludlow Music, Inc.
Used by permission.

Unless otherwise credited, images are from the author's collection and are in the public domain, except for a few whose copyright holders proved impossible to locate.

Requests for permission to reproduce material from this work should be sent to:
Permissions | University of Texas Press
P.O. Box 7819 | Austin, TX 78713-7819
http://utpress.utexas.edu/index.php/rp-form

∞ The paper used in this book meets the minimum requirements of ANSI/NISO Z39.48-1992 (R1997) (Permanence of Paper).

Library of Congress Cataloging-in-Publication Data

Meikle, Jeffrey L., author.
    Postcard America : Curt Teich and the imaging of a nation, 1931–1950 / Jeffrey L. Meikle. — First edition.
        pages   cm
    Includes bibliographical references and index.
    ISBN 978-0-292-72661-1 (cloth : alk. paper) — ISBN 978-1-4773-0859-2 (library e-book) — ISBN 978-1-4773-0860-8 (nonlibrary e-book)
    1. Postcards—United States—History—20th century. 2. Curt Teich Postcard Collection (Lake County Museum). 3. Postcards—Collectors and collecting—United States. I. Curt Teich Postcard Collection (Lake County Museum). II. Title.
    NC1875.U6T456 2015
    741.6'830973—dc23   2015023704

CONTENTS

Acknowledgments vii

1. "They Do Say It's Real": An Introduction to Linen Postcards 1

2. Curt Teich and the Early History of Postcards 13

3. The Linen Postcard: Innovation and Aesthetics 35

4. Landscapes in Linen Postcards: A National Imaginary 69

Portfolio 1: Landscapes 83

Representative Vistas 87
The Southwest: A Regional Aesthetic 119
Travel and Tourism 137
Scenic People 171
Resources 211
Infrastructure and Transportation 241

5. Cityscapes in Linen Postcards: Images of Modernity 275

Portfolio 11: Cityscapes 293

Overviews 297
Skyscrapers 315
Main Streets 335
Landmarks 355
Recreation 383
World's Fairs 401
Accommodations 415

6. From a Rearview Mirror: Contemporary Reflections 441

Notes 465 | *Illustration Credits* 493 | *Index* 495

ACKNOWLEDGMENTS

THIS BOOK HAS BEEN LONG IN THE MAKING BUT NOT INTENsively so until about five years ago. I am most indebted to my wife, Alice, who has been living with postcards for nearly as long as I have, at first with patient indulgence but eventually as an enthusiastic collector of early twentieth-century foreign cards. She has offered valuable suggestions throughout the process and commented perceptively on multiple drafts. Her expertise in genealogical research enriched my understanding of the early American years of Curt Teich and enabled me to contact the son of his leading sales agent, G. I. Pitchford. For so many reasons, this book is for Alice.

To understand how linen postcards were produced, one must consult the Curt Teich Postcard Archives at the Lake County Discovery Museum in Wauconda, Illinois. During several visits there I benefited from the knowledge and tireless assistance of Katherine Hamilton Smith, Debra Gust, and Heather Johnson. Robert Pitchford welcomed me into his home in Palm Desert, California, to examine his father's photographs and papers. Bob and his wife, Vera, shared family stories and generously submitted to being interviewed, along with Bob's sister, the late Marilyn June Maurer. Lawrence Tichnor and Walter Harles offered first-person accounts of the proprietary process of preparing the printing plates for linen postcards. Axel Plank shared his knowledge of the early postcards of Lobenstein. Alan Petrulis, creator of the superb website of the Metropolitan Postcard Club of New York City, offered convincing opinions on the linen printing process.

Comments on sections of the manuscript from Bob Abzug, Andi Gustavson, Steve Hoelscher, and Robert Jackson clarified my thinking. My daughter, Vanessa Meikle Schulman, an art historian, offered a reading of the first half of the manuscript that altered my drafting of the second half. Sally Clarke posed insightful questions about the economics of postcards in response to an early essay. Lisa Schrenk helped with a vexing problem of visual interpretation. Fellow participants in the Humanities Institute Faculty Seminar at the University of Texas, in particular Janet Staiger and Polly Strong, critiqued my presentation and offered useful suggestions. Much later I benefited from perceptive comments from two outside readers, Miles Orvell and one who remains anonymous. Over the years, Tim Davis, Victor Margolin, and the late Peter Hales offered advice and encouragement.

Two early attempts to visualize this project as a whole and drafts of two sections were initially prepared for presentation as papers. I would like to acknowledge invitations to present the annual Reyner Banham Memorial Lecture for

2000 at the Victoria & Albert Museum and to present papers at three conferences: "Representation and Decoration in a Postmodern Age" at the University of Würzburg; "Public Spaces and the Ideology of Place in American Culture," sponsored by the Bavarian American Academy in Munich; and the "Fifteenth Maple Leaf & Eagle Conference on North American Studies" at the University of Helsinki. I also benefited from comments on lectures presented at the Buell Center for the Study of American Architecture at Columbia University, the annual meeting of the American Studies Association of Korea, the University of Southern Denmark, Doshisha University in Kyoto, and the Corcoran Gallery of Art.

From fellow postcard collectors and dealers I have absorbed much information and opinion, mostly through casual conversations at the Capital of Texas Postcard Club's annual shows. I would particularly like to acknowledge Ned Coleman, Richard Eisenhour, Larry Gretsky, Joe Horn, Bing McClellan, and Bill Petersen, some of whom might be surprised to find their names here.

Finally, I would like to thank the University of Texas Press, which has been everything an author could wish. Theresa May expressed enthusiasm for the project early on and encouraged me as I began writing in earnest. Robert Devens took over as editor after Theresa's retirement and saw me through the final stages of writing and revision with astute suggestions and good humor. I would like to thank the copyeditor, Gloria Thomas, whose many small improvements yielded a more readable book. Lynne Chapman, the production editor, supervised the overall flow of a complicated project. Finally, Ellen McKie, the design and production manager, created a book design that highlights the unique appearance of linen postcards.

MIDTOWN NEW YORK CITY "THE GREAT WHITE WAY"

Postcard
America

AS SEEN FROM THE EMPIRE STATE BUILDING OBSERVATORY AT NIGHT, NEW YORK CITY   3A-H654

1

"They Do Say It's Real"

AN INTRODUCTION TO LINEN POSTCARDS

EARLY IN MARCH 1937 A WOMAN IN WESTERN New York received a colorful postcard offering a vivid contrast to the gloom of late winter (fig. 1.1). Sent from Tucson, Arizona, the card illustrates a radiant desert landscape in nearby Sahuaro National Monument. Several majestic saguaro cactuses stand tall against a sky artfully streaked with reds, yellows, and purples. Long shadows, anticipating a gorgeous sunset, cross a dirt road curving toward a distant horizon of purple mountains. Although the recipient's reaction to the card is unknown, the sender conveyed something of her state of mind in the fragmentary style of most such messages. "How come I haven't heard from you," she asked, "do I owe you a letter (as usual)?" Her question demonstrates a basic function of postcards, reminding friends or relatives that one is thinking of them without having to say anything more. She also offered evidence of a common problem with popular forms of visual representation. "Haven't seen this," she admitted, referring to the card's desert scene, "but they do say it's real."[1]

Her expression of doubt may merely indicate a belief that "seeing is believing." From our perspective, however, the postcard's image, composed of bold dark lines contrasting with delicate color washes,

669   SAHUARO NATIONAL MONUMENT, NEAR TUCSON, ARIZONA   6A-H715

FIG. 1.1. "Sahuaro National Monument, near Tucson, Arizona," Teich 6A-H715, 1936

falls midway between the apparent realism of a color photograph and the imaginative license of a watercolor or pastel. An examination of the card's surface reveals an embossed pattern of delicate parallel lines running horizontally and vertically, some more prominent than others, suggesting the weave of an artist's canvas, on which the image is printed. Seen through twenty-first-century eyes, this image represents the general idea of a desert landscape but hardly seems a photographic slice of a particular moment of reality. Even so, this postcard and thousands of others comprise a popular full-color portrayal of the United States during an era often later envisioned as existing in monotone black-and-white. If these cards seem now to fall short of realism, they must have been accepted in their own time as at least approximating reality.

Linen postcards, so called for their embossed surfaces resembling linen cloth, dominated the American market for landscape view cards from 1931 into the early 1950s. By then, competing cards known as "chromes," with shiny surfaces based on Kodachrome color transparencies, were in the process of replacing them. The linen variety, so unlike any other postcards before or since, was originated by Curt Teich & Co. of Chicago and widely imitated by other printers. Based on retouched black-and-white photographs, linen cards were printed by offset lithography on inexpensive card stock in vivid, exaggerated colors. Teich's

C.122—DELAWARE RIVER BRIDGE CONNECTING PHILADELPHIA, PA. AND CAMDEN, N. J.

3A-H963

Fig. 1.2. "Delaware River Bridge Connecting Philadelphia, Pa. and Camden, N.J.,"
Teich 3A-H963, 1933

sales booklets celebrated the "striking note of smartness" of the "linenized effect" and praised these "beautiful miniature paintings" as the most "aristocratic of all post cards."[2] In fact, however, they were printed by the millions, were often sold for just a penny, and were sometimes given away by businesses as promotional items. Linen postcards offered a unique, recognizable vision of America. Whether representing natural landscapes, roadside attractions, or marvels of modern technology, the miniature images of linen view cards, about 3½ by 5½ inches in size, portrayed the American scene as shimmering with promise during the uncertain times of the Great Depression and World War II (fig. 1.2). Their saturated colors provided a popular view of the United States not displayed in grainy newspaper photos, high-contrast *Life* magazine photos, or the stark documentary work of photographers such as Dorothea Lange and Walker Evans.

These colorful postcards remained submerged for decades, hidden away in neglected albums and shoeboxes. Only recently has this alternative vision risen into popular and historical consciousness. Some linen cards have entered museum collections or historical archives after the deaths of original purchasers or recipients. Descendants have inherited and kept others. Most cards that survived natural attrition by now have passed to dealers and collectors through estate sales and auctions. Although postcard collectors have existed since the early 1900s, linen cards have attained status as true collectibles only recently as their era receded into history and their style acquired a desirable retro quality. As for historians, while some have reproduced linen postcards as illustrations in books devoted to other topics, no one has yet fully examined their significance as cultural artifacts. My interpretation of linen postcards involves a dual approach, considering primarily their meanings for the people who initially purchased, sent, received, or saved them, and secondarily their quite different meanings for people who later collected or drew inspiration from them. For a cultural historian, the encyclopedic iconography of these view cards offers a window onto popular middle-class attitudes about nature, wilderness, race and ethnicity, technology, mobility, and the city during an era of intense transformation that was often self-consciously referred to as "the machine age." For a collector, on the other hand, despite the status of these cards as historical artifacts, they may awaken nostalgia for a lost world evoked by colorized images whose details were exaggerated in the first place.

Although postcards might seem simple objects, they have served relatively complex purposes. Acquiring a postcard has often verified one's presence at a tourist site or other location and conveyed virtual possession of that place when a visitor left with its miniature image in hand. Although some tourists have collected postcards as personal souvenirs, others have mailed them to friends and relatives while en route or after returning from a trip. Postcards also facilitated communication with acquaintances in nearby towns during the early twentieth century, when postage was only a penny (half that of a letter), mail was delivered twice daily and in some places even more frequently, and long-distance telephone service was prohibitively expensive. Recipients often discarded such functional cards but sometimes kept them for their images. Cards sent by traveling friends or relatives have often played more problematic roles. Such cards might have aroused envy if recipients had not personally visited the pictured sites, or they might have evoked expanded horizons by suggesting places for future visits. A postcard acquired while traveling and saved for years or decades by the purchaser might later have become a key to reviving personal memories. In some cases, a card's conventionalized image might have served as the only reminder that a person had actually visited a particular place at some point in the past. Finally, for a present-day observer, a collection of stylized postcards from the 1930s and '40s might provoke nostalgia or even suggest an idealized alternate reality or retro-utopia, an enticingly close parallel world.

When considering linen postcards in the context of their own time, we must assume that people who purchased, sent, or received them regarded these views of the American scene as approximations of reality. Any doubt in the phrase "they do say it's real" referred more to the astonishing saguaro cactuses themselves than to the degree of fabrication involved in their portrayal on the postcard. Over the years enough people have marked an X on the window of a hotel or motel room as an indication of where they stayed to suggest acceptance of postcard images as shorthand for reality. According to Caren Kaplan, an anthropologist of travel, tourists are offering "proof of the authentic" and engaging in "a technology of documenting the 'real'" when they select and write postcards.[3] Following her hint, this study traces the development of vibrantly colorful linen postcards as a technology of representation. Between 1931 and the early 1950s, Teich & Co. published about 45,000 unique individual views of the United States in the linen format. Imitators and competitors such as Tichnor Brothers and Colourpicture in Boston, Metrocraft in Everett, Massachusetts, and a score of smaller printers brought the total number of unique linen views to more than 100,000. A conservative estimate suggests Teich and other companies printed in total over a billion linen cards in twenty-five years.[4] The presence of these cards in everyday life was significant even if people often discarded them, and their commercial success indicates popular acceptance of their collective portrait of America.

Because linen cards did not emerge in a vacuum, this book opens with a history of picture postcards beginning with the late nineteenth century. Various earlier types of view cards ranged from individual photographic prints and mechanically printed black-and-white halftone cards to lithographic cards printed in up to sixteen colors. Curt Teich, a German immigrant printer, pioneered the use of offset color lithography for postcards and in 1931 introduced the linen variety, which quickly triumphed over other types in the United States. The linen postcard's unique aesthetic derived as much from new printing methods and economic constraints as from any intention of creating an innovative visual style. After reviewing the linen production process, one cannot help marveling that inexpensive, mass-produced artifacts designed, printed, and shipped out by the thousands from Chicago could project an aura of the local and the particular.

Tension between the generic and the specific becomes obvious when one examines the iconography of the American scene conveyed by Teich and other postcard printers. Natural and rural views, whether of eastern farms and pastures, the Appalachian and Great Smoky Mountains, the desert Southwest, the Rockies, or rugged western scenery, privileged viewers as masters of all they surveyed, sharing a democratic abundance indicated even by the very intensity of the colors in which landscapes were represented. Somewhat indebted to nineteenth-century painting styles of the Hudson River School and more obviously to western paintings by Albert Bierstadt and Thomas Moran, the makers of natural views in linen often drew directly from archives of earlier landscape photographers, as when Teich based cards on images originally distributed by William Henry Jackson or H. H. Bennett. Linen view cards recapitulated and further popularized long-standing notions of picturesque nature and wilderness.

Despite relying on earlier romantic vistas, natural scenes often included modern highways offering easy access by automobile. Emphasizing mastery over nature, the iconography of linen postcards glorified the technology of bridges, dams, and factories. Towns and cities appeared in bird's-eye and skyline views, often at night, when electric light's artificial brilliance emphasized outlines of buildings and window grids. Street scenes portrayed an array of commercial signs, with crowds reflecting an upbeat urban tempo (fig. 1.3). Views of landmarks heralded each locale as unique even though a common visual style conveyed a sense of the generic. Cityscape postcards often echoed the grand-style urban photography of the late nineteenth century, but on occasion they suggested parallels with Berenice Abbott and other contemporary documentary photographers. The extravagant formal qualities of linen cards were especially flattering to the stylized architecture of world's fairs, whose popularity indicated wide faith in technological modernity during the Depression's hard times.

Linen postcards were often used to promote individual roadside attractions, hotels, motels, and restaurants. Such commercial images emphasized the cosmopolitan styles of Art Deco and streamlining (fig. 1.4). The colorful linen process heightened their effects and suggested that machine-age technologies afforded a supremely malleable reality. The production of interior views of hotel lobbies, cocktail lounges, and other commercial establishments frequently relied on paint chips and upholstery swatches submitted by clients to authenticate patterns and colors. Cards with interior views often seem the most realistic of linens owing to their meticulous detail. Their overly fabricated realism, characterized by the painter John Baeder as having a "messed-with" quality,[5] promised access for everyone to exclusive fantasy realms.

Although the American scene of linen postcards belonged mostly to middle-class whites of western European origin, members of ethnic and racial minorities, immigrants, and working-class men and women also purchased, sent, and saved them. While the typical perspective of oversight and mastery may have promised marginalized consumers a degree of inclusion, a significant number of linen cards objectified and romanticized the nation's most visible minorities. African Americans in the South, Native Americans in the Southwest and Southeast, Mexican Americans in Texas and California, inhabitants of various urban Chinatowns, and even white Appalachian mountaineers were represented in stereotypical costumes and activities. They often appeared so passive and mute as to be naturalized into unchanging landscapes (fig. 1.5). Such representations

F I G. 1.3. "Third Street Looking West, Jamestown, N.Y.," Teich 9A-H1881, 1939

F I G. 1.4. "Entrance to Hotel Hollenden, Cleveland, Ohio," Tichnor 67967, n.d.

FIG. 1.5. "Pueblo of Acoma, the Sky City, South of Laguna, N.M.," Teich 6A-H2777, 1936

of minorities counteracted the very modernity often celebrated by linen view cards and in doing so suggested the survival of static pockets of unchanging tradition.

My approach mostly takes postcards of the 1930s and '40s at face value as representations of an alternate world somewhat congruent with realities perceived by their consumers. Behind the scenes, however, clients, sales agents, artists, and printers collaborated in manipulating the black-and-white photographs to which the linen colorizing process was applied. Those Americans who accepted the authenticity of postcard views would have been astonished by what was added, subtracted, shifted, or altered in moving from a glossy photograph through an airbrushed photo and hand-painted watercolor mockup to the five printing plates required for production. Detailed job files for thousands of linen cards printed by Teich reveal manipulations ranging from basic cleaning up or simplifying of images to major transformations with definite ideological intent. Although Teich's photographers and artists were participating in a commercial venture, many took pride in their work as art. The aesthetic they collectively fostered accurately portrays aspects of its era for the very reason that the verisimilitude they took pains to capture often dissolves when closely examined.

Although these artificial images illuminate their era, they also appeal today to collectors and the general public in ways that complicate their authenticity as historical artifacts. Colorful images of Times Square and Grauman's Chinese Theatre, for example, may evoke memories of Hollywood films. Cards illustrating swank nightclubs and streamlined diners may evoke the retro attractions of Art Deco. A card with "Greetings from Asbury Park, N.J." emblazoned across it may recall Bruce Springsteen's first record album even for fans who have never played it on vinyl.[6] Linen postcards appeal to a secondhand nostalgia for a time lost to memory because the people who experience that nostalgia were not yet born when the cards were produced. The mediated quality of that nostalgia reminds us once again of the status of linen cards as artifacts of mass culture. And yet, surviving handwritten messages, however fragmentary or puzzling, also connect these artifacts more directly to social history. But when a particular card was written or received in the mail by a collector's relative or ancestor, then genuine nostalgia may confuse the issue still further, yielding a complex blend of the personal and the cultural.

Nostalgic attraction partly motivates my involvement in this project. Growing up in the 1950s and '60s, I was vaguely aware of these unusual cards as part of the vast universe of material objects. My younger brother was given every postcard that came into the house, of whatever vintage, not only brand new, shiny chromes but also older offerings from grandparents. I was fascinated by a dreary linen card bearing the title "The Legend of the Dogwood" and featuring a religious text surrounded by blossoms, which for years was tacked above a small desk in a summer cabin in northern Michigan belonging to my mother's parents. Only a few years ago, when my mother gave me that card, did I discover that my paternal grandmother had mailed it to my maternal grandmother in February 1958, complaining about frost in Orlando and mentioning an impending trip to Texas to visit my family.[7] My first professional awareness of linen postcards came in the mid-1970s while researching a dissertation on industrial design during the 1920s and '30s. My brother loaned me several cards that had belonged to our grandparents, including one with a night view of a Goodyear blimp floating over the General Motors Building at the Chicago World's Fair of 1933, which I wanted to use as an illustration (see p. 406). I recall spending hours at the typewriter perfecting an interpretive metaphor based on the card's representation of an airship and a mini-skyscraper. When I finally emerged from my grad student office, I witnessed the unbelievable sight of a Goodyear blimp floating serenely over the University of Texas tower.

By the mid-1980s, I had become fascinated by the surreal look of many linen cards. I occasionally bought them in antique shops and junk stores—unused ones with blank backs, the idea being that I would mail them to friends and

C-3—*Flying Fish, Santa Catalina, California*

4A-H449

FIG. 1.6. "Flying Fish, Santa Catalina, California," Teich 4A-H449, 1934

relatives if I ever visited the places they pictured. The unique visual qualities of linen cards had first struck me when I found an odd, nonphotographic, inked-line representation of a flying fish off the California coast (fig. 1.6). The card's sunset hues ranged from purplish rose through greenish yellow to full yellow at the horizon line, and the ocean revealed a subtle array of blues. Perhaps there was also something compelling about the card's message, inscribed by a father to his young children in small-town Texas. "This fish followed us all the way across to Catalina!" he exclaimed, "but this is all we could catch of him." As with the saguaro cactuses, there is a gap, both puzzling and fascinating, between the contrived quality of the scene and the assumption that it represents reality. In any case, I soon became a collector, attracted by the images whether or not the cards had any messages. Over the next twenty-five years I collected some 6,000 linen postcards, acquiring them at flea markets, junk stores, collectors' expos, on family vacations around the country, and at annual shows of the local post-card club.[8] About 4,000 of them carry the Teich name, and about 1,800 of them are addressed and postmarked.

At first my collection contained only images that spoke to me directly, like the flying fish, demanding to be possessed. Up to a point, postcards sought me out, not the other way around. There seems to have been a resonance with child-hood, perhaps a longing for a mythical time before my own existence, when imagined lives of parents and grandparents seemed, if not heroic, then at least reassuringly certain and fixed (despite realities of depression, war, and everyday life). By the end of the 1990s, after fifteen years, the collection had grown so much that I had to keep a checklist of serial numbers to avoid duplicate pur-chases. Some images were so compelling I kept buying them over and over, a fact suggesting things had gotten out of hand. I began to have doubts about rummaging through boxes of old cards with no purpose beyond accumulating more. Eventually the objective concerns of a cultural historian became engaged, however, and my collecting became omnivorous. Dealers and fellow collectors joked about my lack of discrimination, my refusal to settle on a specific topic or two, and my status as a self-described "bottom feeder" rummaging through boxes of bargain cards (initially a nickel or a dime apiece, later a quarter, and then finally fifty cents or a dollar). The collection eventually expanded into a relatively complete microcosm of the subject range of linen postcards.

Even so, it took a long time for me to realize that I could write as a cultural historian about linen postcards. For much of my professional life I had been writing about the period between the world wars—about topics related to that era's visual and material culture. As it turned out, there was much to discern and interpret in the cards themselves, in their range of coverage and manner of representation. Unlike some historians who have written about postcards, I decided I would interrogate them as artifacts. I would interpret the images rather than using them as neutral illustrations of the subjects portrayed. But to consider visual images in the context of the time in which they were created and first consumed opens up issues of intention and reception. How can one determine what commercial artists and printers, many of them German im-migrants, intended to convey through mass-produced images of the American scene? More problematic, how can one recover responses of original purchasers and recipients to ephemeral bits of cardboard intended to be discarded after use? And how does one know one's own collecting parameters are not biased?

Fortunately there are wider resources for a cultural history of linen post-cards than my personal collection. In 1982 Ralph D. Teich donated everything left from his father's company to the Lake County Discovery Museum in Wau-conda, Illinois, which established the Curt Teich Postcard Archives. Those ma-terials include the job files already mentioned, family papers, a privately printed Teich autobiography and family history, sales literature for traveling agents, some in-house newsletters, a detailed company audit and inventory for 1939, a Geographical Index listing all the company's postcards from the early twentieth century onward, multiple copies of nearly every card printed by the company, and sixty-seven large albums with a complete run of the company's linen cards in chronological order. When I first visited the museum, these albums, which are handy for quick skimming, enabled me to track changing styles and themes of cards and to correct for my previously unrecognized prejudices as a collector. Over a week's time I was exposed to nearly 50,000 images, flickering past as a generalized whole. That exhausting, exhilarating process convinced me that linen view postcards do embody a coherent vision of the historical American scene despite a wide range of subjects, mixed motives of thousands of clients, and wide disparities of intention and execution among individual images. That vision now functions both as a significant artifact of the cultural history of a particular era and as a powerful stimulus to nostalgic re-imaginings of the past.

2

Curt Teich and the Early History of Postcards

WHEN THE YOUNG PRINTER CURT OTTO Teich arrived in Chicago from Germany in 1895, the picture postcard barely existed as a commodity. Since the mid-nineteenth century, postal authorities and private entrepreneurs in Europe and the United States had experimented with various forms of postcards. In 1873, for example, the U.S. Post Office began selling blank postcards with an image of a penny stamp preprinted on the side reserved for an address. A private business could buy these official cards in bulk and print an advertising message on the blank side. The innovation proved so useful that the Post Office sold sixty million in the first six months. Sometimes a sender incorporated a decorative border or small illustration in the advertisement. Christmas and New Year's greeting cards appeared immediately. Entrepreneurs also printed cards advertising world's fairs and regional expositions in the 1870s and '80s. Although such cards often included small images of exhibit buildings, they were not sold at the fairgrounds but were used to attract exhibitors and visitors.[1]

All this changed when the World's Columbian Exposition in Chicago introduced the souvenir postcard to Americans in 1893. Officially licensed postcards printed by color lithography were sold to visitors from vending machines in packs of ten for a quarter. With a grand view of the visionary White City's neoclassical buildings across the top and a portrait of Christopher Columbus or some other decorative device on the left, a considerable space remained for a handwritten message. The other side was reserved for a recipient's address and postage. Unsanctioned competitors offered similar cards. Some were printed on government forms preprinted with one-cent postage, but most souvenir cards required a sender to affix a stamp on the address side. Such so-called private cards required two cents' postage, the same as a first-class letter sealed in an envelope. Such an extravagant postage rate ensured that many cards were not mailed but were saved as souvenirs or given as gifts. These Columbian postcards, widely imitated at subsequent, turn-of-the-century expositions, introduced the American public to the concept of colorful view cards.[2]

Postcard Mania Comes to America

Five years later, in 1898, the U.S. Congress encouraged wide use of privately printed picture postcards by authorizing a postage rate of one cent, the same as for prestamped government cards (and half that of a letter). The new law stimulated American participation in a postcard craze already sweeping Europe. A British journalist described the range of subjects as encompassing "the comic, the sentimental, the purely artistic, the scenic, the architectural, the heraldic, [and] the coarse." Except for season's greetings or humorous comics completely filling the message side of a card, most graphics were limited to a decorative arrangement of several tiny scenes around a space left vacant for a handwritten message. Within a few years, led by the United Kingdom in 1902, most governments authorized the so-called divided-back card, with a line down the middle of the back separating a message space on the left from an address space on the right. Postal authorities in the United States were slow to recognize the "greatly increased postal revenues" to be gained by "catering to the fad" and did not approve divided-back cards for domestic mail until 1907.[3] While the penny postal rate made sending postcards affordable, the divided back freed up the whole front of a card for an illustration with plenty of room for a message on the back. The basic format established in 1907 has remained the same ever since.

From 1898 onward, dozens of American printers turned to postcards as the fad spread from Europe to the United States. In that year Emil C. Kropp began publishing cards in Milwaukee with small halftone views printed in a single color and texts reading "Greetings from" or "Souvenir of" this or that place. In 1897 the Detroit Photographic Company had licensed the Photochrom printing process from a Swiss company, thereby attaining continuous gradations of tone, an improvement over the visible dots of halftone printing. After acquiring twenty thousand negatives from the western photographer William Henry Jackson in 1898, Detroit began rendering the American scene in delicately colored view cards, expanding from small vignettes to full-card images around 1900. Even Joyce Hall, later a founder of the greeting card industry with his Hallmark company, dabbled in the sale of postcards as a teenager in 1904.[4]

Within the first decade of the twentieth century, every small town in the United States boasted a shop dedicated to racks of postcards of all sorts—local views, famous world sights, architectural monuments, fine art reproductions, paintings and drawings by illustrators and poster artists, celebrity portraits, holiday greetings, romantic encounters (both staged photographs and artists' renderings), comics, and sometimes relatively tame pornographic images kept under the counter. In one year ending June 1908, the U.S. Post Office reported handling 668 million postcards, a figure rising to 968 million in 1913. Collectors traded postcards with friends through the mail, mounted cards in albums, and even projected them onto parlor walls with devices like Bausch and Lomb's Reflectoscope Post Card Magic Lantern. Not everyone was pleased with this popular new graphic medium. *Atlantic Monthly* complained about the "tame *simulacra*" sent by tourists too lazy to describe their travels. In a more democratic tone *Scientific American* praised view cards for offering people "some idea of the beauties of their own and foreign lands of which they would otherwise have remained in ignorance."[5]

American printers did not benefit much from the fad. Although the postcard industry employed two or three thousand workers in the United States, German printers captured most of the American market—90 percent, according to congressional testimony by a Philadelphia printer in December 1908. He estimated that 700 to 800 million cards had been imported from Germany in 1907, a figure echoed by other witnesses. At the same hearing on import tariffs, another printer sarcastically observed that all the views of the Capitol and other Washington sights sold at the hotel where he was staying during the hearing were printed in Germany. Two months later, a hastily organized trade association petitioned Congress for a duty of 100 percent on imported "souvenir post cards."[6]

German printers had several advantages over Americans. Wages in the lithographic printing trade for everyone from artists and engravers to litho stone polishers and press operators were three to four times higher in the United States than in Germany. Almost all the limestone used for lithographic stones was imported from Bavaria at five times the price paid by printers in Germany. And German printers had built up inventories of lithographic stones for thousands of cards. It cost next to nothing to provide their American sales agents with samples for attracting orders from American distributors. On the other hand, American printers who were new to the business had few samples to show and could not afford to work up a new card without being assured of selling at least 3,500 copies. The trade association estimated that it cost three dollars more to have a thousand cards printed in the United States than to import them from Germany. Even for view cards based on photographs of local scenes, according to a printer who wanted to enter the postcard business, "the fact that the Germans must buy photographs here, reproduce them at home [in Germany], [and] transport them back again, is of very small significance." Everyone in the business, according to a Denver stationer, was "demoralized by the flood of German importations."[7]

Eventually the Payne-Aldrich tariff of 1909, which mostly *lowered* import duties on a wide range of goods, did impose a protective duty on imported postcards, in particular those with images portraying the American scene. The tax on cards with "views of any landscape, scene, building, place or locality in the United States" went up from five cents per pound of cards to fifteen cents, plus an additional 25 percent of overall value.[8] Five years later the government simplified the import duty on view cards by making it a flat twenty cents per pound. By then the revised tariff had done its work. The annual value of imported view cards dropped from $193,000 in 1910 to less than $65,000 in 1912. Among the many American printers filling the vacuum when German companies abandoned the field was Curt Teich, a naturalized German immigrant.

Curt Teich's Background

Born in Greiz, Germany, in 1877, Curt Teich came from a printing and publishing family.[9] His grandfather, Friedrich Teich, a local official and poet, had operated a print shop and published a newspaper in nearby Lobenstein, a picturesque Thuringian town nestled below a castle ruin. Friedrich's son Christian, who had expanded the business by acquiring several regional newspapers, publishing houses, and bookstores, and by purchasing a printing firm in Dresden, returned to live in Lobenstein in 1889. Apparently restless, Christian sold everything but the local print shop and newspaper, which he left his wife, Elise, to supervise while he traveled to Chicago in October 1892 to visit relatives and take in the Columbian Exposition. He did not return home for two years. His son Max joined him in February 1893, and Christian, who enjoyed wandering the streets, provided German newspapers with enthusiastic reports about Chicago's energy and its dazzling world's fair.[10]

Meanwhile Christian's son Curt, after attending elementary school in Lobenstein and four years of a science-oriented secondary school in Dresden, was learning the printing trade and helping run the family business. When Chris-

Compliments of
Curt Teich,
Chicago, Ill., U. S. A., Aug. 1, 1899

FIG. 2.1. Curt Teich, ca. 1899

tian finally returned home to Lobenstein, the two quarreled, and Curt, then eighteen, left for America. Traveling in steerage with no luggage, he arrived in New York in April 1895 and listed his occupation as "compositor." After working briefly in New York to earn traveling money, he moved on to Chicago and found work as a printer. His brother Max, who had established himself in the hotel business during the world's fair boom, loaned Curt the funds to open a print shop early in 1898. The young printer did well enough that he chose to become a U.S. citizen less than two years later, in time for the new century (fig. 2.1).[11]

According to family legend, Teich decided in 1898 to specialize in postcards and thus avoid competition with the hundreds of small job printers who produced Chicago's business forms and handbills. Although that was the year Congress rendered postcards attractive by reducing postage to a penny, Teich's shift toward postcards may actually have occurred gradually and somewhat later. He was certainly familiar with the European postcard fad. During the late 1890s and into the new century, the Teich family print shop lithographed several post-cards, each reading "Gruss aus Lobenstein" (Greetings from Lobenstein) and featuring tiny illustrations of such attractions as the castle and a health spa founded by grandfather Friedrich (fig. 2.2). The existence of these cards suggests Teich's familiarity with the postcard as a product and with its means of production.[12]

In any event, Teich became involved with postcards both as a printer and as a distributor in the early years of the twentieth century. His younger brother Alfred, who arrived in Chicago in 1902, imported cards from Germany for Curt and ran a branch office in St. Louis during the Louisiana Purchase Exposition of 1904.[13] For a while, as early as 1903, they contracted with C. G. Röder of Leipzig to print view cards of Chicago and St. Louis. One such card, dated 1904 in pen by its purchaser, depicts the Tribune Building (fig. 2.3), headquarters of the Chicago newspaper, using fine-grained collotype printing to reproduce a black-and-white photograph in precise detail, with sparing touches of pink, yellow, and light green inks creating a vague sense of colors. The cream-colored card stock is lightly embossed with a dimpled pattern similar to that on the surface of an orange. The overall impression is of elegance.[14]

FIG. 2.2. "Gruss aus Lobenstein," Verlag von Christian Teich, n.d.

FIG. 2.3. "Chicago / Tribune Building," Teich Publication No. 27, ca. 1904

It is uncertain when Teich began printing postcards in addition to importing them, but he reached a turning point in 1904. In March of that year, he and brothers Max and Alfred applied to incorporate as the American Photochrom Company, a name soon changed to Curt Teich & Company (six months later for all practical purposes but not legally until December 1906). In requesting incorporation, the brothers announced the dual purposes of importing and printing postcards—or, as their application confusingly phrased it, "Printing and Litographing [*sic*], Publishing, Importing of Art printing, Manufg & Importing of Souvenir articles." A month or so after forming the company, Curt traveled to Germany to observe up-to-date lithographic techniques. Sailing back to the United States in June 1904 on the Hamburg-Amerika liner *Pennsylvania*, he enjoyed the relative comfort of a second-class cabin while contemplating how innovative German methods of high-volume printing might transform his business.[15]

The Search for Mass-Produced Photographic Realism

Teich and other publishers of view cards faced several problems: how to produce realistic images, how to do so at high volume, and how to reduce the cost of labor and materials. A review of various printing techniques available to postcard publishers in 1904 should provide a sense of the options open to Teich as he returned home and pondered his future. The most direct way to obtain view cards was to print from photographic negatives. So-called real photo postcards (fig. 2.4), as collectors have long referred to them, were often rendered in a sepia tone that now conveys a nostalgic aura they did not originally possess. Printed by hand, one at a time, from a negative made by a local photographer using a large-format view camera, a real photo card offered the ultimate in verisimilitude. In 1902 Eastman Kodak had introduced light-sensitized card stock, making the job easier, and in the following year Kodak democratized the process with the A3 camera, whose roll film and postcard-sized negatives enabled amateurs to turn family photographs into postcards in a home darkroom. Or they could let Kodak do the work for ten cents apiece.[16]

Every moderately sized town boasted a commercial photographer who offered studio portraits printed as postcards and who also usually produced postcard views of the common and the uncommon: main street, public buildings, churches, businesses, school groups, athletic teams, tourist attractions, traveling circuses, celebrations, train wrecks, floods, and rarely (and most notoriously) lynchings.[17] Sold at the studio or in a stationery shop, such cards directly represented a town to itself. For viewers unaware of how a photographer could manipulate an image at the time of exposure by framing and posing or later in the darkroom by cropping, dodging, burning, and retouching, a real photo card promised unmediated reality. Our more complex understanding of representation, which recognizes that a photograph is at least two removes from the moment it purports to capture, did not exist for most people in the early twentieth century. Humorous exaggeration cards depicting subjects such as a huge cucumber filling a railway car or a trout as large as a whale actually served by their obvious absurdity to verify the truthfulness of more ordinary images.[18] Social historians today value real photo cards for their wealth of detail and unselfconscious portrayal of everyday life in specific places during the first two decades of the twentieth century.

FIG. 2.4. Real photo postcard showing a parade in Galion, OH, Galion View, n.d.

Although real photo cards, laboriously printed by hand, supported only local markets, their existence contributed to the publication of mass-produced cards. Traveling agents working directly for German printers or for American distributors of German cards often took their own original source photos, but they also negotiated with local photographers for views likely to sell in volume to travelers and tourists. Sometimes they pirated real photo images, buying them off the rack for their own use and adding instructions for colors if the views were intended for lithography.[19] The challenge all printers faced was how to mechanically reproduce images from photographs while maintaining the realism that photography had conditioned people to expect. At the same time, however, different printing methods yielded different visual styles, and within each style a homogeneity of appearance marked representations of similar subjects, whether main streets, courthouses, or parks, across different regions of the country. As late as 1929, a defender of real photo cards complained that mass-produced view cards appeared "so unnatural" that he "wonder[ed] at the courage of the purchasers and the temper of the recipients." The typical traveler seemed to be "satisfied with any kind of picture which somewhat resembles the scene he has encountered."[20] The process of becoming accustomed to the artificial, the hyperreal, or the surreal, whether by mistaking it for reality or by assuming its superiority to reality, is what it meant for ordinary citizens to be immersed in a culture of visual representation.

Two photomechanical printing processes, the collotype and the halftone, approximated the appearance of original black-and-white photos. Each process created the illusion of photography's continuous tone gradations from white through shades of gray to black, despite the fact that printing ink is a uniform black. Each process worked by mechanically breaking down an image into thousands or millions of discrete elements. Collotype, introduced in the 1850s, was visually more successful.[21] To make a collotype printing plate, a photosensitive layer of gelatin was laid on a thicker layer of gelatin on a sheet of glass. As the top layer dried, it crazed into a reticulated pattern of minute, tightly packed, randomly granular forms. When exposed to light shining through a reversed photographic negative (flipped over to preserve left-right orientation), the photosensitive layer hardened more with greater light exposure, while less exposed areas remained soft and able to absorb more moisture. In the final step, the gelatin was removed from the glass and its back was hardened by exposure to light so as to yield the strength required for use as a printing plate in a flatbed press. When moistened before printing, the saturated absorbent portions repelled oil-based ink, while the more hardened, nonmoistened portions accepted ink and thus printed onto the paper.

Because the minute, granulated forms absorbed varying amounts of ink depending on their degrees of exposure to light, collotype produced a detailed image with fine gradations of tone, from white through gray to black (fig. 2.5). There was something almost organic about a collotype's rich, velvety texture, barely visible to the naked eye. The collotype process yielded an excellent mechanically printed reproduction of a monotone photo, but there were problems. Printing plates of hardened gelatin were relatively fragile, required labor-intensive presses, and wore out after a few thousand impressions, necessitating the fabrication of new plates when popular views were reprinted. Despite the aesthetic advantage of collotype reproduction, as evidenced by thousands of different view cards in both Europe and the United States during the first ten or fifteen years of the century, it was not an acceptable solution for inexpensively mass-producing postcard views.

Halftone, on the other hand, facilitated high-volume printing. As with collotype, the idea was to break up the continuous tone gradations of a photograph into discrete particles of different values, which, when viewed together, would resolve into a visual illusion of continuity (fig. 2.6).[22] In 1878 the American inventor Frederick Ives devised a way of doing this more predictably and mechanically than with collotype. He created the so-called halftone screen by etching two plates of glass with parallel ruled lines and filling the etched lines with dark pigment. He then joined the two sheets of glass in a wooden frame,

FIG. 2.5. Detail, collotype printing, "Municipal Courts Building. Detroit, Mich," Excelsior 1124, dated 1911 in pencil

FIG. 2.6. Detail, halftone printing, Dowler Brothers Pianos, Marion, OH, Feicke-Desch, n.d., postmarked 1913

with the dark lines facing inward and at right angles. The result was a smooth, transparent glass screen covered with small, precise squares similar to those on graph paper. To prepare a printing plate, this screen was mounted in a camera between a reversed photographic negative of the image to be printed and a photosensitized zinc or copper plate. Light shining through the negative created patterns of varying high and low light intensities, which were then diffused by the ruled squares of the screen, casting dots of light (or shadow) onto the plate. The more intense the light, the larger the dots on the plate, though their center points were all arranged in precisely even rows. In the case of completely dark areas of the negative, no dots of light were cast onto the plate's surface. After an exposed plate was chemically fixed and washed, an acid bath dissolved the surface of the plate around the dots, thereby creating a raised or relief surface with which a halftone image could be printed.

Widely adopted during the 1880s, halftone plates were combined with typeset text in printing magazines and newspapers, yielding illustrations with greater photorealism and less artistic intervention than that in the handmade wood engravings previously used to approximate reproductions of photos. Although the printed dots were composed of even-toned black ink, those of largest size clumped together, joining visually to create solid black. The smaller the printed dots, the lighter the tone of gray they seemed to create when inked and printed on paper. Printers learned to make the pattern of halftone dots less visually obtrusive by rotating the screen forty-five degrees and thus shifting lines of dots to the diagonal. Even so, halftone postcards could not disguise the pattern of their making. Indeed, that precise geometry seemed to indicate that the result approximated photography's presumed objectivity.

Lithography and the Colorizing of Monotone Views

A rummage through bargain boxes of any postcard dealer today would yield hundreds of monotone view cards printed in collotype or halftone from the early 1900s through the 1920s, all aspiring to photographic exactitude. Only close inspection would reveal collotype's soft granulation or halftone's mechanized dots. Although mass-produced imitations of black-and-white photos remained common in Europe, colorized view cards quickly became popular in the United States. Virtually all color printing of postcards employed lithography, a process used in the nineteenth century for full-color reproductions of paintings, drawings, and other artwork. Lithography was based on the discovery that grease applied to a flat piece of absorbent limestone would repel water and attract oil-based inks, while an ungreased limestone surface would absorb water and repel ink. Thus a flat, smooth stone could be used as a printing plate when areas to be printed were drawn, stenciled, or filled in with a grease crayon and then chemically fixed. Multiple stones, each inked with a different color, sometimes twenty-five stones in all, could be overprinted on a single sheet of paper to create the infinity of hues needed to reproduce a source as complex as an oil painting. Specialists called chromists, who examined an original artwork and separated out its colors for printing, were engaged in a kind of reverse engineering. Their work required an intuitive artistry derived from experience.

The firm of Currier & Ives had popularized simple lithographs from the 1840s onward, offering more than 7,000 different prints with scenes of westward settlement, farmsteads, everyday life, steamboats, trains, and celebrated disasters, as well as images of prominent citizens. Although chromos, as they were called, comprised a new form of inexpensive mass-produced artwork, the publisher Louis Prang took them up-market during the late nineteenth century with painstaking color reproductions of famous oil paintings and original work by such artists as Thomas Moran, who in 1874 produced a series of watercolor landscapes of Yellowstone National Park to be reproduced by lithographic printing. Even so, the trend in lithography was toward simpler, more mechanized processes yielding ever more colorful—and inexpensive—images. This revolution in visual culture created the advertising poster fad of the 1890s and transformed the appearance of books and magazines. But it extended its most democratic reach with the landscape postcard.[23]

Teich would have known several ways of applying lithography to postcards. Some cards, such as the views he imported from Germany, revealed only minimal areas of one or two colors printed over a black collotype or halftone base, imitating the effect of a partially hand-tinted photo. At the opposite extreme, other cards resembled miniature Prang artworks with ten or fifteen color inks blended through repeated overprinting to yield a thick, saturated image with rich colors submerging the lines and shading of the collotype or halftone base. Most complex were the Photochrom and Phostint processes of the Detroit Publishing Company (as it was known from 1905 onward). Still regarded as "undocumented" and "mysterious," those processes yielded 17,000 individual views over a quarter century. Detroit abandoned the standard black base and overprinted multiple colors in collotype-like patterns using lithographic stones.[24] The challenge faced by anyone seeking to offer full-color postcards while undercutting Detroit's premium price of two cards for a nickel was to define a point between the extremes by limiting the number of overprintings while still achieving a realistic color effect. Reducing the number of colors saved on labor and materials by reducing the number of printing plates that had to be prepared, the number of times that card stock had to be run through a press, and the amount of ink used.

German lithographers who sought to simplify the process were familiar with what is now called CMYK four-color printing, in which three primary colors—cyan, magenta, and yellow—produce complementary colors when two are layered together. Cyan and yellow yield green, cyan and magenta yield a blue-purple hue, and magenta and yellow yield red. Confusing the issue somewhat, the three primaries are often popularly thought of as blue, red, and yellow. Black, the so-called fourth color, was used for outline, emphasis, and shading, and also served as the key or register plate for aligning the color plates during printing, so it is represented by the letter K for "key" in the CMYK abbreviation. Most color view cards destined for the United States were based on various hybrids of CMYK. Rather than exhibiting bright, true colors, as we now envision them, however, the postcard palette of 1900 to 1910 was definitely skewed toward cyan.

Typical of this trend were thousands of halftone-lithographic views imported from Frankfurt, Germany, by Hugh C. Leighton, a distributor in Portland, Maine, who specialized in New England scenes. These hybrid cards combined halftone printing in black with color inks conveyed by lithographic plates. A card illustrating a textile mill along the Kennebec River in Waterville, Maine, postmarked in 1905, can serve as an example (fig. 2.7). Simulating the delicacy of collotype, the printer used an ultra-fine halftone screen of 200 lines per inch for black, with minute dots creating crisp, photographic definitions of the mill, ripples on the water in the middle distance, and foreground details of the shore. The screen was so fine that black halftone dots, relatively widely but uniformly spread, actually fill the sky with an imperceptible texture. The card's colors, which today seem idiosyncratic when compared with those of standard CMYK printing, were quite typical for the time. They were derived from four inks: a delicate aquamarine, red, bright yellow, and a soft peach.[25]

FIG. 2.7. "Kennebec River, Waterville,
Maine," Leighton 1679, n.d.

FIG. 2.8. Detail, "Kennebec River,
Waterville, Maine"

Although the image's colors seem smooth and crisp to the eye, magnification reveals its construction from disparate elements (fig. 2.8). An expanse of solid aquamarine fills most of the sky, but lighter areas of cloud are defined by random stipples of aquamarine. The deep blue green of the river comes from solid aquamarine printed over large oval dots of yellow, known as Ben Day dots after the printer who first used them. Spanning four halftone dots in length and two in width, these yellow ovals are arrayed in staggered diagonal rows with occasional intensity provided by additional yellow stippling. The factory's red brick derives from a combination of vertical rows of red dashes, the same staggered diagonal rows of yellow ovals, and smaller scattershot dots of peach that also extend above the mill building to create a vague sunset effect. The green of trees in the distance derives from merging yellow ovals with aquamarine stippling. Magnification also reveals the importance of halftone shading, with the eye mistaking black for a darker green or red or brown, depending on the overprinted colors and the visual context.

Although German printers reduced the number of printing plates for lithographed postcards from ten or fifteen to four or five (three or four colors plus black), their process remained labor intensive and still required an intuitive grasp of color manipulation. Whether the Germans used traditional lithographic stones or modern zinc plates, each color's printing surface had to be prepared separately by a litho artist working with grease crayons, Ben Day stencils, brushes, and other tools under a magnification of twenty times the original. Despite a consistent overall aesthetic, color effects of individual cards varied considerably. Rather than settling on a standard of three or four colors, printers sometimes shifted colors of ink from card to card to create different effects. For example, magnification reveals that the red stripes in two tiny U.S. flags flying over a postcard view of a courthouse in Detroit derived from individual brushstrokes reproduced in a bright red ink used nowhere else on the card. Even with only four colors instead of ten or fifteen, it still took one litho artist about a week to prepare the plates for a single postcard.[26]

Despite the clash of colorful dots, dashes, and random blobs revealed when one magnifies a typical lithographed card of this era, only a litho artist or printer would have regarded an image in such a fractured way. Thousands of cards produced in a similar palette using similar techniques yielded precise photographic lines and delicate blues and pinks that today seem washed out but that conveyed a sense of heightened realism to purchasers and recipients of these postcards. Even the photographer Walker Evans, who amassed a personal collection of 9,000 postcards, described this genre of "black-and-white photographs subsequently tinted by hand lithography" as offering "some of the truest visual records ever made of any period." Writing for *Fortune* magazine in 1948, he praised them for their "fidelity" and "restraint," especially "in the rendering of patina and the soft tones of town buildings and streets."[27] The aesthetic of the pre-linen color lithographic view card, celebrated by Evans for realism and noncommercial innocence, had been developed by German printers who established it as a standard in both Europe and the United States long before Teich, still a Chicago job printer, was involved in anything more than importing postcards from Germany.

The General Motors of the Postcard Industry

Teich's brief autobiography does not indicate which "up to date lithography" techniques he brought back from Germany in June 1904.[28] A few months later, however, in February 1905, a lithograph artist arrived from Germany to join Teich's firm as head of the art department. Otto Buettner, at twenty-five only two years younger than his employer, was the son of a former manager of the Teich family business in Lobenstein. Four years later Frank Hochegger, an Austrian immigrant in his mid-twenties, took charge of the printing department, eventually rising to senior management. By 1906, Teich's company was printing a series of halftone-lithographic cards of urban sites in Chicago. Mostly based on three-quarter photographic views taken from neighboring buildings, these images exhibited a faded color palette of Ben Day dots and stipples of light aquamarine or green, bright yellow, and dark red over black halftone dots. Given the primitive quality of these cards compared with those the company had earlier imported from Germany, it is not surprising that Teich & Co. remained $75,000 in debt in 1907. As Teich later recalled, they were "in a strange position" because "the more we sold, the greater were our losses."[29]

About this time several developments coalesced to propel the fledgling company out of debt and into leadership of the American postcard industry. For one thing, this new American business staffed by German immigrants benefited from the tariff of 1909. Already able to fill orders in two to three months compared to a minimum of six months required by printers in Germany, Teich could also now undercut them in price. The tariff also brought a profitable relationship with Hugh C. Leighton, the Maine postcard importer. It seems likely that Teich was already the midwestern distributor for the New England business, whose line contained some cards portraying scenes in Illinois, Wisconsin, and Ohio. Whatever the case, Leighton feared the impending increase in the cost of German imports and contracted with Teich to print a new series of cards, with around 1,500 different subjects in all. Mostly views of main streets, public buildings, commercial blocks, churches, monuments, parks, and scenic landscapes in New England, the series also included several hundred views from Florida and a smattering from New York, Pennsylvania, and Virginia. These

FIG. 2.9. "Fitchburg, Mass. Prospect Street, Looking North," Leighton L1457, ca. 1910

cards followed the aesthetic of Leighton's German imports, with crisp halftone detailing and delicate aquamarine and peach skies (fig. 2.9). They marked a significant advance beyond Teich's faded-looking 1906 views of Chicago. Only the omission of "Printed in Frankfort" (as the city's spelling was Anglicized) or "Printed in Germany" and the addition of the prefix L to their serial numbers distinguished Teich-printed cards from Leighton's earlier imports. The Leighton order was so large and the deadline so tight that Teich requested approval from his employees to run two shifts at the plant until the order was filled, making 1910 his first profitable year.[30]

The Leighton contract also tested an innovative printing method, offset lithography, the equipment for which Teich had just installed. Offset lithography enabled faster printing and higher volume without wearing out printing plates. It also stimulated innovations in the art department's preparing of plates for colorized postcards. Traditional lithography had employed horizontal flatbed presses that printed no more than 250 sheets per hour even when mechanized. And lithographic stones wore out so quickly that the Detroit Publishing Company, which typically used nine or ten stones and occasionally as many as fifteen for the velvety colors of its secret process, was continually preparing new editions of its better-selling cards. Even zinc printing plates, which Teich had already adopted, did not last forever.[31]

FIG. 2.10. Teich's first offset printing press, 1910

Offset lithography, a high-speed rotary process, employed zinc plates but only indirectly. To visualize the process, imagine three long cylinders or rollers fixed horizontally, one above the other, with a curved zinc printing plate attached to the upper roller, a thin blanket of rubber covering the middle roller, and the lower roller carrying blank sheets of paper through the press. Turning counterclockwise, the zinc plate on the upper roller was inked at the top of its cycle. As it moved to the bottom of its cycle, it transferred the ink directly onto the rubber-coated middle roller, which was turning clockwise, as the two momentarily converged. This middle roller, now carrying on its rubber surface the ink of the image to be printed, made contact at the bottom of its cycle with the third roller, turning counterclockwise and carrying a sheet of paper. The ink was transferred to the paper, which was then ejected from the press. Meanwhile the upper roller was automatically sprayed with water and re-inked as it continued turning into the next cycle. After one color of ink had dried, the sheets were overprinted with the next. Advantages of offset lithography included greater speed (and thus higher volume), low wear on the printing plates because they touched only resilient rubber (instead of the abrasive fibers of paper), and fewer skilled pressmen.[32]

Teich was pushing technical limits with the offset process. When the original manufacturer of offset machinery in the United States, the Harris Company of Cleveland, could not supply a press with an unprecedented 38 × 52–inch sheet capacity, Teich convinced the upstart Walter Scott Company of Elizabeth, New Jersey, to build one for him (fig. 2.10). The new press required a recently introduced high-speed mechanical paper feeder, and Teich and Hochegger tinkered with the two machines for several months to coordinate them, just in time for Leighton's huge order. In the meantime the company was standardizing the preparation of printing plates. Anyone who now tries to understand why these early postcards look as they do discovers that markedly different processes for preparing color lithographic plates could and did yield similar results on paper. Written descriptions of printing processes from that time are maddeningly incomplete because they assume a working knowledge now lost. However, a journalist who interviewed Teich in 1938 hinted that he had "startled the printing world" in the early days "when he combined printing with lithography."[33] That phrase suggests the black halftone base was printed by letterpress (traditional "printing," as Teich referred to it, with the areas to be printed raised above a plate's surface), while the four color inks were overprinted by offset lithography.

To prepare litho plates for the colors, artists transferred the halftone base (the part eventually to be printed in black) in light blue onto four zinc plates to serve as outlines and guides for the application of color. Each plate was then marked in grease and finally etched with the solids, dashes, Ben Day dots, or random stipples required for its particular color. After scanning and magnifying several Teich postcards from the 1910s and '20s, one discovers increasing regularity of appearance as the search for greater speed and lower labor costs continued. The black halftone screen was reduced from 200 to 175 lines per inch, a change requiring less black ink and visually opening up an image, allowing more of its value to be carried by colors rather than shading. And while Ben Day dots and dashes applied by hand continued to define yellow, peach (or pink), and red, Teich shifted to halftone dots for aquamarine (or light blue), which usually covered an image's greatest area. Screen sizes for aquamarine halftone varied from 133 to 110 lines per inch on two sampled cards from about the same date, indicating a state of flux.[34] The very existence of aquamarine halftone dots suggests that Teich was experimenting with a photomechanical process to replace the traditional labor-intensive hand stippling done by litho artists while maintaining the primary aesthetic effect. Teich himself said he did not patent the new process because it was so "difficult" that "nobody would want to imitate it."[35] Competitors did reverse engineer the process, however, and the trend toward mechanization reached its logical conclusion in the linen postcards of the 1930s.

Before then, during the 1910s and '20s, Curt Teich & Co. became the dominant American postcard printer, the "General Motors" of the industry.[36] The custom-made Scott offset press was large enough to enable Teich to "gang" together plates for thirty-two postcards and print them, one color at a time, on large sheets of card stock, after which they were cut apart and separated. As the size of printing presses increased, the company eventually printed 110 different views on one sheet. This capacity challenged sales agents to secure orders to ensure that the plant was never idle, but the company also printed brochures, letterhead stationery, and advertising blotters. As Teich & Co.'s fortunes rose, its primary American competitor's declined. Unable to maintain market share with the labor- and material-intensive Photochrom process, the Detroit Publishing Company entered receivership in 1924.[37]

Flush with the success of the Leighton order, Teich & Co. continued expanding. In 1911 the firm built a three-story brick plant in a new industrial district on the Far North Side of Chicago. Located on West Irving Park Road at North Ravenswood Avenue, the new plant boasted an impressive Romanesque entry tower but could not long accommodate the growing company. In 1922 a more modern-looking, five-story brick addition, designed by Curt's older brother Frederick, an architect, extended the plant eastward to the next street and enabled a Ford-like flow of work from reception, offices, and mailroom on the fifth floor, to art and photography departments on the third and fourth floors, to pressrooms with thirty printing presses on the first two floors. By then, the former job printer was referring to himself as a "manufacturer." He and his wife, Anna Niether, whom he married in 1909, when he was thirty-two and she not quite twenty, were living in a large three-story Queen Anne house in Sheridan Park, where they raised four sons and a daughter. By 1935 they had moved farther out, to a three-story stucco mansion along Lake Michigan in Glencoe. The family lived according to a German bourgeois ethic of hard work and frugality. A domestic servant recalled with approval that the master of the house occasionally inspected vegetable peelings to make sure they were as thin as possible.[38]

Although Teich prospered by mass-producing landscape views, the standard history of postcards characterizes the period of his firm's rise as one of general decline for the industry in terms of aesthetic quality and economic standing.[39] Most American postcard printers had not fared as well as expected after German imports were eliminated. For one thing, major importers and distributors had ordered surpluses in anticipation of the tariff and eventually had to dump overstocks at a loss. Perhaps more important, in 1912 the F. W. Woolworth Company, a recently consolidated national chain of six hundred dime stores, ordered millions of cards portraying scenes across the United States, mostly commercial streets and prominent buildings. Oddly, Woolworth often relegated its own stores to the background in these views. One of Woolworth's cards, a view of the main street of Marion, Ohio, with buggies and automobiles

Center Street, Marion, Ohio.

FIG. 2.11. "Center Street, Marion, Ohio," Teich A-28104, ca. 1912

along the curb (fig. 2.11), features the F. M. Kirby dime store in the foreground, while Woolworth's is barely visible across the street. Ironically, given the chain's depressing effect on the postcard market, a large sign two doors beyond Kirby's advertises postcards for sale.[40]

Woolworth sold millions of cards at ten cents a dozen, contributing to a saturated market and temporarily driving the general price down to five cents a dozen. At the same time greeting cards with envelopes became popular and replaced greetings printed on postcards. These two developments led to the industry's partial collapse. Fifteen American postcard printers went out of business in 1913, and the National Association of Post Card Manufacturers canceled its annual meeting for 1914. But Teich & Co. thrived by putting its simplified production process and increased printing capacity to work as Woolworth's major supplier. Consolidating that advance and expanding even further required aggressive sales agents who could obtain independent orders from across the country. The company had emerged as the major American postcard printer.

Contrary to criticism from collectors much later, Teich's standardization of the landscape view card during the teens and twenties did not indicate a loss of quality for American postcards. The aesthetic of Teich's hybrid halftone-lithographic printing process remained constant, with the precise photographic details later admired by Walker Evans continuing to project clearly through the colorizing of light blues and pinks. Over the years the cards exhibited only two material changes. The first was the introduction of white borders around all four edges, about three-sixteenths of an inch wide, which saved on ink and allowed cards to be cut apart with less precision. The second was the disappearance of a shiny, lacquer-like finish, visible mostly when a card was tilted in the light, in favor of a harsher matte finish. Around 1915 the firm abandoned the brand name C. T. Photochrom, printed along the line dividing address and message sections, replacing it with the name C. T. American Art. This change might seem minor, but it marked a rhetorical shift away from emphasis on the photographic or technical reproduction of reality, a goal Teich's halftone lithographs had always shared with real photo, collotype, and halftone postcards. The new name for a virtually unchanged process instead emphasized presentation of a miniature art object that might expressively or impressionistically evoke some quality beyond ordinary reality. Although the striking visual impact of brightly colored linen postcards was still sixteen years away, their unprecedented aesthetic was prefigured in the phrase "American Art."

3

The Linen Postcard

INNOVATION AND AESTHETICS

THE LINEN POSTCARD EMERGED FROM NO-where as an optimistic response to the Great Depression's bleakest years. Or so it has seemed to those who comment on linen cards after the fact. For the painter John Baeder, their popular imagery defies the "dark cloud" of the 1930s. The social historian Allen F. Davis observes that while the "bright, romantic, sometimes airbrushed" linen cards might "come as a shock" to anyone accustomed to perceiving the Depression in grim black and white, they do record the way things looked at that time—or, expanding on his comment, the way people wanted them to look. In their guide for collectors, Mark Werther and Lorenzo Mott present linen cards as signs of an American dream replete with "the fruits of abundance" during "a time of hardship and hope." Others who comment more generally on the impact of linen cards typically describe them as projecting a spirit of optimism. The cultural geographer John A. Jakle, who favors linens in a book on night views, maintains that view cards present a "visual modernism suggestive of a better future." Finally, a former curator of the Teich Postcard Archives, Katherine Hamilton Smith, has observed, of the entire run of linen cards, that "what exists here is really America as it saw itself, as it brought itself to this company."[1]

Fɪɢ. 3.1. Curt Teich in his fifties

One cannot help wondering whether Curt Teich (fig. 3.1) recognized the larger import of what he was doing. Did the printer, who at the beginning of the Depression had been a naturalized U.S. citizen for thirty years, set out to create a hopeful portrait of a nation that had offered opportunity to so many members of his family? Did he direct photographers, artists, and printers, many of them also German immigrants, in making a culturally resonant portrait of the nation? Or were they merely doing a job, one postcard at a time? And if that was the case, did they ever realize what they had accomplished? If Teich was largely following commercial instincts, then how did this celebratory vision of the American scene come about? Teich left no clues in his autobiography, noting only that the Depression brought hard times as orders for cards evaporated and New Deal policies increased his labor costs. In response to a loss of business, he personally traveled across the United States and on a junket to Mexico, Panama, Cuba, and the Caribbean to solicit orders. In the meantime, he remarked laconically, "a new color process had been perfected," and "soon the factory was working again full time and everybody was happy." This new color printing process, introduced in 1931 and trademarked as "C. T. Art-Colortone" but universally known by its textured linen finish, was a product of the Depression, but its expression of exuberant optimism in the midst of gloom seems more of a happy accident than an inspired gesture.[2]

The C. T. Art-Colortone Process

The linen card owed its existence to a continuing drive to reduce costs of labor and materials, but it also seems Teich sought to take advantage of new inks that made bright, saturated colors attainable without the expense of multiple lithographic overprinting. Several factors—economic, technical, and aesthetic—joined in a transformation that rendered obsolete the halftone-lithographic cards of the previous twenty years, with their sharp photographic outlines and delicate blue and pink washes. Just as Teich had adopted offset lithography immediately after its practical introduction, he presumably also investigated reports of new so-called watercolor inks introduced in the United States in 1927 by the French printer Jean Berté. Intended for low-volume fine-art printing of posters, greeting cards, and brochures, Berté's water-soluble inks were hailed for "brilliancy of color," an "opaque" quality, and a contradictory "transparency" that produced "many intermediate tones" through overprinting. Observers differed over the degree to which his inks were water-based, with one claiming the name actually referred to a quality in the finished product of resembling watercolor paintings. Berté's tight control over the process did not enable easy clarification. But the effects were so impressive that chemists sought to achieve them through thinner, dye-based inks, which, though containing oils, acted more like Berté's watercolor inks than like traditional pigment-based inks.[3]

However, Teich could not use these "richer and more brilliant color effects" without changing another factor, the card stock he used for postcards.[4] When printed on the smooth paper the company typically used, so-called watercolor inks were absorbed quickly, lost their brilliancy, and yielded a dull, faded product. Teich experimented with card stock that had been run through an embossing roller to impart a surface texture. The idea was to create greater surface area through miniscule ridges and valleys, and thus greater exposure to air after the ink's transfer to the paper, thereby enabling faster drying. Ink remained on the surface as it quickly dried, instead of being absorbed, and finished cards retained the new ink's deep, brilliant hues. The embossed texture required for drying also gave the cards an illusion of having been printed on expensive handmade paper or a miniature artist's canvas.[5]

Evidence suggests some experimentation in search of an ideal embossing pattern. An early card with a low linen serial number, a view of the Hotel Fensgate in Boston from 1931, has a texture imitating that of handmade notepaper, with horizontal rows of shallowly impressed waves barely visible in the background (fig. 3.2). Within a short time, however, Teich shifted to the standard linen embossing of thin, raised parallel lines, arrayed both horizontally and vertically, tightly packed in each direction at about 85 lines per inch (fig. 3.3). Thicker, more visible lines, embossed to slightly greater height, were scattered at varying distances, running along for random lengths before merging back into the finer lines, yielding the illusion of a fabric-like weave. In addition to facilitating quick drying of thin, color-saturated inks, the texture supplied an "added touch of quality," according to the company, and gave the new line of cards its characteristic "linen" nickname. Competing printers introduced "numerous imitations," so many that by the mid-1930s there were few non-linen color postcards being printed anywhere in the United States.[6]

For all the stylishness conveyed by the new inks and texture, they also brought new printing economies. For the first time in the short history of lithographed color postcards, it proved possible to use halftone dots for each color, thereby eliminating the need for labor-intensive litho artists, with their brushes, stippling crayons, and Ben Day stencils. Teich employed the new inks in bright, strong values of cyan, magenta, yellow, and a dark blue used for emphasis and for night scenes. As before, black provided outlines and shading, but with strong, saturated colors it proved possible to use even less shading than before, thereby opening up spaces for greater color emphasis. The linen texture made it possible to reduce the black halftone screen from 175 to 133 lines per inch, which enabled a minor savings in black ink. However, that change made the printed dots more discernible even when printed on the diagonal. But on the other hand, the texturing reduced the visual impact of the dots because they physically wavered over the embossing and because its rectilinear lines interfered with their diagonal patterns. The texture also obscured the halftone dots of the various colors and made it possible to print them at 133 lines per inch as well.

Following the custom for color halftone printing, yellow's screen was set on the vertical, magenta's was tilted fifteen degrees to the right from vertical, and cyan's was tilted fifteen degrees to the left from vertical.[7] Dark blue, when need-

HOTEL FENSGATE — 534 BEACON ST. — BOSTON, MASS.

OVERLOOKING THE CHARLES RIVER AND ITS ESPLANADE

FIG. 3.2. "Hotel Fensgate—534 Beacon St.—Boston, Mass. / Overlooking the Charles River and Its Esplanade," Teich 1A-H107, 1931

FIG. 3.3. Detail, "Delaware River Bridge Connecting Philadelphia, Pa. and Camden, N.J.," Teich 3A-H963, 1933

FIG. 3.4. Detail, "Hotel Fensgate"

ed, seems to have been printed at the same angle as cyan. Tilting the screens ensured that most dots were printed not on top of those of other colors but next to them. That juxtaposition, rather than any overprinting, causes eye and mind to perceive a rainbow of hues in CMYK four-color printing. Viewing a card at 8× magnification, however, reveals phalanxes of cyan, magenta, yellow, and black halftone dots marching at different angles, each sometimes in possession of an open field and sometimes marching at cross-purposes with other phalanxes, interpenetrating, strengthening, or fading out. Individual inks were printed at uniform strength, but halftone dots became larger or smaller, clumping together or thinning out according to shifting patterns of the larger image. We tend to think of blue and yellow forming green, or red and blue forming purple, but in fact, when viewed at the scale of ordinary vision, varying sizes and clumps of interacting dots of different primary colors stimulate a visual illusion of many more colors. Teich obtained a richness of hue similar to traditional hand-printed, fifteen-color lithographic work while using high-speed offset presses and five halftone plates with surfaces defined by photomechanical processes.

To sum up, it is impossible fully to sort out the complicated convergence of factors contributing to the C. T. Art-Colortone process and the triumph of the linen postcard. New inks brought brighter, more saturated colors. An embossed texture enabled those inks to dry quickly, leaving greater brilliancy on the paper and allowing the company to use faster offset presses. Embossing also obscured the halftone dots that had been extended beyond black to encompass three primary colors plus dark blue. Photomechanical production of halftone printing plates eliminated the cost of skilled litho artists. Coarser half-tone screens lowered the cost of etching the plates and brought a small savings in ink. Five-color halftone printing introduced a palette of scores of colors, replacing the washed-out blue and pink of pre-linen color cards. Finally, bright new visuals benefited from the linen finish, which suggested an artist's canvas and conveyed a slight three-dimensional sheen when tilted against the light. It took Teich's staff a while to adjust all these elements. For example, the Hotel Fensgate card from 1931 (fig. 3.4) exhibits colors that seem more natural when compared to earlier, pre-linen views, with brighter reds for brick (differing in sun and shade), varied greens for vegetation, a brighter, less watery blue for the sky, and fluffy white clouds rather than sallow yellow ones. Even so, the image's overall appearance has the vague softness typical of the previous twenty years. But linen cards quickly assumed richer, more saturated tones, sometimes with a hard edge evoking their manufactured status but more often with an exaggeration suggesting an abundant landscape of promise.

To some extent Teich was catching up with a revolution in color printing. In 1907, shortly before the company received the Leighton contract, only 5 percent of full-page advertisements in the *Saturday Evening Post*, a popular family magazine, were in color. By 1930, 50 percent of *Post* ads were in color, and bright hues had transformed the marketing of such consumer goods as automobiles, tableware, and plumbing fixtures. As economic gloom descended over the nation, Teich's success depended on being able to offer the improved "true colors" of the C. T. Art-Colortone process while also lowering production costs so these upbeat views of America could be sold for a penny apiece, the price Teich regarded as a ceiling above which he could not go and stay in business.[8] Despite economic and aesthetic benefits of the new process, however, the linen postcard's success also depended on a larger process of making and selling postcards that Teich & Co. had been perfecting for twenty years. Before surveying the iconography of natural landscapes and urban scenes typical of linen postcards, we need to understand how individual images were captured at unique sites across the country and conveyed to Chicago, how they were processed and transformed according to standard procedures, and how they were finally returned to their points of origin for sale as local souvenirs.

The Role of the Sales Agent

There is some irony in the fact that traveling sales agents propagated the postcard, which was used by their colleagues in other lines of merchandising to communicate with family and friends while on the road. Unlike most traveling salesmen, whose major effort came at the end of the mass-production cycle (that is, placing goods with retailers for sale to consumers), Teich sales agents were often directly involved in conceiving and designing their products. Their major activities, soliciting commissions for local views and convincing local retailers to carry the company's cards, encompassed the beginning and the end of the commercial life of a postcard. A breezy bonhomie pervaded *Curteich News*, an in-house newsletter, which in 1935 reviewed recent successes by twenty-seven agents, some identified by name but others only by nicknames such as "Mailsy," "the Old Maestro," and "the Tennessee Hill Billy," Harry G., who had yet again exercised his "penchant for creating designs that stand out like a beacon on a black night." Sales activities described by *Curteich News* suggest an amorphous division of territories dependent on shifting personnel and differing degrees of ambition and willingness to travel. For a while at least a few agents distributed cards printed by multiple companies. When the magazine *American Business* profiled Teich & Co. in 1938, there were purportedly thirty teams of agents on the road, each with two salesmen and a photographer, though some salesmen were described as taking their own photos. Given the article's dubious claim that photographers revisited sites twice a year, the figure of thirty teams seems wildly exaggerated. The company's auditor's report for 1939 portrayed an orderly division of the country into ten regions, each with a single representative.[9]

Only one Teich sales representative, G. I. Pitchford (fig. 3.5), emerges from obscurity. Although job files documenting thousands of postcards reveal frequent input from many sales agents, only Pitchford appears so frequently in company records at to take shape as a definite personality. His duties, activities, concerns, and problems were typical, but his career was uniquely influential in the development of linen postcards owing to his longevity, his sales region, and his energy as a postcard designer. The territory of this self-described "western representative" eventually included Washington, Oregon, Idaho, California, Nevada, Utah, Arizona, and western Mexico—a region encompassing many of the nation's scenic natural areas and rapidly growing cities. Pitchford's employment with Teich ran from 1913 until his death at eighty in 1967.[10] Born in Ohio in 1887, Pitchford grew up in Duquesne, Pennsylvania, where his father, an English immigrant, worked as a foreman for Carnegie Steel. After studying bookkeeping, "Pitch" worked for two years as a stenographer at the steel mill and then went to Los Angeles, hoping to enter the nickelodeon business. Instead he wound up in 1912, at age twenty-five, working as a postcard sales agent for his wife's stepfather, who had purchased, for next to nothing, the retouched photos and printed postcard inventory of the failed Cardinell-Vincent Company.

The new but short-lived Carlin Post Card Company relied on several printers for pre-linen color views of California—including Teich & Co., to whom Pitchford sent his first order in May 1913. Over the next two years he gradually shifted to working exclusively as a Teich sales agent. In 1915 he wrote a friend

FIG. 3.5. G. I. Pitchford, western representative of Teich & Co.

that he had been "connected with a Chicago house" for the past year and was "getting along nicely." Indeed, he was "a lot better off selling one of the lines direct" than being "in business for myself" (with his father-in-law). He reported having "the whole Coast for my territory" and being "very busy for the last year, spending most of my time on the road."[11] He did not mention that he was also taking the photos for many of the orders he submitted, having taught himself to use large- and medium-format view cameras, with developing and printing done by commercial labs in Los Angeles.

While traveling through their assigned territory, sales agents negotiated several types of commissions. The most lucrative accounts, and the easiest to maintain, were those with regional distributors, such as the Zenith-Interstate

News Company in Duluth and the Western Publishing & Novelty Company in Los Angeles. The latter's owner, Theodore Sohmer, became a close friend of Pitchford's, as did Earl Brothers, a distributor in Boulder City, Nevada, so much so that at some point he presented the agent with the mounted head of a moose he had shot. Such news agencies, as they were called, supplied newsstands with newspapers, magazines, maps, souvenir booklets, and other printed matter, including postcards. After establishing a relationship with an agency, a Teich representative could expect a steady stream of orders for individual local views.

Similar connections existed with organizations involved in promoting tourism. For example, the Fred Harvey Company, operator of hotels, restaurants, and souvenir shops along the route of the Santa Fe Railroad, commissioned hundreds of views of southwestern Indians, their dwellings, and their ceremonies and crafts. Photographic studios in scenic areas, such as Haynes in Yellowstone National Park and H. H. Bennett in the Wisconsin Dells, ordered cards from Teich and provided source photos from negative archives extending back to the late nineteenth century. Occasionally government offices charged with promoting tourism contacted Teich directly. For example, the director of the official news service of Miami invited the company to go through the city's archive of thousands of negatives and even offered to assign photographers to make additional exposures for Teich at no charge.[12]

Usually agents did not have it so easy. "No town," an in-house pep talk exhorted, "is too small for an edition of colorful post cards showing the attractions of the community." Following the company's sales hints, an agent would invite a customer to imagine a revolving wire rack "right inside the entrance to the store, where light strikes at the display in all its fullness," with dozens of cards massed in such a way that "there appears to be an almost limitless variety." Often a druggist, stationer, or proprietor of a department store could be convinced to commission a series of ten or fifteen local views—courthouse, town common or monument square, churches, high school, main street, city park, the birthplace of a historical personage. Flipping through a sample book with 250 cards, an agent would suggest how the most ordinary local landmarks could be rendered attractive, especially when surrounded by generic scenes of pastures, woodland lakes, waves crashing on rocky coasts, palm-framed sunsets, mountains, or desert vistas, depending on the local geography. Consumers tended to accept at face value such generic scenes imprinted with local place names. Ralph Teich, Curt's youngest son, recalled witnessing a man pointing to a generic card and declaring, "This is the spot on lake so and so where we caught that big fish."[13]

An agent would also recommend comic cards themed for vacationers and traveling salesmen, and possibly a large-letter "Greetings from" card devoted to the town or state, with fragments of miniature scenes embedded in the large outlines of the letters spelling its name (fig. 3.6). Finally, he would also push so-

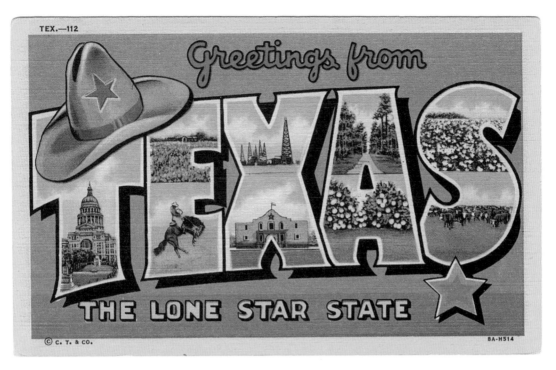

TEX.—112

Fig. 3.6. "Greetings from Texas / The Lone Star State," Teich 8A-H514, 1938

called accordion folders with eighteen different postcard-sized views from the region (also available for national parks, tourist attractions, and cities). Images were printed nine to a side on a long strip of paper that was folded to fit into a cardboard wallet that could be mailed for 1½ cents without a message. Retailing for 10 cents, folders were inexpensive to print because printing plates for the images already existed. A typical small-town order encompassed not only the design and printing of original cards but also a supply of generics, comics, and folders for which Teich already possessed an inventory.

Negotiating with stationers and druggists consumed only a fraction of an agent's time. Much effort also went into convincing proprietors of individual businesses that commissioning a postcard afforded effective, inexpensive advertising. *Sales Pointers*, a ninety-six-page in-house booklet issued in 1935, touted more than thirty commercial endeavors from florists and fish hatcheries to service stations and sporting goods stores as opportunities for go-getter postcard salesmen. In fact the majority of advertising cards, which constituted about a quarter of Teich's total volume of images, illustrated restaurants from humble diners to posh urban retreats, lodgings from tourist courts to luxury hotels, roadside attractions, taverns and nightclubs ("a new, a vast market" after repeal of Prohibition[14]), and occasionally dress shops, jewelry stores, and other retail businesses. Such cards were given away to guests and customers as a means of

FIG. 3.7. "Armour Star Frankfurters," Teich 6B-H2352, 1946

inexpensive publicity. Management also used them to conduct business or confirm reservations.

Teich's sales agents also solicited orders for postcards portraying every imaginable type of product—Armour hot dogs sizzling on a grill (fig. 3.7), a tubular-steel dinette set manufactured in Connecticut, the Indian Model 340 motorcycle, police uniforms from Dubois & Son in New York, and so on. Teich promoted these nonview cards, which often carried printed advertising messages, as central to advertising's "natural endeavor"—"to illustrate the article as it in reality is." Illustrating reality was also the stated purpose of Teich's portrayals of the American scene, whether natural, rural, industrial, urban, or commercial. In fact, however, while exhorting "color conscious" customers to take advantage of an innovative "natural color reproduction" process, the company was actually providing simple tools for projecting an intensified, exaggerated simulation of reality.[15]

A file of G. I. Pitchford's business correspondence from 1912 to 1918 reveals his responsibilities as a postcard sales agent, which remained constant throughout the rest of his career. Although Pitchford worked for Teich, he actually served as a kind of middleman in production and distribution. He was expected to file reports with the company on creditworthiness of new customers and to alert the home office regarding accounts that seemed "unsafe" or "in danger."[16] He wrote letters to new hotels and other establishments in his territory, suggesting how postcards could promote business. Working the other side of the fence, Pitchford tracked down missing shipments for customers and backed up claims of poor design or printing at the plant. Sometimes he wrote to commercial photographers he knew only by reputation to describe photos he hoped they would be able to supply him. Strict about copyright, the company demanded releases for photos submitted with orders. Some photographers sent unsolicited prints for Pitchford's consideration, and on one occasion Curt Teich himself sent an envelope of photos for which he wanted Pitchford to find customers.

Teich sales agents filed weekly reports of visits to regular and potential customers, whether wholesalers who ordered cards or retailers who stocked them. Pitchford kept records on officially printed index-card forms revealing, among other things, that he dealt directly with managers of individual Woolworth and Kress chain stores regarding postcards they stocked on their racks. He was on the road about three-quarters of the time for decades. His itineraries had to be carefully orchestrated to include small retail outlets and souvenir shops as well as major distributors. Often he was told a customer was "working old stock down" and could take nothing at present. Or in a few months they would be ordering "new subjects" and he would "have to go back again." Or he would have to return to "take photos" for a "spring order." On one occasion Pitchford recorded it was "too foggy to take pictures." After another visit he wrote frankly, "This manager is impossible." Even at home, the tapping of his portable Smith-Corona typewriter was a constant, and on one occasion he composed business letters on Christmas Day. A daughter who recalled him as a generous, caring father also reported that "he loved every minute" on the road and "could hardly wait to get going again."[17]

Whether Pitchford and fellow sales agents took their own source photos (typical in the case of local sights, street scenes, minor tourist attractions, and small-town commercial establishments) or clients provided them (usually the case with exterior and interior views of major restaurants and hotels), the agents had to record standardized color information for the art department in Chicago. In 1932 Teich published a color chart as a postcard with thirty-two squares filled with numbered colors (fig. 3.8).[18] Although the client might occasionally report the colors required for a particular card by using this chart, to do so required some understanding of the printing process. In most cases the sales agent pasted a frisket (a sheet of translucent tracing paper) to the upper edge of the back of an 8 × 10 glossy photo and folded it down over the image on the front. After tracing the image's main outlines in pencil on the frisket, he wrote in the numbers of the colors needed to complete the scene, one for each outlined area, sometimes also elaborating in words. The process demanded considerable judgment because some colors were to be printed on areas with no black halftone, others on areas with moderate halftone shading, and others with substantial shading. To record the colors correctly involved an unconscious referencing back and forth from the black-and-white print to the real-life scene as it appeared to the person who was filling in the numbers. As with so much in the linen process, this "paint-by-number" system harked back to nineteenth-century lithography, as when Thomas Moran accompanied watercolors for reproduction by Louis Prang with pencil drawings and color notations, thereby providing an image "that could be easily taken apart and reassembled to resemble the original."[19]

In addition to using numbered sketches, agents relied on experience accumulated over three decades. For example, for a card depicting a passenger train crossing the causeway over Utah's Great Salt Lake, Pitchford advised the art department to take the proper yellow for a Southern Pacific diesel locomotive from an earlier postcard and pointed out "lots of chances for color in the sky" because "deep red sunsets are a regular thing on this lake."[20] Although agents frequently took pains to render colors exactly as they actually were in order to please clients, even forwarding to Chicago samples of wallpaper, drapery, upholstery, paint, and flooring (many of which survive in the job files), they also specified exaggerated effects of cloud, sky, sunset, and water—often quite startling but used so frequently that they became generic to the linen postcard aesthetic.

An agent typically served as a mediator between client and company as to a card's design, relaying instructions and cautions. In addition to specifying colors, he might emphasize elements about which a client was especially proud. For example, Pitchford warned retouching artists not to remove new lighting fixtures from a view of Main Street in Yuma, Arizona, because "these were the reason for remaking this subject!"[21] Agents sometimes marked cropping guidelines on the tracing paper frisket, requested that individual commercial signs in a street scene be emphasized or obscured, or ordered that extraneous buildings on either side of a featured hotel or clothing store be faded out. Often agents participated in the actual design of a card. For example, one agent reported that the proprietor of the Lycoming Hotel in Williamsport, Pennsylvania, admired a sample postcard of the Hotel Ponce de Leon in Roanoke, Virginia. That card featured three small pictures (one showing the exterior, the others a lobby and a lounge). A swirl of arches in the background, vaguely suggesting entryways and windows, joined the three images in a unified composition. Rather than directly copying that card's framing, a move that would have satisfied the client, the agent instead suggested carrying out the "secondary decorating between the pictures . . . with airplane ideas" because Williamsport's largest employer manufactured airplane motors. The resulting card (fig. 3.9) employed a background of stylized forms representing an engine and propeller, factory gears, and bits

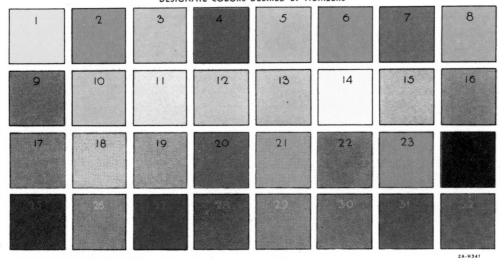

FIG. 3.8. "Color Chart / Curt Teich & Company, Chicago," Teich 2A-H341, 1932

FIG. 3.9. "The Lycoming / Williamsport, Pa.," Teich 6A-H2378, 1936

of archways to frame and integrate views of the hotel's brick exterior, coffee shop, and streamlined cocktail lounge. Although an artist in Chicago mocked up these abstractions on tracing paper, the idea came from the agent in the field, whose innovative suggestion relied on a continually shifting dialectic between local realities as he interpreted them and generic solutions residing in the collective experience of the company's art department and its archive of postcard designs.[22]

Those who consistently and successfully negotiated that process could be amply rewarded. By 1930, for example, Pitchford had moved with his wife, Star, and four children from South Pasadena into a new, custom-built stucco house in San Marino valued at $10,000. His income that year of about $9,000 placed his family well into the top fifth of the nation's households. Although Teich's 10 percent commission on sales did not stretch far during 1932 and 1933, the Depression's worst years, sales in Pitchford's territory rose steadily throughout the rest of the decade, enabling him to build a vacation home at Lake Arrowhead in the San Bernardino Mountains. In 1943, possibly owing to sales of postcards to soldiers, sailors, marines, and defense workers who were on the West Coast during wartime, he received a net income of more than $30,000, which catapulted his family into the top half percent of U.S. households. The one-time "traveling salesman" of 1917 (as his draft card identified him) had become the "western representative" for a "wholesale publisher" (according to the 1940 census).[23] Although Pitchford's career was unique in the Teich sales force, his success points to the unusual significance of sales agents in the postcard industry. What the historian Timothy B. Spears has said of traveling salesmen in general is especially the case with those who worked for Teich. They "universalized the local" because "their assimilation and transmission of knowledge particular to a specific place or culture . . . contributed, in a larger sense, to the creation of a mass society."[24]

From Art Department to Printing Press

If the process of closing a deal and transmitting orders to Chicago differed according to varying situations and client temperaments, a definite routine took over once an order had reached the Teich plant, where about three hundred employees saw it through to completion.[25] On June 2, 1937, for example, a clerk logged in a request from the Dakota News Agency for a white-bordered linen view card illustrating the city hall in Sioux Falls, South Dakota. After assigning an order number and a serial number by which the card would always be identified (in this case 7A-H1798), she typed a "photo ticket" recording the client's name and location, the subject, the initial print run of 12,500 cards, the

client's ownership of the source photo, and key phrases from the agent's color and retouching instructions. This label was glued onto a manila envelope, establishing the card's "job file," which included a rubber-stamped "estimate and work schedule" on which various production steps were recorded. Six days later the order was initialed by the cost department and by an executive, Curt Jr., the founder's oldest son, then twenty-seven years old, who had taken over day-to-day management a few years earlier.[26] That same day, both the composing and retouching departments began work on the card. Compositors prepared letterpress type for a brief caption and serial number for the card's front, and for a line of text for the back identifying the Dakota News Agency as the distributor (and in a sense as the card's publisher[27]). Although this card had no additional text, a descriptive caption (usually written by a sales agent but sometimes provided by a client) often appeared at the top of a card's message section. The agent was also responsible for the brief captions on the front of most cards.

Meanwhile, an artist in the retouching department worked with the 8 × 10 black-and-white source photo of the city hall, which was glued onto heavy cardboard, transforming it into an image from which a black halftone printing plate could be obtained. A surviving photo of the retouching department shows about twenty male artists sitting at rows of individual tables, three or four abreast, extending back along a wall of high windows with light streaming in (fig. 3.10). Most of the artists appear to be in their twenties (a balding older man is visible), and they wear white shirts, ties, vests, and aprons. Incandescent bulbs in metal shades hang from the ceiling. Many of the men were recent immigrants or came from the local German community. Some had attended the School of the Art Institute of Chicago, which emphasized industrial training in general and graphic design for advertising and printing in particular.[28] According to anecdote, strict discipline reigned; however, open seating may have encouraged camaraderie and comments on each other's work.

The retouching artist who worked on the Sioux Falls image confronted an unpromising source photo (fig. 3.11): the image is muted and dingy, with a washed-out sky; a patched-asphalt street takes up much of the foreground, and ill-defined sections mark different surfaces of the blocky WPA-style structure—brick walls with marble facing on the foundation, door surrounds, windows, and infill panels. With the source photo attached to a holder on the back of his table for reference, he used an airbrush, supplemented with fine-pointed brushes of sable hair, to paint directly onto a copy print of the photo. After pasting a translucent frisket over the copy photo with rubber cement, the artist cut an outline around an area to be painted and then carefully lifted the tissue paper from that section of the photo, exposing its surface while the rest of the image remained masked. Using the airbrush, a mechanical device consisting of a handheld pen and nozzle through which paint is forced by compressed air, he

Fᴵɢ. 3.10. Retouching department, Teich & Co., ca. 1930s

Fᴵɢ. 3.11. Source photo, city hall, Sioux Falls, SD,
ca. 1937

Fᴵɢ. 3.12. Retouched photo, June 1937

sprayed a uniform value of gray paint over a selected area. Typically an artist would boost contrasts and open up a source photo's darker areas so that depth or intensity could be conveyed through color rather than through shading. In this particular case, the artist applied various uniform gray-scale tones to wall panels, windows, grass, and pavement (fig. 3.12).

Next, setting down the airbrush and selecting a sable brush, the retoucher sharpened and emphasized lines and edges, painting directly by hand onto the copy photo. If this photo had included signs or lettering, those too would have been outlined for clarity. In this case, the artist chose to simplify and sharpen other structures in the distance on either side. He might just as easily have obscured them by spraying a mist of light gray over them—or deleted them entirely. The artist also brought out a streetlight stanchion and rendered its glass globe more clearly. Following handwritten instructions on the back of the source photo, he cropped the image, airbrushed out three older cars parked in front (probably Model T Fords), and sprayed highlights onto the fenders of four newer sedans, laconically indicated as "OK," which are diagonally parked along the street to the right. In the most obvious touch, responding to the command "put on flags," the artist painted delicate outlines of U.S. flags waving on two previously vacant flagpoles. He also cleaned up the street corner, which in the source photo has a bank of mud or sand extending from the curb into the street, eliminated a weedy strip of grass between the front curb and sidewalk, and in general smoothed the street's paving. A single artist typically did all the work on an image, but some became known for handling such tricky subjects as automobiles, interiors, or atmospheric landscapes. Most jobs remained in the retouching department for about five business days but took only four to eight hours to complete (the estimate in this case being five hours). The department took one week with the Sioux Falls city hall and finished on June 15.[29]

After the retouched image was approved, two things happened. The very next day, the texts to be printed on front and back were pasted up, along with such generic elements added to the back as the words "POST CARD," a rectangle indicating postage stamp placement, and a vertical line of type dividing address and message sections, identifying the card as a "genuine" Curteich C. T. Art-Colortone. Front and back paste-ups were photographed and plates made for relief printing. The image's key, or black, printing plate was also prepared that day. In this step, the retouched photo was rephotographed. The negative thus obtained, which reflected the sharpened details and contrasts of the retouching process, was printed through a halftone screen onto a photographically sensitized zinc plate. Two types of halftone proofs were then printed from this plate—one in black to guide a watercolor artist and four in light blue for later use by a colorist. Using the original color instructions and the proof from the black key plate as a guide, an artist spent ninety minutes on June 17 hand

FIG. 3.13. Hand-painted color proof, June 1937

painting a postcard-sized watercolor of the image. The color proof was then sent for approval to the Dakota News Agency in Sioux Falls. This miniature painting (fig. 3.13), now in the job file, presents the city hall as a blue-gray structure and surrounds it with grass of the deepest green and a dramatic sky with huge cumulus clouds suggesting an approaching storm.

Approval usually came by return mail, but in this case the client objected, complaining that the "blue shading on the building creates an entirely different effect than is natural." Although the marble trim did approach blue in color, the brick was actually "very light colored." The client called for "a much brighter treatment" to make the city hall "stand out as it really does" and make "the card appear more natural." Beyond that, the art department had guessed wrong in trying to clean up the curb; there was no grass strip between sidewalk and street. Even the atmospherics were wrong. The client argued without irony that the "deep colored sky and grass" must be "toned down" because "our South Dakota colors are not so brilliant." In this case a desire for authenticity worked against the exaggeration that gave linen cards their aesthetic resonance.

At this point, notations on the card's manila envelope become harder to decipher. The design was apparently reworked during the first week of July in response to the complaints and then sent to the section of the art department responsible for colorizing retouched black-and-white images. The project remained there for four business days, until July 6, and the colorizing took nearly ten hours. Colorizing was central to Teich's process for making linen cards.

Despite promotional talk of natural or real colors, linen cards relied on what printers technically called "fake color work." Ralph Teich later referred to them dismissively as "our fake color cards."[30] In all fairness, however, he was comparing them to the later chromes, postcards from the 1950s whose colors derived directly from Kodachrome color transparencies, which eventually drove Teich out of business as a late adopter.

The usual method of preparing plates for any four-color halftone printing, then only recently perfected, involved starting with color artwork in oils, watercolors, cut paper, or some other medium. A technician made three separate photographic exposures of the original artwork, in each case using a filter to exclude all but the desired light value (cyan, yellow, or magenta), whose varying intensities were thereby separated and recorded. Printing each of the resulting negatives through a halftone screen onto a photosensitized plate yielded three printing plates, one for each of the three basic colors. Carefully registered printing of these three plates onto a black print from the key plate yielded a color halftone copy of the original color artwork. The process was different for linen postcards, however, because the original (the retouched photo) was not in color. Teich boasted that their process avoided the need for "expensive colored [hand-tinted] photographs or costly drawings or paintings" as source images and did not employ "expensive process color plates" produced with elaborate filters. Teich's fake colorizing was a proprietary variant of a process so different from printer to printer that an 800-page printing manual from 1921 devoted only two vague sentences to it.[31]

When the Sioux Falls city hall project reached the colorizing department in July 1937, the process was apparently even more standardized than the retouching process. According to anecdote, Teich's colorists were female workers segregated from male retouchers on a different floor of the plant. Like the men, some of them had trained at the Art Institute. Vera Berdich, for example, a printmaker who later taught at the institute for thirty years, supported her education in the mid-1940s by working for Teich.[32] In 1931, however, when the firm created the linen postcard process, Teich had recruited the original colorists, all male, from Germany. Tichnor Brothers, the company's main competitor, duplicated Teich's linen colorizing process around 1936 by offering higher wages to four of Teich's colorists. Two years later, when a Tichnor brother and one of his sons established the rival Colourpicture after a family dispute, they recruited two more German colorists from Teich. These hijacked colorists, or color separationists, as they were also called, probably had reputations for technical innovation and served as supervisors of the routine colorists who did most of the work. While lithographic color separation had traditionally involved rigorous analysis and experiential intuition, the whole point of the linen process was to lower costs by reducing colorizing to a rote procedure. Even so, given the complexity of some

color effects, it seems likely that those projects were handled by more skilled, experienced colorists, who could invest a mechanical process with conscious artistry.

The colorist assigned to the simple, straightforward Sioux Falls city hall project used the revised watercolor proof only as a general guide and worked on four postcard-sized sheets of heavy white paper. Each sheet had the key, or black halftone base, of the entire image printed in a faint blue ink visible to the eye but not to a camera lens. During the colorizing process, each sheet was used to define the intensity of one of the four colors to be used in printing (cyan, magenta, yellow, and dark blue). In front of the colorist were eight to ten bottles of numbered red-hued inks ranging from just the faintest hint of pink (#1) through progressively darker pinks and reds to a full, rich red (#10, let us say). The fact that these inks were in various shades of red had no connection whatsoever to any red in the final image. The point was to create a progression of shades from no tone to full saturation.

The colorist also had a color chart with swatches of dozens of colors that were routinely required for postcard images. For each color swatch the chart listed the intensity number of the ink to be used for each of the four printing hues in order to yield that exact color when all four were printed over the black halftone base. For example, obtaining the blue in the reflection on the fenders of the nearest car parked by the Sioux Falls city hall probably required intensity #5 in cyan, shading into #6 just above the tires, while attaining the brownish gray of the pavement alongside the car probably required intensity #5 or #6 in both yellow and magenta, and #8 in cyan. Neither required any dark blue, which was, however, required for the roof, lower side panel, and windows.[33] Comparing areas of color on the watercolor proof with swatches on the color chart and presumably working on one sheet at a time, the colorist painted by number, filling in various shapes with the differing intensities of inks required for each hue. In each case, for each of the four printing colors, the result was an image in which the deeper the tone of ink, the greater the intensity of that particular hue. When the colorist had finished inking the four sheets, they left the art department on July 6, about a month after the order was received in the mailroom.

At that point the camera department took over, photographing each of the four variably reddish sheets, one for each printing color. Each exposure was made through a halftone screen onto a photosensitive glass plate, creating a screened negative conveying the intensity of that particular CMYK color. After each exposure, the halftone screen in the camera was rotated to the proper angle for the next color using a Bassani device, a patented machine leased by the firm in 1930 or 1931. The Bassani process refined halftone dots, reportedly making them seem half their actual size, and ensured that dots of different colors would usually be printed not on top of each other but adjacent for the most convinc-

ing optical illusion of multiple colors. Sometimes, for a demanding client, the four glass negatives for an image were used to make zinc printing plates from which a color proof of the postcard was printed with a small proofing press and sent to the client for approval. In most cases no such printed color proof was made. Instead each glass negative was ganged, or assembled in a frame, with those representing the same color in other postcards. By the 1940s, 110 cards per sheet was the standard. The entire frame of glass negatives was exposed onto a single large photosensitive zinc plate, which became the printing plate for that particular color, and the process was repeated for the other three colors.

Job file entries do not disclose dates of printing and shipping, but Teich promised delivery three to eight weeks after a customer's approval of the watercolor proof,[34] meaning most cards were delivered one to two months after being ordered, perhaps a bit later. Because glass negatives had to be ganged with those for other cards, delays sometimes occurred in assembling enough views for a specific print run. On the other hand, when the company was swamped with orders, sales agents competed for space, as in the case of one named Baumann, who "can't wait to mail 'em in, so he has to wire [send a telegram] to hold a space on a sheet."[35]

With completion of a ganged printing plate for each of the four colors, the Sioux Falls card was finally ready for printing. In 1937 the plant consisted of at least twenty presses of various sizes, including four Harris offset presses, two of which printed two colors in one operation, thereby cutting press time and drying time.[36] The 12,500 large sheets of heavy paper stock of this print run moved through a relief press for the front and back texts of the assembled cards and then through offset presses for the five colors of the images (including black). After being cut apart and separated from the other 109 images, stacks of crisp new cards representing the Sioux Falls city hall (fig. 3.14) as somewhat duller and grayer than in the initial watercolor proof, were packed in cardboard boxes totaling 125 pounds in weight and shipped by rail to the Dakota News Agency.

Throughout the development of the Teich linen process, from bright watercolor inks and embossed paper to fake color separation and Bassani-generated halftones, the goal was greater efficiency, more mechanization, and de-skilling of labor to reduce costs and maintain enough of a profit margin to stay in business during the Depression. The economic edge was razor thin for postcards sold for a penny or two at retail or given away as promotional items.[37] In 1936, Teich would have charged the Dakota News Agency $4.50 per thousand for an order of 12,500 of this "local view post card" (or about $56.00 total, with the buyer paying for shipping). A minimum order of 6,000 cards would have cost $6.50 per thousand, and subsequent reorders of the same card would have cost less than the original orders ($3.50 per thousand for an additional 12,500 and $4.50 per thousand for 6,000). Advertising cards, including views of res-

CITY HALL, SIOUX FALLS, S. D.

7A-H1798

FIG. 3.14. "City Hall, Sioux Falls, S.D.," Teich 7A-H1798, 1937

taurants, hotels, and tourist attractions, cost more because they required more painstaking production work. An order of 12,500 advertising postcards would have cost $8.00 per thousand for new work and $5.75 for reprints.

Even charging more for new orders than for reprints, the company lost money when preparing new printing plates. Ralph Teich recalled, "We would be willing to spend enormous sums of money on a particular card, to get the card the way the customer wanted it. . . . we lost our shirt."[38] With new plates costing from $45 to $75 depending on the subject, the company recovered its losses only when a customer reordered the same card.[39] Motivation to please clients ran high, and job files contained frequent warnings about satisfying fussy demands. Given that retail prices, wholesale prices, and production costs differed only minimally, the Teich plant had to churn out postcards nonstop to maintain a slim profit margin. At a single moment in time, at the close of business on the last day of 1939, the company's "work in process" encompassed orders for sixteen million cards.[40] The genius of the C. T. Art-Colortone linen process, which applied mass production to popular imagery through rationalized photography, retouching, colorizing, printing, and distribution, lay in the fact that an economic imperative yielded not only a formulaic genre of representation but also a unique, colorful aesthetic that celebrated an American scene charged with optimism.

The Linen Postcard Aesthetic

Today, more than eighty years after they were introduced, linen postcards clearly seem to possess their own aesthetic. When explaining my collecting to people with no particular awareness of these cards, I find it sufficient to mention bright colors, embossed textures, exaggerated visual qualities, and striking sunsets. Most people recall having seen them, recognize them as a type, and are vaguely aware of their era. Writers who have recently mentioned Teich postcards, whether out of nostalgia, because of a neutral historical interest, or by way of lamenting photography's betrayal in the service of cultural homogeneity, all agree that these inexpensive cardboard views encompass a coherent vision. Most observers mention the conundrum of airbrushed shapes and vivid colors' purporting to represent reality through effects that now seem unreal, surreal, or, paradoxically, hyperreal.

The cultural historian Leah Dilworth, commenting on fake-color postcards in general, has described how colorizing images derived from black-and-white photos "made them seem both more 'real' (more natural) *and* more like paintings (more like art)." Owing to "painterly application of color," each of these "mass-produced image[s]" seemed "individual, original, singular." For the artist John Baeder, linen cards are "not just 'postcard reproductions.'" Instead they flowed from the printing presses retouched and colorized as "instant surreal paintings in miniature." According to him, "they function on the other side of reality" as "visual entertainment" and "pure fantasy." More to the point, their "heightened visual unreality" itself "becomes *a* reality." In that sense, what the cultural historian Peter Bacon Hales regards as representation's betrayal by "a sanitized, uniform vision" might also be viewed as an alternate realm with its own aesthetic reflecting an ideology of utopian desire realized on a miniature scale. The British artist and collector Tom Phillips, who has written several books on twentieth-century postcards, would agree with Baeder and Hales that postcards typically reflect "the vernacular aesthetic of a period." Postcards in general do represent a culture in "the way it wishes to be seen" because people "vote . . . with their small change" for the "vision" they desire. His argument assumes that only postcard styles with public approval survive in the marketplace. Notwithstanding this democratic perspective, Phillips also believes the linen postcard aesthetic verges on modernist expression. Referring to a 1940s image of a cocktail lounge in Kansas City, he points out "the uniquely American alchemy by which a black & white photograph becomes [a] crystalline abstraction."[41]

The British art historian Richard Morphet stated similar views as early as 1974. Later the curator of modern art at the Tate Gallery, Morphet contributed a brief introduction to a catalog for a traveling exhibition of 2,000 postcards

printed between 1930 and 1960 that was originated by Hofstra University's Emily Lowe Gallery. After noting the "deliberateness" with which postcards were "contrived" and "marketed," he marveled that the finished products were so "extraordinary and puzzling in terms of commercial appeal." Approaching the heart of the matter by assertion rather than proof, Morphet observed that postcard publishers seemed to be "secretly serving some quite different aim than profit, more imaginative and poetic, and diametrically opposed to the requirements of the majority of the postcard-buying public, [and] yet were curiously achieving great commercial success in that very market for reasons unrelated to their aims."[42]

Nothing in promotional material or client correspondence suggests that anyone at Teich & Co., least of all the founder, possessed a secret motive or conceived their purpose as anything more than presenting dramatic colorized views of American landscapes and cityscapes. Curt Teich suffered two heart attacks in 1939 and relinquished control of the forty-year-old company to his son Curt Jr. Although Ralph Teich recalled his older brother as a "little Napoleon" whose decisions entailed "all sorts of goof-ups,"[43] the linen aesthetic remained unchanged into the early 1950s—as if the company went on autopilot after establishing the Art-Colortone process. And yet somehow, almost in a single instant, without forethought or conscious intent, the founder and his associates created an "imaginative and poetic" aesthetic appealing not only to contemporaries but also to those who later sought historical insight or nostalgic connection through humble artifacts emerging from obscurity.

Any understanding of how those who produced linen postcards might have conceived their aesthetic impact must be obtained at a tangent by reading between the lines and across the images. In a sense, tracing the linen aesthetic over space and time is the agenda of this book, which interprets particular examples of the iconography of linen cards ranging from natural and rural landscapes to modern scenes of industry and urbanism. Despite the lack of any sophisticated interpretation by the company, there seems to have been a general sense of the linen postcard's aesthetic accomplishment. In April 1933, two years into the linen process, at which point the company was still churning out vastly more pre-linen C. T. American Art cards, Curt Teich implored sales agent G. I. Pitchford to "push the C. T. Art-Colortone line strongly" in California. Jobbers in Florida were "enthusiastic" about the new product, he reported, and they intended to "go ahead stronger than ever for the coming season." Aware of the linen card's obvious contrast with anything else on the market, Teich insisted that "the public will buy these pretty C. T. Art Colortone post cards readily."[44]

An emphasis on color ran throughout the company's newsletters and booklets for sales agents. In 1933, for example, *Curteich News* compared the colors of linen postcards to those of the buildings at the world's fair that was then the

WF-17   HALL OF SCIENCE, CHICAGO WORLD'S FAIR

3A-H518

FIG. 3.15. "Hall of Science, Chicago World's Fair," Teich 3A-H518, 1933

talk of Chicago, the Century of Progress International Exposition. The designer Joseph Urban had employed twenty-four saturated colors in bold patterns to unify the fair's modernistic architecture, with its striking, even confusing, forms (fig. 3.15). The writer was pleased that the company had been "able to perfect this latest color process just in time" for the fair, presumably so the company's souvenir postcards would be up to the task of representing it. Art-Colortone offered a veritable "Century of Progress in color reproduction, an advancement in lithography which, a few years ago, we did not dream was possible."[45] Celebrating both the Century of Progress and the new Art-Colortone process, the upper

506—Santa Fe's "Super Chief" Traveling thru the Orange Groves, California

© CURT TEICH & CO., INC.   OB-H678

FIG. 3.16. "Santa Fe's 'Super Chief' Traveling thru the Orange Groves, California,"
Teich 0B-H678, 1940

border of the company's letterhead stationery in 1933 featured a fanciful, color-ful, nearly futuristic view of Chicago's skyline, with Buckingham Fountain in the foreground—and a view of the Teich & Co. plant enclosed in a diamond-shaped frame to the right.

Two years later, the in-house newsletter observed that magazine advertising, mail order catalogs, and Hollywood's first full-color movie indicated a "color-conscious" society conducive to the success of linen cards. While a later cultural historian might have suggested an analogy to *The Wizard of Oz* (1939), with its transformation from the dull black-and-white landscape of Kansas to the Tech-nicolor wonder of a magical fantasy realm, *Curteich News* merely predicted in 1935 that the first full-length color movie, an adaptation of William Thackeray's novel *Vanity Fair* entitled *Becky Sharp*, was "going to make millions of people . . . more responsive to colorful presentations." The author advised sales agents to emphasize the company's "forty years of experience" in design, encompassing an "originality of thought peculiar to post card presentations" and an ability "to create . . . outstanding and individual designs for any subject." Several months later, more aggressively, the newsletter pointedly asked, "Do you suggest de-signs when you sell, or are you too anxious just to bag an order?"[46] The newslet-ter's occasional reminders about design beg the question of how much credit for

the linen style should be assigned to the art department and how much to the agents who mediated between those who commissioned images and those who manufactured them. Indeed, once a rationalized production process was established at the plant, so formulaic that the linen postcard comprised a genre of representation, then the individual client, the specific view, and the sales agent became overriding variables in the equation.

A postcard commissioned in 1940 by the Western Publishing & Novelty Company in Los Angeles affords an opportunity to focus on this issue before we explore in detail Teich's imagescape of the American scene. This particular card, captioned "Santa Fe's 'Super Chief' Traveling thru the Orange Groves, California," embodies so many qualities of the linen genre that it could be described as hypertypical (fig. 3.16). We view the scene from a low perspective, as if crouching on the right-hand track of a dual railway line. On the left track looms a Santa Fe diesel locomotive in bright orange-red and yellow livery, pulling a string of passenger coaches along a curving diagonal. An orange grove stretches back on the left and right, its shiny green leaves and bright orange fruit overhanging the tracks to create a bower through which the train appears about to burst. In the distance, framed by the foreground oval of branches, is an apparently snow-capped mountain range, behind which an otherwise blue sky with fluffy white clouds is suffused with sunset's yellow-orange glow. Colors are rich and saturated; lines are crisp and clear, especially the outlines of individual leaves (derived from the source photo) and the black lettering and logo outlines on the front of the locomotive (derived from retouching). Even the wooden ties are photorealistic, with shifting black halftone shading that adds richness to the brown coloration. Shiny gray rails suggest a long continuous sweep running without limit. When one turns the card in the light, the embossed texture breaks up any potentially distorting reflections and instead creates depth and luminous richness. The back caption announces "one of the Santa Fe's great fleet of streamliners with gleaming stainless steel coaches . . . passing through the Orange Groves of California, 39¾ hours from Chicago."

This is one of those cards Werther and Mott describe in their 2002 guide for collectors as "stunners," images that have "a soul," that possess "a combination of wonderful and dynamic composition, detailing, graphics, subject matter, elegance and style, printing quality, contrast and color." Beyond this postcard's latter-day attraction for collectors, however, it also possesses considerable cultural resonance. Mike Davis, a sardonic Marxist historian with two books theorizing the catastrophic demise of Los Angeles, could almost have been thinking of this specific image when he observed that for decades "postcards and orange-crate labels" had promoted an "idyllic image" of "homes and orchards soaking in sunshine at the foot of snow-peaked mountains"—and "unlike so much else about the region, it was not entirely fake."[47] Ironically, however, Teich's image

of the Super Chief passenger train moving through orange groves in Southern California on its way to Chicago was as fake as could be, thanks to manipulations by western representative G. I. Pitchford.

Among scholars who have examined the job files, opinions differ regarding the aesthetic autonomy of agents, photographers, and artists involved in the production process. Thinking more of retouching and colorizing artists than of photographers, Mark Pascale, curator of prints and drawings at the Art Institute of Chicago, has maintained that although Teich artists "were grunts on the job ladder," archival materials suggest that "they went beyond their responsibilities and injected their own talents" into their work. Focusing on the agent-photographer's role, Peter Bacon Hales argues, on the other hand, for a loss of aesthetic responsibility. Admittedly Pitchford's artistry behind a camera did not approach that of such landscape photographers as William Henry Jackson, but one can still question Hales's statement that "all the 'artistic improvement' occurred within the factory, according to stereotyped specifications devised by the company itself," thereby reducing the agent-photographer's role to "little more than a rudimentary sketching process."[48]

Pitchford's career suggests otherwise. Although it took considerable organizational efficiency for him to cover his vast territory, he often made dozens of exposures of the same scene—to cite two examples, Fremont Street in Las Vegas by day and night with shifting arrays of autos and pedestrians, and a panoramic vista across Avalon Bay on Santa Catalina Island under different lighting and weather conditions—seeking perfect postcard images. He mastered such landscape conventions as the diagonal sight line and the use of overhanging branches as a framing device to the point that they became automatic. But he also experimented with street scenes taken from a driver's-eye perspective, crouching under the black cloth of his view camera, tripod-mounted in the middle of a street, as cars swept by in both directions. He made a point of incorporating the automobile into the landscape, whether on curving mountain roads or on city streets defined by flowing neon. In the limited tradition in which he worked, his compositions often moved beyond competence and displayed artistic merit. Because he remained inside the parameters of the postcard trade, however, his work exhibited little of the engagement with human subjects that might have extended its documentary significance. Even so, Pitchford's exposure to the geographical variety of his large region and his role in selecting a wide range of different postcard views contributed substantially to the linen aesthetic and its portrayal of the American scene.

In this particular case, the Santa Fe Super Chief card, Pitchford played a major design role. The image was not based on his original photography, which did form the basis for scores of other Teich cards, but on a collage he composed by cutting out and combining elements from at least seven different black-and-

FIG. 3.17. G. I. Pitchford, photo collage for Teich 0B-H678

white photos (fig. 3.17). These bits and pieces encompassed the train and two tracks, the mountains and sky immediately above, two sections of orange grove on the left, at least two more along the right, and a close-up of oranges and leaves over the right-hand track. In Pitchford's handmade collage the train was moving from left to right, but he apparently thought the scene worked better with the train moving from right to left, so after completing and photographing the collage, he reversed the image; this is why the Santa Fe logo appears backward. This reversed image of his collage is what he submitted to Chicago with his name stamped on the back as the photographer. The Super Chief view was not Pitchford's only collage: the technique was so central to his vision that he kept an envelope stuffed with bits of cactuses and other desert plants cut from miscellaneous photos and ready for use.

After completing the collage of the Super Chief, Pitchford sketched the logo and engine colors in red and yellow colored pencil on a piece of frisket paper, indicating that the lettering should be reversed. Some of his instructions were for colors, such as "stainless steel" for engine skirting and passenger coaches, a "golden color" for oranges, "blue gray" for the "very distant" mountains, and "lavender & pink" for the tiny bushes in front of the orange trees on the right. Other trees visible in the distance on the other side of the train were "just a little too high" in the photo and had to be reduced, but Pitchford found the "shadows

about right" on the track. Finally, taking for granted the art department's expertise with generic elements, he advised them to "fix up the sky." Although the collage was somewhat rough, with obvious seams and bits of track missing from the corners, it was sufficient for a retouching artist, who glued fragments of two photos of clouds onto a copy of Pitchford's print and added a few more oranges. With this image Teich's western sales agent proved himself a knowledgeable interpreter of landscape conventions and an expert postcard designer. Indeed, Pitchford's employers thought so highly of the design that they intended to copyright it, but somehow that was not carried out.

Few other designers of linen cards employed collage to construct imaginary scenes with no direct analog in reality. In most cases a card was based on a single source photo. Even so, other agents and artists transformed their sources in ways that resonated with the intentions expressed in the Super Chief image. For one thing, despite the projective motion of the Santa Fe locomotive through an idealized landscape, the image is mostly flat, and its attractiveness is more a matter of dramatic juxtaposition of bright colors than creation of a realistic illusion of depth. The earlier American Art cards, owing to greater reliance on meticulous detailing conveyed through fine-screened halftone shading, did a better job of conveying a photorealistic illusion of depth. To compare Pitchford's original photographic collage with the postcard made from it is to recognize the degree to which the Art-Colortone aesthetic merged, flattened, or collapsed figurative elements. The paste-up collage exaggerates depth by the physical edges of its parts, with those of the locomotive, for example, or the overarching orange branch, being laid over others. Within such single components as the foreground branch, details of individual leaves, such as the contrast with an orange or the sheen of a reflective surface, are clearly discernible. In the image as translated from collage to postcard, however, details are reduced to essentials; they are as streamlined as the form of the locomotive itself. This effect derived partly from the smoothing of the collage by airbrushing during the retouching process. It also owed something to the miniaturization of the postcard format, which reduced the surface area of the image to roughly one-quarter that of a standard 8 × 10 photographic print.

This visual effect of streamlining or reducing to essentials was typical of much commercial design during the 1930s, whether in automobiles, domestic appliances, or the architecture of movie theaters, nightclubs, and restaurants. The linen aesthetic thus conformed to the era's dominant design motifs, a fact that may have contributed to the genre's success. Whatever the case, the look of Teich's linen cards remained unchanged into the mid-1950s, by which point it was obsolete. Kodachrome-derived cards with sharp outlines and shiny surfaces echoing the tailfins and swooping rooflines of postwar design had captured the postcard market by then. As orders declined, whether for new linen cards

858   THE STREAMLINER PASSING THROUGH A CALIFORNIA ORANGE GROVE.

FIG. 3.18. "The Streamliner Passing through a California Orange Grove," Longshaw 858, n.d.

or for reprints of old ones, Teich had trouble ganging together enough cards for a particular print run, and orders sometimes took months to fill. Ralph Teich claimed that his brother Curt Jr. was slow to emulate such competitors as Colourpicture and Dexter Press in the switch to chromes. The company limped along until shortly after Curt Sr.'s death at age ninety-six in 1974, when it was sold to a greeting card publisher.[49]

For the quarter century after 1931, however, the linen type of postcard developed by Teich and imitated by Tichnor, Colourpicture, Metrocraft, and other, much smaller companies outnumbered all other types in the United States. The Chicago plant led the market owing to a rationalized production and distribution process, along with greater technical and aesthetic proficiency than that demonstrated by competitors. Anyone tempted to dismiss Teich's product as merely generic might compare the Santa Fe Super Chief card designed by Pitchford with a direct knockoff printed by the Longshaw Card Company in Los Angeles (fig. 3.18). Many Longshaw images of Southern California fascinate because they render landscapes through an outlandish glow (see p. 134). But Longshaw's version of a "streamliner passing through a California orange grove" is truly generic, lacking any resemblance to an actual railway locomotive and lacking even a convincing logo. Instead the train suggests an artist's illustration from a children's book with a vaguely anthropomorphic, ghostlike cab, wispy vapor trailing back from the wheels, tracks sketchily delineated, and a backdrop with mountain and sky less realistic than those of Teich's image, which by comparison appears nearly photographic.

Such direct copying by postcard publishers was common but not usually so poorly done. The Teich card, by contrast, offered viewers a proud sense of mastery of a gloriously modern technology, a diesel locomotive moving with clean, smokeless ease through bounteous agricultural wealth. The mountains suggested America's rich natural landscape, available for visual consumption by the Santa Fe's passengers, comfortably seated and air conditioned as they traveled across the continent at speeds surpassing a hundred miles an hour. After taking them through the orange groves, the Super Chief whisked them through Arizona and New Mexico, stopping at Albuquerque to allow them to purchase Indian curios, and then headed out across Colorado's southeastern corner, through the wheat fields of Kansas, and on across northern Missouri and Illinois to the midwestern metropolis of Chicago, second only to New York and perhaps Los Angeles as exemplar of a forward-looking machine age. Encompassing natural and cultivated landscapes as well as an evocatively modern transportation machine, this hypertypical image serves as an appropriate bridge to a consideration of the iconography of linen postcards.

4

Landscapes in Linen Postcards

A NATIONAL IMAGINARY

EARLY IN 1940 THE FOLKSINGER WOODY GUTHrie penned the words to a song that became something of an alternative national anthem. "This land is your land, this land is my land," the song's best-remembered line declared, "from California to the New York Island, from the Redwood forest to the Gulf Stream waters." After connecting named places across the nation, from natural wonders to its greatest metropolis, the singer imagined an idealized landscape as he envisioned walking a "ribbon of highway" through "diamond deserts" and looking over an "endless skyway" into a "golden valley." He then evoked the glory and tribulation of the agricultural heartland with "wheat fields waving" and "dust clouds rolling," and he sensed a future deliverance "as the fog was lifting." The rest of the song reflected Guthrie's left-wing political identification with the economically dispossessed and his righteous anger at their plight. The song's title itself, "This Land Is Your Land," proclaimed the singer as presenting the land to its rightful owners, reminding them of its boundless promise, and inviting them to retake possession of it.[1]

Coming at the end of the 1930s, "This Land Is Your Land" belonged to one of the Depression's most characteristic expressive genres: the representation of the nation to itself. The first verse's list of locations evoked the democratic vistas of the poet Walt Whitman by standing in for an entire catalogue of all the varied landscapes of the American scene. When cultural historians discuss national representations during the decades between the world wars, they often emphasize two quite different efforts at representing the nation to itself, one through photographic images, the other mostly through prose, both of them funded by the U.S. government. Working for the Farm Security Administration (FSA), documentary photographers such as Walker Evans, Dorothea Lange, and Russell Lee recorded the lives of southern sharecroppers, Dust Bowl migrants, and other survivors of Depression hard times. Evocative black-and-white images, many of them now iconic, celebrated ordinary citizens as stoic figures possessing dignity and quiet heroism. When the agency's mission shifted with the approach of World War II from documenting the dispossessed to promoting the American way of life, its images continued to suggest that the nation displayed in its current adversity the same qualities of character that had enabled it to thrive and endure well into its second century.[2]

Equally celebratory was the Federal Writers' Project, an agency of the Works Progress Administration (WPA) that prepared guidebooks to all the states, many cities, and several distinct regions and major highways. Organized around driving tours, the state guides emphasized the depth of historical tradition in even the smallest villages. While describing ethnic diversity and particularities of local landscapes and experience, the guidebooks also sought to portray evidence of an ethos of progress shared throughout the nation, whether revealed in new agricultural techniques, in new highways, bridges, and dams, or in the vibrant life of cities and small towns. Overall, the American Guide Series offered a comforting vision of a modernizing nation anchored in the stability of a living past. As early as 1937, with only a few of the state guides published, the prominent public intellectual Lewis Mumford proclaimed the project as "the first attempt to make the country worthily known to Americans."[3]

By then, linen postcards with colorful images representing the American scene were already commonplace. Teich & Co. had published more than fifteen thousand different views in six years, and competitors added to the total. The revolving wire rack in any dime store presented an eye-catching display, an abundance of bright, jarring swatches that attracted notice but never resolved into an integrated pattern. A browsing shopper would not have focused on the whole but on an individual card or two, making a split-second decision about which was most compelling. Linen cards, designed to attract random attention at the point of sale or to portray the essence of a restaurant, motel, or tourist attraction, were never intended to convey a coherent vision of the American scene. Neither, on the other hand, were FSA photographs meant to comprise a comprehensive American portrait, though Roy Stryker, the project's supervisor, did devise a checklist of typical aspects of small-town life for his photographers. For the most part, his staff's images were distributed piecemeal to newspaper and magazine editors.[4] Although several socially progressive books of FSA photos were published in the late 1930s and early '40s, a sense of their comprehensive documentary vision came only with historical hindsight. As for the volumes of the American Guide Series, while each was meant to be regionally comprehensive, their impact was also piecemeal, state by state, as readers who could afford the luxury of tourism used individual guidebooks to plan their travels.

Let's return for a moment to that wire rack of linen postcards, slowly turning. Even if its random juxtaposition of images was visually chaotic, its circular shape signified a closed universe of representation. However, most cards were eventually dispersed individually through the mail, with many discarded almost immediately and others shunted into albums and shoeboxes. The physical sense of totality that a large body of postcards today conveys is an illusion imposed by collectors and dealers. Even so, Teich and his competitors did construct an American scene unified by a common aesthetic and by an unspoken consensus regarding what was worth representing and what was not. Informed by opinions of clients, distributors, and sales agents as to which subjects, perspectives, and treatments would sell best, the total output of linen postcards converged around a sense of what mattered most to Americans in the landscapes they inhabited and passed through, or what it was they desired to see abstracted and reflected back to them. No more partial or incomplete than FSA photographs or WPA guidebooks, though defined by parameters more commercial and popular, the American scene of linen postcards had the advantage over officially sanctioned counterparts of being inexpensive, widely available, and the earliest in circulation during a period when extreme economic and social insecurity had provoked a national cultural identity crisis.

As if responding to that crisis, the linen aesthetic presented bright, colorful, upbeat images. Unlike Guthrie, who intended his anthem as a politically charged alternative to the cloying words of Irving Berlin's instant classic "God Bless America," a song then popular on the radio in a vibrant recording by Kate Smith, Teich and other postcard publishers offered a wholly optimistic interpretation of the American scene. The need for success in the marketplace ensured that linen postcards addressed common assumptions of ordinary citizens. Linen images challenged few opinions and posed few questions. If their landscapes and cityscapes seemed more vivid than reality itself, that effect came from a focusing and exaggerating of their photographic sources, and from a flattening or obscuring of any details that might have complicated or confused a simple acceptance of surface reality. Despite the unprecedented colorized aesthetic of Teich's America, its iconography was conventional, even traditional, offering reassurances about the national landscape's continuing promise. The photographer Walker Evans may have attacked linen postcards as "gaudy boasts" with no "feeling for actual appearance," but more typical was the response of a visitor to Utah's Bryce Canyon who bought a card shimmering with pinks and purples and then hastily scrawled in pencil, "This is just the way it looks."[5]

Although we may discern a problematic gap between the landscape viewed by this tourist and its representation on a mass-produced postcard, that gap likely did not exist for the card's purchaser. Contemplating a more iconic landscape in 1930, that of the Grand Canyon, an author of popular Western stories, Hoffman Birney, wondered "if all the postal cards that have been sent away from there" might actually "fill" the canyon. Echoing Birney, the visual culture theorist W. J. T. Mitchell has mused, "Could we fill up Grand Canyon with its representations?" More to the point, he wonders "how many photographs, postcards, paintings, and awestruck 'sightings' of the Grand Canyon will it take to exhaust its value as landscape?" That value was already exhausted for an earlier culture critic, Daniel Boorstin, who described American society in the early 1960s as overwhelmed by unreal, inauthentic images. The Grand Canyon as popularly experienced had become, in his sarcastic phrase, "a disappointing reproduction of the Kodachrome original." For Boorstin, the gap between reality and representation was wider than the canyon itself. Despite the improbability of anyone's ever regarding an image of the Grand Canyon as more awe-inspiring than the reality, there is no doubt that perceptual experience of the canyon has been mediated, or at least informed, by an accumulation of past visual representations.[6] Coming after a long series of changes in methods for bridging the gap between real landscapes and graphic reproductions, makers of linen postcards had more than two centuries of conventions to draw upon. They could paraphrase, reference, and abstract from the images of earlier media as they created uncomplicated forms that seemed to speak to the present moment. The formal landscape conventions glossed by images on linen cards were familiar to consumers as well as producers, even if not many people could have articulated those conventions.

The Picturesque Landscape Tradition

Many view cards employed conventions of landscape representation familiar to middle-class Americans since the mid-nineteenth century. Revealing the nation to itself had been a primary motive of the fine arts from the earliest colonization by the English in Virginia. John White's watercolor sketches of native inhabitants, painted in 1585 and circulated in Europe as engravings, began a tradition of satisfying curiosity about America's natural wonders among those who stayed home. White was the forerunner of many painters and later photographers who over the next three centuries accompanied explorers and surveyors of the wilderness just beyond the zone of settlement.[7] Most nineteenth-century artists viewed America's unfolding wonders through eyes conditioned by a picturesque landscape tradition extending back two centuries to Salvator Rosa's dark, brooding portrayals of torrential streams and jagged peaks and Claude Lorrain's gentler, melancholy views of calm lakeshores, crumbling ruins overrun by vines, and distant mountains obscured by haze. According to the British aesthetic theorists William Gilpin and Uvedale Price, both writing shortly before 1800, the picturesque style emphasized nature's irregularity as superior to classical symmetry through such compositional devices as rough shapes and textures, a tangled tree to one side serving as a frame, a diagonal vista across water to a distant horizon, and tiny human figures in the foreground through whose point of view observers could project themselves into the scene of a landscape painting.

The picturesque tradition proved essential in representing America to itself. During the early nineteenth century, untrained artists entertained popular audiences with panoramic paintings hundreds of feet long, slowly unwound on canvas-backed scrolls to portray, for example, a journey down the Mississippi. Ordinary people decorated their homes with inexpensive landscapes lithographed by Currier & Ives. In the meantime, the upper class visited studios of landscape painters such as Thomas Cole, a leader of the Hudson River School of artists, whose members envisioned rural upstate New York in terms of the wilder reaches of Germany's Rhine valley. As the century progressed, landscape painting took on the American West's larger-than-life attributes, with Frederic Edwin Church, Albert Bierstadt, and Thomas Moran producing vast canvases inviting viewers to move outside the comfort of the picturesque and stand in awestruck wonder before a painted scene whose immense sublimity nearly rivaled that of the natural original on which it was based.

Most late nineteenth-century Americans had little access to such large-scale representations of Yellowstone, the Grand Canyon, or even Niagara Falls, though special exhibitions of some paintings attracted so much publicity that they were crowded with viewers. Most people interested in landscape views depended on multicolored lithographic reproductions of paintings, on large prints sold by photographers (often framed as artworks), and toward the end of the century on magazine illustrations by well-known artists or anonymous illustrators. The photographer William Henry Jackson, who like Moran had served as an artist with the U.S. government's survey of the Yellowstone region in 1871, parlayed that experience into a major commercial enterprise. Jackson relied not only on his own work but also on that of a team of assistants and on negatives purchased from other photographers. Into the early twentieth century, regional photographers, among them Carleton E. Watkins in northern California, T. J. Hileman in Montana, and H. H. Bennett in Wisconsin, thrived by selling picturesque and sublime views.

However, making American landscapes accessible to more people required reproducing them inexpensively in reduced formats. Before the advent of postcards, nothing popularized picturesque conventions so well as the stereopticon, a hand-held device for viewing twin photographic images of the same scene taken from minutely different positions and mounted side-by-side on a rectangular card. Peering through the viewer, which had a separate magnifying lens for each eye, a user perceived an illusion of three-dimensional depth and felt physically drawn into the resulting space. The stereopticon became an instant fad at its introduction in 1851. Fifty years later the leading American producer, Underwood & Underwood, was reportedly manufacturing twenty-five thousand stereograph cards per day. Historians have frequently noted the irony of an abundance of views of the expansive American landscape stacked in a basket in every middle-class parlor, domesticated, reduced to the status of commodities, and ready for casual viewing.[8]

The scope of romantic landscapes diminished further with the postcard fad soon after the turn of the twentieth century. The Detroit Photographic Company led the way by acquiring Jackson's inventory of negatives, and other postcard publishers bought up negatives and prints from local photographers across the country. It was not unusual to find a view that had formerly been offered to well-heeled clients in a large frame and then mass-produced for the middle class in stereograph format finally fully democratized as a postcard. While some photographers, more successful and commercially savvy ones, retained copyright to their images, others sold their prints and even negatives outright. Collectors often come across several cards based on the same photographic image, variously retouched and altered by different publishers, yielding postcards with widely differing degrees of verisimilitude of outline and color. Many individual images migrated down through the years, appearing first in the hazy collotype hues of the Detroit Publishing Company, then in the delicate peach and light blue washes of Teich's pre-linen cards, and finally in the vibrant, more saturated colors of Teich's linen process—at each phase moving further from the original photo's precise details and taking on greater flatness.

The landscape postcard marked a diminishing significance even more pronounced than that of the stereograph. While a basket of stereograph cards in the parlor had invited the act of viewing as a special occasion, to be indulged privately or shared with family and friends, the postcard invited no more than a momentary glance. Even so, many conventions of landscape representation remained constant throughout the shifts from expansive large-format oil painting to photographic print to disposable postcard. Reduced to basics, the linen

FIG. 4.1. Vitaly Komar and Alex Melamid, *America's Most Wanted*, 1994

view card democratized aspects of landscape representation that extended back nearly three centuries. At the same time, however, the commercial choices of the American public simplified and transformed the conventions that most often came into play. As a Teich sales agent advised when proposing a major revision to the image on an existing postcard, the "competition brought out a [similar] card . . . and it sells."[9]

Before yielding to a temptation to regard linen view cards as an expression of the lowest common denominator, however, let's consider them briefly in light of a survey of attitudes about the visual arts conducted in 1993 by the polling firm Marttila & Kiley for the Nation Institute, a branch of the liberal journal *The Nation*. Armed with a statistical analysis of responses of a thousand people to more than a hundred questions about their aesthetic preferences, two straight-faced émigré Russian conceptual artists, Vitaly Komar and Alex Melamid, created a single artwork they referred to as the "most wanted painting in America." Selecting from many variables, they combined the respondents' preferences for a "realistic" over a "different-looking" style, for natural outdoor scenes, abundant water, wild animals instead of domestic animals, and, in the case of human figures, for fully clothed historical subjects (as opposed to nudes). The resulting oil painting (fig. 4.1), an ironic parody of the traditional picturesque landscape,

Greetings from St. Charles, Michigan

FIG. 4.2. "Greetings from St. Charles, Michigan," Teich 5A-H2288, 1935

boasts a view extending diagonally upward to the left, across a lake with blue hazy mountains on the opposite shore, framed by a large clump of trees on the left and a single tall, irregularly shaped tree on the right. Three figures in casual contemporary clothes, a young woman and two young men, move from the foreground toward two deer standing in the water to the far right, while George Washington incongruously stands in full historical garb, gazing in an uncertain direction.[10]

Intended to raise a smile, Komar and Melamid's absurdly literal visualization of late twentieth-century poll results differs little from some picturesque linen postcard landscapes. In the mid-1930s, for example, Teich published a series of generic images with the series title "Rural Scenes" printed vertically on the back. These cards could be sold anywhere from the mid-Atlantic states up through New York and into the Midwest. One card portrays a small herd of Holstein cattle straggling home toward a golden sunset (fig. 4.2).[11] Teich artists here used several motifs later identified by Marttila & Kiley as "most wanted." In the postcard view, a river, the image's central feature, meanders up a diagonal slope toward the upper left, dividing bucolic pastureland in the foreground from a continuous clump of picturesquely variegated trees and shrubbery on the opposite bank. The composition is set off on the right by a single tree taller than the others, extending outside the frame. In the far distance, to left and right, beyond the clumped trees, appear glimpses of a range of hills in hazy blue and gray. The sun's yellow globe, beginning to slip below the horizon, radiates horizontal streaks of golden orange that merge upward through a fainter orange to a dull yellow.

This particular card with its lush coloration almost perfectly embodies the pastoral mode of the picturesque. However, its image is mundane compared with those of many other linen cards, even boring. It is significant for its typical or representative quality, for its evidence of a progression of formal conventions leading from seventeenth-century landscape paintings, through nineteenth-century photographs and stereograph views, and eventually to Komar and Melamid's tongue-in-cheek rendering of contemporary visual taste. Purchasers and recipients of the card may have regarded its image as conventionally pretty. However, linen postcards probably would not have succeeded in the market-place if they were all so dull and formulaic. Nor would collectors now find them fascinating. Nor would it be possible to engage in an extended interpretation of their historical significance.

This bucolic card's main problem is the simple fact that it is so completely generic, not only in the sense that it could be overprinted with "Greetings from St. Charles, Michigan" or any of thousands of other locations, but also that there is nothing striking about it, nothing that grabs attention and distinguishes it from other formulaic landscape views. On the other hand, however boring some generic scenes may be, there are others that possess compelling power. A cultural historian who wishes today to discover—or construct—a representation of the American scene through linen cards must somehow identify the unique and specific within the generic. That process involves selecting a relative handful of images from among a possible universe of more than a hundred thousand examples. Not only must each selected image be typical of a formulaic genre, it also must possess a unique quality that justifies the attention.

Hybrid Forms: Locating the Unique within the Generic

The selection principle behind the roughly 150 postcards individually featured in this book's two portfolio sections (on landscapes and cityscapes) was hardly scientific. A more random sampling would have resulted by taking the first 150 linens from an unsorted box of cards recently acquired by a dealer; or by opening one of Teich & Co.'s chronological albums and taking every tenth card, up to 150. The images obtained by either method would be too ordinary, too bland, or too faulty in design to warrant reproduction and interpretation. One might also have applied formal content analysis to all of Teich's linen cards, arriving at a minutely categorized typology. There would still have been the problem of selecting those few cards to serve as illustrative examples. My preference has been to rely on a thorough knowledge of the full range of images derived through years of thumbing through boxes of dealer cards and, in a more focused way, by paging through all of Teich's linen albums. Some selected cards are here because they were convincingly designed, others because their effects were technically innovative, others because they were culturally revealing, and still others because they are too striking to be ignored. The problem, of course, is how to justify representing an entire genre by relatively few specific examples—particularly when historical and personal motives must be sorted out.

Tension between the specific and the generic often comes up in theoretical discussions of photographs and the images derived from them, such as those on postcards. The individual photograph, a unique exposure, has always purported to convey the true reality of a particular subject at a definite place in a single otherwise irrecoverable instant of time. Yet the uniqueness of any photo is overwhelmed not only by artistic and representational conventions inherited from earlier media or developed for new media, but also by the sheer volume of the total number of existing photos, forever increasing at an accelerating rate.

In 1980 the French critic Roland Barthes characterized most photos as conventional by referring to them as each being defined by and existing within a *studium*, a more or less rational set of intentions and forms generated by a culture and legible equally to producers and consumers. Occasionally, however, he found that an extraordinary element within a photo, often a seemingly minor detail, bypassed conscious reason and spoke to him directly, unmediated. This *punctum*, as Barthes referred to it, "rises from the scene, shoots out of it like an arrow, and pierces me." Unrelated to the general cultural structures of the *studium*, the wholly personal experience of the *punctum* encompasses "what I add to the photograph and *what is nonetheless already there*." This irrational, even mystical, agency operates from "a kind of subtle beyond—as if the image launched desire beyond what it permits us to see."[12]

Similar reactions, though not so intellectualized, are common in discussions of photographic images. For example, Paul Vanderbilt, a former curator at the Wisconsin Historical Society, described how he assembled a book juxtaposing his own landscape photos with historical photos and short texts. His selections for *Between the Landscape and Its Other* (1993) came from "stockpiles of photographs old and new, formal and casual, good and bad," each of which possessed "some *hidden* value, something inviting but not obvious." Vanderbilt may have been aware of Barthes's *punctum*, but Walker Evans had also said something similar long before Barthes's famous meditation on photography. During a public lecture at Yale University in 1964, Evans insisted that documentary photography is good only when a quality he called "the lyric" is added. That oddly named element, according to Evans, is "usually produced unconsciously, and even unintentionally and accidentally by the cameraman." It is something beyond the photographer's conscious manipulation, some fugitive quality inhering in the situation or in the moment when the camera shutter-release button is pushed. Although Evans's lyric quality derives immediately from the producer of a photo, it does seem related to Barthes's *punctum*. Finally, giving this quality a bit more substance, the photographer Edward Weston declared that "there is a reality—so subtle that it becomes more real than reality," which was what he claimed to be "trying to get down in photography."[13]

Even mass-produced postcard images occasionally evoke similar nonrational responses. The literary scholar Naomi Schor regarded her collection of monotone postcard views of Paris from the early twentieth century as a mostly objective record of daily life. Sometimes, however, an image offered more than mundane information. "Here and there," she wrote, "a detail of street life arrests one's glance in the manner of the Barthesian *punctum*." The painter John Baeder reported a similar sensation while rummaging through postcards at flea markets. He found himself attracted to "images that appealed to me for reasons I wasn't aware of at the time," images that "touch[ed] me somewhere in my psyche." Finally, there is that term "stunner," used by collectors Werther and Mott to refer to linen postcards they regard as "having a soul." Although they define a stunner as a card with superlative aesthetic qualities, their insistence on the word "soul" suggests the matter is not so clear-cut. In a sense, you know one when you see it.[14]

In Barthes's scheme of things, the culturally determined *studium* defined the predictable realm of the generic. The *punctum*, on the other hand, arose from some aspect of a photo that touched his psyche directly and nonrationally. The example he cited involved his reaction to a photo of his deceased mother, a unique personal experience no one else could directly comprehend. On the other hand, the experiences of Schor and Baeder, of Werther and Mott, indeed my own experiences, as well, suggest that a culturally determined image can also evoke personal *punctum*-like reactions. Barthes would have countered that it is the predictable *studium* that comprises the cultural material in an image. However, the predictable often goes unnoticed. A familiar, dull, or boring image, such as Teich's view of cows at sunset, arouses little attention. But among the generic views whose grounding is in the culture, there are also occasional images possessing some quality that, like Barthes's *punctum*, "rises from the scene, shoots out of it like an arrow, and pierces" the viewer. I make no apology for occasionally relying on that complex personal experience in my selection of images.

To claim that linen postcards represented the nation to itself during a disruptive era marked by great social and cultural uncertainty is not to argue that the resulting portrayal was accurate in its details or unprecedented in its conclusions. Composed of thousands of views, many of them compelling but the majority of them rather dull, the American scene of Teich and his competitors was a hybrid construction. Any survey that is not exhaustively complete must emphasize cards that for whatever reasons make strong impressions. It must acknowledge that lackluster cards also attracted purchasers, often for utilitarian postal purposes, but then it must mostly ignore them. In support of the claim that unusual images can serve, when taken together in a group, as a microcosm of a more predictable universe of representation, one might suggest that they highlight certain typical, even common, traits and characteristics that are present in less expressive images but that tend to remain submerged and less noticeable. Extraordinary images help clarify the ordinary.

Even so, there remains the problem that some linen cards may fascinate today precisely because they engage twenty-first-century preoccupations. The last chapter of this book addresses the contemporary significance of linen postcards for those who find them attractive. But for now, the main concern is interrogating a selection of historical images on the basis of how they might have been originally experienced or understood. Most of those selected for inclusion here possess some slightly exaggerated feature, some quality that acts in the manner of Barthes's *punctum*, announcing itself with a clarity that is absent from more typical linen cards, those whose intentions or meanings are weak, muddied, or confused. Unusual images may shed light on predictable images—but ultimately they must be viewed in the larger historical context of the culture that gave rise to this genre of popular representations of the American scene.

Portfolio 1

LANDSCAPES

Two extensive portfolios of linen view cards are at the heart of this book. The first, which follows here, is devoted to landscapes; the second is devoted to cityscapes. The distinction between landscape and cityscape is a bit casual, considering that geographers regard cities and towns as comprising landscape as much as mountains, lakes, or wheat fields. Landscapes are here understood as representations of wilderness areas, national parks, rural scenes, roadside tourist attractions, highways and bridges, even industrial zones—anything, in other words, that travelers might have driven through, stopped to visit, or merely observed along the way as they moved from place to place for business, for pleasure, or in search of work. Images of members of minority groups who were viewed by some tourists and by postcard producers as part of the scenery also appear in this portfolio. All of the images included here share at least one quality marking them as cultural sights: someone, somewhere, regarded each one as significant enough to be portrayed on a postcard and offered for sale. Although linen landscape cards possess so many generic qualities that a relatively small sample can stand for the whole, each of the cards selected for illustration here also justifies its presence on its own terms. Some cards facilitate analysis of technical matters of reproduction and printing; some reveal aesthetic decisions regarding cropping, collaging, retouching, or colorizing; and others lend themselves to cultural interpretations extending beyond an individual image.

Each of the two portfolios consists of a series of reproductions of individual cards. Following each card are two or three paragraphs of description and interpretation. The accompanying text is more than a caption and less than an essay. It places its image in aesthetic, historical, or cultural contexts that shift from one card to the next. Each pairing of image and text may be read in isolation. However, there are frequent allusions forward and backward, and themes develop not so much by linear narrative or logical argument as by accumulation and association. There are often visual or topical segues as one paired image and text lead to the next. The effect of moving through an entire portfolio should simulate the experience of paging through a large album of postcards, selected and organized for various purposes. The overall intent is to create, through arrangement and juxtaposition of images and texts, a multidimensional understanding of the cultural work of linen postcards.[1]

The following landscape portfolio is divided into several loosely defined sections. The first, entitled "Representative Vistas," presents a selection of natural scenes from across the United States to suggest the geographic diversity portrayed by Teich and other linen postcard publishers. Most of the time, whether depicting rugged western mountains and pristine lakes or the domesticated scenery of New England and the Appalachians, photographers and art departments worked within the parameters of the picturesque and sublime styles that had long dominated American painting and photography.

After this introduction to the general range of linen landscapes, a section entitled "The Southwest: A Regional Aesthetic" presents a sequence of views from a single region to facilitate comparisons across different representational styles. The common cultural concept of the possessive gaze of an observer from a scenic overlook is developed through multiple images. Not all landscape cards represented the American continent's natural grandeur. Others, gathered together in the next section, "Travel and Tourism," portrayed common experiences of travelers, presenting the road and automobile as central features of otherwise natural scenes. The section also covers attractions and accommodations ranging from national park lodges to roadside cabins and tourist traps that emerged in response to the development of automotive landscapes.

Like the figures of people frequently used on linen postcards to provide a sense of scale or to enliven a scene, travelers and tourists were assumed to be of European descent. But many cards portrayed individuals whose stereotypical markers of race or ethnicity seemed so distinctive, and in some instances so exotic, that they became part of the scenery, in a theme explored in the next section, "Scenic People." From African Americans picking cotton to American Indians dressed in supposedly native costume, such representations often objectified and naturalized their subjects as part of the landscape. Patronizing, often racist images, which also encompassed Mexican Americans and urban Chinese Americans, gave white Americans a comforting sense of unchanging traditional hegemony.

Another major category of cards, on the other hand, emphasized change. Images gathered together under the heading "Resources" celebrated a technologically progressive nation engaged in exploiting natural wealth through agriculture, mining, and industry. Such positive views of extraction and manufacture, which were to appear only rarely on postcards in the second half of the twentieth century, suggest a society that accepted the notion of living in a machine age. The natural landscape itself was often transformed, or increasingly transcended, by bridges, multilane highways, dams, railways, and airplanes—images of which, represented in the section "Infrastructure and Transportation," portrayed multiple ways of moving toward the city, the dominant landscape of modernity and the subject of the second portfolio.

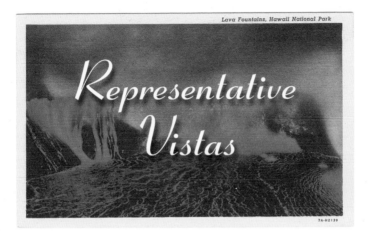

Lava Fountains, Hawaii National Park

Representative Vistas

7A-H2139

3A-H789

UNTITLED

TEICH 3A-H789, 1933

MANY LINEN POSTCARDS EMPHASIZED THE VIEW FROM A MOV-
ing automobile but few as effectively as this generic representation of a back
road snaking in a lazy reverse S-curve along a forested lakeshore. Despite tree
shadows falling across the roadway, evoking memories of the strobe effect of
driving through alternating lines of sun and shade, the sun-drenched white
fence hugging the steep shore pulls our eyes smoothly along the sinuous road
into the center of the image. Simple arrangements of halftone dots in Teich's
standard five colors (cyan, magenta, yellow, dark blue, and black) produce a
colorful rendering of autumn leaves, wildflowers, dappled sunshine, variegated
shadows, and a bright blue sky yielding to picturesque haze along the far shore.
The card must have sold well because Tichnor directly copied this image with
less convincing colors, intrusive black outlining, and an awkward attempt at
roadway shadows. Two years after publishing the original view in 1933, Teich
produced a new card based on a less compelling photograph of the same lakeshore road. Views like this were intended to appeal to motoring tourists or casual Sunday drivers. The total mileage of paved roads in the United States had
doubled between 1920 and 1930, and the number of registered automobiles had
increased from roughly 8 million to 23 million (or one passenger car for about
every five Americans). Although one can imagine walking along this lake road,
the image probably appealed mostly to motorists. Two journalists observed in
Harper's in 1933, "We are not a knapsack, open-air people" but instead "want
to view the scenery through the windows (usually closed) of a two-door sedan."[2]

"BEAR LAKE AND GLACIER GORGE /
ROCKY MOUNTAIN NATIONAL PARK, COLO."

TEICH 4A-H1864, 1934

"I CHOSE THIS CARD FOR YOU BECAUSE IT LOOKS SO MUCH LIKE an oil painting."

This simple, direct comment opens a message inscribed on the back of a postcard of Bear Lake in Colorado, addressed by a married woman in the eastern part of the state to a male correspondent in New Mexico but never mailed. She observed that from her home "on the plains" she had a "year-round" view of the Rockies' "snow-capped peaks" and said she had visited the park several times. The scope of this image recalls the grand sublime landscape tradition of such painters of the American West as Church, Bierstadt, and Moran. Unlike most national park views, which usually carried a local photographer's copyright, this view was not credited, but the pains taken by Teich's art department suggest that the Sanborn Souvenir Company in Denver, whose name appeared on the back as the card's distributor, was a demanding client.[3]

Delicate and precise in its detailing, the image effectively represents the reflection of mountains, glaciers, trees, and rocks in cool lake water, conveying both the apparent spatial depth of those features and the water's depthless surface, depending on how one chooses to focus. Complexity of line and subtle color gradations suggest the brushwork of an oil painting, an effect reinforced both by the card's obvious canvaslike texturing and by the borderless printing, which was available at a marginally higher cost. A scene whose original would have evoked awe at nature's sublimity, and whose portrayal in a large-scale oil painting would have inspired a sense of majesty, here becomes one of those "beautiful miniature paintings" touted by the Teich sales force. However, to believe that this postcard resembled an oil painting was to question its photographic verisimilitude. Like the conflicting depth and surface of the reflection represented by this particular image, documentary precision and artistic expression often wavered back and forth in linen landscape views. The question of whether contemporaries valued linen cards for representing reality or for expressively, even fantastically, augmenting it cannot be settled. Indeed, an ever-present oscillation between realism and artifice, both within a single image and across the full body of linen views, served as one of the attractions of this hybrid genre.[4]

PHOTO BY HILEMAN

4100   GRINNELL GLACIER, GLACIER NATIONAL PARK   5A-H195

"GRINNELL GLACIER, GLACIER NATIONAL PARK"

TEICH 5A-H195, 1935

T. J. HILEMAN WAS ONE OF THOSE PHOTOGRAPHERS CLOSELY associated with a particular national park, having moved to Kalispell, Montana, just outside Glacier National Park, in 1911, one year after the park was established. Trained as a photographer in Chicago, he became an official photographer for the Great Northern Railway, which brought prosperous midwestern tourists to the park on its main line from Chicago to Seattle and lodged them in the rustic-themed but sumptuous Glacier Park Hotel, owned by the railroad. Hileman, who was known equally for landscapes and portraits of Blackfeet Indians, opened a photo service in the hotel to process photos taken by visitors. Teich received orders from the Glacier Park Hotel for many linen cards based on Hileman's prints. The art department took great care with Glacier views, which were credited to the photographer.

The photographic print on which this card was based possesses an ethereal grandeur, with low contrast nearly effacing billowy cumulus clouds rising behind and over the striated mountain, and long, vague shadows projecting across the glacier. That same ethereal quality was maintained and perhaps even heightened in the postcard, owing to wavering shades of blue in the sky and over the ice and an atmospheric dusting of yellow fogs and highlights merging to near green. A close look reveals long free-form strokes and blobs of color texturing and contouring on the ice, almost as in a pastel sketch. On the other hand, the black halftone derived from the retouched photo emphasizes bare rock, especially in the outcropping at the right foreground, where an otherwise impressionistic image becomes overly photorealistic. The overall effect remains unspoiled, perhaps even enhanced, by the fact that this particular card, despite the care lavished on its design, was printed off-register and the error was not caught by quality control. However, this was one of those situations when reality did not live up to its representation. Writing in 1937 to a woman living south of Harrisburg, Pennsylvania, a man called Henry reported he had walked five miles up a "beautiful" trail only to find that "the glacier is only a deep pile of dirty snow turned to ice."[5]

CRATER LAKE NATIONAL PARK, OREGON

887   "THE PHANTOM SHIP SAILING INTO THE SUN"

"Crater Lake National Park, Oregon / 'The Phantom Ship Sailing into the Sun'"

Teich 7A-H996, 1937

MANY VIEW CARDS OF DAYLIGHT SCENES, WHETHER ILLUSTRAT-
ing landscapes, cityscapes, or individual buildings, boasted a sunset sky consisting of a bright orange glow at the horizon merging smoothly into a paler orange
above that, and then a bright yellow, a fainter yellow, and sometimes even a
purple or greenish purple. However, few linen cards equaled the effects of this
view of Crater Lake, which goes way beyond what the British critic Reyner Banham once referred to as "the cheapo charm of [American] postcard sunsets."[6]
Despite this card's dramatic appearance, it reveals little of the reality of Crater
Lake, which fills the caldera, or crater, of a sunken volcano whose nearly circular rim is more than five miles across, rising one to two thousand feet above the
water level.

In this view over the lake, past a jagged island called the Phantom Ship to
the opposite shore, nothing indicates we are looking at anything more than a
typical mountain lake. Even the caption on the back refers only to how sunset
and shadow transform the island (actually part of the rim of an older volcano)
into the semblance of "a full rigged ship sailing into the sun." But with this astonishing sunset as its subject, the card did not need to inform purchasers and
recipients about the natural wonders of Crater Lake. Instructions from the field,
probably sent by Teich's western representative, G. I. Pitchford, had directed
the art department to create a silhouette effect for the foreground tree by making it "very dark green almost black." More crucial to the card's success was the
vigorous command "Put as much color in this as possible." The artists created an
apocalyptic vision of fiery orange clouds roiling through the sky and liquid fire
spreading over the lake's surface like magma. It was all a bit more than anything
seen in the real world, and yet one wonders if anyone noticed that.

875   CRATER LAKE NATIONAL PARK, OREGON

THE PHANTOM SHIP   PHOTO BY WESLEY ANDREWS

"CRATER LAKE NATIONAL PARK, OREGON / THE PHANTOM SHIP"

TEICH 7A-H984, 1937

PROCESSED BY TEICH AT THE SAME TIME AS THE PREVIOUS card, this one presents a serene image of the volcanic island in Crater Lake with a sky reminiscent of the light aquamarine washes of the pre-linen era. To the lower left of the island, which is 163 feet at its highest point and some 300 feet long, a small boat affords a sense of scale and offers a point from which to imagine viewing the island. This image also affords an example of the shifting scales Teich's retouching artists and colorists had to keep in mind as they worked to render visual effects both printable and perceptually legible. One may focus closely on the lake's reflection without losing any pictorial resolution—that is, without the wavering likeness on the water's surface morphing into patterns of colored halftone dots. The middle-ground effect of the volcanic rock is less certain, ultimately refusing to come into focus if one moves the card close to the eye. And as for the background shore, whose indistinctness seems appropriate at the intended viewing distance, it dissolves into messy abstract patterns of dull colors when viewed at close range. Although critics from Walker Evans to Peter Bacon Hales have faulted linen postcards for a mechanized destruction of photographic creativity, an image such as this demonstrates the nearly intuitive artistry of the linen process (if, in this case, one ignores the unconvincing cottony fluffs that pass for clouds).

"A Redwood Burl / Redwood Highway, California"

Teich 5A-H781, 1935

THE REPRESENTATION OF LIGHT DISTINGUISHED LINEN CARDS from other varieties—real photo prints, pre-linen color lithographs, and chromes from the 1950s. Different intensities of white indicated the presence of light in black-and-white source photos. As retouching artists worked on a photo, they could enhance discrete sources of light such as lamps, headlights, or open windows, improve contrasts, and define areas of diffusion. Some effects, such as sunset or moonlight, were used so often they became formulaic. A sales agent would merely scribble "sunset effect" to obtain the desired result. But color artists faced greater challenges with natural landscapes in which light was directed, filtered, or suffused in ways that might be unique to a single image.

No color codes or scribbled phrases directed the artist who colorized this scene of California redwood trees. Viewed quickly, the card's image conveys a sense of sunlight streaming from a break in the trees behind the wide trunk to the right, filtering through a mass of needles and dappling the surface of another trunk behind as it radiates downward. Irregular diagonal striping suggests changing intensities of light conveyed in printing by subtle proportional shifts in the mixing of different colors. Rather than provoking awe at the sublime, this interpretation of nature invites the eye inward, engaging a viewer with the play of light, opposing a "meticulously [rendered] foreground to a remote, veiled distance" and "encouraging a sustained absorption in the image in place of an active movement through it." These phrases from the art historian Angela Miller describe the effects of landscape paintings by such mid- to late nineteenth-century artists as Sanford Gifford and John Frederick Kensett, often referred to as Luminists to distinguish them from Church, Bierstadt, and other painters of the sublime. The "impulse toward miniaturization" and emphasis on a "light suffused atmosphere" promoted by Luminists were also often reflected in the miniature landscape genre of linen postcards.[7] In this case, however, a closer look leaves one wondering where those shafts of light emanate from, but also marveling at the merging of yellow and light blue halftone dots to create the delicate light green branches feathering out from the slender redwood trunk rising on the left. That creative effect, conveyed without any reliance on the black plate derived from the source photo, originated with a colorist who in this case infused the standard rote colorizing process with a considerable degree of artistry.

Lava Fountains, Hawaii National Park

7A-H2139

"Lava Fountains, Hawaii National Park"

Teich 7A-H2139, 1937

ALTHOUGH MOST LANDSCAPE VIEWS PRODUCED BY TEICH AND other postcard companies followed the picturesque aesthetic, a subject occasionally proved so unprecedented that the artist abandoned all preconceptions. That was the case with this representation of lava spewing from an unidentified Hawaiian volcano—a view whose subject might have remained a mystery to most recipients had it not been identified by a caption. Except for night views of city skylines and steel mills, no other linen card relies so heavily on saturated black halftone dots, and in those other cases the night sky is usually composed of dark blue as well as black. Nor does any other card have so much of its surface area covered by only red and black. Without precedent to fall back on, the colorist relied on a garishly hand-painted source photo provided by the customer, K. Maehara of the Camera Craft Shop in Hilo, Hawaii, and a command, scrawled on the job file: "Be sure & use brightest red!"

Production of this card was delayed because the customer rejected an initial color proof. The "fountains of fire" appeared "too lumpy" and had to be rendered "a little brighter." Indeed, the central fountain on the proof looks like a blood-red cauliflower. Although the final corrected image contains tiny fringes of yellow at the tops of the central lava fountain and the lava flow on the left, recent color photographs suggest that most such eruptions present as much yellow as red, especially when viewed at night. The smoke seems well rendered, both the dense brownish cloud floating above the volcano's crater and the more nebulous gray in the upper left. However, without any direct experience of the phenomenon being illustrated, the artist blindly followed the hand-painted source in wrongly allowing the brown cloud to float behind the red on the left—not realizing the wall of red indicated lava flowing from a fissure near the top of the volcano's solid cone, rather than a lava fountain spewing upward. Even so, the result is a hellish image portraying, almost realistically, an awe-inspiring, surreal natural event neither they nor most of the people who received the card in the mail had ever actually experienced.

J:——ROCK OF AGES AND CAVE OF THE WINDS BY ILLUMINATION.

NIAGARA FALLS.

1299

"ROCK OF AGES AND CAVE OF THE WINDS BY ILLUMINATION / NIAGARA FALLS"

METROCRAFT 1299, N.D.

CURT TEICH IN 1938 DECLARED NIAGARA FALLS THE COMPANY'S second most popular subject, followed by Yellowstone's Old Faithful geyser and the Grand Canyon. The top seller was not a natural scene but the White House in Washington, DC.[8] One could have argued that Niagara Falls was also not a natural scene. Surrounded by hydroelectric plants, factories, and tourist attractions, and visited by hordes of tourists, Niagara had generated a cluttered, human-centered landscape.

Dozens of postcards illustrated every aspect of Niagara: Horseshoe Falls seen from above as if an observer were about to plunge over; catwalks snaking close to certain death; a viewing terrace on the Canadian side; the huge turbines of a generating plant; and the *Maid of the Mist* tourist boat. Most popular was Niagara's most dramatic artificial feature, nightly illumination by searchlights playing colored lights over the surging water, a regular attraction since 1925. Captions on the backs of many cards emphasized not only the spectacle's beauty but also human control over nature. Three Teich cards from 1932 to 1950 bore the same text, describing the "kaleidoscopic playing of multi-colored lights upon the turbulent spray" and declaring that "Niagara with the help of Man illuminates itself into a gorgeous splendor."[9]

This unique view was printed by Metrocraft of Everett, Massachusetts. Its caption clumsily announces a "new enhancement of America's beauty resources" as the Falls' power was "taken from them, brought under the control of man, and then turned back upon the power creator itself," yielding "a new beauty, ten-fold greater than any beauty known at the Falls before man took hold to conquer them for service." The turgid phrasing does not do justice to the astonishing image, which suggests an expressionist art poster. Pictorial elements do not cohere realistically. The yellow rock on the left, with weathered surface rendered accurately from the black plate, anchors a billowing cascade of equally realistic water pouring into a void composed of undulating abstracted bands of unearthly colors slanting across the frame. Horizontal streaks of gray cloud in a deep blue sky emphasize the flatness of the waterfall, which becomes a skin peeled away from reality.

What the historian David E. Nye says of the actual illumination can be applied as well to this extraordinary image. Colored spotlights "permitted the landscape to be edited, simplified, and dramatized," enhancing the central attraction and effacing insignificant surroundings.[10] This modernist rendering reduces Niagara to an abstracted expression of both its natural energy and the electrical energy it generates. The image offers an extreme example of the linen aesthetic's tendency to smooth away reality's extraneous detail.

N223:–A BEAUTIFUL REFLECTION. LAKE SANTEETLAH,WESTERN NORTH CAROLINA

44647

"A Beautiful Reflection. Lake Santeetlah, Western North Carolina"

Metrocraft 44647, n.d.

ALTHOUGH TEICH & CO. PRINTED MANY STYLIZED OR OTHER-
wise unrealistic images, their landscape cards hewed closely to what passed for
realism in the universe of offset halftone lithographs based on colorized black-
and-white photos. That was not always the case with other printers. Metrocraft,
the company that rendered Niagara Falls in a dramatic expressionist mode, also
printed this view of Lake Santeetlah, a meandering, many-fingered body of water formed in 1928 by the damming of the Cheoah River in the Appalachians.
Similar in composition to Teich's view of Bear Lake in Rocky Mountain National Park (see p. 90), this image also situates a viewer as if in a boat, looking low
across the water to a lakeshore with higher ground to left and right, and it also
emphasizes the reflection of the entire scene in the lake's surface.

Otherwise there is little similarity between the cards. Metrocraft rendered
the shore in dense photorealistic black halftone dots overprinted in a bright,
iridescent green, while cotton-ball cumulus clouds loom up beyond the horizon. The reflection is even more disruptive to any sense of verisimilitude, with a
wedge of sky and cloud opening downward to an ominous subterranean dimension below the shallower layer of reflected greenery. Even so, the deep, gaudy
colors possess a compelling quality, regardless of their failure to resolve into a
convincing landscape representation. Metrocraft printed this postcard for the
Asheville Post Card Company of Asheville, North Carolina, a major publisher
that contracted out the printing of most if not all its cards. This is one of Asheville's few postcards to credit the printer, but many others exhibited the same
odd aesthetic of dense halftone photorealism overlaid by deep, rich, often hal-
lucinatory color. Those probably also came from Metrocraft.[11]

Moonlight Scene of Moccasin Bend and Chattanooga, Tenn. From Lookout Mountain   183

17.322

"Moonlight Scene of Moccasin Bend and Chattanooga, Tenn. From Lookout Mountain"

Colourpicture 17,322, n.d.

Night views posed problems for linen postcard publish-
ers. A landscape with little artificial light, such as the one represented here,
yielded a black-and-white photograph with little detail or contrast, and streetlights and automobile headlights in urban scenes typically produced exposures
with too much glare to be usable. As a result, artists usually fabricated a night
view by retouching and colorizing a daytime source photo so it would appear as
a night view.[12] Stylized effects of moon, cloud, and stars created a generic look
as common as the orange sunsets of so many daytime views. The bright yellow
moon of this image differs from hundreds of others only in the dramatically
unconvincing wisp of cloud drifting across its surface, seeming oddly to cast a
shadow on it.

Although portraying the view from a scenic overlook, this eastern landscape evokes a feeling more of contemplation than of possessive mastery. The
Tennessee River's foot-shaped bend, looping around below a bluff at the top of
Lookout Mountain, encloses a patchwork of agricultural fields of varying luminous shades of green. The city of Chattanooga gleams unrealistically in the
moonlight to the upper right, almost as if a stray sunbeam is breaking through
a storm cloud. There is something of the quality of an illustration in a children's
book to this image, which seems simultaneously simplified and exaggerated.
The card bathes a factual representation of a prominent geographical feature
in a magical storybook light. An unusually long back caption ignores the landscape. Instead it describes the locale as the site of a major Civil War battle, referring to "the War Between the States" in deference to the southern sympathies
of most potential purchasers despite the fact that Colourpicture, the firm that
produced the card, was located in Boston. Even so, it would seem the moonlight
pastoral was the main attraction.

The Fern Garden in Cold Water Canyon, Wisconsin Dells

© H. H. BENNETT STUDIO

"THE FERN GARDEN IN COLD WATER CANYON, WISCONSIN DELLS"

TEICH IB-H2236, 1941

SOME LINEN POSTCARDS APPEAR MORE PHOTOREALISTIC THAN others, often because a greater area is determined by black halftone dots directly derived from the source photo. Other than black, the major hue in this view of a narrow canyon in the Wisconsin Dells is the green of ferns growing from narrow shelves and crevices formed by eroding layers of sandstone, nearly every one of them sharply outlined in black. Teich artists added little to the central image defined by the original photograph taken by H. H. Bennett, who made thousands of pictures of the Wisconsin Dells from the 1870s until his death in 1908. Although Teich had relied on several photographers during the pre-linen era for source photos of the Dells, including Bennett, all their many linen cards were commissioned by the H. H. Bennett Studios and based on his original prints. During the 1910s Bennett's survivors had commissioned heavily retouched, wholly unrealistic color lithographic cards for resale at the Bennett Studios, but by the 1930s they were demanding photorealism. The order for each in a series of five linen views of the Dells in 1934 carried the blunt instruction "Do not do too much retouching." The job files contain source photos with such minimal retouching (for greater contrast or clarity) that one must hold them against the light to determine that any paint at all has been added.[13]

Although this card from 1941 closely follows the source photo, two details reveal art department interventions. In the first, the rustic walkway looks too smooth and seamless to be constructed of wood, perhaps the result of an effort to visually simplify a part of the image regarded as insignificant. An artist's touch is also reflected in the treatment of the trees in the distance, rising against a pale blue sky in a gap between the canyon walls. Examined up close, the trees suggest a fanciful watercolor sketch similar in effect to the delicate feathering of the California redwoods (see p. 98). Viewed from a normal distance, however, they suggest light and air beyond the canyon's cool, dark confines. More to the point, they contribute a three-dimensional depth effect, a layering of foreground walkway, sandstone cliffs, and background trees reminiscent of the view through a stereopticon—an unusual illusion of depth for a linen image.

Echo River 360 Feet Underground in Mammoth Cave, Kentucky

OB-H147

"ECHO RIVER 360 FEET UNDERGROUND IN MAMMOTH CAVE, KENTUCKY"

TEICH OB-H147, 1940

Although not a landscape in a strict sense, the interior of a cavern dramatically lit by torch or electricity edging off into darkness affords a scene reminiscent of Gustave Doré's engravings of hell for Dante's *Divine Comedy* or Piranesi's *Carceri* prison etchings, with their vast, gloomy interiors. Most caverns commercialized for tourists in the nineteenth and twentieth centuries acquired a series of fanciful or dread-inducing names for passageways, chambers, and noteworthy formations. Mammoth Cave had its Black Snake Avenue and Bottomless Pit, its River Styx and Charon's Cascade. No tour was complete without a moment when the guide, after requesting complete silence, extinguished all illumination and plunged visitors into a palpable darkness unlike anything experienced above ground.

One of the major problems with a cave tour was the near impossibility of photographing it. Most families that could afford a sightseeing trip during the Depression also possessed an inexpensive Kodak to document their travels, but because such cameras were ineffective under low light conditions, postcards were the only option for a visual record of a cave tour. Other than the eerie electrical illumination, with its indeterminate sources, this image of Mammoth Cave portrays a scene little different from the earliest tours in the 1840s, when guides conducted visitors by torchlight along the River Styx and Echo River. Careful as always with reflections, Teich's artist also included rocks and other variations on the riverbed. The dramatic contrast of deep blue and rich yellow brown added visual interest to a cave whose dull walls lack the reflective opalescence of active stalactites and stalagmites. A back caption notes the presence of "several species of eyeless fish" and observes that the Echo River was "the largest body of water yet discovered in Mammoth Cave," thereby suggesting the cavern's virtually limitless extent—a conclusion visually reinforced by the appearance of a current entering at the lower right foreground.

"SUNSET ON A FLORIDA LAKE"

TEICH 5A-H1273, 1935

THE SOUTH DID NOT EVOKE AS COHERENT A PORTRAYAL ON LIN-
en postcards as the West or even New England. With the exception of Florida,
the Great Smoky Mountains, New Orleans, and such attractions as Colonial
Williamsburg and Lookout Mountain, the South possessed few long-range
tourist destinations. Excluding Florida and Texas, the former Confederate states
were not among Teich's major income producers.[14] Southern towns generated
typical views of city squares and monuments, but the region yielded few scenic
cards beyond the generic. The most common southern landscape cards portrayed riverbanks, mangrove swamps, Spanish moss, and atmospheric effects
nearly as dense as the vegetation. This lush sunset over a shimmering tropical
lake in Florida possesses irregular blots of deep orange and purple in the sky,
all moodily transformed as reflections in the water. The image emerged in response to a supervisor's prosaic instruction "Make pretty sunset," but the result,
which resembles an original watercolor, echoes typical forms and colors of post-
impressionism and German expressionism that might have been familiar to a
commercial artist trained at the Art Institute of Chicago.

While most Teich linens bore the trademark C. T. Art-Colortone, this one
is imprinted with the unusual C. T. Art-Colortone De Luxe—as if the company
was experimenting with a new, more exclusive process. No printed title mars
the image (a frequent flaw with borderless cards). Instead it appears on the
back. Dozens of other cards portrayed similarly generic southern landscapes.
Referring to the image on an earlier Teich pre-linen card, with a caption that
announced "beautiful scenery along the banks of a river in Dixieland," someone
wrote, "This may be along the St. John's or any of the numerous other rivers but
it is very like several I've seen."[15]

55—A Breaker on Atlantic Ocean

3A-H1205

"A Breaker on Atlantic Ocean"

Teich 3A-H1205, 1933

WHILE MANY MIDDLE-CLASS AMERICANS WITH TWO WEEKS OF vacation and savings to spare drove to view natural wonders of mountains and lakes, others headed for seaside resorts. There are hundreds of linen postcards portraying the ocean in myriad ways—waves and surf, bathing beaches, palms silhouetted at sunset, coastal highways, moonlit bays, sailing ships on the horizon. Many are generic cards that could be sold on the Atlantic coast, along the Gulf Coast from Florida to Texas, in Southern California, and even on the Great Lakes, sometimes with a local town's name added along the bottom. Teich released a series of cards titled "Ocean Scenes" in 1933 followed by ten "Bathing Scenes" cards in 1934, ten "Surf Scenes" cards in 1938, ten "Water Scenes" cards in 1938, and several other series. This particular ocean card was printed for the Jersey Supply Company in Atlantic City, but Teich also captioned the same view, under the same serial number, as representing breakers at Daytona Beach, Florida. Local distributors often overprinted generic scenes with town names in black letterpress or rubber stamp. In 1934, for example, Teich published a close-up of bathers relaxing on a beach as they watched others "bathing in the surf." Perhaps attempting humor, a distributor overprinted the lower margin with "Greetings from Seymour, Ind.," a town located 220 miles south of Lake Michigan, the closest place one could view water all the way to the horizon.[16]

This image reveals a classic linen late afternoon sky, with orange along the horizon merging into brownish yellow, a tinge of green, and finally light aquamarine. As with many linen landscapes, a diagonal splits the scene, in this case a cresting wave with a flock of gulls punctuating a line extending toward the upper left. The artist seems to have taken pains to capture the wave's spray almost as the painter Winslow Homer might have done. Even more impressively, the image conveys through a blurry blue-green foreground, nearly devoid of defining black halftone dots, the vague opacity of seawater, sand, and debris stirred up by the previous wave receding from the shore. For greater realism, the water in the distance should have had a dull greenish hue, but water in the world of linen postcards is nearly always a deep, bright, satisfying blue.

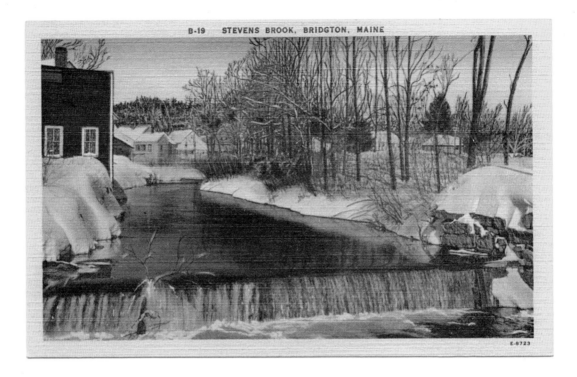

B-19   STEVENS BROOK, BRIDGTON, MAINE

E-8723

"STEVENS BROOK, BRIDGTON, MAINE"

HARTMAN LITHO SALES E-8723, N.D.

NOT ALL LINEN LANDSCAPE CARDS PRESENTED BREATHTAKING
vistas with extravagant, atmospheric lighting. Much depended on the region
of the country being portrayed. Views of the Northeast in general and New
England in particular tended to be understated but often effective. This scene
evokes the crisp air, chill quiet, and placid stasis of a winter afternoon. Bridgton
was a small town spread out along Stevens Brook, which ran for two or three
miles from Highland Lake to Long Lake, nearly parallel fingers of water filling
deep glacial striations. Against a background of frame houses in the distance,
the corner of a red-brick building efficiently references the textile mills established during the nineteenth century in every town with enough fall in elevation
to drive a millwheel. Bridgton, which appears idyllic in this view, became a summer resort area soon after the postcard was published.

The publisher of this card, Hartman Litho Sales in Largo, Florida, was one
of many small publishers that issued cards with the same type of serial number:
the letter E followed by a hyphen and four or five numerals. Others included
Eastern Photo Litho in Lowell, Massachusetts, William Jubb in Syracuse, New
York, J. P. Walmer in Harrisburg, Pennsylvania, and, most notably, Asheville
Post Card Company in North Carolina. The font used for the words "Post Card"
above the address section is identical to one commonly used by Metrocraft,
whose artists and printers were probably responsible not only for this card but
for all postcards in the "E" series. In any event, a skillful artist seems to have improved the image. Individual lines of every branch and twig, and of the edge of
the brook, whose dark borders suggest snow banks undercut by moving water,
reveal the emphasis of the retouching artist. The image's delicacy and restraint
are more typical of light pastel pre-linen cards. The mill's solidity, the stream's
immediate presence, and the large rock on the right all contrast effectively with
the houses, whose more muted tones convey a sense of receding distance and
depth. The picturesque convention of the diagonal view to the upper left is employed. The image resonates with the quiet sense of decay that had marked New
England regionalism since the Civil War, reflected in the so-called local color literature of the late nineteenth century and in the poet Robert Frost's oft-quoted
lines "The question . . . / Is what to make of a diminished thing."[17]

893. DEATH VALLEY, CALIFORNIA

The Southwest

A REGIONAL AESTHETIC

659—SMOKE TREES ON THE DESERT, CALIFORNIA. SALTON SEA. 260 FEET BELOW SEA LEVEL. IN THE DISTANCE

1A-H441

"Smoke Trees on the Desert, California.
Salton Sea. 260 Feet below Sea Level,
in the Distance"

Teich 1A-H441, 1931

JUDGING BY TODAY'S OFFERINGS OF VINTAGE POSTCARD DEAL-
ers, views of the Southwest and West comprised a major proportion of linen
images of the American scene. However, sales figures do not confirm that observation. In 1939, the only year for which records exist, the company sold 618,700
"scenic" cards in Massachusetts and 161,500 in Minnesota, but only 85,250 in
California and 12,000 in Arizona.[18] Perhaps eastern and midwestern cards were
discarded as routine correspondence, while western cards with dramatic landscapes were saved by tourists as souvenirs or by folks back home who received
them in the mail. Whatever the case, the linen landscape postcard attained its
most characteristic aesthetic in portraying the American West.

This desert view is nearly a generic, one of many illustrating cactuses, yuc-
cas, palm trees, or smoke trees. However, a thin blue line on the horizon, almost
a mirage, situates this as a specific spot near the Salton Sea, a large body of salt
water, below sea level, sixty miles inland from San Diego. Smoke trees seem to
have been a popular subject, but their nebulous forms proved hard to capture,
or perhaps they shifted hues with changes in the light. When ordering a new
view in 1937, Pitchford warned the art department that smoke trees "are not
green" but "rather a silver-gray-green—that from a distance resembles smoke."[19]
The resulting card represented the trees with off-green cotton puffs for leaves—
as opposed to this earlier card, from 1931, which exhibits a bluish purple and
conveys more of a sense of individual leaves. Dull colors ranging from green to
blue to red for creosote bushes and sagebrush offer a subtle visual foil to the
smoke trees. But the card's major effect is a creative variation on the typical
linen sunset, here reflected from a vast cloud formation.

Such colorful images do not convey the monotony and misery of driving
across the desert in hundred-plus heat before cars were air-conditioned. To understand that situation, we have the messages. One correspondent reported it
was so hot crossing the California desert, "we had to hold a wet rag [to] our
nose." Another described "traveling the dessert [*sic*] at night on account of the
baby." And a third complained about such "desolate country," concluding, "the
Lord did a poor job when he dump[ed] this mess in Calif."[20]

MT. SAN BERNARDINO, GREYBACK AND MT. SAN JACINTO

A-16 FROM HIGH GEAR ROAD TO LAKE ARROWHEAD, CALIFORNIA 7A-H1399

"MT. SAN BERNARDINO, GREYBACK AND
MT. SAN JACINTO / FROM HIGH GEAR ROAD TO
LAKE ARROWHEAD, CALIFORNIA"

TEICH 7A-H1399, 1937

AUTOMOBILE TOURISM AND HIGHWAY CONSTRUCTION PROMOTED
access to scenic overlooks with "breathtaking" vistas formerly accessible only on foot
or by pack animal. Even after the advent of Sunday drivers, travelers from San Bernardino to Lake Arrowhead had to take a hazardous gravel road known as the Rim
of the World Highway. They negotiated endless switchbacks in low gear (or driving
backward in reverse on the steepest grades). All that changed in the mid-1930s with
completion of the paved High Gear Road, so called because one could drive it in high,
or third, gear at relatively normal speed.[21] Looking out from this rustic rock parapet
at a mile-high elevation, one could see Southern California's highest peak thirty-five
miles to the east-southeast.

This image's composition is unusual in placing the figure of a young woman so
prominently as a frame and implicit point of view. Her posture suggests nonchalant
confidence in her ability to encompass and possess the landscape. The art historian
Albert Boime has defined "the magisterial gaze" as an expression of a "fantasy of
domain and empire" that places a "spectator" looking down from a "ledge or crest,"
subjugating "boundless reality" and "carv[ing] out unity, harmony, and order from
endless vistas." Usually the magisterial gaze is a possessive male force. Here, however,
it is a woman who looks over the landscape—her hair open to the breeze, one hand
on her hip, the other hand draped over a knee. She is wearing pants, hiking boots,
a loose white blouse open at the throat, and a casual jacket. In the background an
elderly man hunches on the wall, head bowed, contemplating the vista, perhaps with
regret. But the woman looks directly across the image's horizontal flow, her pose and
gaze suggesting mastery.[22]

Even so, one gets a sense, with the freestanding parapet totally isolated from everything below, that this woman, despite her outdoorsy clothes, may have ridden up
in high-gear comfort like everyone else. The new road had tamed the San Bernardino
Mountains and rendered their vistas available to anyone in Los Angeles with access
to a car. This image, placing the figure of a woman, however healthy and vigorous, in
the position usually taken by a man, suggests a domestication of the sublime. A female tourist browsing a postcard rack could purchase this mass-produced, miniaturized image and then, after taking possession of it, casually tuck it away in her purse.

In fact, the card's job file reveals that sales agent Pitchford required a pretty model to dress up the mountain view. The young woman's image was actually cut from
another photo and collaged onto a photo of the overlook. Not only had the model not
hiked up to her perch, she had quite likely never been there at all. "Preserve features
of girl as much as is possible," Pitchford requested, "so face will look natural." But the
landscape itself required further softening. "There is a lot of distance here and view
is very impressive," the sales agent observed, but he also warned, "do not outline too
harshly." Avoid "vivid greens," he suggested, in favor of "olive tone, gray greens and
some brownish green." Above all, he concluded, wrapping this already domesticated
landscape in the guise of women's fashion, "distant mountains have some mauve
tones and look very much like velvet."

H-4219 THE WATCHTOWER AT DESERT VIEW, GRAND CANYON NATIONAL PARK, ARIZONA

"THE WATCHTOWER AT DESERT VIEW, GRAND CANYON NATIONAL PARK, ARIZONA"

TEICH 7A-H652, 1937

AMERICAN NATIONAL PARKS WERE BECOMING MORE ACCESSI-
ble by car at the same time Curt Teich was developing the linen postcard process.
Initially partnerships between the federal government and various railroads had
opened up the parks to affluent visitors. A two-hour train ride northward from
the Santa Fe Railroad's main line brought tourists to the Grand Canyon's El
Tovar Hotel, run by the Fred Harvey Company in association with the railroad.
Auto travelers also enjoyed Harvey amenities along twenty-five miles of roadway on the canyon's South Rim. The Watchtower at Desert View, the subject of
this card, exemplified a coherent southwestern vision that was orchestrated for
Harvey by the designer Mary Colter.[23] Although framed in steel, the seventy-
foot tower, completed in 1932, took inspiration from ruins of Pueblo watchtow-
ers and was built from uncut natural stone. A faux ruin on one side lent a suggestion of authenticity. The tower's amalgam of Native American pastiche and
Arts and Crafts rusticity reflected a desire to naturalize the tourist experience,
to disguise modern interventions in the landscape by blending them with the
timeless canyon.

Visitors had an array of Teich cards to choose from, most illustrating the
canyon, others the tower, and still others the wider region's Navajo and Pueblo
Indians—all displaying a distinctive "Fred Harvey" logotype in cursive on the
back. Within a few years Teich had printed more linen views of the Watchtower
than might be expected, essentially showing the same thing from different perspectives. Although Harvey enjoyed a monopoly on what was sold in the company's souvenir shops, competing vendors also needed views of this distinctive
site. Teich produced images of the Watchtower and of the canyon in general for
the photographer J. R. Willis of Albuquerque and the news agent Harry Herz of
San Diego. Teich also printed Grand Canyon postcards for Lollesgard Specialty
Company of Tucson and Phoenix, and for Verkamp's curio shop, a competitor of Harvey's on the South Rim since 1906. That Teich prepared at least five
complete—and different—sets of Grand Canyon images serves as a reminder
that the company's American scene evolved piecemeal in response to individual
commissions. Only in hindsight does it approach coherence.

H-4220   THE KIVA, DESERT VIEW, GRAND CANYON NATIONAL PARK, ARIZONA

"THE KIVA, DESERT VIEW, GRAND CANYON NATIONAL PARK, ARIZONA"

TEICH 7A-H694, 1937

A NEARLY CIRCULAR ONE-STORY ROOM PROJECTED OUT FROM the Watchtower at Desert View, serving as a reception area and souvenir shop. Despite its large windows and panoramic canyon view, Colter intended this space to replicate a kiva, a ceremonial structure that would have been located underground, accessible only to the initiated. As portrayed in this image, various details set a quasi-Indian scene: a circular fire pit (nonfunctional), large drums stretched with skins, and a rustic wooden ladder (representing the only entrance down into an actual kiva). For modern tourists, a working fireplace with rawhide-covered benches offered heat on cold days, and tables and chairs invited relaxation. As this postcard's caption admits, the similarity to a prehistoric kiva, otherwise complete "in all details," did not extend to the "great windows overlooking the magnificent panorama of Canyon and Desert."

At one of these windows we find a tourist couple. Even at the small scale, Teich artists managed to suggest they are stylishly dressed, the woman in a long coat and cloche hat, sitting in the window embrasure, and the man standing, wearing a driving cap, hands thrust in his trench coat pockets. Despite their surroundings, they radiate calm urbanity. Their possessive oversight of the sublime wonders below them is casual and taken for granted. They lack even the trappings, fully though misleadingly exhibited by the woman at the High Gear Road overlook (see p. 122), of having earned the right to mastery of all they survey. Their dress and pose suggest an enervated domesticity whose focus is not the landscape but the interior of the Watchtower itself. As a woman informed a male correspondent in Dallas in 1938, after purchasing this card and settling into the exact location of the woman pictured on it, she was "sitting on this little bench" and "having a nice time." As for the view, only fuzzily rendered, the retouched photo reveals that its vague canyon features were added freehand. In the source photo a tree blocks the view from the central window, and the other windows are blank owing to overexposure.

"GRAND CANYON FROM MORAN POINT"

TEICH 8A-H1582, 1938

This image, based on a photograph taken at Moran Point, ten miles west of Desert View, is typical of Grand Canyon views in its luminous clarity. As if the art department wished to lavish attention on the shifting colors of the canyon itself, they avoided the gaudy sunset coloration of so many linen postcards, opting instead for an affectless sky of robin's-egg blue along the card's upper edge, conveying a sense of dry desert clarity. This card's borderless printing emphasized an intention of representing reality unframed, despite a reference in the back caption to "the illustrious artist and pioneer painter of the Canyon" Thomas Moran, whose work interpreting this landscape had given the site its name. A visitor needed only a "glimpse . . . under full sunshine to realize the astonishing beauty and coloring which so delighted the artist."

But if the caption writer partially mediated reactions to the canyon by filtering them through references to a legendary painter, artists in Chicago labored to convey a draftsman's sense of the representation of direct perception. While Moran had presented the Grand Canyon in shimmering curtains of liquid color inspired by the seascapes of the British painter J. M. W. Turner, Teich's artists conveyed unusual precision of form and shading derived ultimately from the retouched source photo. Black halftone dots of the key printing plate defined with utter clarity each horizontal stratum of rock and vertical mark of erosion. Only in the lower right corner was the illusion of painterly draftsmanship negated by a couple of rock faces rendered in white, thus revealing the photographic skeleton of their imaging. Otherwise the sense of direct artistic verisimilitude distinct from that of the photographic is maintained, particularly as white limestone cliffs in the distance fade and shimmer along the horizon. The aesthetic composition of this image, its subtle shifting of complex color tones, based as always on a blending of halftone dots in the basic colors, serves as evidence of the artistry of linen postcard colorists at their best. However, that conclusion must be tempered by the observation that this level of care and attention was rare in the general universe of linen postcards, most of which displayed the results of a less creative, more mechanical colorizing process.

921   THE QUEEN'S COURT, BRYCE CANYON NATIONAL PARK, UTAH

3A-H221

"THE QUEEN'S COURT, BRYCE CANYON NATIONAL PARK, UTAH"

TEICH 3A-H221, 1933

MORE TYPICAL OF THE ARTISTIC QUALITY OF LINEN IMAGES OF southwestern rock formations is this view from Bryce Canyon National Park, one of dozens of cards Teich produced for Deseret Book Company in Salt Lake City, a Mormon publishing house and bookstore that commissioned most of the printer's Utah views. The park was established in 1928 after lobbying by the Union Pacific Railroad and local boosters who projected a tourism circuit connecting southern Utah with the Grand Canyon's North Rim. In 1933, when this card was produced, in the depths of the Depression, the annual number of park visitors had dropped 20 percent since 1931, but by 1935 the number had doubled to 63,700, and it continued rising steadily. Most visitors now came by car and used the lodge and other facilities owned by a subsidiary of the railroad.[24]

Bryce Canyon lends itself to dramatic presentation in color, with vivid contrasts between a limpid light blue sky, dark green pines along the eroded rim, rust-red and pure white limestone formations, and brownish-yellow sand. The column of rock framing the view on the right echoes picturesque landscape conventions but fails to provide a sense of scale. Other Teich images of the park in the 1930s and '40s better reveal the delicate play of color variations in the horizontal strata common to a single group of formations. But none of them provides such an accurate impression of a "maze of grotesque figures uprising from the floor of Bryce Canyon," according to this card's back caption, which uses words still found in brochures and websites devoted to the park. Although the image is devoid of human presence, the caption invites a viewer to subordinate the canyon to literary or cultural conceits, to subsume it into narrative by regarding its formations as "many hundreds of groups about which ones [*sic*] fancy weaves many fairy-tales"—the Queen's Court being one of the most impressive.

NATURAL COLOR REPRODUCTION FROM KODACHROME

COPYRIGHT STEPHEN WILLARD

Twenty-Nine Palms Oasis, California

1B-H2599

"TWENTY-NINE PALMS OASIS, CALIFORNIA"

TEICH 1B-H2599, 1941

ALTHOUGH LINEN POSTCARDS REMAINED DOMINANT INTO THE late 1940s, this 1941 view of a site now also known as the Oasis of Mara, located north of the then–newly established Joshua Tree National Monument, indicates the direction that view postcards would take during the second half of the twentieth century. The photographer Stephen Willard, a Teich customer throughout the linen era, commissioned cards to sell at his studio in Palm Springs. Willard was known for using oil paints to colorize enlargements of his black-and-white photographs of desert views. With a selection of postcards he could offer miniature versions of his work to visitors who did not intend to purchase a hand-painted photo. That Willard wanted his cards to appear classy is evident from the fact that he paid fifty cents extra per thousand cards for a die-cut "deckle edge" simulating handmade paper.

This card's palette of colors departs from standard linen colors. Warm hues, orange and yellow, are replaced by a cool blue tinge that seems more realistic to twenty-first-century eyes. This card (and others prepared for Willard in 1941) proclaims itself a "natural color reproduction from Kodachrome," but the process was more complicated. Eastman Kodak's 35 mm Kodachrome film for color slides had been introduced in 1936. Willard apparently would photograph a scene with two cameras, using both the new color film and black-and-white film, and then use the resulting color slide as a guide when painting colors onto a black-and-white print. Teich's job file for another Willard postcard, an image of smoke trees from 1939, contains both Willard's signed color painting on a black-and-white print and an identical black-and-white print used by the retouching artist, who followed an injunction to "do no unnecessary retouching." Teich's colorist was told to "see oil painting att'd" when preparing the color printing plates for that card.[25] Thus even Willard's so-called Kodachrome cards were based on the standard Teich process for colorizing black-and-white photos. However, this scene's colors ultimately derived from the slide film Willard had exposed at the Oasis of Mara. Although it took years for shiny chromes based on color photography to overtake linen cards and drive Teich out of business, the cards produced for Willard in 1941 marked the first shift away from the dominant warm colors of the linen postcard aesthetic.

893. DEATH VALLEY, CALIFORNIA

"Death Valley, California"

Longshaw 893, n.d.

MOST LINEN POSTCARDS, THOUGH ARTIFICIALLY COLORIZED, attempted to convey a heightened sense of reality. The popular understanding of photographs like those on which linen cards were based held that photos do not lie. Producers of early real photo postcards played on that belief by constructing humorous composite images showing a giant ear of corn or a giant eggplant filling a horse-drawn wagon. The momentary disorientation triggered by such images depended on the apparent evidence of a violation of the natural order. Linen postcards later featured similar subjects, such as a man standing on a potato large enough to fill a railway flatcar.[26] Today such linen cards seem pointless. How could people have accepted them even momentarily as representations of reality when their colorized images, even without giant vegetables, often seemed extravagantly unreal?

One also wonders what to make of this wildly surreal interpretation of Death Valley. Its predominant colors, purple and yellow, echo those of Teich's smoke trees (see p. 120), and both scenes encompass desolate land and scrubby vegetation, but there is no other point of comparison. Today this image suggests an imaginary scene on Mars, or a radioactive landscape from a post–World War II science fiction movie, not anything a tourist driving across the desert would have recognized. Printed by the Longshaw Card Company of Los Angeles, this view of Death Valley, with its slashing diagonal perhaps intended to divide areas of sun and shade in late afternoon, possesses an uncompromising unearthliness. Whether the product of incompetence or of a visionary sensibility, the image is accompanied by a back caption referring to "weird and colorful scenery." Most of Longshaw's cards portrayed urban scenes in Los Angeles and San Francisco with vivid colors and dramatic expressionist forms, and most exhibited greater verisimilitude than this extreme image. Unfortunately no message reveals how its purchaser regarded it.

7A-H1608

Travel and Tourism

29187   CANYON LODGE LOUNGE   COPYRIGHT BY HAYNES INC.; YELLOWSTONE PARK, WYO.

264-B—Erosion of the Ages, Bad Lands, So. Dak.

1B-H1325

"EROSION OF THE AGES, BAD LANDS, SO. DAK."

TEICH 1B-H1325, 1941

PICTURESQUE CONVENTIONS REMAINED OPERATIVE AS THE CAR entered the wilderness. In this desolate view of South Dakota's Badlands, a tiny auto stands in for the banditti roaming Salvator Rosa's seventeenth-century paintings and focuses a viewer's attention on the landscape's immensity. A cool color palette intensifies the sense of isolation. The road replaces the meandering stream of typical picturesque landscapes. Its main straightaway forms a diagonal line merging smoothly with the sunlit edge of a rising promontory of rock, leading the viewer's gaze upward from left to right. Crossing the diagonal at an acute angle is a nearly horizontal line formed by a shelf of rock running through the central massif near the center of the image. As these two lines cross, they create a flattened X dividing the image into four parts of unequal size, with the road's meander outlining a triangular wedge on the lower left. In effect the two left-hand arms of the X define the car's direction of travel as it moves diagonally upward along the roadway from left to right and then, rounding the bend, shifts to a diagonally upward motion from right to left, moving out of sight behind a hill.

These effects, which seem forced and mechanical when described, and were probably not intentional, emerged from the convergence of landscape and photographer at the precise moment the source photo was taken. Even so, they suggest two contradictory interpretations: first, the conformity of roadway and traveler to the natural landscape, and second, the bending of the landscape itself to human desire and control. Teich's retouching artist went beyond the photographer's intention when he meticulously emphasized each vertical post of the guardrail that keeps drivers from plunging over the edge. The image thus reinforces the presence of human control in the loneliest, most desolate of landscapes. Linen postcards that featured the road and car as extending modernity into a natural scene proved so numerous they formed a distinct subgenre.

T-7

Mt. Lemmon Road, near Tucson, Arizona

OB-H2616

"MT. LEMMON ROAD, NEAR TUCSON, ARIZONA"

TEICH OB-H2616, 1940

OTHER THAN THE ROAD, THE CAR, AND A DRAMATIC REVERSE S-curve, not much connects this postcard with that of the Badlands. Rather than being overwhelmed by desolation, the automobile here assumes physical and visual centrality in a luminously glowing landscape. Partially cropped in the direction from which it travels, the car assumes a dynamic relationship to the rest of the image. The composition invites a viewer to assume the driver's perspective, looking over a long, curving vista to the city of Tucson on the horizon, which is emphasized by a "halo effect" Pitchford asked the art department to "preserve." The back caption represents the car as returning from an outing on the completed portion of a new highway that was to run from Tucson to the top of Mt. Lemmon. Seven years under way at the time the card was published and later known as the Catalina Highway, the road was not finished until 1950.[27]

This image, with a pre-sunset glow on the horizon conveyed more delicately than was often the case, remains within the parameters of the linen aesthetic. A raking horizontal light illuminates the edges of cactuses viewed from behind and renders luminous the desert flowers and plants on the hillside. Pitchford insisted that the "effect of the sun shining thru the needles" in the source photo "must be preserved." Rippling shadows suggest washboard erosion of the hard-packed dirt visible just in front of the car. The depth and texture of the road surface is unusual in linen cards, indicating careful work in the art department for a card based on an atmospheric photo taken by Pitchford. Above all, the image conveys a sense that natural landscapes are best experienced by car, indeed, that the automobile offers access to an expansive, limitless American scene. No one knew that better than the well-traveled Pitchford, whose 1940 Buick sedan energized this view.[28]

G. I. PITCHFORD, *MT. LEMMON ROAD, TUCSON, AZ*, CA. 1940

©28478—OLD FAITHFUL INN AND GEYSER, YELLOWSTONE NATIONAL PARK

COPYRIGHT BY HAYNES STUDIOS INC., BOZEMAN, MONTANA

"Old Faithful Inn and Geyser, Yellowstone National Park"

Teich 5A-H515, 1935

ALTHOUGH HUNDREDS OF LINEN POSTCARDS DEPICTED SCENES
purporting to be wholly "natural," untouched by human presence, an equal
number portrayed human interactions with nature. In this view from Yellowstone National Park, the bulk of the Old Faithful Inn overwhelms the park's
most famous natural feature, the geyser for which the hotel was named. Although the card affords a poor example of the linen aesthetic, given the sallow
horizon hue, muddied sky, poorly delineated geyser spray, and reliance on dull,
undifferentiated fields of color for building, wagon, and driveway, its composition is significant for the subordination of Yellowstone's primary natural wonder to the need for human control and comfort. The Old Faithful geyser was the
third most popular subject for postcards, according to Curt Teich, but this view
turns up frequently enough in dealers' offerings to suggest many visitors wanted
to recall the structure from whose veranda, according to the back caption, one
could observe the geyser erupting with a regularity mimicking the clockwork of
modern times.[29]

Opened in 1904, the Old Faithful Inn awed visitors with its sheer size, its
vast open lobby (seven stories high, with four levels of balconies), and its massive 500-ton fireplace. Though built of natural materials, undressed logs and
rough stone, the structure so thoroughly dominates this image that the geyser,
situated at the end of a formal vista, looks artificially sited, as much a matter
of human whim as a 300-foot artificial fountain installed along the lakefront
of Geneva, Switzerland, in 1891. And if the rustic Old Faithful Inn almost invites one to regard it as an extension of nature, then one must account for three
automobiles rendered so tiny as to be barely visible, but also physically closer
than anything else to the natural energy of the geyser. The automobile, the central technological focus of twentieth-century American modernity, was the very
means of bringing visitors to Old Faithful and its modern accommodations. The
horse-drawn "Yellowstone wagon" in the lower right corner, used to transport
park visitors from 1890 until the advent of motorized buses in 1917, was just
another frontier prop.

7A-H1608

29187   CANYON LODGE LOUNGE

COPYRIGHT BY HAYNES INC., YELLOWSTONE PARK, WYO.

"Canyon Lodge Lounge"

Teich 7A-H1608, 1937

THIS VIEW OF THE LOUNGE AT CANYON LODGE IN YELLOWSTONE makes it appear so vast as to compete with the Old Faithful Inn. The general emptiness and lack of functional definition suggest the open provisional space of a medieval hall or Silk Road caravansary. In fact, Canyon Lodge was a modest one-story log building with lodge, dining, and office facilities for visitors traveling by car and staying in nearby cabins. Located at what is now Canyon Village, the complex was constructed in the mid-1920s and used until 1957. The image places a viewer looking up a kind of arcade or colonnade that recedes nearly to infinity. Side chairs with rush seats lean against each column in a clump at odds with any useful arrangement. Most of the interior space is light and airy owing to a row of open doors along the right through which sunlight streams in. Although the image is highly photorealistic, based mostly on lines and shadings from the black printing plate, with a dusting of yellow-brown color for warmth, the open door on the lower right seems out of scale. The actual door was obviously quite high, but the simplicity of its framing as rendered by a retouching artist gives it the appearance of an ordinary house door. A person walking through such a door into the room would be way too large for the otherwise realistically rendered chairs.

This violation of scale recalls children's bedtime stories, perhaps "Goldilocks and the Three Bears" or even Lewis Carroll's *Alice's Adventures in Wonderland*. The image's disconcerting quality also resonates with a strange description from Henry David Thoreau's *Walden* (1854) of an imaginary domestic interior, of which this is the opening line: "I sometimes dream of a larger and more populous house, standing in a golden age, of enduring materials, and without gingerbread work, which shall still consist of only one room, a vast, rude, substantial, primitive hall, without ceiling or plastering, with bare rafters and purlins supporting a sort of lower heaven over one's head." This image, like those of many other national park interiors, evokes a mythic quality, supporting the historian Alfred Runte's observation that national parks offered an "opportunity to acquire a semblance of antiquity through landscape."[30]

99 "PLEASE SIR, I'M HUNGRY"

2A-H679

"'Please Sir, I'm Hungry'"

Teich 2A-H679, 1932

Nothing reveals the significance of the machine in the wilderness so well as this view of a black bear leaning on the side of a closed car, begging a handout. The car following behind suggests that traffic jams reported on Yellowstone Park roads during the 1950s as drivers stopped to interact with bears actually began much earlier. Photos from the later period reveal a considerable difference, however. Postwar tourists greeted bears with windows rolled down and heads stuck out, and people got out of their cars to approach the bears on foot, smiling and taking snapshots. In this image the sheen on the window reveals it is nearly closed. No passenger's face is discernible. The automobile becomes a protective cocoon of modernity, its uniform blue-black finish at odds with the irregular jumble of trees in the background. Even the roadway exhibits an unnatural uniformity instead of the granular asphalt or rolled pebble texture visible in photos from the 1930s. The road thus becomes a smooth extension of modernity, conveying tourists in complete comfort through the wilderness of the park. As for the bear, although its general form and shaggy coat, with individual tufts of fur clearly rendered, convey a sense of realism, the retouching artist seems to have humanized its face, conveying a hint of personality through gleaming eye and curling lip. Bears were not the only animals featured on linen postcards. But except for a tangle of alligators on display in St. Augustine, Florida, most such images portrayed scenes tourists would never have encountered, such as a rattlesnake swallowing a rabbit, a gila monster climbing vertically up a barrel cactus, a horned lizard and its young, or a close-up of a Brahman bull.[31] This image, however, is a record of what a tourist could have snapped with a Kodak if doors and windows had not been closed up tight.

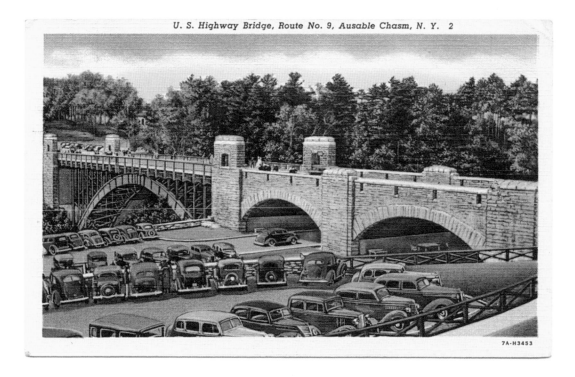

U. S. Highway Bridge, Route No. 9, Ausable Chasm, N. Y. 2

7A-H3453

"U.S. HIGHWAY BRIDGE, ROUTE NO. 9, AUSABLE CHASM, N.Y."

TEICH 7A-H3453, 1937

ALTHOUGH THE ARRAY OF COLORS AMONG THE AUTOMOBILES IN
this postcard is striking, there is no escaping the fact that its subject, despite a
caption emphasizing the bridge, is actually a parking area. The ability to travel
by car to see sights whose enjoyment was previously limited to local residents
was novel enough that a parking lot full of cars could interest tourists and
their correspondents. Ausable Chasm is located in the heart of the Adirondack
Mountains, only three miles from Lake Champlain. The waterfall and gorge
on the Ausable River had been a regional site for nature pilgrimages since the
1870s, but only in the 1920s, with the expansion of recreational auto travel, did
the site begin to attract large numbers of visitors.

Neither the image nor the brief caption (there is no descriptive caption on
the back) reveals that pedestrians standing on the steel arch of the bridge, facing south (toward the left), could look upriver toward a high, wide triple waterfall. If they crossed the road and looked the other way, they could observe
the fast-moving river before it turned sharply to the right, out of sight, into a
narrow, tortuous sandstone gorge bordered by wooden walkways, bridges, and
overlooks. The postcard's announced subject is the bridge itself, an example of
WPA civil engineering completed in 1934. Its slashing line divides the parking
area from the lush vegetation beyond, the only evidence of the natural realm
that tourists and Sunday drivers had come to enjoy. The river is not even visible
in the image. Shortly before the bridge opened, a local newspaper reported that
the project's "parking spaces" would "accommodate hundreds of automobiles,
making it unnecessary for cars to stop on the bridge while the passengers are
viewing the chasm a hundred or more feet below."[32]

"WHY SHOULD I BOTHER"

TEICH 7A-H2401, 1937

POSTCARD RACKS ACROSS THE COUNTRY WERE STOCKED WITH humorous cards referred to as "comics" to distinguish them from "scenics." In a single year, 1939, Teich & Co. sold nearly equal numbers of each, 6.9 million comics and 6.5 million scenics. However, the number of scenic designs outnumbered comic designs by fifty to one—which means a typical comic sold far more copies than a typical scenic.[33] Most of the humor involved travel and vacation: motoring, trailers, outhouses, beaches, fishing, nudist camps, and tents (with nude females casting silhouette shadows on their sides). More than 425 comic designs, about half of Teich's total number, were sketched and painted by Ray Walters, a newspaper editorial cartoonist educated at the Art Institute of Chicago, who began designing cards in 1932, when he was about fifty, and continued through 1946.

This postcard is typical of Walters's output. His males were grinning, red-nosed, buck-toothed, sometimes loutish figures, while his females were young, blonde, and voluptuous with prominent nipples, unless portrayed as middle-aged, in which case they were plump like the woman in the background here, facing the other direction. Many of Walters's comic cards and those by Teich's other comic artists employed humor now regarded as sexist or occasionally misogynist. In this example a lone wolf male has parked a tiny one-man trailer on a spit of tropical beach (in Florida, on the Gulf Coast, or in Southern California) in front of a larger trailer from which a bathing beauty has emerged as the object of his leering attention. The stickers on the man's trailer, boasting of visits to eighteen states and three cities, and the sentiment of the doggerel verse clearly promote a leisurely life of aimless wandering. One would never guess that thousands of homeless citizens were roaming the nation during the Depression—hitchhiking, riding the rails, and driving beat-up cars in search of work. Whether bought by affluent vacationers or by people driven by necessity to keep moving, this postcard and others in a series of twenty cards called "Trailer Comics" indicated a population that liked to regard itself as footloose. The experience of travel was at the heart of Teich's American scene.[34]

P. G. 17   MUNICIPAL TOURIST CAMP AND COMMUNITY HALL ON CHARLOTTE HARBOR, PUNTA GORDA, FLA.

6A-H1198

"Municipal Tourist Camp and Community Hall on Charlotte Harbor, Punta Gorda, Fla."

Teich 6A-H1198, 1936

Gerald Cleveland, *Municipal Tourist Camp,*
Punta Gorda, FL, 1936

MOST TOWNS ESTABLISHED MUNICIPAL TOURIST CAMPS DURING
the 1920s for auto campers. These typically charged no rent as the towns wanted
to encourage retail purchases by visitors. The town of Punta Gorda, on Florida's
western coast near Sarasota, opened a camp beside a public fishing pier. The
permanent structure in the background in this image was a community center
built by WPA labor in 1933 using traditional log construction. The card's back
caption boasts of a location where "every variety of salt water fish" could be
caught "in abundance," yet it was "within one-half block of the business district."

Examination of several photos taken in 1936 by Gerald Cleveland, a local
photographer, reveals a decision by Teich or the client to manipulate the camp's
image by excluding tents and showing only trailers. Two of the photos reveal at
least six tents, several of them sprawling affairs, scattered through the camp (see
photo at lower left). Taken at different times, the photos show nearly complete
turnover in the trailers, but the tents remain constant—suggesting that campers who lived in them were long-term residents. A third image, on a halftone
black-and-white postcard mailed in 1936, shows at least five tents. By contrast,
Teich's source photo, also taken by Cleveland, shows no tents at all. But another
taken by Cleveland on the same day from a less advantageous angle reveals a
single tent off to the left.[35] Selecting from among Cleveland's photos, someone
decided to exclude tents and thus suggest a tidier, more affluent clientele than
existed in reality.

According to elderly locals interviewed in 1996, most camp residents during the Depression were midwestern farmers fleeing winter, living along the
water and eating from tin cans. The woman who mailed this card to wintry
Bridgeton, New Jersey, in January 1938 described the camp as "just the place
for me" and was certain her correspondent "would feel better" if she were to "get
a trailer and be down here with these folks." The historian Warren Belasco has
shown that "poor people began to turn to semi-permanent gypsying" during
the Depression, "not for romance, but as a way to deal with serious economic
and social problems." This card offers evidence of a popular vacation practice
and living arrangement but also reminds us that linen postcards often relegated
harsh aspects of everyday life out of sight and out of mind.[36]

THE OAKS TOURIST COURT — 1650 STEWART AVE., S. W. — ATLANTA, GA.
For Tourists Only

6A-H2537

"THE OAKS TOURIST COURT—1650 STEWART AVE., S.W.—ATLANTA, GA. / FOR TOURISTS ONLY"

TEICH 6A-H2537, 1936

Teich classified postcards commissioned by businesses not as "scenics" but in a separate category of "advertising" cards. Travelers staying at the Oaks Tourist Court in Atlanta picked up free cards in the small office building, and the management used them to confirm reservations, to thank travelers for their patronage, and for routine business correspondence. Apparently the first tourist court on the city's south side, situated on two combined U.S. routes, the Oaks was built in 1934 at the beginning of a travel boom during which the number of tourist courts in the United States increased from 9,800 in 1935 to 13,500 in 1939. As motorists shifted from adventurous pioneering to a practical desire to get from one place to another quickly and efficiently, according to Belasco, they sought "accommodations that were economical yet comfortable, simple yet convenient, and intimate yet selective."[37] Individual cabins or cottages offered a miniature home away from home and the assistance of a neighborly owner/manager living on or near the site. According to an awkwardly worded blurb, the Oaks offered such amenities as "fireproof, steam heat, private bath, innerspring mattresses."

More care went into the construction of this image than was the case with those of many tourist courts on linen cards. Bright red brick, deep blue roofs, dramatic shadows, sylvan surroundings, and variegated pavement together yield a picture of an attractive place where one might have enjoyed staying for a night. The Art Deco chevron motif heightens the effect by focusing attention on a panoramic letterbox and substituting bright colors for the uniformly gray pavement usually portrayed in front of such establishments. The art department was ordered to "show trees in rear" and "leave out building in rear," referring to a large ranch-style house, the home of the owners, which appeared in other linen cards of the Oaks from the 1940s and '50s and would have appeared here in the upper left. The slogan "For Tourists Only" promised a respectable clientele, but by the 1980s the area along Stewart Avenue containing the Oaks and other motels of similar vintage had declined into a vice district.[38]

ELECTRICAL AND MUSICAL FOUNTAIN

NELSON DREAM VILLAGE — U.S. HIGHWAY No. 66 AND No. 5 — LEBANON, MO.   6A-H769

"ELECTRICAL AND MUSICAL FOUNTAIN /
NELSON DREAM VILLAGE—U.S. HIGHWAY NO. 66
AND NO. 5—LEBANON, MO."

TEICH 6A-H769, 1936

FOR MANY SMALL BUSINESS OWNERS, SEEING THEIR ESTABLISH-
ments on colorful postcards printed in Chicago must have occasioned pride. Arthur Nelson thought so highly of the tourist oasis he was creating where the new
U.S. Route 66 ran through the family apple orchards outside Lebanon, Missouri, that he ordered four views in 1934 and another six in 1936. Nelson had
opened a gas station at the site in 1926, followed by eight small white tourist
cabins and in 1931 a hotel, the Nelson Tavern, whose urbane interior belied the
name. In 1934 he commissioned postcards with views of his well-landscaped
establishment and his family's two-story stone house. By that point he was already building the Nelson Dream Village across the highway from the hotel and
gas station. Twelve small high-pitched cottages, faced with flat, irregular slabs
of sandstone in a popular regional style, were arranged in a V whose open end
faced the north side of 66. A large fountain anchored the center of the development, and a long narrow building at the back provided garages for guests' cars.

The postcards Nelson ordered in 1936 included this one and five others,
portraying front and rear views down one arm of the V, two individual "guest
houses," and a central view of the fountain. The art department closely followed
source photos and did an excellent job of lightening and detailing front porch-
es obscured in shadow in the originals. The only marked difference between
source photos and finished cards occurs in this image, where five or six thin
jets of water at the photo's left edge become a generous spray shooting up and
arcing outward. Although one might today regard the Dream Village's rustic
stonework as evocative of Ozark hillbillies, still a common theme for local tourist traps, Nelson aspired to the rural domesticity of the English countryside,
with the scalloped deckle edges of the cards contributing a touch of class. "Few
are the good places in this area," Duncan Hines announced in his guide for "dis-
criminating" travelers in 1941, "and this happens to be one of them."[39]

BUCKLEY'S
Texaco Service
301 F. N. W.   CHILDRESS, TEXAS

If You Can't Stop — Wave.

"BUCKLEY'S TEXACO SERVICE / 301 F. N. W. / CHILDRESS, TEXAS"

NATIONWIDE POST CARD CO. F18268, N.D.

ONE MIGHT EXPECT THAT LINEN POSTCARDS ADVERTISING SER-
vice stations were as common as those for tourist courts and restaurants. In fact
they were rare. A gas station was not a destination but a momentary stop along
the way—except when travelers were waiting for repairs, an event not likely
to be commemorated by a souvenir postcard. Most service station proprietors
did not bother with postcards of their establishments. This exception, Buckley's
Texaco station, was located on a U.S. highway running through Childress, in the
southeast corner of the Texas Panhandle. The card, with its caption "If You Can't
Stop – Wave," seems intended more for locals than passing travelers.

Nationwide Post Card Company, located outside Dallas, specialized in cards
for small-town businesses across the Midwest. Although carried out with a visual style indebted to Teich's art department, as in the delicately variegated greens
of these trees and shrubs, most Nationwide cards featured expanses of dull,
uniformly colored pavement and unimaginative skies. The company continued
producing linen cards well into the 1950s, after many companies had shifted to
shiny chromes, almost as if intentionally portraying places trapped in the past.
The styling of the cars suggests the late 1940s or even early 1950s. Beyond that,
the card emphasizes Childress's lush vegetation and the modernity of Buckley's
Texaco, with its white porcelain-covered, steel-panel walls, accented with horizontal pinstriped streamlines, and its prominent "Rest Room" sign heralding
an oasis of reassuring order amid the highway's uncertainty. The industrial designer Walter Dorwin Teague consciously intended such impressions when in
the mid-1930s his office produced prototype Texaco station layouts that were
adopted for use throughout the United States.

This building still exists in Childress but can barely be matched to the image. The front and side doors and the outlines of walled-in service bays are still
inscribed on a dilapidated structure with no gas pumps, a faux mansard roof,
and signs suggesting its final use as a convenience store, closed and abandoned.
One or two trees straggle behind the building, and a glance from the intersection reveals dusty, windswept desolation in all directions—prompting a question of whether the building's wider surroundings ever looked as lush as in this
image.[40]

Qualla Park Shop, Cherokee, N. C.

"QUALLA PARK SHOP, CHEROKEE, N.C."

[TICHNOR] 76007, N.D.

THE EXPANSION OF HIGHWAY NETWORKS AND INCREASE IN vacation mileage driven by ordinary Americans stimulated the construction of roadside attractions. But long-distance motorists often had little incentive to stop. As early as 1930 an auto-camp proprietor reported that the "main topic" of messages on postcards left by guests for him to mail was "how many miles were covered for the day and how many they expect to make the next day."[41] Greater ease of travel on better-paved roads tempted motorists to drive greater distances in a fixed amount of time. Tourist traps had to be bright, even garish, to attract motorists with long distances to drive.

The Qualla Park Shop in Cherokee, North Carolina, next to the Cherokee Nation's reservation and just outside Great Smoky Mountains National Park (established in 1934), was typical of such places. This card, noteworthy for a clearly reproduced Coca-Cola sign, is oddly effective for a relatively colorless image. The scrubby hillside nearly fills the backdrop normally taken by sky effects. The roadway takes up minimal space in the image, and the building itself, with its strangely opaque, perhaps screened, upper windows, inspires little interest. Instead, the eye is drawn to an array of tiny, indistinct forms beneath the first-floor overhang—representing tables, rugs, handmade brooms, a beach umbrella, rustic pots, and even two revolving metal postcard racks. To examine this image closely is to see few truly identifiable objects and a lack of realistic colors in a mix of unconvincing yellows and reds. But to draw back until the entire image is encompassed in one's line of sight is to be reminded of the uncanny ability of linen postcard colorists (this time at Tichnor in Boston) to create a miniaturized simulacrum of reality.

San Antonio, Texas, Where the Sunshine Spends the Winter

East Room of the Famous Buckhorn Curio Store. Originally Buckhorn Bar—Established 1881

5A-H589

"SAN ANTONIO, TEXAS, WHERE THE SUNSHINE SPENDS THE WINTER / EAST ROOM OF THE FAMOUS BUCKHORN CURIO STORE. ORIGINALLY BUCKHORN BAR—ESTABLISHED 1881"

TEICH 5A-H589, 1935

A PENCHANT FOR COMBINING EDUCATIONAL UPLIFT AND COM-
mercial entertainment extends back to the natural history museum Charles
Willson Peale established in Philadelphia in 1786 and forward to the tourist attractions of the interwar years. This postcard reveals that intention at the Buckhorn Curio Store in San Antonio. The clutter on the walls is repeated in the back
caption, with 177 words filling two-thirds of the space normally left blank for a
message. Albert Friedrich, son of an artisan who made horn furniture, opened
the Buckhorn as a saloon sometime in the 1880s and displayed a growing collection of horns, antlers, preserved animal freaks, and other natural curiosities.
In 1922, in response to Prohibition, he reestablished the Buckhorn in a different
location as a museum and souvenir store.[42]

Like most business interiors on postcards, this one is without clerks or
customers, an inner landscape with flowing cabinet surfaces and empty aisles
in sharp contrast to walls bristling with animal heads and horns. According
to the caption, the Buckhorn was "more of a Museum than a store," comprising "a Natural History exhibit without equal," including the head and rack of a
seventy-eight-point buck, a stuffed gorilla, a full Texas longhorn with eight-foot
horns, and pictorial designs and verbal mottoes "formed of the rattles of thousands of Diamond-Back Rattle Snakes." The latter, created by Friedrich's wife,
are vaguely represented in the narrow panels below the animal heads along the
left wall. More obvious are the "Mexican hand-made pottery, drawn-work and
Serape" visible on the counter, "typical curios and souvenirs of the South-West
and Mexico." As with the Qualla postcard, the artist suggested a more colorful
scene than in fact was being portrayed. The card's most telling feature is its
paradoxical emptiness. Heads, antlers, horns, ceiling fans, pottery, serapes, and
an armadillo project into a void. The room's physicality is barely suggested by
a sparse floor pattern and parallel lines on the ceiling. The architecture is schematic, suggesting a superabundance of stuff existing in a timeless void.

RJ   FAMOUS GREEN BENCHES, ST. PETERSBURG, FLORIDA

"FAMOUS GREEN BENCHES, ST. PETERSBURG, FLORIDA"

[METROCRAFT], N.D.

MANY POSTCARDS SENT FROM FLORIDA AND SOUTHERN CALI-
fornia were purchased by retirees fleeing the cold winters of the Northeast and
upper Midwest. St. Petersburg, located midway up Florida's western coast,
proved a particular draw. The population of this self-declared "sunshine city,"
augmented by retired people who had permanently relocated, increased from
about 14,000 in 1920 to 40,000 in 1930 and 61,000 in 1940. Among the city's
unique features were rows of green wooden benches so "famous" they were featured on dozens of postcards published by several companies. Fifty benches in
front of a real estate office around 1910 had gradually multiplied throughout
the business district until they could accommodate fifty thousand people at one
time.

Although most cards of St. Petersburg's downtown include a few younger
people sitting among the retirees, this image reveals a phalanx of older folks,
women in Sunday dresses and men in suits and panama hats. The card's publisher, which I believe to be Metrocraft because their typical fonts appear on
the back though the card is identified only by the name of Rutland's department store, seems to have lacked Teich's emphasis on disguising faces in crowd
scenes. This card is noteworthy for the improbably varied array of rich, bright
colors in the clothes and cars, next to which the sallow complexions of the sit-
ters introduce a sour note. Most striking is the image's sheer crowdedness. St.
Petersburg appears as a single vast parking lot for cars and people, stretching to
the horizon.

Any thoughts of beach recreation recede as this concourse of seated retirees
paradoxically suggests the perpetually moving crowds of the modern metropolis, with their differing intentions and unpredictable effects. According to Florida's WPA guide, the benches served not only to spark discussions of weather
and health problems but also as "the open-air offices of the promoter, the hunting grounds of the real-estate 'bird dog,' a haven for the lonely, and a matrimo-
nial bureau for many," leading to their prominent place "in fiction, swindles, and
divorce courts."[43]

Nightly Scene at the Shuffleboard Courts in Mirror Lake Park, St. Petersburg, Florida. "The Sunshine City"

"Nightly Scene at the Shuffleboard Courts in Mirror Lake Park, / St. Petersburg, Florida, 'The Sunshine City'"

Tichnor 67242, n.d.

The Florida WPA guide remarked on the "illusion" in St. Petersburg "that life gets off to a good start at 75, not 40." Referring to the famous green benches lining the city's sidewalks, the guide contended that "for the most part sitting is but an interlude" in a life of "energetic participation in outdoor recreation." At first glance this card illustrating the St. Petersburg Shuffleboard Club seems dark and devoid of eye-catching forms. Nearly half the image is taken up by a wide perspective view across empty dull-brown courts, and the upper edge portrays a deep blue-black night sky. The more carefully one looks, however, the more one finds a scene of hurricane-like intensity. Branches of trees seem shaken by a torrent of wind, all the more apparent when illuminated in the truncated cones of the electric lights. Figures of the shuffleboard players, stylized through outline emphasis by the retouching artist, are frozen in various positions as if by strobe light. Several, such as the woman in pink on the left side, are caught in the act of shoving a "biscuit," or puck, down the court with a long-handled "tang." Even the man at the far left, who somehow, through the retoucher's art, really does appear elderly, is extending his tang, readying himself for a shot. Despite the wide, empty expanse of the courts, the image seethes with energy as the wind-blown trees frame what viewers can imagine are brief, controlled bursts of energy pulsing piston-like across the courts. If one knows, as a daytime Teich view from 1939 reveals, that the club consisted of three such ranks of courts arrayed in long parallel lines, then the sense of intense energy, in a game often thought of as a nonphysical pastime for the elderly, becomes even more compelling. As a correspondent wrote on this card to someone in South Weymouth, Massachusetts, in February 1944, the club boasted 5,275 members ("200 more than it was last week"), and its 105 courts were "occupied all through the day and at night." The image possesses an almost nightmarish quality.[44]

Hall of Waters' Dispensary, Excelsior Springs, Mo., Missouri's National Health and Pleasure Resort

8A-H1273

"Hall of Waters' Dispensary, Excelsior Springs, Mo., Missouri's National Health and Pleasure Resort"

Teich 8A-H1273, 1938

NOT ALL RESORT TRAVEL WAS FOR VACATION OR ENTERTAIN-
ment. The search for health drove the ill and the hypochondriac of the middle
and upper classes to such traditional spas as Saratoga Springs, New York; Hot
Springs, Arkansas; and Excelsior Springs, Missouri—all of which were represented by linen postcards. Although hydrotherapy came under the suspect
rubric of alternative medicine as the American Medical Association sought to
rationalize the profession, water cure was still big business in the 1930s, with
major sites combining the functions of both medical center and vacation resort
(as this postcard's caption proclaims). The mineral springs in and around the
town of Excelsior Springs, northeast of Kansas City, had been attracting the ail-
ing since their discovery around 1880. Twenty local springs produced water of
varying mineral content used for drinking, bathing, bodily irrigation, and bottling. The city government, which had taken over the springs, obtained federal
funding for the Hall of Waters, completed in 1937, a large building in the WPA
style that encompassed swimming pool, treatment rooms, a bottling plant, and,
projecting to one side, the one-story Hall of Springs, represented in this postcard, with water from several different springs piped in for drinking.

This image's muted tones seem appropriate to a place of recuperation.
While the card suggests an airy interior with abundant greenery visible through
windows and doors, recent color photographs indicate greater transparency
between inside and out.[45] The postcard, on the other hand, suggests a filtered
sunlight reacting with rich browns and dull, mottled blue-green tiles to create
a calm mood of peace and reflection. Although one can almost make out facial
features of the two men seated to the lower right, they are shaded and protected
by their hats, just as the hall itself shades and protects its visitors. A careful
retouching artist might have removed a lone foot projecting from an otherwise
obscured figure on the right, but its disembodied presence lends photographic
realism.

870 Black Rock Beach, Great Salt Lake, Utah

Scenic People

8A-H2750

W-14—Orton Plantation near Wilmington, N. C.

OB-H37

"ORTON PLANTATION NEAR WILMINGTON, N.C."

TEICH OB-H37, 1940

FOR MANY AMERICANS THE OLD SOUTH EVOKED NOSTALGIA
for a traditional way of life that seemed attractive in the face of intense economic,
social, and cultural changes fueled by ongoing modernization and urbanization.
Postcard views of the South tended to present the region as a fortunate place
where time stood still while the rest of the nation experienced the machine age.
Orton Plantation was a definite place but could easily have exemplified the lost
plantation Tara as fantasized in Margaret Mitchell's *Gone with the Wind* (1936),
a million-seller novel promoting nostalgia for the South. The house at Orton
was built in 1735 by the wealthy son of a colonial governor and was expanded
with two side wings in 1910. Extensive gardens developed during the 1920s and
'30s were opened to the public as a tourist attraction.[46] The caption describes
"beautiful trees, festooned with Spanish Moss," and "exquisite gardens, artistically planned," with "Azaleas, Camellias, Rhododendrons and other beautiful
shrubbery." The house gleams with whitewashed purity beneath the canopy of
a huge old live oak, with sun-drenched oaks behind and lush bushes in front. A
woman and her daughter, dressed in period costume, stand in front of the Greek
Revival mansion. The mother looks toward an older woman stooping beneath
a parasol to examine some blossoms. The vibrant colors of this sun-drenched
but cool and shady scene suggest opulence derived from the South's nurturing
climate and from the presumed natural grace of its traditional aristocracy.

A purchaser or recipient of this card could have taken vicarious comfort from
Orton's rich associations without ever being reminded that its historical wealth
as a rice-growing plantation was based on slavery. However, Teich's mostly immigrant artists and printers did portray a racially oriented South. *American
Business* reported in 1938 that, "as might be expected, southern pickaninny and
cotton picking scenes are popular."[47] By definition such representations of African Americans do not obviously qualify as landscapes but instead often fall
into the art history category of genre pictures. Even so, as with most linen cards
portraying members of economically and socially marginalized minorities, the
individuals represented in such images were naturalized and objectified as part
of the scenery.

"A Busy Day in the Cotton Field"

Teich 6A-H1932, 1936

OVER THE YEARS TEICH PUBLISHED MULTIPLE SERIES OF POST-
cards portraying black life in the South. Most views suggested African Americans were happy and contented as agricultural laborers, but an occasional card
emphasized conditions of poverty. This image of a family at work appeared in
a series of ten cards called "Cotton Picking Scenes" from 1936. Earlier that year
the company had produced series titled "Happy South Scenes" and "Southern
Pickaninny Scenes." Although the number of different African American views
is trivial compared with the total number of linen views, they were reprinted
frequently. Indeed, this card is a reprint, probably from about 1940, without
the original linen card's white border. Most such images were based on earlier
photographic artwork for pre-linen cards going back as far as the first decade of
the century. Southern blacks were thus portrayed as frozen in a social structure
of white supremacy unchanged since the antebellum period.

Briefly glancing at this view from a considerable distance, one can almost
imagine a happy family frolicking among wildflowers. Billowing trees rendered
as in a picturesque watercolor lead to a gray haze creating an irregular horizon
with a delicate, postcard-perfect sky. The setting suggests a pastoral scene, but
these figures are black workers, not white middle-class day-trippers. Even so,
they appear to be enjoying a relaxing afternoon, not engaging in backbreaking
labor. Only one person, presumably the father of the children in the scene, appears to work, bent over and pulling cotton bolls into a nearly invisible sack. Two
children look down as if in contemplation. Another adult, perhaps the mother,
stands behind, regarding her progeny without a care. This image implies that
black sharecroppers shared strong family ties among themselves and with white
planters who apparently offered them a satisfyingly pre-industrial livelihood.
Although the image, by invoking family ties, invites a viewer to see fellow human beings whose concerns are universal, it also places its African American
subjects within the landscape as just another regional feature. They are as much
objects of a possessive gaze as any mountain, lake, or cityscape.

MY OLD LOG CABIN

S-434

6A-H445

"MY OLD LOG CABIN"

TEICH 6A-H445, 1936

LINEN IMAGES FEATURING INDIVIDUALS WERE RARE UNLESS
the figures belonged to racial or ethnic minorities. Most such cards presented
their subjects as exotics inseparable from the landscapes they inhabited and
placed them in poses reminiscent of early nineteenth-century genre paintings.
Teich's series "Happy South Scenes" belonged to the genre tradition—though
scholars of popular representation of African Americans also regard such images as evidence of a pseudo-ethnographic approach common in the late nineteenth century.[48] Postcards in the series portrayed family life around sharecroppers' cabins. This card, "My Old Log Cabin," would have evoked memories of
theatrical versions of Harriet Beecher Stowe's *Uncle Tom's Cabin*. That connection was reinforced by another card in the series, a portrait of an old man directly identified as "Uncle Tom."[49] Stowe's character was in the prime of life, but
it was common in popular adaptations to portray him as elderly to make him
clearly unthreatening to whites. In "My Old Log Cabin" a fragile Uncle Tom
chops wood in a yard littered with debris. The woman in the doorway is understood to be his wife. The image was meant to suggest a scene common anywhere
in the South.

Such postcards followed a tradition of stereotypical views of black life presented in *Harper's Weekly* engravings in the 1870s, Currier & Ives lithographs
in the 1880s, and stereograph cards in the 1890s.[50] This image originated with
the British firm Raphael Tuck & Sons at the turn of the century. The Tuck series
"Old Folks at Home," printed in Germany and sold in the United States, included six photorealistic color lithographic postcards, five of which were based
on photos of the same elderly couple posing around this dilapidated cabin. By
1911 Teich had appropriated Tuck's wood-chopping image, originally known
as "Four Score Years and Ten," had renamed it "My Old Log Cabin," and had
printed it as a detailed but less photorealistic pre-linen card. Teich reprinted the
image several times in various pre-linen formats, and this linen version from
1936 was further reduced in detail. When Asheville Post Card used the image
for a linen card in the 1940s, the yard became solid green, the axe blade was a
neutral white, the background figures became daubs of color, and the old man's
beard looked like cotton. At each remove from the original photo, with new
cards based on old cards, the image became less a portrayal of posed individuals
and more a stylized expression of popular myth.[51]

SOLID COMFORT   S-433

"SOLID COMFORT"

TEICH 6A-H444, 1936

ALTHOUGH POSTCARDS LIKE "SOLID COMFORT" ARE NOW CON-sidered racist, some white purchasers must have believed the "Happy South Scenes" cards treated subjects with respect. This portrait of a woman smoking a clay pipe offers a companion piece to "Uncle Tom." The source photo is lost, but Teich printed a version of the image in 1910 for Hugh C. Leighton, part of the huge order establishing Teich & Co. as a major producer. A year later the same card appeared under the Teich imprint.[52] The woman in this 1936 version belies the claim for a "Happy South." She is solid and compact, cradling hands that have known hard work. Her homely face seems contemplative, not mind-lessly "happy." However, colorful cottons suggest an aesthetic flair some viewers would have considered a racial characteristic of African Americans.

The Leighton version was printed mostly in black halftone with realistic facial features. The woman's dress was in daubs of orange-red Ben Day dots. When the art department prepared this linen image in 1936, they had no source photo and so retouched a photo of the earlier card. The rendering of the wom-an's chin as gouty came from a misinterpretation of dark shadows in the origi-nal. Her dress became more colorful and was split into separate blouse and skirt. Folds of fabric became rounder, more organic. The steps, dark and dingy in the original, acquired wood graining. With the strong colors of the woman's garments contrasted against the lines of the steps, the image seems almost a compositional study.

However, the title ironically invites comparison of the woman's brief rest with everything the middle class expected of "solid comfort." Not all linen por-traits of black women granted even this limited degree of respect. The "Happy South" series also featured a woman sitting on a porch, combing fingers through a child's hair. The card was cruelly titled "Aunt Venus Hunting"—a title derived from the image's photographic appearance around 1880 on a stereograph card entitled "An Hour's Search; Or, Aunt Venus Hunting for Florida Fleas." Detroit Photographic put the same image on a postcard in 1901, and Teich was using it by 1912. On one copy of this 1936 linen card, a correspondent inscribed a line in the lower border claiming she "saw this in real life as we drove along—be-lieve it or not."[53] Such unchanging images, derived from fifty-year-old source photos that were staged in the first place, reinforced a notion of the South as a picturesque region with lifestyles and race relations untouched by modernity's forward rush.

THE BLACKVILLE SERENADE

S-425

6A-H455

"THE BLACKVILLE SERENADE"

Teich 6A-H455, 1936

GIVEN THE PATERNALISTIC DEFENSE OF RACE INEQUALITY, IT IS not surprising that popular imagery represented black children as lazy, immature pleasure seekers. Teich's "Southern Pickaninny Scenes," produced simultaneously with "Happy South Scenes," includes "Dinnertime," with six grinning boys devouring huge watermelon slices. Another, based on a 1901 photo, shows three boys eyeing a fourth, who hoards half a melon. To their plaintive question "Give Us De Rine?," he responds, "Ain't Goin' Be No Rine." The series featured adolescent boys too old for constant parental supervision and too young to threaten middle-class whites. Even so, activities like gambling and gluttony suggested they would soon become immature adults. In "Seben Come Eleben" nine energetic young men swagger, sprawl, and gesture in an artfully posed tableau of a game of dice. The eight rambunctious young men in "A 'Lasses Party" imitate their elders in colorful hats and suspenders while guzzling molasses from an upturned barrel.[54]

Strangest of all is this view of six musicians playing homemade guitars and a fiddle while two other young men sing. In a surreal touch, an alligator stands among them with conductor's baton and sheet music, apparently singing. Alligators often appeared in African American–themed comic cards, as in the common example of an alligator treeing a fat-lipped, bug-eyed man. Teich also pandered to racist sentiment with the scurrilous "Chocolate Drop Comics" series—each card presenting a caricature of a pudgy black child, head turned in profile, viewed from behind with bare bottom rendered as an upside-down heart-shaped form posed on a chamber pot, outhouse seat, or fence post, and accompanied by a supposed dialect rhyme.[55] The humor in "The Blackville Serenade" is subtler. The alligator, printed in dull gray, recedes from view behind the saturated colors of the young men's clothes, and an observer would have done an incredulous double take after finally noticing the alligator. The title was borrowed from a *Harper's Weekly* engraving from 1883, "A Blackville Serenade," one in a series by illustrator Sol Eytinge that lampooned urban blacks for imitating upper-class white society. Even liberal whites regarded Eytinge's caricatures as sympathetic despite fat lips, silly grins, and sprawling figures.[56] Teich's use of the title suggests the continuity of "Southern Pickaninny Scenes" with a long tradition of racist comic representation. However, even with daubs of red on their lips, the young men retain a photorealism that humanizes them in a way not possible with racial stereotypes produced by freehand illustrators.

LA-19   TYPICAL OF EARLY LOS ANGELES—OLVERA STREET, LOS ANGELES, CALIFORNIA

6A-H2613

"TYPICAL OF EARLY LOS ANGELES—OLVERA STREET, LOS ANGELES, CALIFORNIA"

TEICH 6A-H2613, 1936

MEXICAN AMERICANS APPEARED IN POSTCARDS MOSTLY AS objects of the tourist gaze. Their concentration in the Southwest rendered them as exotics to many Anglo-Americans. In the late 1920s a preservationist had turned an alley in Los Angeles into a Mexican-themed outdoor market to save the city's oldest surviving adobe house. The new pedestrian way, paved in brick and tile, was renamed El Paseo de Los Angeles, but the public called it Olvera Street. The caption on this card romanticizes the scene and objectifies its subjects by describing the street as "typical of Old Mexico—an interesting quarter of colorful Bazaars, where vendors display their quaint pottery, candle and basket novelties."

Although colorizing could enhance a source photo, in this case its advantages were lost. The original black-and-white photo by Padilla Studios employs sharp contrasts to animate individual details—human figures, facial features, dress, clay pots, balcony railings, canvas sunscreens, even leaves on the tree. When colorized, these details merge into a muddy mélange. Even so, a burst of color serves as backdrop to the figures of two señoritas whose energy reverses the usual diagonal sightline, which here projects outward toward the lower left. One woman adjusts her hat while sauntering forward in a white dress with a tiered skirt whose blue accents simulate subtle contrasting motions. The other strums a guitar, adding sound to a festive environment. A heavy older woman with long black hair represents a stereotypical señora.[57] Four other figures emerge from the background. Two men wearing sombreros are coded as Mexican. One is behind the young women, his tie suggesting a mariachi musician. The other is a vendor gesturing toward a pot. His female customer is one of two obvious Anglo-Americans. The other, her tall male companion, looks past and beyond the apparently insignificant commercial transaction. In the shift from source photo to postcard, the Anglos became more conservative and commanding. The woman's sleeveless summer dress became a darker dress worn over a high-necked shell. Her companion's walking cane was deleted to make him appear more vigorous. Replacing a straw hat with felt made him appear businesslike. Although these Anglos may be enjoying a moment of festive leisure, they are individuals of substance. The Mexicans, on the other hand, whether charming or deferential, perform entertainment and service roles defined by a society that regards them as picturesque.

C-4   *Agua Prieta, Sonora, Mexico, Across the Border from Douglas, Arizona*

4B-H55

"AGUA PRIETA, SONORA, MEXICO, ACROSS THE
BORDER FROM DOUGLAS, ARIZONA"

TEICH 4B-H55, 1944

FEW LINEN POSTCARDS PORTRAY AN URBAN LANDSCAPE AS bleak as the one in this image of a Mexican border town that owed its existence to the construction of a copper smelter on the U.S. side in 1902. Although isolated in the desert, the town comprised a gritty industrial scene. For the most part the image is realistic. The view is low to the ground, raking across weeds and hard-packed dirt to a ragged line of rocks edging the roadway. Beyond the checkpoint on the right is the Mexican customs house, a substantial brick structure crowned with a clock tower and surrounded by vegetation—an oasis in a washed-out scene. Agua Prieta's main street extends in the far distance, a jumble of buildings and parked cars barely suggested by the image's halftone dots. On the left is a cafe advertising Coca-Cola. If not for the image's single departure from verisimilitude, a sketched-in pair of buildings surmounted by a Mexican flag, a viewer could have assumed the entire business district echoed the cafe's exterior of dirty whitewash. The card is almost unique among linen urban views in one respect. Unlike hundreds of images for which Teich sales agents specified deletion of utility poles, this view emphasizes ramshackle poles leaning this way and that. One stands at the very center of the image, rising from waste ground across from the checkpoint.[58]

In contrast to the festively garbed señoritas and entertainers featured in most images of Mexicans (and Mexican Americans), this view presents a woman and her daughter, rendered as brown-skinned, walking from the U.S. side toward the Mexican town. Their ordinary dresses suggest everyday reality. The fact that they are shown in mid-stride indicates definite purpose as opposed to the lazy "mañana" attitude attributed by some Anglos to those south of the border. Although the Mexican government buildings and their landscaping project a civilizing presence, desolation reigns elsewhere. It seems the point was to demonstrate Mexico's utter poverty by means of dirt, weeds, rocks, and crooked utility poles. And yet central to the composition, viewed from a respectful distance, are the purposeful figures of mother and daughter—quite ordinary and yet extraordinary in the face of common stereotypes.

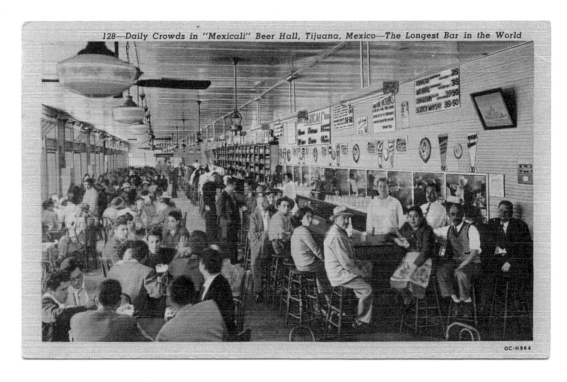

128—Daily Crowds in "Mexicali" Beer Hall, Tijuana, Mexico—The Longest Bar in the World

"DAILY CROWDS IN 'MEXICALI' BEER HALL, TIJUANA, MEXICO—THE LONGEST BAR IN THE WORLD"

TEICH OC-H964, 1950

G. I. PITCHFORD, *INTERIOR, LA BALLENA, TIJUANA, MEXICO*, CA. 1950

ANGLO-AMERICANS' STEREOTYPES OF MEXICO ENCOMPASSED more than pretty señoritas and peasants dozing under sombreros. Tijuana, across the border from San Diego, became famous for forbidden pleasures after successful crusades against alcohol, gambling, and prostitution in the United States. Postcard publishers offered views of the many saloons along Tijuana's Avenida Revolución, most notably La Ballena, with its 215-foot bar (sometimes known as "the Mexicali" by the brand of beer it sold or more frequently and simply as "the Long Bar"). Three different cards from the 1920s portrayed "the longest bar in the world" with a few male drinkers leaning on the bar and a narrow room with no tables extending to the vanishing point. In 1928 Teich integrated women into the scene with elegant Anglo ladies in furs standing among Anglo suits—an image revised as a linen card in 1935.[59]

This view of La Ballena from 1950, regarded by western representative Pitchford as an "IMPORTANT SUBJECT," is unusual because it offers realistic close-ups of people who look directly at the observer. Unlike many linen images, whose large expanses of uniform color lack realism, every bit of this image is filled with realistic detail. The job file's retouched photo suggests little was changed from the original photo. Eyes, eyebrows, hats, and cuffs were exaggerated for legibility, and lettering was made more readable. Recognizable individuals remain undisguised. Although ethnicity is uncertain, there seems to be a Latino manager in a tie, an Anglo barman, several Latinos sitting around the curve of the bar, and several Anglo patrons beyond them. People at the tables appear to be of varying ethnicity, with a table of Latinos at the lower left. La Ballena seems to have offered a welcoming environment where Mexicans mix with Anglos.

However, this apparently photorealistic card presents an illusory image. Pitchford's personal archive reveals he took several photos at different times from the same position. The postcard is based on a collage of two different photos—a fact that the retouched photo in the job file is too smoothed over to disclose. The line between the joined images runs up the aisle dividing the tables from the bar. To the right, the postcard is based in every detail—even facial expressions and folds of cloth—on a photo from Pitchford's archive (see photo at lower left). But to the left of the line, that archival photo shows not the people who appear in the postcard but a different group. In the photo, the front table is occupied not by men with their backs to the viewer but by two couples directly facing the camera. All four individuals are people of color. One couple is of uncertain ethnicity, but the other, a smiling woman and a pensive man, are dark-hued African Americans. Several blacks sit at tables immediately behind them in company with Latinos and Anglos. Tijuana may have been a wide-open town, but for U.S. consumption it was portrayed through Pitchford's collage as racially segregated. While Mexicans may have seemed picturesque in their home territory, blacks belonged only in southern genre scenes and elsewhere were subject to erasure.[60]

GRANT AVENUE, CHINATOWN, SAN FRANCISCO, CALIF.   63

"Grant Avenue, Chinatown, San Francisco, Calif."

Teich 7B-H1120, 1947

UNLIKE OTHER MINORITY GROUPS REGARDED AS PICTURESQUE, Chinese Americans were distinctly urban, having been forced into ghettos by discrimination. Several cities had "Chinatowns," with San Francisco's being the best known. To white Americans, the Chinese seemed distinctive for their facial features, traditional dress, and a social insularity partly chosen, partly enforced. Before the 1906 earthquake destroyed the original Chinatown, white opinion regarded it as a maze of opium dens, gambling houses, and brothels to be avoided except by slumming tourists. That stereotype flavored white perceptions of Chinatown even as rebuilding yielded a welcoming themed environment carefully planned by Chinese community leaders. The district's new main street, Grant Avenue, offered restaurants catering to non-Chinese patrons with such Americanized dishes as chop suey, featured on a vertical sign in this card from 1947.

Pride of place goes to a lamppost emulating a Chinese lantern with pagoda roof and hanging bells—one of forty-three erected by local merchants along Grant Avenue in 1925.[61] Neon signs emphasized by the retouching artist promote several restaurants, not only Hang Far Low, known to Chinese Americans for authentic cuisine since 1875, but also Lotus Bowl and Chinese Village, both oriented toward non-Chinese patrons. According to the caption, Chinatown's "gorgeous Bazaars, with their bewildering variety of colorful, exquisite and alluring Oriental merchandise," attracted visitors, but ideas of an alluring forbidden world lingered. The man on the lower right, with shirt collar flared over his jacket, expresses that underworld idea in the guise of a postwar hipster. Similar figures frame other street views. For example, a Teich night scene from 1934 shows a young man, hand in pocket, lounging next to a lamppost. And a daytime view by Longshaw portrays a woman in a green Mandarin jacket and baggy pants, leaning from a balcony and beckoning the viewer to explore Grant Avenue. There is nothing suggestive about her demeanor, but the informal pose in a pajama-like outfit would have recalled common Chinatown stereotypes.[62]

This Teich card from 1947 presents a striking new theme. Flags flying from buildings, so common in urban views as to seem invisible, here become a statement of Chinese American loyalty to the American-supported government of Nationalist China (soon to be defeated by the Communists). More subtly, painted crosswalks and the single word "SLOW" indicate that Chinatown's inhabitants, whatever the case in the past, have become law-abiding Americans.

CHINESE CHILDREN, CHINATOWN, SAN FRANCISCO, CALIF.

60

8A-H2820

"CHINESE CHILDREN, CHINATOWN,
SAN FRANCISCO, CALIF."

TEICH 8A-H2820, 1938

ALTHOUGH CHINATOWN STREET VIEWS PRESENTED A MODERN
scene of automobiles, neon, and western dress, images of individuals emphasized quaint dress and lifestyle. As early as 1932 a postcard caption correctly
proclaimed the "silk and embroidered costumes" of seven children to be worn
mostly for "celebrations."[63] However, this similar card from 1938 presents colorful quaintness as an everyday matter. The caption claims Chinatown's "narrow
streets continually echo to the shrill cries of native children, many of whom
are gaily costumed." These children, awkwardly posed, stand with light flooding their unnatural faces. Despite photorealistic features from black halftone,
a yellow-green wash distorts their skin, distinguishing them from the pinkish
beige of European Americans. There is no attempt to disguise their identities.
Their parents could have recognized them—or, decades later, adults might have
picked out their own distorted childhood likenesses on a souvenir stand.

Many linen images of Chinese Americans were based on pre-linen cards
dating back to 1912. Source photos cannot be easily traced, but most images are
in the style of Arnold Genthe, a German photographer who arrived in San Francisco in 1895. Even at that time, the brightly costumed children he liked to photograph were dressed for special occasions such as Chinese New Year. Genthe
himself regarded his images as nostalgic memorials to the "Old Chinatown" lost
in the destruction of 1906. However, books of his photos published in 1908 and
1913 set a long-standing tone for popular representations of Chinatown as an
alluring destination both quaint and forbidden.

A frontal view of a smiling "soothsayer" recycled by Teich in 1940 portrays
a man in long jacket and skull cap, dressed identically to and with similar features as a man shown in side view in the Genthe photograph *The Fortune Teller*,
which was published in 1908. Another linen card, from 1932, shows a man in
traditional long jacket and felt hat, reading notices plastered on a wall as he
holds the hand of a festively dressed child. The boy is turned, looking at the
viewer, in a tableau echoing a sequence of photos by Genthe. Such linen images
differed from Genthe's in only one major detail. After the Chinese Revolution
of 1911, Chinese American men had abandoned the single long braids of hair,
known as queues, that made them appear so distinctive to white Americans.
The instructions for adapting a 1910 postcard image to create a new card in
1935 asked the retouching artist to "remove Ques [*sic*] from the men in picture." Otherwise, the picturesque tourist Chinatown of postcards remained unchanged for decades.[64]

"DANCE OF THE MAGNIFICENT LION, CHINATOWN, SAN FRANCISCO, CALIF."

TEICH 8A-H2834, 1938

"PICTURESQUE COSTUMES, CHINATOWN,
SAN FRANCISCO, CALIF.," TEICH 2A-H795, 1932

TRADITIONAL CHINESE FESTIVALS DREW TOURISTS TO A PIC-
turesque, exotic scene, but dancers proved hard to capture in a static medium. A
1938 series of views included the golden dragon dance, with several men under
a decorated tailpiece sinuously following their leader in an ornamental headpiece, and the lion dance, which involved two dancers, one wearing an extravagant headpiece, the other holding a short tailpiece. With a source photo taken
from an upper window, the dragon dance was viewed so obliquely as to waste
much of the image on the street surface.[65] By contrast, the lion dance of this image immediately draws attention to the gorgeous mask with green features outlined in pulsating yellow. Shops in browns and blues and a varied street surface
contribute a liveliness lacking in the dragon dance postcard.

However, a cursory glance reveals human figures rendered as cartoons. The
source is not a photo but a sketch by E. A. Burbank, an artist known for ethno-
graphic portraits of American Indians taken from life between 1890 and 1910.
Released in 1934 after seventeen years in a mental hospital, the elderly Burbank lived in San Francisco and sold sketches to various publications—most of
them not drawn from life but based on other images.[66] This lion dance occurs
at a recognizable corner (Fat Ming stationery shop long remained at 903 Grant
Avenue). Burbank may have sketched the lion mask and background from life,
but he also borrowed bits from earlier Teich cards. The small girl leaning into
the frame derives from the previous card's image, which had appeared as a non-
linen card at least by 1928, while the freehand sketch of children in the upper
left was based on several people in a card entitled "Picturesque Costumes" (see
at lower left). The grotesque lion mask may animate the image, but these human figures are unconvincing.

In forwarding Burbank's sketch to Chicago, Pitchford addressed the racial
status of the two men on the right. Regarding the man holding the tail, he wrote
that his "face could be made to look more like a Chinaman," and he ordered
"same here" for the man on the far right. The "forehead should slant," he suggested, and instead of the Roman nose of Burbank's sketch, the figure should
have a "small nose and slant eyes." Apparently a sallow, yellow-green complex-
ion was not enough to indicate otherness in the tourist fantasy of Chinatown.

H-1933—FRED HARVEY INDIAN BUILDING AND SANTA FE STATION, ALBUQUERQUE, NEW MEXICO

"FRED HARVEY INDIAN BUILDING AND SANTA FE STATION, ALBUQUERQUE, NEW MEXICO"

TEICH 8A-H477, 1938

AMERICAN INDIANS OFTEN APPEARED IN POSTCARD VIEWS AS natural accessories of the landscape, looking out over vast distances like the banditti of the European picturesque tradition. Such images afforded opportunities to observe native peoples in their element—in the wild, so to speak. Indians portrayed on such cards appeared as nature's noblemen, strong and independent, but images representing Indians with whom tourists actually came into contact tended to present them as docile, even domesticated.[67]

The Fred Harvey Company furthered this transformation as it incorporated Native Americans into a fabricated narrative of the Southwest for tourists traveling by the Santa Fe Railroad. In 1902 the company opened the Indian Building in Albuquerque, located between the railway station and the new Alvarado Hotel. Constructed in Mission style to emphasize Spanish colonial heritage, the Indian Building was filled with weavings, beadwork, pottery, and baskets, most for sale to visitors, and artisans gave demonstrations. Before entering, tourists passed by vendors displaying wares along the sidewalk. Emily Post, later a famous etiquette columnist, wrote in 1916 that "dozens of vividly costumed Navajos and Hopis" would appear "out of nowhere . . . ten minutes before the California Limited" arrived at the station.[68]

In this image of railway passengers examining handicrafts, most of the Indian vendors are women. They figuratively kneel before white patrons, and their backs are turned toward the viewer. The tourists are well dressed. Only one man is in shirtsleeves, and he seems to wear a tie. Most women wear summer dresses, with two in suits. Near the center of the line of travelers, at the image's focal point, a woman holds a purse—the source of the largesse for which the native artisans have gathered. Along the left is the gleaming modern train that has brought the travelers to their brief scheduled encounter with carefully curated natives, and to which they will return laden with souvenirs. Tourists must have taken snapshots of the Pueblo Indians they encountered here. Indeed the man in shirtsleeves has a camera around his neck. But no one is actually taking pictures. Indeed, few linen cards show anyone taking a photo. There was no need for photos when a visit could be recalled through brightly colored postcards—including ones with images of the museum-like rooms of the Indian Building.[69]

"How Navajo Indian Rugs Are Made"

Teich 3A-H710, 1933

"Now the Indians / Take the Pictures," Teich 9A-H1251, 1939

THIS VIEW OF A NAVAJO WOMAN WEAVING A RUG IS TYPICAL OF postcards of Native American artisans. Similar images of traditional native crafts around the globe were a staple of turn-of-the-century stereograph publishers, who intentionally addressed an educational need by portraying human diversity in exotic colonial lands. Native crafts appealed to westerners, who also sought escape from modernity in the handmade furnishings of their own culture's Arts and Crafts movement. Although most linen views offered visual representations of sites visited, some followed the earlier educational format. A long description of wool carding, thread winding, dyeing, and weaving fills half the message section of this card. Vertical warp threads are portrayed so clearly in the image that one can envision the weaver passing the horizontal woof thread between. She seems intent on her task. A viewer looks over her shoulder, at her work, without having to consider her as an individual. The background recedes from clarity into an impressionist dappling of leaves reminiscent of watercolor. Despite the informative precision of the caption, the viewer is invited into a timeless reverie. Not all the world has yielded to modernity.

Other linen views of American Indian artisans similarly portrayed them as vehicles or conduits of their work. In one portrayal of four adults weaving, working leather, and making jewelry in Harvey's Indian Building, only two small children look in the viewer's general direction. For an image of four Navajo sand painters sitting around their work, Pitchford asked the art department to retouch a boldly staring individual so as to "indicate this man's eye looking downward." Even a full-on portrait of a jewelry maker using a hand-powered thong drill on a piece of turquoise, an image based on a photo emphasizing every line in his aging face, captures his eyes as abstracted, not exactly looking down but not gazing at the viewer. Such images portrayed southwestern Indians as docile and unthreatening, a far cry from Geronimo's warlike Apaches.[70]

Although linen postcards rendered Native Americans as objects of the tourist gaze, that relationship did not go entirely unexamined. This view of a Navajo weaver was based on a photo taken by J. R. Willis, who sold hand-tinted, framed enlargements to the public. Willis was a former political cartoonist who had opened a studio in New Mexico for oil paintings and photos. In 1939 Teich published a comic card based on a sketch by Willis. Against the backdrop of a Pueblo dwelling appear an absurd tourist couple in shorts, short sleeves, and silly grins. The skinny man carries binoculars and wears a camera around his neck. The heavy woman carries a large purse. Both have comical sun hats. A buxom Indian woman sits near a stack of pots for sale. Looking over her shoulder and grinning, she addresses a child at her feet, "Run Get Mama's Camera, Quick!" Although Willis was frankly expressing a low opinion of tourists, the main caption, "Now the Indians Take the Pictures," allowed those same tourists to misunderstand the humor as absurdity rather than sarcasm.[71]

Ok 8   Navajo Indian Chief

16772

"Navajo Indian Chief"

Colourpicture 16772, n.d.

GENERIC IMAGES OF AMERICAN INDIANS WERE ALREADY COM-
mon in postcards when Teich introduced the linen variety in 1931. Before 1920,
however, especially in real photo cards, representations of Native Americans
tended toward realism. Although cards based on studio photos sometimes bore
evidence of clothing and props provided by a white photographer, most images
of everyday life portrayed native people as they actually looked or wished to be
represented. Such cards were produced locally for local residents, and they had
to portray people and situations, even Indians, in ways purchasers would recognize as real. But around 1920 the local demand for realism lost its influence
as the postcard market became national in scope. War bonnets, teepees, and
other equipment of Plains tribes became common markers of "Indian-ness" to
be used even when representing southwestern tribes—to the point that Hopis
or Navajos sometimes adopted them when performing for whites or interacting
with tourists.[72]

This portrait of an unnamed "Navajo chief" wearing the feathered war bon-
net of a Plains Indian is typical of such hybrid generic images. He grasps the
rung of a ladder leaning against a rough adobe exterior, which a viewer is meant
to understand as the wall of a pueblo—though Navajos did not live in pueblos.
To further confuse the issue, the postcard was distributed by Mid Continent
News in Oklahoma City, the capital of a state with many Indian tribes but few if
any Navajos and no adobe pueblos at all. Colourpicture may have sold the same
postcard to multiple distributors in widely separated geographical locations.
Whatever the case, this particular card was sold as a representative image in
a state for which it was entirely inappropriate. For most tourists, however, this
costumed figure corresponded with the popular conception of an Indian chief.
This was not the fierce, defiant chief of national mythology, however. Instead,
despite the fact that much of his face is in deep shadow, his features reveal he
is an older man, no longer a threat. His presence next to a pueblo wall further
marks him as a leader of a domestic people known for their crafts, not for their
prowess as warriors. Finally, the deep red light bathing the wall behind the aging chief suggests it is sunset time for American Indians—if not literally a vanishing race then a remnant existing beyond modern life's space and time.[73]

"TYPICAL INDIAN PRINCESS"

TEICH OB-H346, 1940

THERE IS NO BETTER SYNONYM FOR "GENERIC" THAN "TYPICAL," used by Teich to characterize a young Indian woman whose portrait reveals one cliché after another. There is no evidence the image was recycled from earlier cards. In such cases the job file usually lists prior cards by serial numbers and may contain examples of them. This card's job file contains only a heavily re-touched photo bearing no evidence of being collaged. The card was probably based on a single photo taken during the 1930s, carefully composed for iconic effect. There is no distributor name, but the original order came from a news agent in Eau Claire, Wisconsin, and the card was postmarked in Sault Sainte Marie, Michigan—suggesting this was a generic sold in the Great Lakes region. Tourists browsing postcard racks would have thought of Minnehaha, the lover of the title character in Henry Wadsworth Longfellow's popular poem *The Song of Hiawatha*, which romanticized Indian life along the "shining Big-Sea-Water" of Lake Superior.[74]

The young woman poses in a teepee's entrance. She wears a long, fringed buckskin dress with a beaded yoke, a matching beaded bag, and what seem to be beaded moccasins. She stands with a hand on the teepee as if in confident possession. In the other hand she holds a paddle, suggesting both her prowess and her independence. A canoe projects into the frame—indicating easy access to traditional transportation. The teepee itself, untypically painted with designs from nature, stands barely three feet from a shore composed of rock rubble. The water visible at the bottom edge situates the scene on a lake or river, though one imagines such a site as easily flooded by rising water or wind-driven waves. It seems unlikely a teepee would have opened directly onto a waterway rather than out of the wind and toward the campsite's other equipment. The shore is thick with bushy trees, but two birch trees with white bark establish the location as somewhere in the north woods. Taken together, these details create a mytho-logical portrait more appropriate for an illustrated edition of *Hiawatha* than for a postcard claiming to portray a "typical" scene in the life of an American Indian woman.

D.C.21—Fur Trading in the Everglades of Florida

© CHAS. C. EBBETS

"FUR TRADING IN THE EVERGLADES OF FLORIDA"

TEICH 9A-H995, 1939

THE SEMINOLES OF FLORIDA, WHOSE ANCESTORS RETREATED into the Everglades in 1858, may be the only Native Americans to avoid generic portrayal on postcards. They lived in small matriarchal villages on humps of land rising from swampy water, in open-sided dwellings framed with cypress logs and thatched with palmetto leaves. While the women prepared food, tended hogs, and used treadle sewing machines acquired in the 1890s to produce brightly colored patchwork clothes that made the tribe distinctive to whites, the men hunted otters, deer, and alligators from dugout canoes. Although the Miccosukee, as they called themselves, had never signed a peace treaty with the United States, they accepted tourism on their own terms early in the twentieth century.[75]

This scene emphasizes the Seminoles' patchwork garments (women's skirts and men's jackets in eye-popping colors), viewed against a neutral backdrop of green palm fronds, gray-green thatch, and a sky devoid of distracting clouds. The image is photorealistic, based largely on the black key plate. The Seminoles' faces are enriched with color, while the white fur trader is rendered in a near gray that contrasts—visually and metaphorically—with the colorful Indians. The Seminole trader's Stetson hat marks him as a leader, the white man's equal in negotiating. The source photo was taken by Charles C. Ebbets, a Miami photographer whose documentation of Seminole life in the 1920s and '30s yielded many linen postcard views.[76]

More than other Native Americans, the Seminoles were regarded as "primitive," still following the "tribal lure" of their "ancestors," in the words of a Tichnor card's caption.[77] According to Teich's caption, they relied on "fur and hide trading" as their "chief source of income." In fact, however, tourism and handicrafts already provided the Miccosukees' main connection to the larger economy. As early as 1919 a white entrepreneur organized a Seminole camp near Miami as a tourist attraction. After completion in 1928 of the Tamiani Trail, an east–west highway across the Everglades, entire villages relocated just off the road, charging admission to tourists, selling handicrafts, and accepting tips for photographs. By 1939, when this card was published, there were thirteen Indian-run attractions, a major segment of Miami tourism. And yet postcards still presented the Seminoles as primitive hunter-gatherers—part of the natural landscape of the Everglades.

"'WHERE EAST MEETS WEST' / MUNICIPAL AIRPORT, ALBUQUERQUE, N.M."

TEICH 1B-H231, 1941

Although linen views of natural landscapes often included the highways that brought travelers into contact with otherwise inaccessible scenery, views of American Indians tended to portray them as if they inhabited environments untouched by modern times. Even so, popular promotions of technological progress occasionally juxtaposed native peoples with the latest transportation machines. In Florida, for example, Seminoles from the Everglades were taken for a ride on the Goodyear blimp *Defender* in 1929, and two years later a group of Seminoles were hired to paddle dugout canoes to meet a Pan American Clipper seaplane as it landed at Miami. Contrasting the extremes of "primitive" Indians and modern technology was the point of this image as well.

Here are two Navajos gazing, apparently in awe, at a DC-3 in front of the two-year-old Albuquerque Municipal Airport. According to the back caption, the Indians are "amazed at seeing 'chi-di-nah-tah-ee' (wagon that flies) at close range." The pueblo-inspired architecture of the terminal intensifies the gleaming aluminum plane's intrusive presence in a scene described by the caption as "where east meets west." But as so often is the case, the situation was more complicated. For one thing, the people who posed for the source photo were actually wearing store-bought shoes, not the moccasins indicated on the card. The woman was wearing laced oxfords with moderately stacked heels, the sort of shoe any practical woman might have selected for everyday use. Sketches from sales agent "R.M." directed the art department to provide "regular Indian moccasins . . . quite flat on bottom with no heels." More to the point, the two models have been identified as Helen Lowley Emerson and her brother Mike Lowley, two Navajos who worked in the terminal's Fred Harvey gift shop, demonstrating the tinsmith's craft. Airplanes were thus nothing new to them, and they were unlikely to be contemplating the technological sublime, though they may have been complicit in conveying that impression to travelers and tourists.[78]

870 Black Rock Beach, Great Salt Lake, Utah

8A-H2750

"BLACK ROCK BEACH, GREAT SALT LAKE, UTAH"
TEICH 8A-H2750, 1938

M-111 HAVE A SWIM WITH US AT MIAMI BEACH, FLORIDA

PHOTO BY FRANK BELL

5A-H910

"HAVE A SWIM WITH US AT MIAMI BEACH, FLORIDA,"
TEICH 5A-H910, 1935

MEMBERS OF RACIAL AND ETHNIC MINORITIES WERE NOT THE only scenic people appearing on linen postcards. The subject of beach resorts allowed publishers to portray scantily clad young white women in socially acceptable poses. This view of fourteen so-called bathing beauties running toward the viewer at Great Salt Lake would be typical of the genre if not for their small scale in relation to the overall image. The card also offers yet another example of manipulation in the making of linen cards. Black Rock was a private resort on the lake's south shore just west of Salt Lake City. The order came to Teich from Deseret Book Company by way of Pitchford, who likely took the source photo, which shows a mostly empty beach at midday. The sales agent asked the artists to put "strong reds in sky" for a "sunset effect," but more importantly instructed them to "put in bathers . . . as per sample attached or any other group that might be adaptable." In the resulting image, enthusiastic young women enliven an otherwise dull scene. As it turns out, they are exactly the same women who had romped through the surf at Miami Beach in an earlier card, from 1935. Someone in the art department retrieved the retouched photo from the Miami Beach card's job file, rephotographed it, cut out the group of bathers, collaged them onto Pitchford's photo of Black Rock Beach, retouched everything, and then sent the image to a colorist, who decided for some reason to change the color of one bathing suit and add stripes to three others.

The resulting postcard proved popular enough that Tichnor stole the image and made a freehand copy, also a sunset view, in which two men in swim trunks replace the two fully clothed men standing by the parked cars in Teich's view. An entirely different group of six young women run in a straggly line toward the viewer in the Tichnor image, probably because Teich's image of the Miami Beach bathing beauties was copyrighted by its maker, Frank Bell, a photographer at the *Miami Daily News*. Even so, Bell's name does not appear on Teich's Black Rock card, or on several other Teich cards documenting the further adventures of these well-traveled bathers. In 1939 they appeared on a generic card in a circular frame superimposed over four smaller, rectangular frames enclosing miniature images of waves breaking, fishing, boating, and water skiing. Printed with an enlarged caption of "Greetings from" or "Scenes at," variants of this card promoted Wrightsville Beach, North Carolina; Asbury Park, New Jersey; and Hampton Beach, New Hampshire. Two years later, in 1941, the running women reappeared across the upper margin of a large-letter card bearing the legend "Greetings from Carolina Beach" in letters enclosing other miniature beach scenes. Those who guided production of images at Teich must have believed they had found an ideal expression of wholesome female beauty in this group.[79]

Physical Hardening Program Builds up New Recruits in Training, Constitution Field,

U. S. Naval Training Center, Great Lakes, Illinois

OFFICIAL U. S. NAVY PHOTOGRAPH

2B-H1025

"PHYSICAL HARDENING PROGRAM BUILDS UP
NEW RECRUITS IN TRAINING, CONSTITUTION
FIELD, / U.S. NAVAL TRAINING CENTER,
GREAT LAKES, ILLINOIS"

TEICH 2B-H1025, 1942

THE YOUNG WOMEN PHOTOGRAPHED AT MIAMI BEACH HAD PRE-
sumably signed models' releases. Most individually recognizable women who
posed in close up for other linen cards, playing tug-of-war, water skiing, or
leaning seductively against a cypress tree, had also signed off.[80] No matter how
freely postcard publishers might represent individuals from racial and ethnic
minorities, especially when taken from source photos buried in long chains of
past postcard images, they usually drew the line at individually recognizable European Americans. Exceptions were made for celebrities and, more relevantly,
for individuals in exotic garb and surroundings, such as cowboys, Appalachian
basket weavers, and Amish farmers—nonracialized to be sure but available for
scenic appropriation as members of cultural minorities. Indeed, images of visually distinct, nonmainstream white people often came from publishing histories
as tangled as those of images of African Americans or Chinese Americans.[81]

Mainstream white males, on the other hand, typically remained invisible in
linen postcards, indistinctly rendered in crowds or employed as tiny figures to
establish the scale of a landscape or urban view. Rarely do linen postcards focus
on white male bodies as directly as on attractive white female bodies. When
they do, as in this image of naval recruits doing calisthenics during World War
II, the emphasis is not on the individual but on man in the mass. Beyond the tilt
of a cap or the length of a pant leg, nothing distinguishes these sailors one from
another in their perfect group harmony. The nation can take pride in its young
manhood, brilliantly white in bright sunlight flooding the parade ground. Most
other linen images prepared for sale in post exchanges and in communities host-
ing military installations also portrayed masses of young white men in identical
uniforms, marching, drilling, falling in outside barracks, or sitting in worship.
If shown more informally, reading in a base library or lined up in a mess hall,
their crisp uniforms still rendered them as anonymous parts of a larger social
effort to which they had subordinated their individuality.[82] These young white
men are scenic people only in the abstract.

511 PRODUCERS IN THE FAMOUS SIGNAL HILL OIL DISTRICT, LONG BEACH, CALIFORNIA

Resources

5204   CHERRY PICKING SCENE, DOOR COUNTY, WISCONSIN

5A-H2681

"CHERRY PICKING SCENE, DOOR COUNTY, WISCONSIN"

TEICH 5A-H2681, 1935

WHEN THIS POSTCARD APPEARED IN 1935, IT HAD BEEN ONLY fifteen years since the U.S. Census Bureau declared a majority of Americans to be living in urban rather than rural situations. Some people in towns still depended on home canning of vegetables and fruits as a food source during the Depression. But the people portrayed here picking their own cherries on a peninsula in Lake Michigan seem to be comfortably well-off vacationers or day-trippers and not agricultural workers or town dwellers supplementing their food supply. The women are wearing fashionable hats and summer dresses in various light colors, while the men have shed their jackets but are otherwise well dressed. Despite extreme retouching of the faces, two women are clearly portrayed as smiling—happy in their momentary occupation of harvesting cherries.

The image is festively colorful with wildflowers scattered among the small plants carpeting the orchard and tiny cherry blossoms pinpointed among bunches of equally tiny cherries in the foreground tree. The vanishing point of the ragged aisle fades into a delicate but typical linen sky appropriate for a lazy summer day in a low-key resort area. This image was not new but was recycled from earlier postcards published in economically more expansive times—a Teich pre-linen from 1924 and its own source, a real photo card of the same scene that had been heavily retouched as part of Teich's earlier production process. Both cards were included in the job file for this linen card along with the command to "shorten and modernize the dresses."[83] The retention and updating of the image in 1935 indicates there was a market for views of middle-class Americans enjoying the fresh rural air of the upper Midwest.

A West Texas Ocean of Wheat at Twilight

PHOTO 1497-E   COPYRIGHT, 1935 BY MCCORMICK CO.   5A-H2434

"A WEST TEXAS OCEAN OF WHEAT AT TWILIGHT"

TEICH 5A-H2434, 1935

LINEN POSTCARDS CELEBRATED MODERN PRODUCTION, WHETH-
er agricultural or industrial, along with relaxation and picturesque reflection.
Although images of farming, mining, and manufacturing boosted local pride of
people who worked in or profited from those activities, such cards also appealed
to travelers and tourists. This view was distributed by a photographer in Amarillo, at the center of a wheat-growing area in the Texas Panhandle. Although
the source photo was tame, even boring, Teich's artists enhanced the image with
an apocalyptic tone. They airbrushed the photo with seething clouds and then
juxtaposed two contrasting color fields—the roiling wheat's electric brownish
yellow offset by the clouds' deep blue-black. The wheat's unearthly illumination
seems generated from within, with the only obvious natural light proceeding
from a narrow band of sky along the horizon tinged with sunset's red, orange,
and pink.

It is hard to imagine a more dramatic representation of this agricultural
landscape's sheer immensity, nearly engulfing two men in the middle distance.
Those figures provide a measure of scale, as in the picturesque tradition, but also
evoke the sublime terror of exposure to lightning and tornado. The postcard has
its greatest impact when viewed from the standard distance. A closer look reveals two flaws, the most obvious being the odd lack of a head beneath the hat
of the man on the right. More significant is the art department's failure to clearly render a windmill and several farm buildings visible on the horizon in the
source photo. That failure reinforces a sense of the inhuman scale of modern agriculture—with factory farming displacing single-family farms and mechanized
plowing contributing to topsoil erosion and Dust Bowl dirt blizzards. Visibility
in Amarillo was reduced to zero on several occasions only months before this
postcard was ordered. Although the card's back caption praises modernity by
extolling "millions of acres of waving, golden grain" harvested "by great, modern
combine-harvesters," the image suggests destructive natural and human forces
and may have provoked viewers to recall the ongoing human tragedy of the
Dust Bowl.[84]

57   KANSAS CITY STOCK YARDS, KANSAS CITY, MO.

7A-H2280

"Kansas City Stock Yards, Kansas City, Mo."

Teich 7A-H2280, 1937

THE EXPOSÉ OF MEATPACKING IN UPTON SINCLAIR'S NOVEL *The Jungle* (1906) was still fresh in older people's minds when this card appeared. He had introduced readers to the industry by having his protagonist tour a packing plant. Such organized tours were common at Armour and Swift by the turn of the century, evidence that Americans were curious about the mechanization of agricultural processes. This overview of the cattle stockyard in Kansas City, which covered 160 acres of bottomland west of downtown, brings an aesthetic of clarity to a scene infamous for noise, stench, and filth. The entire landscape, all the way to the horizon, is an expanse of pens, alleys, and chutes, some stacked up on two and even three levels. Clean draftsmanship applied to fence lines and roof surfaces suggests orderly control imposed on the random disorder of individual cattle. The patterning of corridors and chutes, so like a conveyor-belt system, offers a twentieth-century visual parallel to the illustrations of rational processes in the eighteenth-century French *Encyclopédie* or, more pertinently, to the engravings used by *Harper's Weekly* during the mid-nineteenth century to render manufacturing processes in panoramic views, promoting feelings of comprehension and mastery. In fact, the postcard reveals little of the stockyard's actual operation—with the supremely important railroads suggested only by a tiny rail bridge over the Kansas River in the upper left.[85]

Clear, cool sunlight renders each detail with precision, though in fact the source photo blurs at the edges and presents the dumb energy of seething cattle as barely contained. Although the postcard retains an industrial haze along the skyline of Kansas City, it softens with typical linen colors a horizon that in the source photo appears dense with polluting smoke. Viewed by tourists and travelers who may not have visited the stockyard but who found the card in a rack with other city views printed for the news agent Max Bernstein, this image reassured them the mechanized supply of beef was under rational control.

511   PRODUCERS IN THE FAMOUS SIGNAL HILL OIL DISTRICT, LONG BEACH, CALIFORNIA

1A-H393

"PRODUCERS IN THE FAMOUS SIGNAL HILL OIL DISTRICT, LONG BEACH, CALIFORNIA"

TEICH 1A-H393, 1931

THIS VIEW OF THE SIGNAL HILL OIL FIELD, A MORE PUBLICLY accessible site of extraction of resources than the Kansas City stockyard, projects a more chaotic impression. Overlooking downtown Long Beach, with the Pacific Ocean a mile away, this field had expanded rapidly after discovery of oil in 1921. Located in the urbanizing environs of Los Angeles, Signal Hill became a site that visitors to the region wanted to drive through, an industrial analog to the orange groves that inspired scores of postcards. The oil fields of Texas and Oklahoma also inspired many postcards, sometimes generic, as when Teich published a series of ten cards titled "Oil Field Scenes" in 1935, but just as often quite specific, as with views of wells on the grounds of the Oklahoma state capitol and governor's mansion. While some cards illustrated a single well, sometimes fully gushing and on one occasion on fire and about to explode, the massed derricks of Signal Hill offered a dramatic subject because they were crammed onto small residential lots in what had been a partially built suburban neighborhood.[86]

Although this view emphasizes modern abundance as much as Teich's stockyard view does, it suggests not rational precision but dark romanticism. The derricks' outlines and their oddly contrasting colors merge in a muddy expressionist haze. Puffs of smoke or steam augment the mood while also suggesting a sense of real-time motion and raw industrial power that linen representations mostly lack. The image remains somewhat murky, however. Only photographs reveal that the horizontal bar on the lower left represents a long, narrow refinery building, and that the taller structure to its right is a storage tank. A few small buildings are faintly present among the oil wells, with only two at the extreme left suggesting two-story suburban houses—reminders of how close this dark vision of extractive abundance was to sunny Southern California's more typical attractions.

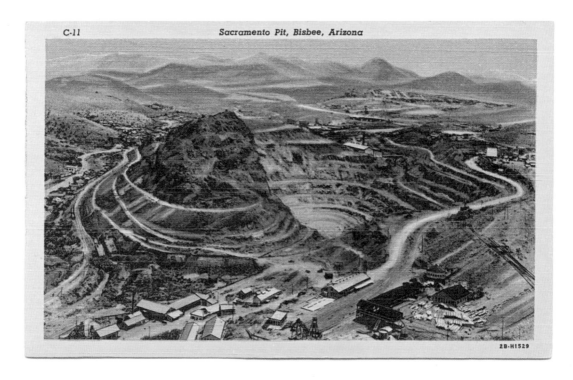

C-11   Sacramento Pit, Bisbee, Arizona

2B-H1529

"SACRAMENTO PIT, BISBEE, ARIZONA"

TEICH 2B-H1529, 1942

SOFT, GRAY MOUNTAINS ON THE HORIZON OF THIS VIEW OF AN open-pit copper mine suggest an idealized landscape. Green foothills seem more appropriate to rural England than to an Arizona desert. The backdrop is unusual given Pitchford's efforts to make certain Teich's artists got everything right. Initial blasting at the Sacramento Pit began in 1917, the same year Phelps Dodge Corporation arrested 2,000 striking workers at gunpoint in Bisbee and deported 1,300 by train. Since then, half the mountain had been blown away and a 435-foot hole dug. In contrast to the natural surroundings, which recede from view, the image emphasizes human intervention in the landscape—the deep pit with concentric terraces, roadways snaking around the mountain, and a sprawling array of buildings indicated by strong lines and smooth planes.

Pitchford provided the usual tracing-paper frisket and marked up an earlier, pre-linen postcard as a color guide. But when the Tucson distributor Holger Lollesgard, a personal friend, rejected the handmade color proof, Pitchford sent an exasperated screed to Chicago. What was rendered as a "wavering yellow strip" on the left was in fact "the highway, an asphalt road, the main highway, which must be shown," and which could be discerned "if you will put your [magnifying] glass on the picture." To the right of the meandering highway was a creek, and to its right a railroad track, both essential. The bottom of the pit was "green-gray talus slopes, NOT YELLOW AS YOU HAVE IT"—but even so it was "streaked with occasional splotches of yellow, sulphurous-looking stuff." A frisket pasted over the rejected proof specified various areas as "gray green . . . green gray . . . more reddish or rust . . . redder . . . a little yellow . . . open space gray—slightly greenish." The artists complied, though the image lacked the scale to implement Pitchford's request for "several cars" on the highway. The postcard may not successfully integrate shifting colors, artist-drawn details, and picture-book backdrop, but it does highlight the coliseum-like excavation and its cutaway hillside, which Pitchford had requested be indicated by having the "cleft in mountain shown by strength of color." All in all, his search for accuracy was misguided. The Sacramento Pit had closed a decade earlier, in 1931. More recent photos—not only by Russell Lee of the FSA in 1940 but by real photo postcard publisher Burton Frasher in 1939—revealed it as already abandoned, its terraces crumbling away.[87]

Hull Rust Crushing and Screening Plant, Hibbing, Minn.

7A-H3536

"Hull Rust Crushing and Screening Plant, Hibbing, Minn."

Teich 7A-H3536, 1937

"Greetings from Hibbing Minn.," proclaimed a large-letter card published in the 1940s, one of the few Teich cards with no serial number. Unlike most large-letter cards, that one contained no images of courthouse, main street, monument, or public park within the outlines of the letters spelling the town's name. Instead the tiny images within the letters promoted the mining industry of the Mesabi Iron Range and its civic benefits—with capsule glimpses of the vast Hull-Rust pit mine on the north edge of town, a steam shovel loading ore, a railway yard for assembling ore trains, and a city auditorium and elementary school paid for by the Oliver Iron Mining Company. The card's main image, arrayed below the city's name, was an aerial view of the high school, an elegant neoclassical structure that had cost the mining company nearly $4 million in the early 1920s.

Among the slivers of images within the letters of Hibbing's name were two taken from this view of an ore-processing plant outside the Hull-Rust mine— a fragment showing a gondola car on a high trestle and another showing the plant's diagonal roof. This card was one of many ordered by the *Hibbing Daily Tribune* during the linen era, along with a souvenir accordion folder of the "Missabe Range" that collected ten mining scenes, five town scenes, and two scenes portraying canoeing in Minnesota's pristine North Woods. This view, presented from the dramatic perspective of someone standing on the lower tracks along which crushed ore left the plant, shows a steam locomotive pushing cars loaded with ore to be processed along a slashing diagonal whose abrupt termination on the right, amidst the rosy haze of a typical linen sky, provokes an observer to wonder just what, exactly, is happening here. The hillside's lush weedy vegetation and the bushes surrounding a manager's shack on the lower right offer a reassuring contrast to the desolation of the mine's actual landscape, which an engineering journal described in 1948 as "pocked with huge open pits that suggest the craters of the moon."[88] Indeed, the image is rendered with clarity and delicacy that belie the heavy industry of mining and the deafening noise of mechanized ore processing and railway shipping.

17:—LOADING SULPHUR AT DOCKS. GALVESTON, TEXAS.

Photo by Verkin

42451

"LOADING SULPHUR AT DOCKS.
GALVESTON, TEXAS."

METROCRAFT 42451, N.D.

THIS POSTCARD ALSO PORTRAYS A SINGLE MOMENT IN AN EX-traction process few people who purchased the card would have witnessed. The popularity of such images suggests some Americans were intrigued by modern industrial processes and sought behind-the-scenes knowledge. This view of sulfur storage and transport on the docks at Galveston was popular enough that when Galveston Wholesale News Company switched from Metrocraft to Tichnor as a printer in the late 1940s or early '50s, the new supplier copied this card down to the last detail. Examples of both printings now frequently turn up in the offerings of postcard dealers. Cotton and wheat were higher-volume commodities at Galveston than sulfur, which had been extracted in the Texas Gulf Coast region since the teens, but substantial new deposits were discovered during the 1920s and '30s. Rather than mining sulfur by traditional means, companies like Texas Gulf Sulphur injected hot water into shafts drilled into underground deposits, pumped up the sulfur-laden water, and then extracted the mineral in a process yielding a nearly pure substance whose bright, artificial golden color lent itself to dramatic illustration.[89]

This image has an almost abstract quality, with large wedges of yellow contrasting with the sky's standard peach and aquamarine. Even so, the black-plate detailing of railroad cars and tracks, of the cranes and their track, and of the ship moored across the end of the dock (complete with a flag at the stern) remind a viewer that sulfur is being transferred from gondola cars onto a ship. But for all the "you are there" realism of the image, it conveys little information about what is actually happening. Cranes are transferring gleaming sulfur from the train cars to the huge bins on either side, but the next step, moving the mountain of sulfur in the foreground to the ship in the distance, goes unexplained. An image that promises to clarify an unfamiliar process instead remains no more than a romanticized expression of modernity.

Loading Cotton for Export at Houston, Texas

9A-H1476

"LOADING COTTON FOR EXPORT AT HOUSTON, TEXAS"

TEICH 9A-H1476, 1939

Unlike the loading of sulfur at Galveston, this bustling image of cotton being loaded onto a freighter in nearby Houston would not have taxed anyone's understanding. Moving a heavy cotton bale by hand with a dolly was traditional labor. One could imagine cotton being loaded exactly the same way a century earlier. The only difference that might have puzzled a viewer is that all seven workers are white—also the case with the source photo. However, the absence of black stevedores did not necessarily reflect a desire to avoid the issue of race. Houston had long had both white and black longshoremen, with segregated teams working staggered hours so as not to overlap. This white crew was no more unusual than the black longshoremen in a series of photos of a similar loading operation taken by FSA photographer Russell Lee in the same year.

The postcard portrays a chaotic scene, with workers moving in contrary directions and a rope line abandoned on the dock, where it could trip someone or foul a dolly. Pulling a bale on a dolly was the most traditional moment in a somewhat mechanized process. As revealed by Lee's photos, cotton bales were unloaded by dolly from trucks or train cars, suspended from a moving conveyor that took them inside to a compressor, mechanically pressed to one-third their original volume, and then loaded onto individual dollies, which stevedores pulled outside to a waiting freighter. At that point, a line from the ship was secured to the top of the dolly, which was winched up the ramp. On the ship three compressed bales were roped together, winched further up, and then lowered into the hold, where they were wrestled by hand into final shipping position.[90] Little of that process appears in this image, one of the few linen postcards to portray the physical labor of individuals. That a retouching artist obscured their faces seems ironically appropriate because they become part of the landscape, objectified as the energizing aspect of a vivid, colorful scene.

UNLOADING BANANAS, FROM SHIP SIDE
NEW ORLEANS, LA.

"UNLOADING BANANAS, FROM SHIP SIDE / NEW ORLEANS, LA."

TEICH 7A-H3126, 1937

WATCHING THE UNLOADING OF A BANANA BOAT FROM SOUTH America ranked among the major tourist attractions of New Orleans and had long been a popular postcard subject. Early pre-linen lithographic cards had shown a line of stevedores, each with a huge bunch of bananas slung over a shoulder, walking down a gangplank, and a line of empty-handed men returning in the other direction for more bananas. By the 1920s mechanization had arrived on the docks. Conveyor belts carried bunches of bananas up from a ship's hold, over the railing, and down the outside of the ship (as illustrated on the left side of this image). Another belt carried them past inspectors who culled overripe or damaged fruit for local sale. Eventually the bunches were carried (by hand? by hand cart? by conveyor?—this image is ambiguous, and contemporary descriptions and photographs are conflicting) to refrigerated railroad cars backed up, as shown here, on multiple tracks running perpendicular to the docked freighter. The WPA guide to New Orleans, published in 1938, titillated tourists by reporting that tarantulas and small boa constrictors often emerged from the bunches.[91]

This view of the process, which belongs to a behind-the-scenes documentary tradition, derives from a large-format photograph by H. J. Harvey, active in New Orleans from the early teens into at least the early twenties. Teich was not the first postcard publisher to use the photo, which formed the basis for a pre-linen view by E. C. Kropp—a card with more vibrant colors and less clumsy detailing. Even so, Teich artists closely followed the photo, a copy of which exists in the job file. As was often the case, they smoothed and simplified the scene, making it appear more efficient by cleaning up leaves, straw, and other debris from the floor and by eliminating a large, splintered hole from a rotten board in the foreground. As for the issue of race, the breakdown of whites and blacks in the postcard remains the same as in Harvey's photo, with African Americans indicated here mostly by not colorizing the faces, leaving them gray. The exception is a man dressed in blue near the center of the image whose face has been colorized.

T-5—Ore Docks, Two Harbors, Minn.

"ORE DOCKS, TWO HARBORS, MINN."

TEICH 9B-H1647, 1949

TRANSFER OF MESABI RANGE IRON ORE FROM RAILROAD CARS into freighters occurred not only at Duluth's large harbor but also thirty miles northeast along Lake Superior's north shore at Two Harbors, Minnesota. The main dock featured in this image was No. 6, the first steel-framed ore dock on the lake. When it was completed in 1909, five wooden-framed ore docks extended into the lake. By 1916, two had been rebuilt in steel and the others destroyed. Unlike the image of the banana docks at New Orleans, which drew observers into a busy, noisy, peopled scene, this view of a freighter being loaded with iron ore uses conceits of the picturesque landscape tradition to convey contemplative tranquility. The docks and ship seem painterly as they jut on a diagonal toward the receding backdrop of a delicate linen sky. Bits of leafy branches to either side and a foreground of vegetation frame the composition. Although several gravity-loaded chutes are lowered to the freighter, a viewer does not think to imagine the grinding rumble that would have been audible even at this distance.

Earlier views of the site, both photographic and lithographic, do not shirk from portraying an industrial landscape. Indeed, they emphasize a bay filled with artificial structures and in some instances present the observer's viewpoint as a railway embankment on this bluff in the foreground, mostly denuded of vegetation. Whoever took the source photo for this card reached the overlook by walking along the tracks to the bluff, which today still lacks any other access. By the late 1940s, however, enough vegetation had grown up to allow the photographer to ignore the railway and instead record a lush natural scene. Deep, vibrant blues and greens contribute to a process of encompassing the industrial realm within an older, forgiving natural landscape. For whatever reasons—whether visual or conceptual, aesthetic or sentimental—an owner of this unsent postcard found it compelling enough to tack it up for display, leaving a tiny hole at the top. The image seems to have been admired more as a composition—a picture—than as a source of information.

Mills along the Canal, Lewiston, Maine

7A-H3861

"MILLS ALONG THE CANAL. LEWISTON, MAINE"

TEICH 7A-H3861, 1937

THERE WERE AS MANY POSTCARD VIEWS OF FACTORIES AND manufacturing as of agriculture, mining, and shipping. Factory tours remained a staple of corporate publicity, and a postcard may occasionally have served as a souvenir of such a visit. More often, however, travelers drove past on a highway, looking down a valley or across a river at an industrial site, enjoying the experience of the sublime familiar to tourists at the Grand Canyon or Yosemite. However, this view looking north along a canal in Lewiston, Maine, suggests a tranquility perhaps more apparent today than in 1937, when the Bates cotton mill occupied multiple buildings and employed thousands of workers. Even so, the image emphasizes the pastoral setting of red-brick mill buildings on the left and worker housing on the right. Delicate branches of what appear to be elm trees form a bower over the canal, which shimmers with carefully colorized reflections.

Such pastoral settings in New England industry derived from the placing of early nineteenth-century mill towns at pristine sites along rural waterfalls and from an ideological desire to embed textile mills in restorative natural surroundings.[92] But by the late nineteenth century, introduction of steam power and an influx of immigrants had transformed New England textile towns into less tranquil spots. The calm of this image may have played to past notions of the pastoral New England mill town. The artist-generated automobile on the right, replacing an old Model T in the source photo, today seems the only reminder of the twentieth century. But local residents would have known that the arched bridge, which now seems a relic of bygone days, was only ten years old. Completed in 1928, the Wiseman Bridge at Chestnut Street was a concrete structure whose representation in gleaming white may have been intended as a marker of modernity.

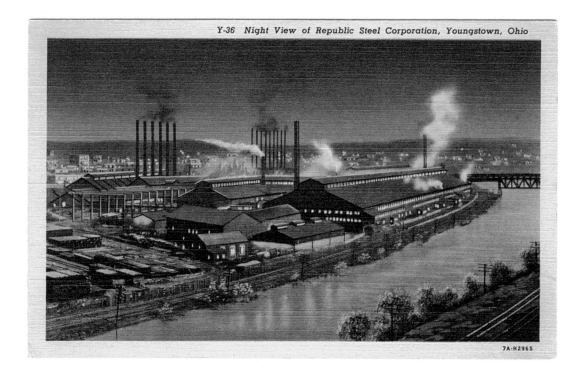

Y-36 Night View of Republic Steel Corporation, Youngstown, Ohio

7A-H2965

"NIGHT VIEW OF REPUBLIC STEEL CORPORATION, YOUNGSTOWN, OHIO"

TEICH 7A-H2965, 1937

POSTCARDS OF INDUSTRY FELL MOSTLY INTO TWO CATEGORIES.
While some presented aerial views similar to the engravings of factories that had graced corporate letterheads around the turn of the century, even more were night scenes like this image of the Republic Steel plant at Youngstown, Ohio. Taken from the Market Street viaduct over the Mahoning River, this view is typical of a mini-genre that portrayed a factory from across a river, usually with railroad tracks running diagonally across a lower corner (suggesting a train passenger's panoramic viewpoint) and plumes of gray smoke, often augmented by intense red-yellow flames, visible against a deep blue-black sky. Similar views of Youngstown Sheet and Tube's Campbell works and of a steel mill near Warren, Ohio, exhibited apocalyptic intensity—the former with more than a dozen red flares, some of them seeming to engulf entire buildings, the latter with a fierce glow emanating from behind the entire plant. However, this view's industrial energy is surrounded by—and thus softened by—a lighter blue along the horizon, suggesting the glow of city lights, and by the lighter blue of the river with its faint reflections.

Someone at the Youngstown News Agency who ordered the card in October 1937 may have hoped a calming image would moderate the negative impact of industrial violence that had engulfed the region four months earlier. After the so-called Little Steel companies declined to follow U.S. Steel's lead in signing a union contract, workers had struck at Youngstown and several other steel-producing cities. Republic's security forces had killed two workers and wounded thirty-five on June 19, leading to a declaration of martial law and the arrival of 4,500 troops to break the strike. The explosive energy of nighttime factory views is here brought under control, just as the strikers were. Rather than recalling labor unrest, purchasers of this card might have echoed the sentiments of the sender of a card illustrating a different steel mill, near Pittsburgh, who asserted that "although it is never given any publicity, . . . this is the most beautiful scene Pittsburgh has."[93]

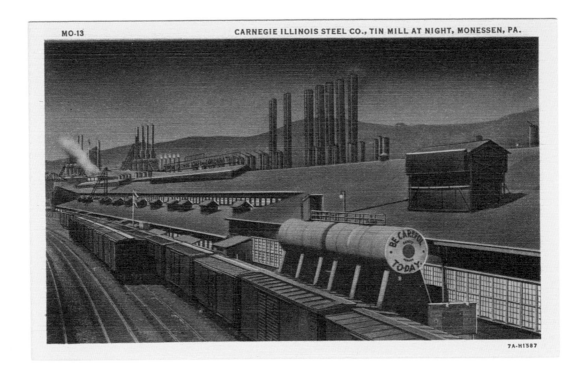

MO-13　　　　　　　CARNEGIE ILLINOIS STEEL CO., TIN MILL AT NIGHT, MONESSEN, PA.

7A-H1587

"Carnegie Illinois Steel Co., Tin Mill at Night, Monessen, Pa."

Teich 7A-H1587, 1937

THE MILLS OF MONESSEN, PENNSYLVANIA, YIELDED POSTCARDS
even more dramatic than those of Youngstown. A small city of about twenty
thousand, Monessen filled a horseshoe bend in the Monongahela River thirty
miles south of Pittsburgh—a location with many opportunities for long-distance
views across water to large industrial sites. Photographers who took real photo
views in the early twentieth century usually set up their cameras with exactly
that intention. However, the creator of the source photo for this view of a tin-
rolling mill (where tin-plated steel for "tin" cans was made) ignored the obvious
vista. Although the mill hugged the river just inside the horseshoe's northern
curve, the photographer instead set up on the opposite side of the plant along
some railroad tracks. The close crop on both ends excludes the mill's surroundings and focuses attention on its lines, planes, and geometric forms. A plume of
smoke rises in the distance in the finished postcard and a small smudge emerges from the nearest stack. The image lacks the apocalyptic fire of most night
views of industry. The only illumination is electric light glowing evenly from
gridded windows running the factory's full length—suggesting orderly activity
inside the plant. If not for the textures of roofs and doors of railway cars and
the admonition to "be careful today," the entire image would project a smooth,
abstract sense of efficiency. Even the hills' irregular silhouette serves more as a
contrasting border than a reminder of the larger world in which the mill exists.
Although many linen postcards lack human figures, not many present scenes so
completely composed of artificial elements, with no hint of the organic. This is
a popular variant of the precisionist realm defined by Charles Sheeler's *American Landscape* (1930) and *Classic Landscape* (1931)—paintings that portray
abstract industrial forms as inherently perfect and self-contained. Ironically,
however, the rolling mill, which had operated for forty years, suffered multiple
work stoppages and closed for good in December 1937, a few months after the
postcard's publication—almost immediately rendering the card obsolete.[94]

MC307   *View of the Hot Strip Mill*

at the Irvin Works located on the Monongahela River

"VIEW OF THE HOT STRIP MILL / AT THE IRVIN WORKS LOCATED ON THE MONONGAHELA RIVER"

TEICH 9A-H372, 1939

INCONCEIVABLE ENERGY SUFFUSES THIS IMAGE OF RED-HOT steel flowing from a production line in a continuous rolling mill south of Pittsburgh. Carnegie-Illinois Steel's Irvin Works had been in operation just over a year when Minsky Brothers, a wholesaler of general goods in Pittsburgh, submitted large orders of 25,000 for this card and a second one featuring the same plant in a daytime aerial view. The source photo for this card showed a well-lit behemoth emblazoned in five places in large, blocky letters with the single word "Mesta," the name of its Pittsburgh manufacturer. In addition to asking for removal of the name, instructions directed the art department to "show strip of steel red hot" and to "make night view if it will show better than day view."

Those commands came in the unlikely handwriting of western representative Pitchford, who had grown up five miles away in Duquesne, another mill town in a bend of the Monongahela River. Pitchford's father, George, had been a steelworker in England before immigrating and eventually retired from Carnegie as a foreman at the Duquesne steel mill. Whatever had brought the fifty-two-year-old postcard salesman back to his childhood home, he must have wanted to do justice to a subject his deceased father would have enjoyed seeing. Although the completed image minimizes the brutal heaviness and deep grime exposed in documentary films on the steel industry, the contrast of the glowing red-yellow ribbon of steel with the burnished purple-black machinery successfully transfers to a colorized medium the white-hot intensity of molten steel originally captured in black and white. Careful details, such as the spray of water for removing scale as the steel emerges from the machine, render the postcard more legible than the source photo. In composing the caption, Pitchford provided more information than most readers would have wanted. The actual point of the image was not to document but to evoke the technological sublime—not so much through the visual impact of red-hot steel as through the controlling power of the machine, whose rendering by the art department elevated it from an expression of brute force in the source photo to an emanation of rational organization and control in the postcard.[95]

Infrastructure and Transportation

71965

19—Suspension Bridge, Cincinnati, Ohio

3A-H288

"SUSPENSION BRIDGE, CINCINNATI, OHIO"

TEICH 3A-H288, 1933

FROM HISTORICAL STRUCTURES WITH GRANITE ARCHES TO modern marvels with steel trusses, bridges appeared in scores of postcards—often as central subject but sometimes as visual passage to a featured landscape or as background detail. New bridges attracted public notice during a period of federal WPA construction that supported expanding auto traffic and stimulated economic recovery. Instantly famous structures such as New York's George Washington Bridge (1931) and San Francisco's Golden Gate Bridge (1937) shared the limelight with regional landmarks such as the Coos Bay Bridge in Oregon (1936) and the Huey P. Long Bridge over the Mississippi at Baton Rouge (1940). But older bridges also offered fit subjects for postcards, especially if they were among a city's prominent features.

That was the case with a monumental suspension bridge crossing the Ohio River at Cincinnati. Designed and built by John A. Roebling of Brooklyn Bridge fame, and completed in 1867, the bridge was the subject of a Detroit Publishing postcard around 1905. Many more followed—all taken from Kentucky, from one side or the other of the bridge's massive southern pier, with or without shanties in the foreground and steamboats passing underneath. Teich's linen image from 1933 bathes the old bridge and the city on the opposite shore in the golden light of nostalgia. Although shadows on both piers indicate a light source high in the northeastern sky, the honey-colored limestone and the yellow-orange haze over the city would have suggested late afternoon to most viewers. Intricate details of cables, decking, railings, and ornamentation give the bridge, however idealized, a realism lacking in the stylized rendering of Cincinnati. Even the iconic forms of the city's two new skyscrapers, the pyramidal roofline of the Central Trust Bank Building set against the taller Carew Tower, recede into the haze in the presence of Roebling's bridge. Compared with skylines of earlier postcards, Teich's rendering seems doctored to make the city appear farther away than in actuality. The bridge appears as a burnished monument to a larger-than-life past.[96]

102   Lift Bridge and Ship Canal at Night,
Duluth-Superior Harbor

"LIFT BRIDGE AND SHIP CANAL AT NIGHT, / DULUTH-SUPERIOR HARBOR"

TEICH 7A-H1068, 1937

WHILE SOME LINEN IMAGES ASSUMED THE INDUSTRIAL INTO A premodern aesthetic of nature, others acknowledged an independent aesthetic for modern industrial structures. That was the case with this view of Duluth's Aerial Lift Bridge, constructed in 1905 to rejoin to the city an inhabited six-mile spit of land that defined the city's natural harbor—through which a short canal had been cut in 1871. The original "bridge" was a large gondola suspended by long cables from the steel superstructure, carrying up to 350 people in a one-minute crossing as it was moved from roadway to roadway. There was a world's fair extravagance to the engineering feat, and its steel fretwork recalled the recent technological marvel of the Eiffel Tower. After traffic overran capacity, the gondola was replaced in 1930. A horizontal lift section, visible here along the waterline, was raised 390 feet when a freighter entered or left the harbor.

Although watching the huge freighters was a popular pastime, many postcard views presented the bridge alone, without a passing ship, as a phenomenon. This card's caption describes it as "a mecca for tourists at any time of day" but as "unusually attractive at night." The view is from one of two promenades extending into the lake from the sides of the short canal. An observer looks back toward the bridge, which is bathed in gray light tinged with lavender—a unique effect for a linen postcard. The bridge's left pier and street lamps on the far promenade reflect in the water with wavering lines whose boldness suggests a precisionist nocturne. Everything, from the bridge's detailed tracery and the sky's unearthly hue to the effects worked with street lamps and reflections, implies a dedicated attempt to achieve a "beautiful miniature painting."[97] However, the source for this atmospheric card was not a black-and-white photo but instead a printed image, somewhat larger than a postcard, derived from a photomechanical reproduction of an artificially colorized photo, and printed on paper with a shimmering, grained surface. Typed instructions told the artists merely to "see colored photo," which must in fact have been a tourist souvenir. The artistry thus preceded Teich's involvement. Even so, this particular view, one of twenty-two mostly typical scenes ordered by a local distributor, conveyed an aura of modernity.

PA-119   *Moonlight on Pennsylvania Turnpike*

"America's Super Highway"   1B-H346

"MOONLIGHT ON PENNSYLVANIA TURNPIKE / 'AMERICA'S SUPER HIGHWAY'"

TEICH 1B-H346, 1941

POSTCARD VIEWS OF AN AMERICAN SCENE VISIBLE FROM THE highway proliferated with the increase in travelers whose goal was to reach a particular destination quickly. One standard journey-focused message bragged that the writer had "made the trip in 13 hrs (600 miles)." Another—complaining or exulting—announced that "we left Missouri last nite and [are] still on Route 66 all the way now." Although postcards reflected an automotive society, few images represented only the highway. Views of the Pennsylvania Turnpike marked a notable exception. With a segment opened in 1940 running nearly from Pittsburgh to Harrisburg, two-thirds of the way across the state, the turnpike was the nation's first major limited-access highway. The absence of cross streets, stoplights, railway crossings, and driveways on the four-lane turnpike seemed miraculous. Even with a speed limit of seventy miles per hour that was imposed after a brief trial period with no limit at all, travel time between the two cities was cut from 5½ to 2½ hours.[98]

This night view of "America's Super Highway" was ordered from Teich five months after the turnpike opened. Smooth, flat concrete spreads across the full frame of the image, stretching to the horizon. The overpass (a design used throughout the turnpike's length) visually emphasizes the lack of intersections at grade. So new was the concept of a divided highway that the art department had to be told to put "green lawn in center of roads." Three continuous receding lines of reflectors may now look absurdly emphasized, but they mark off swift movement along the road's continuous uniformity. An instruction to "leave clouds natural as in photo" reflected a need for visual contrast in an otherwise featureless space. And while the caption praises the "engineering achievement" of a "completely safe and speedy traffic artery," the job order's request for a generic "moonlight view" romanticized a scene that soon enough became something to be suffered through as quickly as possible.

PA-125

Portal and Tunnel on Pennsylvania Turnpike

"America's Super Highway"

1B-H400

"PORTAL AND TUNNEL ON PENNSYLVANIA TURNPIKE / 'AMERICA'S SUPER HIGHWAY'"

TEICH 1B-H400, 1941

AMONG THE PENNSYLVANIA TURNPIKE'S ATTRACTIONS WERE its seven long tunnels, which kept the highway nearly level throughout the Allegheny Mountains with a maximum grade of 3 percent as opposed to the 12 percent of some mountain roads. Four lanes merged into two at each tunnel, one in each direction—a situation unchanged until the 1960s. Circumstantial evidence suggests that this image represents the Allegheny Mountain Tunnel, about six thousand feet long. The job file contains a competing Tichnor postcard portraying the entrance to that tunnel at night (similar but from a different angle), on the back of which someone wrote, "We should try to get this subject."

Even more than the view of the roadway in moonlight, which portrays grass, trees, and shrubbery, the tunnel in this image offers no hint of natural surroundings, whether organic or inorganic. Triple arches that define the entrance appear set in a black void. Echoing curves move the eye from left to right with the portal arches and then with the roadway as it disappears in the distance. Judging the tunnel's scale becomes difficult with no car in sight—and was probably even harder for anyone who had never experienced such a tunnel.

Working from a straightforward black-and-white night photo, Teich's artists created a complex mix of subtly shifting hues and shades for roadway, walls, and ceiling. The back caption provides information about the tunnel's use of both sodium-vapor lights and mercury-vapor lights but then shifts to an aesthetic comment about how the latter "produce a daylight effect forming a perfect contrast and silhouette the entrance to the tunnel." The image's stillness encourages a meditative mood unavailable to anyone actually experiencing the tunnel from a car. The final instruction to the artists commanded, "Do not remove dark shadows, leave it natural as it is." As so often with linen postcards, especially those with modern technological subjects, the meaning of "natural" was ambiguous.

U-10   U. S. Highway 80 and S. P. R. R. Bridges across Colorado River entering Yuma, Arizona

2B-H1578

"U.S. Highway 80 and S.P.R.R. Bridges across Colorado River entering Yuma, Arizona"

Teich 2B-H1578, 1942

THESE BRIDGES WERE NOT NEW WHEN THIS POSTCARD WAS PUB-
lished in 1942, with the highway bridge dating from 1915 and the rail bridge
from 1923. Even so, the image of paired steel trusses extolled American engineering expertise and the opening of the nation to settlement. The Southern Pacific Railroad first bridged the Colorado River at Yuma in 1877, and passengers
still traveled the line's Sunset Route from Los Angeles to New Orleans in the
1940s. The highway bridge carried traffic over the Colorado, the border between
California and Arizona, as part of the nation's southernmost cross-country route
from San Diego to St. Augustine. Replacing a ferry, the bridge served briefly as
the only highway bridge over the Colorado—a distinction that earned its nickname as the "Ocean-to-Ocean Highway Bridge." That name is still used today
even though a new bridge opened 150 miles to the north on Route 66 in 1916,
and a third was built by 1930.

While many images of bridges situate them statically in the middle distance,
this image benefits from dramatic juxtaposition of rail and road. Differing levels
and angles allow the rail bridge to loom up as it shoots diagonally to the left,
while the auto bridge is foreshortened from a viewer's head-on perspective. As
with many complex structures, the retouching artist has delineated the bridges'
beams and struts in a way that yields a hyperreal quality. But the overall image is unconvincing despite efforts by Pitchford and his friend Lollesgard to
achieve an exacting realism. Submitting a pre-linen card from 1928 as a guide,
Pitchford asked the art department to "wipe out the Red Bldg" because "it is no
more." They were also to "show [the] white center line . . . but be sure it tapers
away in the distance." Among several objections to a color proof, the Tucson distributor Lollesgard criticized "a notch left in the vertical wall of the buff-colored
building [as] seen through the bridgework"—which made the wall look like "a
jig-saw puzzle." As printed, the card reveals little evidence at all of a building behind the rail bridge, and the white line appears so fresh as to have been painted
the day before. Despite lapses in realism, however, the image captures a dynamism that still appears in recent photos of the paired bridges.[99]

BOULDER DAM AND LAKE

5A-H1428

"Boulder Dam and Lake"

Teich 5A-H1428, 1935

No public works project during the Depression attract-ed more attention than Hoover Dam (mostly referred to as Boulder Dam un-til 1947), whose construction in a deep canyon on the Colorado River between Nevada and Arizona took place from 1931 to 1936. The goals were controlling floods, impounding water for desert irrigation, and generating electricity for the Southwest, but the dam also provided a sublime experience for tourists both during and after construction. "Boulder Dam surpassed even our wildest imag-inings," reported a visitor on a card mailed to Oklahoma; it was "truly a man-made marvel." And an Ohio farm woman who was not usually at a loss for words reported the dam was simply "too large to describe." Roughly 750,000 people visited during 1934 and 1935, the same number recorded at the Grand Canyon, and many bought postcards. Teich issued fifty-one views of the dam between 1935 and 1953, with initial orders totaling 832,000. A series of nineteen cards ordered in July 1935 for the dam's dedication two months later included views based on construction photos even though final pouring of concrete had already occurred. Many images, including this overview of the upstream face, portrayed the dam before Lake Mead filled up behind it.[100]

Pitchford took pains with this image, perhaps because his friend Earl Broth-ers ran the tourist-oriented Boulder Dam Service Bureau as a federal franchi-see. The agent rejected the first color proof, maintaining there was "not enough contrast in colors"—which was the only way to "show . . . there is a canyon be-yond the dam . . . very steep and deep." The original design had "too much of the lighter colors," and he asked the art department to "liven it up" with areas of red, reddish brown, and chocolate. As printed, the rocky terrain appears variegated. Shifting patterns of color define juxtapositions of depth not only in the canyon but also in the surrounding mountains, whose texture becomes fine enough at the horizon nearly to merge with the sky. The result is a delicate landscape con-trasting with the dam's gray presence. Its irregular concrete surface is subtly de-fined photographically by the black plate and artistically by a gradual shift from green to yellow highlights down the left side. This is one of those occasions—however restrained—when the linen process revealed itself as an independent form of illustration.

Transcontinental Highway across Boulder Dam

© DESERT SOUVENIR SUPPLY

1B-H2433

"TRANSCONTINENTAL HIGHWAY ACROSS BOULDER DAM"

TEICH 1B-H2433, 1941

ALTHOUGH MOST HOOVER DAM CARDS PORTRAYED ITS DESO-
late setting or vast size, some emphasized recreational potential. Lake Mead's
surface, reproduced in the deepest blue, offered a cooling contrast to a barren
landscape experienced by summer travelers in triple-digit temperatures. Pitchford, who was responsible for securing most if not all Teich orders for images
of the dam, was a boating enthusiast whose cards promoted Lake Mead as a
boater's paradise. As early as 1936, with the new lake's surface risen not even
halfway up the back of the dam, Teich printed a vertically oriented card showing
a cabin cruiser moving below the tall columns of two water intake towers. Two
years later, the company's offerings included a sailboat viewed against the crest
of the dam, with the lake risen to near capacity, and a launch traveling along
Lake Mead's farthest reaches at the Grand Canyon's western edge.[101]

The emphasis in this image is on water as a visual refuge for auto travelers. Pitchford even ordered the deletion of a rowboat and a small tourist boat
appearing in the source photo so as not to distract from the pristine lake. The
deep blue surface, defined not by the irregular shoreline of most lakes but by
the elegant artificial curve of U.S. 93 along the top of the dam, nearly fills the
frame. Unlike most source photos, this card's was cropped to remove the sky,
possibly because the rugged, rock-strewn horizon would have emphasized the
site's desolation rather than the dam's pure geometry and the lake's clear beauty.
Although tiny human figures are portrayed in a notched overlook, gazing down
below the dam, the primary message for a viewer of the postcard, whose vantage
point is defined by a bit of rock in the lower right corner, is the inviting, nearly
miraculous presence of so much cooling water in such a dry location—and its
visual accessibility to tourists driving across the dam along a major "transcontinental highway."

ARIZONA SPILLWAY AND HIGHWAY BRIDGE, BOULDER DAM

6A-H2031

"Arizona Spillway and Highway Bridge, Boulder Dam"

Teich 6A-H2031, 1936

MAKERS OF POSTCARD IMAGES WERE PROBABLY NOT ALWAYS aware of their effects. A case in point is this remarkable portrayal of a spillway at Hoover Dam as an assemblage of abstract geometrical forms arrayed in sharp contrast to the rugged natural landscape. Among thousands of photographs taken by Pitchford are many exhibiting considerable artistry. However, most of the time he worked as if he had internalized an array of templates for typical postcard views that would succeed in the marketplace. There is no definite evidence that Pitchford took the source photo for this card. Nor did he emphasize its dramatic juxtaposition of forms and textures when interpreting it to the art department. Instead he merely requested a "natural concrete coloring" for the spillway and observed that the "cliffs form a colorful background." There is no way of knowing whether sales agent or artists realized the image's extraordinary quality.

A recipient who had not seen the dam might have wondered what was being pictured here. The functions of the V-shaped concrete trough, the dark opening at its end, the apparent catwalk above, and the three-sided black structures and towers to the right are not obvious. All one can assume is that a viewer would have noticed an engineering work of unknown size, extent, and purpose set in a natural landscape. The back caption offers no help when it boasts that "the largest battleship could be floated in this structure." A keen observer might have noticed tiny curved forms representing roofs of three cars along the apparent catwalk and realized it was actually an auto bridge. In fact the highway from Arizona to Nevada ran along the left, across the bridge, behind the crenellated horizontal line on the right side of the image, and from there onto the top of the dam, which an observer standing at this vantage point could have seen by turning to the right. Lake Mead eventually submerged the terrain represented on the card's lower right, but for the moment the image offered the stark contrast of streamlined technological modernity imposed on antediluvian rock.

G. I. PITCHFORD'S PHOTO *HOOVER DAM*, CA. 1935, ALSO EMPHASIZES THE CONTRAST OF RUGGED NATURE AND UNNATURALLY SMOOTH ENGINEERING.

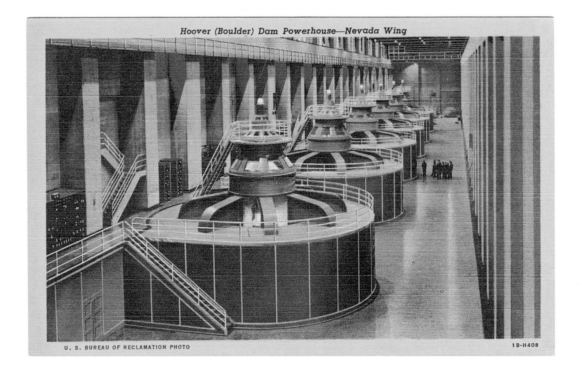

Hoover (Boulder) Dam Powerhouse—Nevada Wing

U. S. BUREAU OF RECLAMATION PHOTO   1B-H408

"HOOVER (BOULDER) DAM POWERHOUSE—
NEVADA WING"

TEICH 1B-H408, 1941

FROM THE TOP OF HOOVER DAM ONE COULD LOOK DOWN ITS vast surface and see two powerhouses, so distant as to seem like toys, one hugging each side of the canyon. Their immensity became apparent only from below. After riding an elevator down 500 feet, as 2.5 million people had done by mid-1937, tourists could gaze the length of the turbine hall portrayed in this image. Humming quietly, seven turbines generated electricity while a light above each indicated its operating status. Concrete columns along the sides possessed an orderly classical symmetry, and in this image tiny figures reveal the scale of the enterprise. Control panels on the left suggest human labor reduced to a minimum, and the polished floor, devoid of grease and dirt, reveals hydroelectric power as clean and pure. The line of turbines approaches infinity, but at the end of the hall a hazy cone of light reinforces a reverential mood.

Although most views of the dam emphasize its massive physicality, this view of the powerhouse projects a smooth, efficient, even immaterial energy. Fourteen years later, in 1955, after the advent of the nuclear age, the photographer Robert Frank employed a postcard of Hoover Dam in a quite different representation of technology, energy, and the American scene. While driving across the nation shooting black-and-white photos of life on the margins, a project yielding his book *The Americans* in 1958, Frank photographed a revolving postcard rack at a souvenir shop near the dam. Arranged top to bottom on the small, three-slot wire rack were chrome postcards portraying the Grand Canyon, Hoover Dam, and an atomic mushroom cloud billowing over Yucca Flat, Nevada. The narrative sequence of Frank's image runs from the canyon's majestic natural beauty, to the dam's technological dominance of nature, and finally to the disastrous outcome of humanity's urge for limitless energy. The lurid red cap of the mushroom cloud as it appears on the shiny color postcard published by Mike Roberts of Berkeley, California, becomes in Frank's black-and-white photo a blot, a black hole torn in the fabric of existence. Not published until 1972, Frank's image reversed the optimism typical of portrayals of technology on linen postcards.[102]

Chicago—Railroad Center of the World 81

Kaufmann-Fabry Photo

71965

"CHICAGO—RAILROAD CENTER OF THE WORLD"

TICHNOR 71965, N.D.

AS ALREADY NOTED, THE LINEN POSTCARD WAS AN AUTOMOTIVE medium. Many landscapes and tourist attractions were accessible only by car, a form of travel enabling people to personalize routes and travel times. Passenger rail service offered a dense web of connections but little flexibility. Ridership had declined steadily since 1920. By 1933 railroads had lost two-thirds of their passengers, though travel increased later in the decade and spiked upward during World War II. Despite the decline, hundreds of thousands of people filled station waiting rooms, bought postcards, and scribbled reports back home even if only to complain of being "almost black" from the coal soot of "those dirty trains."[103] Railroads fought the decline by introducing streamlined passenger trains, some repurposed but others newly designed. Diesel locomotives such as those that pulled the Santa Fe Super Chief were lightweight and cleaner, used less fuel, and eventually replaced steam locomotives on most passenger routes.

Even so, steam engines remained too central to everyday life to evoke the nostalgia felt in a later era. Indeed, this postcard presents five powerful locomotives, belching smoke and hissing steam, at the very center of Chicago, the "railroad center of the world" with fifteen major lines converging on it. The card is based on a photo taken at night in 1937 by Adolph Presler, who worked for commercial photographers Kaufmann & Fabry, with clients including the Illinois Central Railroad. By that time, as wires above the tracks suggest, the railroad's downtown freight yard, which ran in a sunken cut through Grant Park next to Lake Michigan, was electrified, and freight cars were shunted by electric locomotives. Given that steam locomotives were no longer used in downtown Chicago, Presler's photo *Five Titans* seems to have been purposely staged. Illinois Central publicists liked it so much they put it on the cover of the company magazine. As a postcard this image of five powerful engines posed against a backdrop of Michigan Avenue skyscrapers emphasized the dynamism of modern rail transport. Ironically, the locomotives actually hauled freight trains, not passengers, but most purchasers of the card would not have known that.[104]

Main Waiting Room, Union Station, Omaha, Neb.

7A-H2480

"MAIN WAITING ROOM, UNION STATION, OMAHA, NEB."

TEICH 7A-H2480, 1937

DURING THE FIRST THIRD OF THE TWENTIETH CENTURY MANY
cities witnessed construction of so-called union stations combining several railroads under one roof so passengers transferring from one line to another did
not have to travel across town between two stations. Serving as a city's gateway,
a union terminal typically boasted grand architectural gestures ranging from
Beaux-Arts neoclassicism in Washington, DC (1907), and Kansas City (1914) to
Art Deco in Omaha (1931) and Los Angeles (1939). This image of Omaha's waiting room is typical in its emphasis on accurate rendering of decorative flooring,
woodwork, chandeliers, and, above all, colors, here taken from a hand-tinted
photo provided by the customer. However, this view is different from many station interiors in its emptiness. Unlike interior views of other types of buildings,
which are usually unpeopled, those of train stations usually portray passengers
sitting on benches, standing in conversation, or buying tickets. In this case daylight filters through high windows in a room whose far clock reads 4:35 p.m.—a
time of day when the space would have been filled. Teich had already used the
source photo in 1931 for a non-linen card ordered soon after the station's dedication—presumably an architectural photo taken from a low angle to encompass both the starburst mosaic and the chandeliers.

The card's purchaser, a young woman writing to a brother in Manistique,
Michigan, in December 1941, had momentarily entered a calm space, a respite
from the incessant jostling of rail travel. She had arrived from points west and
was "stopping over" so she could "make application for train stewardess." Presumably she was applying to the Union Pacific Railroad, headquartered in
Omaha, which in 1935 began hiring registered nurses as stewardesses to assist
the elderly and women with small children. Eventually she made her way to the
rival non-"union" Burlington Station, a large neoclassical structure, where she
mailed the card before boarding a train to Chicago on the Burlington line. As
an anxious afterthought she added a question, asking her brother, a week after
Pearl Harbor, whether he had "heard any more from [the] draft board?" Waiting rooms were soon filled to capacity as World War II consumed the nation's
attention.[105]

H-4563—DINING CAR OF THE SANTA FE'S EL CAPITAN

"DINING CAR OF THE SANTA FE'S EL CAPITAN"

TEICH OC-H653, 1950

No railroad was better known for luxurious service than the Atchison, Topeka & Santa Fe, which ran trains along a southern route from Chicago to Los Angeles or San Francisco. The Santa Fe's flagship train was the Super Chief, a photo of which Pitchford had collaged onto an orange grove in 1940 (see figs. 3.16, 3.17), three years after introduction of lightweight stream-lined equipment. Composed entirely of Pullman sleepers with lounge and dining cars, the Super Chief carried no coach passengers and was known for its Holly-wood clientele. In 1938 the railroad introduced a coach-only streamliner called El Capitan. Intended to supply inexpensive travel at high speed (under forty hours to reach Los Angeles from Chicago), the train boasted reclining seats, a lounge car, and Fred Harvey dining facilities. "Inexpensive" did not imply "bud-get," however. A one-way ticket from Chicago to Los Angeles ran $44.50 (meals extra), nearly a third of what an Ohio family of four had spent in 1936 during a three-week round-trip driving vacation to the same destination.[106]

In 1948 the Santa Fe introduced this dining car on the El Capitan, with table service for twenty people and counter space for fourteen more. Unlike most people portrayed on Teich cards, the models here were hardly retouched as the image moved from the railroad's official source photo to the printed postcard. Even the African American waiter appears as a unique individual. However, the dining car was transformed significantly by the art department as compared both to the source photo and to a Santa Fe brochure, used for color guidance, which featured a color photo with the same models in slightly differ-ent poses. Reflections in windows and in mirrored panels were deleted for the card. A calendar hanging above the couple on the left was removed. Frames and legs of chairs, appearing in the brochure as metal simulating wood, became sleek, shiny metal in the postcard—a machine-age touch more typical of the 1930s. Even the decorative motif above the windows, in reality a line of blocky aluminum stampings representing a daisy chain of stylized kachina dolls and eagles, appeared indistinctly as if not to distract attention. The intent was a visual streamlining of the interior, divorcing El Capitan from the outside world (nothing is visible from the windows) and reinforcing a sense of smooth, imper-ceptible motion.[107]

838   Greyhound Bus Terminal, Pittsburgh, Pa.

2B-H1369

"GREYHOUND BUS TERMINAL, PITTSBURGH, PA."

TEICH 2B-H1369, 1942

DESPITE THE BLEAK REPUTATION OF BUS STATIONS TODAY, BUS travel shared the machine-age glamour of trains and planes during the 1930s. Greyhound had emerged as the major player in a new industry after consolidating regional companies such as the Blue Ridge Lines, referenced in this image. Not burdened like some railroads with station architecture mired in the past, Greyhound could promote itself through modern architecture as well as modern equipment. This postcard is one of many portraying Greyhound stations across the country from Evansville, Indiana, to Clarksdale, Mississippi. Although each was different, they all shared a streamlined look that branded them as an upscale accessory of modern life.

The Pittsburgh terminal, opened in 1936, was one of several designed by Thomas W. Lamb, an architect known for pioneering the exotic movie palaces of the 1910s. As a designer whose career focused on the movies, Lamb applied his talent for themed environments to creating futuristic sets for people on the move. Nothing disturbs a sense of flowing motion in this image. Teich's artist emphasized an architectural motif of long horizontal lines ending in a curve—as in the first floor's plate glass, the ribbon window along the second floor, and the railing above the loading platform. Even the building's curved corner (setting off the entrance) and a curve in the pavement at the front of the loading platform are carefully delineated and shaded. The bus's paint scheme complements the building's visual effects. As prescribed by Greyhound industrial design consultant Raymond Loewy, painted teardrops curve back in flowing streamlines from each wheel well. The company's signature shade of blue defines the bus (which was operated by a Greyhound subsidiary), the terminal's signs, and even the sky. The retouching artist followed orders to eliminate the source photo's "wires and blurred people" but then left abstracted lines of streetcar tracks as if to emphasize smooth flow from right to left along a slightly inclined diagonal. Vertically oriented buildings behind the terminal recede through a softening of lines and hues, while scattered clouds balance their presence. An aesthetic appropriate for expressing fast transport defines both the terminal and the image that represents it.[108]

50   La Guardia Field, New York, N. Y.

1B-H2481

"LA GUARDIA FIELD, NEW YORK, N.Y."

TEICH 1B-H2481, 1941

THESE TWO SILVER DC-3 AIRLINERS SEEM TO RUPTURE THE fabric of an otherwise stereotypical image—almost like the wartime cargo-cult fetishes of a few years later. The complicated forms of the main terminal building, then two years old, are carefully rendered. A retouching artist has highlighted the numerous lines of control tower, roofline, windows, railings, and light stanchions. A colorist has effected a transition from sun-drenched honey-colored brick on the left to shaded brick on the right. People lining the observation walkway exhibit bright dots of color typical of a crowd—so different from dull black-and-white crowds in newspapers and magazines. Aside from the plane's shadow, the tarmac displays a variegated hue that often eluded postcard artists but was essential for believability. Finally, the sky is both total linen effect and delicately illusionistic. A vague robin's-egg blue shifts in tone, becoming lighter around the cottony gray-white clouds tinged underneath with salmon pink. Working backward from the position of the plane's shadow in the source photo, Teich's artists created a harmonious lighting effect encompassing sky, building, and ground in a manner displaying the linen colorizing process at its most convincing.

Against all that appear the silvery airliners. Unlike the abstract geometrical forms of the Hoover Dam spillway (see p. 256), whose shading and texture suggest material forms composed of heavy concrete, these airplanes possess an otherworldliness that the linen process cannot quite capture. Their bright reflective forms seem a matter of color's absence, as if conveyed through some new reverse or negative photographic process. They are minimally defined, mostly by unretouched elements printed in black—windows, circular shadows at the fronts of engines, wing lines, wheels and struts, and clumpy people. It would be hard to find another linen postcard with such large areas printed in a blinding white. Despite the skill with which a colorist has used shifting blue-gray to indicate the curvature of unpainted aluminum, the two DC-3s pop out from the otherwise hypernormal linen backdrop as avatars of the era's modernity—almost beyond representation. It is hardly surprising that people thronged to New York's new airport and paid a dime apiece to watch from the observation walkway as these magical forms rose into the sky.

M-26   HUGE GLOBE OF THE EARTH, PAN-AMERICAN AIRWAYS TERMINAL, MIAMI, FLA.

THE GLOBE IS 31½ FT. IN CIRCUMFERENCE AND WEIGHS 6,500 LBS.   PHOTO BY GERECKE

"Huge Globe of the Earth, Pan-American Airways Terminal, Miami, Fla. / The Globe Is 31½ Ft. in Circumference and Weighs 6,500 Lbs."

Teich 6A-H1643, 1936

THE SOPHISTICATION OF AIR TRAVEL IN THE 1930S, WHEN ITS expense was beyond the purchasing power of most Americans, appears in this interior of the Pan American Airways seaplane terminal in Miami. Located on Dinner Key in Coconut Grove, south of downtown, the building opened in 1934 for passengers traveling to the Caribbean and Central and South America by the famous Clippers, "flying boats" that took off and landed on water. Although the terminal served 50,000 passengers per year, there is no sense of urgency in the image, which projects a leisurely pace appropriate for recreational destinations like Havana and Nassau. A clerk is assisting a small group at the counter, but four people who gaze at a huge globe could easily have been nonflying visitors.

Photographs of the building's white stucco exterior reveal crowds gathered outside and on roof terraces. The Pan American terminal was a tourist attraction averaging 30,000 nonflying visitors most months, a figure rising to 100,000 during high season.[109] The site had a country-club approach along a palm-lined boulevard ending in a broad circular drive. In addition to watching Clippers take off and land on water, visitors could also watch them being pulled by tractor from a hangar to a launch ramp. Surviving home-movie footage suggests a festive mood. Writing on this card, a tourist described "two girls . . . being loaded into a fine car by 2 gentlemen & 2 porters." Their luggage "filled the trunk" and was "piled high" in the back seat. Perhaps the young women enjoyed their moment of quasi-celebrity as much as the tourist enjoyed watching them.

This image possesses an aura of luxury, with cool hues suggesting an oasis in Miami's tropical heat. The room's spaciousness invites the eye and mind to linger, perhaps to meditate on the history of flight since Leonardo da Vinci's proposed flying machine is visible in the mural above the winged clock. The distributor who ordered this card as part of a large general stock of Miami views expected it to be "our best seller this winter," with sales of 100,000 or more. There was a definite market for images of urbane modernity among those who vicariously experienced its most luxurious elements.

M-232   BIDDING "BON VOYAGE" FROM THE CAUSEWAY, MIAMI, FLA.

PHOTO BY G. W. ROMER

1933

3A-H613

"Bidding 'Bon Voyage' from the Causeway, Miami, Fla."

Teich 3A-H613, 1933

THIS IMAGE OF MODERN TRANSPORTATION ON THE CAUSEWAY between Miami and the barrier island of Miami Beach has an apocalyptic quality. Anyone ignorant of local geography would have had difficulty imagining what might attract such heavy traffic—or why a crowded highway would run along a narrow spit of land going nowhere. The cars are black and boxy, from the Model T era, and so crammed together as to suggest the anonymity of a crowd. A few obscure palm trees do not dispel an industrial mood reinforced by a railway line running up the median (in reality streetcar tracks). An ocean liner steams away, its smoke merging with a purplish-black cloud and spreading pollution in a sky whose saturated colors represent an extreme for linen sunsets. Although the caption indicates that people in cars have gathered to watch the departing liner, the image also seems to suggest the motorists are fleeing a disaster that the boat passengers are effortlessly putting behind them. Floating over the scene is a Goodyear blimp, carrying its few passengers clear of whatever might threaten below.

The card differs markedly from the source photo by G. W. Romer, a local photographer. The original appears even more industrial than the card, with utility poles strung along the track. In the far distance of the source photo is the Goodyear blimp that made sightseeing flights from the western end of the causeway. That tiny object was removed by a Teich artist and replaced by a larger view of a blimp seen from the side. As for the ship, the *Arandora Star*, it was a British luxury liner that made cruises to Florida and the Caribbean. Thus all the details of the card, even the blimp, conform to what Miami tourists might have encountered. The postcard does portray Miami's coastal environment and the ease of modern transportation. However, the motorists are physically divorced from that expansive environment on a dark, gloomy highway, confined to their cars and condemned to traffic. A hint of doubt runs through some of the representations of the city and modernity in linen postcards, to which our attention now turns.[110]

5

Cityscapes in Linen Postcards
IMAGES OF MODERNITY

NATURAL AND RURAL LANDSCAPES MAY HAVE predominated in the lyrics of Woody Guthrie's song "This Land Is Your Land," but the American scene of linen postcards also encompassed modernization during an era widely referred to as "the machine age." Guthrie's "ribbon of highway" was often newly constructed, running over dramatically engineered bridges, looping across hydroelectric dams, skirting the glare of steel mills, and offering panoramic views of expanding cities and their skyscrapers. A journalist who interviewed Curt Teich for *American Business* in 1938 reported that in linen cards "the wonders of nature vie with tall city buildings for popularity."[1] Just as views of wilderness and natural wonders drew on traditional conventions of landscape representation, views of cities and towns relied on representational strategies that had developed in tandem with modern life over the previous hundred years.

The photographer Berenice Abbott returned to the United States in 1929 after an absence of eight years. Living in Paris to escape what she regarded as America's vulgar materialism, she had earned a reputation for portraits of such modernists as Jean Cocteau and James Joyce. Although intending only a brief visit to New York, Abbott

FIG. 5.1. Berenice Abbott, *Department of Docks and Police Station, Pier A, North River, Manhattan; May 5, 1936*

became "mad with joy" when she encountered "new things that had cropped up in eight years."[2] Overwhelmed by the city's transformation as skyscrapers replaced low commercial buildings, the thirty-year-old photographer decided to stay in New York and document the changes. Eventually she received support for the work from the Federal Art Project, a branch of the WPA. The photographs she made under government auspices beginning in 1935 yielded an exhibition at the Museum of the City of New York in 1937 and a book two years later, both entitled *Changing New York*. Many of Abbott's images expressively juxtaposed new bridges and skyscrapers with gritty warehouses, crumbling row houses, and street scenes little changed from the previous century. However, a few of her photos isolated and focused on such icons of modernity as Rockefeller Center, which was the city's most popular postcard subject.[3]

Although Abbott's relatively few such images differ little from picture postcard views of New York, she expressed disdain for popular imagery, insisting her photos captured "a reality superior to guidebook wisdom" and were "far more profound than the postcard view of the Empire State Building." As she saw it, postcard images lacked "the contrasts, the paradoxes, the anomalies" that would provide "vital and interesting material for future historians." Even so, the third photo in her book *Changing New York* foregrounds a souvenir stand overflowing with postcards (fig. 5.1).[4] Located just outside Pier A, near the tip of Manhattan, where celebrity passengers arrived by police launch from incoming ocean liners, the stand offered dozens of idealized views of the city, many of them recognizable in the 1936 photo as specific linen postcards. On the right side of the photo, a man contributes to Abbott's clever commentary on representation by taking a snapshot of the terminal building. Despite her disdain for postcards, this opening to *Changing New York* acknowledges their power. The image functions as the book's metaphorical arrivals terminal by presenting the rack of cards as a self-limiting microcosm her photos are about to challenge, complicate, and expand. The postcards she documented here portray a streamlined perfection without the grit, decay, and energy of the real city, the one that visitors entered through Pier A, the one Abbott strived to capture with her camera.

Viewing the Nineteenth-Century City

Some of the earliest nineteenth-century representations of American cities paralleled those by which the nation made visual sense of natural landscapes. Unlike European cities or those of the East Coast, which had developed over centuries and seemed to possess an organic integrity, American cities of the Midwest and West began as haphazard affairs hastily thrown up, expanding in a process of creative destruction, with even relatively permanent structures like city halls, courthouses, and churches lasting no more than a decade or so before being replaced by new construction. Chicago, for example, developed in sixty years from a frontier outpost into a sprawling city, the center of midwestern trade and manufacturing, whose leaders had envisioned its utopian future in the white neoclassical structures of the World's Columbian Exposition in 1893.[5] Nineteenth-century boosters of other new settlements did not hesitate to misrepresent them as bustling metropolises, hives of industry where any ambitious migrant could grasp material fortune. From the 1820s to the end of the nineteenth century, printers produced so-called bird's-eye views of virtually every American city, town, and hamlet, some 2,400 places altogether. A typical bird's-eye view, usually in color after about 1850, was a lithograph based on a meticulous imaginary drawing encompassing an entire locality rendered in perspective from an impossibly high point of view (fig. 5.2). Such a print showed local geographical features in detail, such as streets in the standard grid pattern and individually recognizable buildings, all conveyed in an illusion of three-dimensionality with the precision of a mapmaker. Although bird's-eye views did

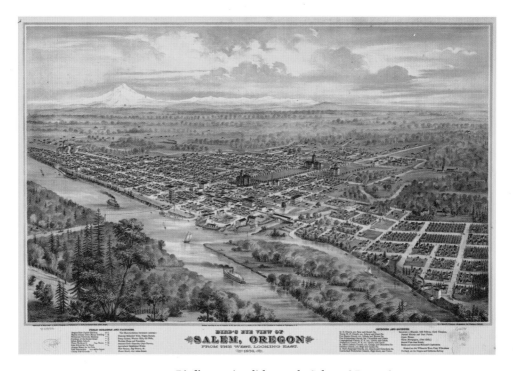

FIG. 5.2. Bird's-eye view lithograph, Salem, OR, 1876

not follow picturesque landscape conventions, they typically embedded a city or town in a pristine natural realm defined by ocean, lake, river, or mountains.[6]

As happened with natural landscapes, the introduction of photography substantially transformed and popularized urban views. From the very beginning photography was used to encompass a city as a whole, to unite its diverse array of often conflicting bits and pieces, much as the collection of postcards at Pier A later offered a vision of unity and uniformity.[7] Around 1850 daguerreotypists began imitating the effects of bird's-eye city views by aiming their cameras from upper-story windows, looking over rooftops or down a street. Other daguerreotypists recorded panoramas of such cities as Cincinnati and San Francisco by exposing multiple plates, one after the other, arranged to yield a continuous picture that could reach six feet in length. These multi-plate panoramas, which were intended to promote a sense of unity, even grandeur, also inadvertently revealed the ramshackle quality of much urban construction. While an artist could idealize a city by altering details in a bird's-eye lithograph, a daguerreotypist had no choice but to record what was in front of the camera. Because a panorama presented an extended horizontal continuum without a break, it often revealed less than perfect details. However, framing devices at each end—a harbor, a ring of background hills, thick vegetation—could circumscribe a city, no matter how provisional or chaotic, within a picturesque framework.

Eventually such panoramic images gave way to an approach the historian Peter Bacon Hales refers to as "grand-style urban photography," which came to prominence during the Gilded Age of the late nineteenth century as upper- and middle-class Americans sought to invest rapidly growing, socially chaotic, perpetually unfinished cities with a veneer of European high culture.[8] The emphasis shifted to views of individual sites presumed to represent civilized progress and civic pride: courthouses, city halls, boulevards, central squares, memorials, churches, libraries, museums, railway stations, hotels, parks, and promenades. At the same time, new photographic processes yielded multiple prints from one negative, as opposed to a daguerreotype's single copper plate. Reproducibility became economically even more feasible after development of mechanical techniques for transferring photographic images to printing plates, such as collotype, photogravure, and halftone. The sense of a coherent city became even more compelling when grand-style photographers began publishing collections of their photos in albums or books, at first by tipping individual prints into a volume that was otherwise typeset and printed, but later by mechanically printing images directly onto the pages. The first book to portray a single city through graphic images was G. R. Fardon's *San Francisco Album* (1856), whose subtitle promised "photographs of the most beautiful views and public buildings." In 1894, when S. B. Frank compiled the *Chicago Art Portfolio* from prints acquired from anonymous photographers and converted to inexpensive halftones, there were enough such books to constitute a genre. By then, many of the books' urban images were also widely disseminated for mass consumption as stereograph cards. Within a few years, postcards completed the process of democratization.

Rather than enclosing and presenting everything, whether orderly or chaotic, as the panorama had done, grand-style urban photography focused on desirable features and excluded everything else. Typical images, which were taken from the vantage point of an upper story, either singled out a prominent building viewed at an angle or encompassed an imposing street along a commanding diagonal similar to that of picturesque landscapes. Often a photographer combined both approaches by anchoring a grand building in the context of its surroundings, with its preeminent position creating a hierarchy that organized an otherwise often chaotic urban scene. The packaging of albums, individual prints, and stereograph cards offered, in Hales's suggestive phrase, a protective "*cordon sanitaire*" that excluded visual signs of poverty, class, race, and social conflict.[9] Like perspectives from scenic overlooks in the West, such images gave viewers a feeling of mastery. No matter how chaotic their actual experience of the modern city, its photographic representation left them feeling in control, even smugly comfortable, as observers of a scene whose permanence as an image flattered their faith in slow, inexorable progress.

The end of the nineteenth century witnessed a new way of viewing the city. About 1890 the first so-called skyscrapers, vertically oriented buildings of ten stories or more, began materially and perceptually transforming the modern city. Steel framing, electric elevators, and the telephone enabled architects to build upward, creating new spaces in crowded city centers to house office workers required by expanding companies. New York, Chicago, and other major cities kept rising higher as each year brought greater numbers of taller skyscrapers. Journalists, artists, photographers, and the general public became aware of the "skyline," a word that formerly referred to the horizon line where earth and sky meet but that had come to indicate the dramatic outline of a city's vertical buildings, irregularly massed, which from a distance offered a new way of encompassing a city's totality.

As opposed to the bird's-eye view, which possessed elements of abstraction and precision, the skyline appealed to emotion and evoked a romantic response. Early reactions to the city's new form embedded it in older landscape traditions. In 1892 a journalist proclaimed the skyline "seen at night by a boat on the water" as "the most picturesque of all sights that New York offers." Twenty years later the illustrator Joseph Pennell described "the towering splendor of New York" as "a composition . . . finer than Claude ever imagined or Turner ever dreamed." To comprehend the newly transformed city, observers often referred to skyscrapers as mountains or cliffs and to the streets they overshadowed as canyons, thereby incorporating unprecedented urban reality into terms suggested by the West's natural landscapes. Even Montgomery Schuyler, the nation's leading architecture critic, admitted in 1897 that "while the architectural excellence of the skyline must be sought in the parts, and not in the unattainable whole, it is in the aggregation that the immense impressiveness lies."[10] Although a picturesque aesthetic thus dominated the tradition of representation on which the creators of urban views for linen postcards depended, by the 1930s that aesthetic had also assumed a technological dimension.

Viewing the Machine-Age City

Teich and other postcard publishers had a century of examples to follow when creating bird's-eye and skyline views of cities, and when promoting prominent civic and commercial monuments through high-angle street views. However, the linen postcard appeared in 1931, during the machine age, an era when Americans self-consciously came to terms with modernity in the fine arts and in commercial mass media. Although the concept of the skyscraper was familiar by 1890, it was not until the 1930s that there were buildings towering high enough above the streets, more than a thousand feet, to retain their impressiveness throughout the twentieth century. A score of new skyscrapers were completed during the late 1920s, most of them clad and ornamented in a partly streamlined, vaguely cubist, wholly stylized Art Deco mode that proclaimed their modernity. Although the stock market crash of 1929 halted most private construction, New York City continued rising during the 1930s, with the Chrysler Building completed in 1930 and the Empire State Building in 1931. The complex of buildings comprising Rockefeller Center was under construction throughout the decade. These unprecedented structures formed an impressive assemblage in mid-Manhattan and stimulated new ways of perceiving urban experience.

One of the most influential visions of the modern skyscraper city came from Hugh Ferriss, an architectural renderer in demand among New York developers and architects for his moody, expressionist presentation drawings. In 1929 Ferriss published *The Metropolis of Tomorrow*, a book illustrated with a selection of his commissioned renderings of actual buildings and with fantastic visualizations of urban trends carried to extremes. His monotone charcoal work emphasized dark crystalline structures emerging from a hazy dusk (fig. 5.3). Such visual tropes as the picturesque massing of buildings and the reduction of human figures to insignificant markers of scale, both employed by Ferriss, were essential to linen city views.

However, historians of machine-age urbanism have deemphasized the gloom of Ferriss's widely published renderings, focusing instead on electric light's transformation of the night city into a shimmering vision powerful enough to inspire awe. David Nye, for example, has described a shift in perceptions of the sublime from the natural to the technological realm. Formally defined by the philosopher Edmund Burke in 1757 as both a psychological state and an aesthetic category, the sublime encompassed the immensity and incomprehensibility of such natural phenomena as precipices, waterfalls, and volcanic eruptions. In Nye's view, large engineering works also projected sublimity during the nineteenth and twentieth centuries. He has proposed the geometrical sublime as a category encompassing skyscrapers, bridges, and other artificial structures large enough to "dominate nature through elegant design and sheer bulk." After nightfall, however, the machine-age city entered the realm of the electrical sublime as artificial illumination "dematerialized" and "glamorized" the city, "giving it a semi-abstract cubist skyline that contrasted with its often drab daily appearance."[11]

Similar meditations on artificial light mark a series of recent cultural histories of twentieth-century urban perception. Dietrich Neumann, an architectural historian, focuses in *Architecture of the Night* (2002) on how architects and lighting designers used colored spotlights to dramatize the geometric setback shapes of Art Deco skyscrapers. Covering a full range of representations of New

FIG. 5.3. Hugh Ferriss, *Radiator Building,*
ca. 1925

FIG. 5.4. Georgia O'Keeffe, *New York, Night,*
1928-1929

York in modern literature, art, and photography, William Chapman Sharpe's
New York Nocturne (2008) characterizes the electrified "skyscraper city" as "a
fantasyland of desire." John A. Jakle, the author of *City Lights* (2001), suggests
that most postcard views of skyscrapers presented their subjects as phallic and
thus gendered them as male. Sharpe, on the other hand, genders the overall city
of this period as female, a conclusion he reaches partly through interpretations
of two striking portrayals of urban illumination by female artists—significant
enough to be summarized and expanded upon here.[12]

Both Georgia O'Keeffe and Berenice Abbott worked from high points of view, looking across or down into an illuminated city. O'Keeffe's oil painting *New York, Night* (1928–1929) (fig. 5.4) almost ignores a phallic skyscraper directly opposite the viewer, whose vantage point is a window in O'Keeffe's apartment in the Shelton Hotel. The tower rises sturdily with a steep penthouse roof bathed in a lurid red glow that actually suggests male preening rather than confident mastery. While the tower is mostly dark, other buildings are punctured by tiny red and yellow rectangles of illuminated windows. Equally if not more provocative than the tower in creating an erotically charged darkness is the street, flowing far below in a diagonal running sharply from the lower left to the upper right of the narrow vertical painting. This metaphorical vagina, glowing molten red from the lights of distant automobiles and neon signs, transforms the city into a warm, organic female body in vibrant opposition to Ferriss's chilling inorganic towers. Sharpe describes *New York, Night* as "domesticating the Upper East Side by enveloping it in a warm, ember-toned darkness."[13] O'Keeffe's city does come across as both erotic and fertile, but her interpretation of urban night seems ultimately more seductively erotic than domesticating.

Abbott's photograph *New York at Night* (1934) embodies a similarly spectacular free-floating urban desire (fig. 5.5). Looking down at a forty-five-degree angle from the Empire State Building, Abbott captured a vertical image of about twenty office towers of various sizes and shapes. Her camera points so fully downward that none of the sky is visible. Seen from a distance, outlines of buildings are revealed only by electric lights shimmering, pulsing, and exploding from myriad windows, and by zigzag silhouettes of towers of other buildings cutting in front of illuminated walls. Abbott's downward gaze inverts the usual phallic view of assemblages of urban buildings. For her as for O'Keeffe, the city becomes a female body—warm, glowing, inviting, if also a bit overwhelming. Abbott's view suggests an organic essence underlying the city's artificial constructs. In both works Sharpe finds "the street as a strong diagonal element that unsettles the city's rectilinear grid," an effect reinforced in Abbott's photo by her decision to shoot across or against the city's street grid, thereby turning rational abstraction into a decorative diamond pattern. In both cases Sharpe locates the aesthetically compelling quality of the image in "the power of the downward female gaze."[14]

At this point one is reminded of the ruggedly dressed but stylish young woman in Teich's postcard from 1937, gazing from a scenic overlook down into the mountain-bordered basin of the San Bernardino Valley (see p. 122), and of the art historian Angela Miller's interpretation of works such as *Kauterskill Clove*, a Luminist painting by Sanford Gifford from 1862 that portrays a wooded hollow in the Catskill Mountains. Gifford's image offers a view into "a great light-filled spatial chamber" as the sun's light and heat "hollow out a great

FIG. 5.5. Berenice Abbott, *New York at Night*, 1934

well at the center of the composition . . . a cavity in place of a mountain." For Miller "this womblike space seems fully animate, its generative force touched into life by the warmth and light of the sun."[15] Abbott's fantasia of urban night parallels Gifford's painting, gendering the city as female in opposition to the obvious trope of phallic skyscrapers. A similar downward gaze sometimes appeared in images by commercial architectural photographers, such as Samuel H. Gottscho's *Night View, North, from RCA Building* (1933), which is a view down from the Rockefeller Center toward converging diagonals of brilliantly lit streets bordering Central Park.[16]

As already noted, Sharpe views this shift in gendered representations of the city from male to female as a form of domestication. By that he means that the city has escaped the artificial male disciplines of the grid and perspective. Instead it is infused with unruly organic vitality. In another sense, however, to domesticate a landscape, whether natural or artificial, rural or urban, means exactly the opposite—that is, to bring it under control, more as a wife or mother traditionally ordering her household, and not as a seductive woman of the night. However, the female sexuality implied in O'Keeffe's *New York, Night* and Abbott's *New York at Night* subverts traditional domestication—that of the bird's-eye, high-angle, and skyline perspectives, by which the modern city's energy was often contained, limited, and directed.

Postcards served to domesticate the landscapes they represented, making them comprehensible and compassable, whether by conforming images to genre conventions or by miniaturizing them to pocket size. Domestication in that sense was one of the postcard's primary cultural functions. The fact that postcards were more often bought and sent by women than by men, or at least more often saved for posterity by women, suggests a genre of representation more attractive to women, one whose very images were somehow domesticated and also actively working as a domesticating force within the culture.[17] On the other hand, to spin this thought in a different direction, the concept of the domestic also suggests the active presence of individual human beings, real people, imperfect by definition, for whom the impersonal city forms a backdrop against which to act out personal desires, domestic and otherwise, sometimes subversive—desires that often do not conform to the commanding visions of urban order. At the height of the machine age, with the electrical sublime casting a shimmery glow over skyscrapers and streets, an element of doubt entered the picture. However bright a city's illumination, its edges faded out into vague shadows and occasionally complete darkness.

Imagining the City Noir

All the way back to nineteenth-century lithographic bird's-eye views, individual people played a relatively minor role in most representations of the city. Grand-style photography focused on monumental buildings, wide boulevards, and spacious parks—all with a view toward channeling the behavior of individual citizens, who appeared as insignificant strolling figures. As for representations of the machine-age city, whether emphasizing breathtaking skyscrapers, dynamic asymmetrical skylines, or awe-inspiring illumination, most reduced individual people to tiny ciphers measuring the city's immense scale—when human figures could be discerned at all. However, a new form of urban representation turned the gaze toward crowded mean streets and even meaner back rooms that a century of urban views had aimed to hide and eventually, by means of reform, to expunge. The concept of noir, in Hales's phrasing, encompassed "the murderous and the voyeuristic, combining urban vice and sin, corruption and cruelty with the voyeur's excited gaze."[18] That gaze focused directly on individual people, many of whose relationships, even manipulative or violent ones, involved the domestic realm, often literally but sometimes in a metaphoric sense, as with gangland "families." Either way, the city, earlier presented as mostly empty, became a stage or film set, awaiting the arrival of actors to make it complete.

The most shocking noir images revealed dissonant scenes that had been covered up, contained, or shunted to the margins, such as sleeping New York slum dwellers exposed in dark, dirty, overcrowded rooms by the flare of the photographer Jacob Riis's flash powder in 1890, their images provoking calls for urban reform that grand-style images had failed to bring about. Forty-five years later, beginning in the 1930s, the tabloid photographer Weegee used the glare of flashbulbs and a Speed Graphic press camera to capture slumped bodies of murder victims. These had been ordinary people, often overweight or aging, viewed now with hair and clothing in disarray, lying in their own blood.[19] In depicting such figures, presented as both anonymous and all too specific, urban photography moved beyond the grand tradition's *cordon sanitaire* and beyond the limit of what the impersonal postcard genre could portray. The new style's visceral immediacy, its in-your-face portrayal of imperfect humanity, could never have a direct analog in mass-produced commercial postcards, with their celebratory intent.

Even so, paradoxically, through the very absence of people, linen postcards participated in the expressive visual representation of a noir sensibility by providing empty sets onto which viewers could project personal desires, expectations, fears, even narratives. It had long been common for small businesses to commission photos of the interiors of their premises. In a typical such view, proprietor and employees were lined up in the foreground or stationed behind sales counters. Such images now inform social historians about consumption habits, interior design, advertising graphics, and clothing styles. But when translated to linen postcards, similar images of business interiors such as those of restaurants, nightclubs, hotel lobbies, and retail shops usually remained devoid of people (fig. 5.6). Interiors were empty, as they rarely were in real life, but were otherwise precise in every colorized detail thanks to samples of paint, wallpaper, and upholstery sent to the Teich art department in Chicago. Such interior images inadvertently convey a sense of the uncanny. A viewer is present during a moment of stopped time, just as someone is about to enter the frame or something is about to happen. It is the emptiness, as well as the sense that any fear or fantasy might be projected onto an incomplete scene, that gives these noir postcards psychological or cultural power.

Such reactions are similar to those evoked by many of Edward Hopper's paintings. Whether in the iconic *Nighthawks* (1942), which casts an electric glare over the denizens of an all-night diner, or in such works as *Office at Night* (1940) and *Hotel Lobby* (1943) (fig. 5.7), Hopper expressed a noir sensibility by placing the nondescript figures of alienated city dwellers into interiors not

Fig. 5.6. "View of Lobby, San Carlos Hotel, Pensacola, Fla.," Teich 2A-H22, 1932

Fig. 5.7. Edward Hopper, *Hotel Lobby*, 1943

so different from those of Teich's linen postcards. However, Hopper frequently introduced a sense of motion, portraying passengers on an elevated train, people looking from furnished rooms onto the tracks, or a momentary voyeuristic glimpse into an apartment window as if the viewer were traveling past by train.

The urban historian Christine Boyer has summed up rapid transportation's psychological impact by describing how it "erase[d] the traditional sense of pictorial enclosure as the cityscape was transformed into a series of fleeting impressions and momentary encounters." Against this "kaleidoscopic arrangement of images and forms," the grand urban narratives of late nineteenth-century photography had struggled unsuccessfully to contain and order the city.[20] Even the *flâneur*, the modern pedestrian enshrined in art, literature, and cultural theory, a neutral, alienated observer who abandoned the elevated train's flickering perspectives to wander on foot, still experienced such radical shifts in point of view as to lose a sense of overarching continuity in space or time. Inhabitants of the noir city existed in a state of perpetual circulation that photographs could capture and preserve, that movies could represent dynamically, but that individual postcards mostly failed even to suggest. On the other hand, a group of postcard images such as those documented by Berenice Abbott on Pier A could just as easily suggest random juxtaposition as urban order. It all depended on one's perspective.

Revisiting the Unique and the Generic

Every small city boasted a skyscraper confirming its participation in machine-age modernity. There were many such skyscrapers, the Industrial Trust Tower in Providence, Rhode Island, for example, and the Lincoln Tower in Fort Wayne, Indiana, both of them the tallest buildings in their states when completed in 1927 and 1930. And yet, this discussion of genres of urban representation has relied mostly on New York. Most images of smaller cities and towns, including those on linen postcards, portrayed scenes and assumed perspectives similar to those of major cities. Most American cities and towns of whatever size shared similar characteristics—the grid pattern, a main business street, the presence of such monuments as city hall, courthouse, library, churches, and parks for orderly relaxation and release. Recalling his travels in the American West, the British novelist J. B. Priestley in 1937 observed that "every village and tiny town" looks "like a bit of a city that has just detached itself." With "the drug stores, the eating-houses, the hotels, all blazing with colored lights," a foreign visitor could easily conclude, even "a hundred miles from anywhere," that someone "had contrived to pick out a block from Sunset Boulevard, Los Angeles, and drop it down there."[21] Boomtowns had long strived to present themselves as settled, civilized communities by emulating institutions, architectural styles, and forms of representation of larger cities. What signified urbanity in New York, Chicago, or Philadelphia also did so in Seattle or Kalamazoo. Even a small town, however provincial, replicated on a smaller scale much that existed in larger cities. An objective cataloging of a small city's streets and physical structures would have paralleled that of a major city.

Just as nineteenth-century urban views shaped the actual appearance of subsequent settlements, they also influenced styles of graphic representation that in turn shaped perceptions of smaller, less significant locales. When Teich devised the linen postcard in 1931, the company could have prepared a standard set of views, differing only in local details, for any town or city. Traveling sales agents photographed each town through the same generic blinders. Artists in Chicago applied the same airbrushing and atmospheric effects to places that might have appeared quite different to travelers passing through. This generic quality has engaged Jay Ruby, a visual anthropologist who in 1988 was the first scholar to address the social impact of mass-produced postcards. After examining cards portraying rural Juniata County in south-central Pennsylvania, Ruby concluded that when "agents of large publishing firms . . . produced a postcard of a rural county seat, the tiny hamlet was symbolically transformed into a miniature version of a 'city'—that is, a place with banks, schools, and other important public buildings; a place where streets divided and defined order; a place of commercial accomplishment; where houses were arranged in neat, orderly fashion." No matter the size or population, a series of view cards "reassured communities of membership in a larger world by replicating the same subject matter"—in other words, by transforming them into "Everywhere, USA."[22] Those images, as they became ever more generic in moving from the specific details of real photo cards to the formulaic effects of linen cards, presumably influenced how local residents conceived their own towns, and how they hoped to see them transformed in actuality.

That is the argument of Alison Isenberg, a cultural historian who has interpreted mass-produced postcards as supporting the goals of two successive groups of urban reformers who tried with somewhat different motives to remake the American downtown business district. Both groups hoped to domesticate, channel, and control public behavior of local citizens—much as grand-style photography had sought to domesticate large cities. During the 1910s and '20s, progressive women's groups ("municipal housekeepers," as Isenberg refers to them) directed beautification campaigns that sought to extend the moral influence of the middle-class home over public life by paving streets, banishing vice through street lighting, removing immigrant street vendors, and excluding working-class loiterers prone to spitting. By the late 1920s, however, local businessmen in chambers of commerce had taken over this movement, casting it not as a moral issue but as an attempt to increase revenue flow by creating "a dignified and simplified retail corridor" that would appeal to middle-class white shoppers.[23]

Referring to Teich job files as evidence, Isenberg maintains that local revitalization plans prepared by city-planning consultants directly influenced main street postcard views, locally commissioned, which in turn provided business leaders with ammunition for their campaigns. The artists in Chicago "labored in the field of municipal housekeeping" as they "touched up photographs to repair broken-down sidewalks, to remove offending utility poles or signs, and to pave streets—improving the streets' physical realities." In 1913 a planner hired by Raleigh, North Carolina, even noted approvingly that color lithographic postcards of the city's business street "show it with wires and poles removed," an improvement he in turn recommended to city fathers. The result, according to Isenberg, in postcards if not always in reality, was "an unobstructed, sweeping corridor view" or "a clear commercial vista in which the eye could travel, like a consumer, uninterrupted by the bodies of other shoppers and by the constant bother of hawkers and 'cheap' sidewalk sales tactics." Such representations might be regarded as a kind of visual streamlining, a reducing of unique American main streets to a single generic form in the service of ideology.[24]

Not everyone approved of this development. When Walker Evans complained in 1948 of the "aesthetic slump" into which postcards had fallen, he was referring in general to linens and in particular to their portrayal of downtowns. The photographer admired what he regarded as the verisimilitude of pre-linen images. His remarks in the article he published in *Fortune* magazine in 1948 expressed nostalgia both for a lost American scene and for the defunct medium he believed had accurately captured it. Among eighteen pre-linen cards reproduced in full color in the article (all published before 1920), five street scenes feature prominent utility poles, some tilted at alarming angles, and one shows electric wires cutting directly across the image. These cards reveal no evidence of any effort to idealize the places they portray and indeed little or no retouching. Referring to one image, Evans enthused, "These, precisely, are the downtown telegraph poles fretting the sky, looped and threaded from High Street to the depot and back again." (For a similar image, see fig. 2.11.) Evans admired the "purity" and "fidelity" of these "humble" images, which he regarded as "honest beyond words," comprising "some of the truest visual records ever made" and conveying a "feeling for actual appearance of street, of lived architecture."[25]

Following Evans, one could make a case that pre-linen lithographic cards, despite their colorizing, reinforced the realism that real photo cards had already established in representations of towns and cities. A similar truth-telling motive, though of an entirely different order of magnitude, later inspired the documentary photographers of the Farm Security Administration. A shooting script from around 1940, by which point the FSA was celebrating American life rather than exposing social problems, prompted photographers to record "fire hydrants, traffic signs, hitching posts[,] . . . watering troughs, . . . wagons and horses, . . . men loafing and talking[,] . . . tired women & children waiting to go home," and other specific details of everyday life.[26] Although seeking a common American story, FSA photography was promoting the same uniqueness of place for which Evans later expressed nostalgia.

By then, Teich and other linen postcard publishers were producing a widely distributed generic vision of small cities and towns. Despite their bold colors and forms, these images were visually and conceptually reduced, brought under control, universalized, and idealized. Everything was modern and up to date. Unlike the pre-linen cards that Evans admired, linen views erased the remnants of premodern life that FSA photographers were instructed to document. Linens also erased any aspects of modernity—utility poles, power lines, water tanks, delivery trucks, and beat-up Model T cars—that would otherwise have detracted from an impression of streamlined efficiency. Perhaps most significantly, linen cards also encapsulated in generic form most of the modes of urban representation evolved over the previous hundred years.

Typical approaches ranged from the bird's-eye view, now offered as a panorama from an airplane, to the abstract distancing offered by a high-angle shot from a skyscraper. Broad vistas defined by rows of parked cars extended diagonally to distant vanishing points. Urban landmarks, ranging from railway stations to hotels, were often abstracted against a neutral backdrop, with other buildings either removed entirely or rendered in a hazy manner. Street surfaces, in reality composed of variably surfaced asphalt or concrete, seemed poured of a smooth artificial substance that banished any reminder of uneven brick or filthy mud. Pedestrians, included for scale, dotted the sidewalks of some linen views. Even so, automobiles constituted the major medium of circulation, often so dominant as to forecast the exclusion of pedestrians from future cityscapes. The automobile also provided some linen cards with a new urban perspective— the streetscape viewed from a vehicle cruising through traffic.

In all these ways, the old and the new, the linen postcard standardized and mass-produced an idealized, perceptually streamlined view of the American urban present and future. Not as realistic as a photo or a pre-linen lithograph, the urban vision of the linen postcard was based on a plausibility that made its limited focus acceptable, attractive, and even desirable. Its very status as a mechanized, mass-produced, and fundamentally modern visual medium enhanced its cultural influence. Even in urban views whose locally unique details were obvious, the comfort of familiar generic perspectives, frames, and forms, repeated over and over again, conveyed a power that might be defined as cultural verisimilitude.

Portfolio 11

CITYSCAPES

THE CITYSCAPES OF THIS PORTFOLIO LEND themselves to a more obvious arrangement than the landscapes of the first portfolio. As before, pairs of images and texts lead by accumulation and association, rather than by linear narrative or logical argument, to a multidimensional set of observations on linen postcards as carriers of cultural meaning. The most obvious conclusion to be drawn from an array of cityscapes on linen postcards is that inhabitants of cities and towns of all sizes desired to be viewed as having the same up-to-the-moment modernity as New York, Chicago, or Los Angeles. Unlike landscape views, which tended to follow a common picturesque model, with each site's uniqueness defined by differing geological features and vegetation, cityscapes came in a variety of distinctive types. All urban locations, regardless of size, from major cities to small towns, could claim to possess similar physical features. There was not much formal difference between representations of a skyscraper in New York and a much smaller one in Hot Springs, Arkansas, or between views of a major commercial street in Los Angeles and the single shopping street of Norfolk, Virginia. While images within a single type, regardless of scale, were often formally similar, cityscapes came in a greater array of types than landscapes did. To organize these types, I begin outside or above the city, looking at it from a distance, and then move past the tall shafts of skyscrapers to major streets and boulevards, eventually focusing on key landmarks and institutions of government, commerce, and culture.

Just as a revolving rack of colorful linen postcards promised a complete world in miniature, so too did a bird's-eye view or skyline card selected from that same rack. Images in the opening section of this portfolio, "Overviews," present views of cities seen from across an expanse of water, from above, from upper windows of commercial buildings, and from the top of the world's tallest building. Although the city often appeared as an artificial construct, other images that embedded the city within the organic realm of nature possibly alleviated anxiety about modern life's change and discontinuity. As primary symbols of modernity, the monoliths of this portfolio's second section, "Skyscrapers," offered a more aggressive reassurance. While some urban overviews, especially those taken from great distances, suggested harmonious cooperation, linen images of skyscrapers celebrated the competitiveness of American business before the 1929 stock market crash. Such images portrayed isolated shafts rising from a sea of lower buildings or from out of nothing. Night views only further emphasized a sense of abstraction by obscuring a skyscraper's Art Deco detailing, which might otherwise have softened its stark impact.

As the postcards in the section "Main Streets" suggest, not all linen cityscapes possessed the abstraction of some skyscraper images. No matter the size of a city or town, views of its commercial streets were intended to convey an impression of energetic activity, but images from smaller towns inadvertently often suggested the opposite. Even in those cases, however, the main street served as a spine, both a conduit of traffic and a means of visual access to the city's individual attractions and services. While some views of main streets echoed nineteenth-century urban photos in being taken from the upper window of an adjacent building, many were taken from the sidewalk. A few dynamically positioned an observer as if looking through a car windshield into the flow of traffic. For the most part, however, postcards presented in the next section, "Landmarks," adopted the static perspective of grand-style urban photography. Three-quarter views emphasized the imposing stature of courthouses, post offices, museums, libraries, churches, and other public buildings. Although each fountain or memorial statue differed in minor ways from those of other cities, their similarly framed images suggested membership in a shared national culture of public uplift. By contrast, places of amusement and relaxation, presented in the next section, "Recreation," released people from everyday social constraints. Parks and beaches (the latter often fully urbanized) appeared in postcards as colorful places marked by a promiscuous mixing of all sorts of people.

To include a "World's Fairs" section in a portfolio of cityscapes is to accept the period's own understanding of an exposition as a material embodiment of utopian visions of the future city, an idea that had first emerged at the World's Columbian Exposition in Chicago in 1893. Most postcard views of the Chicago Century of Progress International Exposition forty years later presented a cityscape of futuristic architecture, banishing any hint of the organic or the natural. Even foreign-themed commercial attractions purporting to embody quaint traditional cultures actually succeeded more in emphasizing their designers' clever modern artifices. The general sense of artificiality climaxed with dozens of unrealistic, even fanciful, views of the New York World's Fair of 1939 printed before the structures they portrayed were even built so that the exposition could be promoted in advance with postcards.

The optimistic aura of wish fulfillment pervading the iconography of most linen view cards reached an apotheosis of sorts in images of urban hotels and restaurants, in images of interiors of hotel lobbies, dining rooms, and cocktail lounges. The final section, "Accommodations," documents the portrayal of these artificial stage sets for modern living but then concludes on a more sobering note with two images whose modest, unassuming features recall the uncertainties of the era's lived social realities.

50   Cuyahoga Valley, Industrial Center, and Main Avenue Bridge, Cleveland, Ohio

Overviews

(C)   Courtesy of Butler Aurphotos, Inc., Cleveland, Ohio   67973

121   LOWER MANHATTAN AS SEEN FROM GOVERNOR'S ISLAND, NEW YORK CITY

2A-H114

"LOWER MANHATTAN AS SEEN FROM GOVERNOR'S ISLAND, NEW YORK CITY"

TEICH 2A-H114, 1932

THE INEXORABLE RISE OF SKYSCRAPERS CREATED THE SKYLINE view, but it was enhanced in New York by the fact that the city is built on islands and peninsulas, whose shores and heights afford multiple opportunities for gazing across open water to dramatic assemblages of buildings. The city's dynamic energy and rhythm, encompassed in the 1920s by the phrase "the jazz age," appeared in the procession of discontinuous vistas perceived from a moving automobile. For a pedestrian, however, the skyline offered a distancing from the city, reducing barely controlled human and technological chaos to a picturesque composition inviting contemplation.

This 1932 skyline view embraces the whole "big apple," as the city has been known from about 1920 onward, a phrase suggesting juicy ripeness and nature's rich bounty. Although exhibiting a pleasing irregularity, the skyline forms nearly a bell curve with a right-of-center focal point established by the adjacent towers of the Bank of Manhattan Trust Building and the Irving Trust Company Building, both recent additions to the city at that time. The skyline diminishes to either side, is bookended by somewhat taller buildings, and then shades into green as if the city merges with the natural realm. The picturesque setting with its irregular tree branches and neatly trimmed hedges reinforces the trope of the city as a machine domesticated by a surrounding garden. The embossed linen texture contributes a sparkle to the water and to the pointillist black dots of the windows from which the buildings are visually constructed, distancing a viewer even more from gritty streets, advertising signs, and crowds of pedestrians.

The source photo for this card was taken from Governors Island, an army post inaccessible to civilians, so the view was available to tourists, ironically, only through postcards. Teich artists recycled it for another card in 1944, stripping away the foreground and using only the pyramid of buildings rising from the harbor. Without hedges and trees to provide depth, the city in that card seems a two-dimensional backdrop lacking substance. A bold caption superimposed over sky and water announces, "Just Arrived in New York / The Wonder City."[1]

84   MIDTOWN NEW YORK CITY "THE GREAT WHITE WAY"

AS SEEN FROM THE EMPIRE STATE BUILDING OBSERVATORY AT NIGHT, NEW YORK CITY   5A-H654

"Midtown New York City 'The Great White Way'
/ As Seen from the Empire State Building
Observatory at Night, New York City"

Teich 5A-H654, 1935

UNLIKE THE SKYLINE VIEW FROM GOVERNORS ISLAND, THIS night view does not present Manhattan from a contemplative distance but instead plunges the viewer into a roiling apocalypse. The image suggests Berenice Abbott's photo *New York at Night*, also a view from the Empire State Building (see fig. 5.5). Both face northward from just past Broadway's diagonal intersection with Sixth Avenue. A huge building rendered in blue gray near the center of the card also appears in the upper right of Abbott's photo, glowing more luminously than any others. The two images date from the same time, with Abbott exposing her negative on December 20, 1934, the shortest day of the year, in order to capture a night image during business hours with maximum illumination, and the postcard appearing in 1935. Anyone confronted by these two images would recognize similarities, but there are considerable differences. While Abbott's vertical image forces a viewer to look straight down, the postcard reassures by allowing a sweeping horizontal view that creates a distance from the maelstrom below. The card also includes a bit of the observation deck parapet in the lower left, grounding us, while Abbott's dizzying perspective affords no such respite.

Even so, Teich's view is unprecedented in avoiding traditional landscape and cityscape forms—as if the electrical sublime required new formal qualities. Lurid channels of orange yellow flow like lava through the streets, with small clouds in the upper right suggesting smoke from unseen conflagrations. The image relies heavily on the black plate, augmented by light and dark blues to add visual richness. Viewed from far away, the buildings seem solid, though they shimmer and glow. Examined closely, they resolve into hundreds of tiny rectangles, yellow on black or black on yellow, with each line delineated by a retouching artist, leaving a visual impression that intense heat has melted away the buildings' curtain walls. Only steel girders remain, glowing with an evanescence as compelling as Abbott's nocturne. Sending this card to a seven-year-old daughter in 1949, a couple reported that it "shows a lot of N.Y.'s tall buildings when they are lighted up at night—like hundreds of giant Christmas trees."[2]

SAN FRANCISCO NIGHT VIEW, BAY BRIDGE AND BATTLESHIP SEARCHLIGHTS AND LIGHTS OF OAKLAND, 13

BERKELEY, ALAMEDA IN DISTANCE

"SAN FRANCISCO NIGHT VIEW, BAY BRIDGE AND BATTLESHIP SEARCHLIGHTS AND LIGHTS OF OAKLAND, / BERKELEY, ALAMEDA IN DISTANCE"

TEICH 8A-H2813, 1938

THIS 1938 BIRD'S-EYE OF SAN FRANCISCO IS A TYPICAL URBAN night scene. The source photo was taken from Nob Hill, looking east down California and Pine Streets toward the San Francisco–Oakland Bay Bridge. The city lacked Manhattan's massed skyscrapers, and the image centers on the Russ Building from 1927. At 436 feet (one-third the height of the Empire State Building), it remained the city's tallest building until 1964. Unlike the chaotic view of mid-Manhattan in the previous card, this image is anchored to a detailed foreground and to the horizon line. Its light projects a warmth stemming from varied coloration and emanates a sense of control. A yellow glow predominates along the streets and rises partway up major buildings, suggesting floodlighting. Accents of blue gray (for marble and limestone) and dark red (for brick) color the sides of buildings whose outlines are more solidly delineated than mid-Manhattan's dematerializing structures.

Unlike most night scenes, this was not based on a daytime photo but on a night shot. Pitchford directed the art department, "Put in lights as per attached photo." Over the Russ Building he wrote, "Illuminate This Bldg," and the major structure to its far right bore the legend "Lighten this Bldg." On the bridge he specified a "yellow glow" for "Sodium lights" along the roadway, "white lights" along the cables, and red above each pillar. Other requests included scattered "neon signs" in the lower left for Chinatown. An arrow pointed to the San Francisco Ferry Terminal at the extreme left with an injunction, "This is important," apparently prompting an artist to spotlight the terminal's tower. Pitchford also requested "a few Neon signs down [California Street]," where seven red marks suggest theater marquees.

Such dots of color are lost in the general illumination. More striking are twenty-one searchlights rising from tiny lines indicating warships in the bay. These crisscrossing rays came not from the photo but from pencil lines Pitchford marked on the frisket. Their white lights contrast with the yellow glow and create a festive quality. The back caption asserts that "these radiant night shafts . . . accentuate the lights of Market Street"—which in fact is completely obscured by buildings along its diagonal path. This image, the product of an experienced designer, lacks the dizzying plunge of the previous card's view from the Empire State Building but is striking all the same, even with its conventional composition.

50 Cuyahoga Valley, Industrial Center, and Main Avenue Bridge, Cleveland, Ohio

(C) Courtesy of Butler Airphotos, Inc., Cleveland, Ohio

67-973

"CUYAHOGA VALLEY, INDUSTRIAL CENTER, AND MAIN AVENUE BRIDGE, CLEVELAND, OHIO"

TICHNOR 67973, N.D.

GEORGE INNESS, *THE LACKAWANNA VALLEY*, 1855

THE MOST STRIKING ASPECT OF THIS BIRD'S-EYE VIEW OF Cleveland's industrial district, across the Cuyahoga River from downtown, is the fact that the image is suffused with green. The tiny reproduction of Terminal Tower on the left, crowning what seems a small city center, fails to convey the structure's actual size. Completed in 1928, it remained the nation's tallest building outside New York until 1964. Despite the immense scale of the view, taken from a plane by Butler Airphotos, it has an almost pastoral quality, with the city itself appearing as a compact village. Even the railroad yard in the left foreground and the waste ground to the right, flanking the river as it flows toward the viewer and then into Lake Erie, almost suggest pastureland. The image emphasizes the meandering river, its organic form contrasting with but also complemented by the delicate tracery of the city's three major bridges, providing an industrial variation on the classic small-town white picket fence. A close look at the industrial land inside the river's two loops reveals warehouses, small factories, and tiny streets lined with worker houses, all carpeted in green and encompassed by bright blue water. Near the horizon smoke rises faintly from chimneys of indistinct steel mills and merges with the natural haze of distance.

There is a parallel to George Inness's painting from 1855, *The Lackawanna Valley* (see at lower left), which the cultural historian Leo Marx famously interpreted as employing picturesque landscape conventions to naturalize a steam locomotive meandering through a meadow outside a railway town with a roundhouse and plumes of machine-shop smoke merging with the horizon's haze.[3] Although the scale of Cleveland's industrial activity is much greater, nearly filling the image, there is still a sense in which everything harmonizes or coexists with a surrounding natural environment. Finally, it is important to note the view's artificiality. It seems tinkered with as much as any artist-rendered nineteenth-century bird's-eye view. Although the image is based on a photo, every detail for the black plate has been outlined and emphasized by Tichnor's artist. Only considerable manipulation was capable of transforming a black-and-white photo of this gritty panorama of modern industry into a pastoral idyll.

NEW VIADUCT AND SKYLINE, BALTIMORE, MD.   6A-H2213

"New Viaduct and Skyline, Baltimore, Md."

Teich 6A-H2213, 1936

WHILE SOME VIEW CARDS OF URBAN SCENES SITUATED THEIR subjects in natural surroundings, others emphasized the city as artificial construct. Beyond a few scattered clouds, this self-described skyline view of Baltimore contains no hint of nature, not even a tree. As opposed to scenes already considered, this image conveys a solid urban fabric. Buildings are well-defined blocks composed of strong fields of contrasting shades of red, brown, orange, green, and beige—arranged according to detailed color instructions. Several landmarks appear on the horizon, including the city's tallest structure, the Baltimore Trust Company Building from 1929. On the left, City Hall's neoclassical dome is superimposed over the ornate clock tower of the Maryland Casualty Company Building. For the most part, however, the image focuses on nondescript buildings whose strong details—piers, spandrels, dentition, window shades, parapets, chimneys, even billboards on a shop and a sign above the Sealcote Roofing Company—yield a dense composition. Together, tending up the hill to the right, they produce a vivid sense of reality and a simultaneous impression that everything is too clean and colorful to exist outside an idealized world.

However, the image is flawed by the visual inadequacy of its key feature— the "new viaduct" cutting across the lower right. Known as the Bath Street Viaduct when completed in 1936 and now called the Orleans Street Viaduct, the flyover extended less than half a mile westward from East Baltimore across a railroad yard. Perhaps seeking to portray the technological achievement and kinetic experience of the viaduct before its actual completion, an artist had collaged a photo of an elevated highway onto the corner of a photo of Baltimore's skyline. While the concrete piers seem realistic, the retouching artist gave the road a texture-less uniformity that jars with the formal richness and colorful textures of the scene it overlooks. The artist also replaced three wholly realistic automobiles in the small photo with five elongated toylike cars, identically styled and poorly detailed. Their two-dimensional flatness contrasts unfavorably with the cars parked below. One wonders whether purchasers noticed the dissonance of the two sections or had internalized the imperfections of linen postcards as natural.[4]

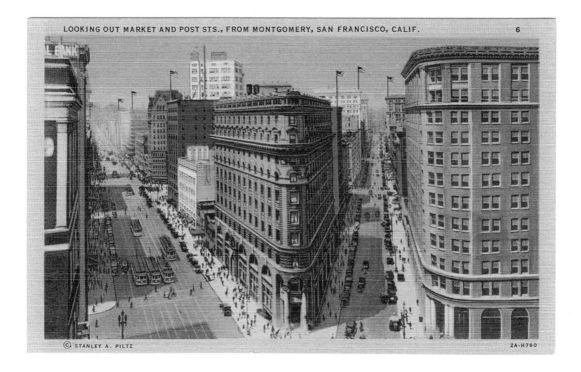

LOOKING OUT MARKET AND POST STS., FROM MONTGOMERY, SAN FRANCISCO, CALIF.   6

© STANLEY A. PILTZ   2A-H760

"Looking Out Market and Post Sts.,
from Montgomery, San Francisco, Calif."

Teich 2A-H760, 1932

THIS VIEW FROM SAN FRANCISCO ECHOES NINETEENTH-CENTURY grand-style urban photographs. The classic high-angle street view possesses a visual coherence lacking in the discordant image of Baltimore's viaduct. A high perspective emphasizes architectural monumentality. Vehicles and pedestrians are so distant as to muffle any thought of noise, hustle, and grime. The view is to the west, focusing on the flatiron shape of the Crocker Building, which cleaves the intersection, emphasizing smooth visual flow all the way to the horizon. Endless vistas were common in grand urban views after Baron Haussmann's creation of Paris's wide diagonal boulevards. In this case, however, the viewer's commanding gaze emanates not from a civic monument like the Arc de Triomphe, the panoptic center of an empire, but from an anonymous commercial building. And the intersection's sharp angle derives not from an overarching urban plan but from the accident of two skewed grid systems meeting at an angle along Market Street.

Even so, this popular view expressed a similar grandeur. Often photographed, it was published as a stereograph card soon after the Crocker Building's completion in 1891 and appeared on early postcards. Teich based this card on a source photo from Stanley A. Piltz, a local photographer who demanded high quality for scores of California views commissioned from Teich. The horizontal orientation, emphasizing panoramic scope, differs from earlier vertical images that focused directly on the Crocker Building. A Mediterranean light emanates from a robin's-egg blue sky and bathes sandstone and brick structures along the streets. The image's delicacy, manifested in the hazy fadeout at the horizon, derives from limited reliance on black and subtle deployment of color. Both approaches are typical of the earliest linen postcards before more solid, saturated color fields became standard, as in the Baltimore image.

Viewed from a normal distance, this postcard suggests realism. Up close, however, there are discrepancies, such as overly regular white lines for streetcar tracks, the lack of overhead wires for streetcars, and perhaps the six flags projecting above the horizon. Although the frequency of flags in linen urban views suggests unreality, historical photographs often feature them.[5] In this case the flags, invoking triumphant nationhood, reinforce the imperial sweep of a grand urban view.

23 — TIMES SQUARE AT NIGHT, NEW YORK CITY

Photo by Ewing Galloway

"TIMES SQUARE AT NIGHT, NEW YORK CITY"

MANHATTAN 23, N.D.

SOME REGIONAL COMPANIES SUCH AS LONGSHAW IN LOS ANGE-
les and the Manhattan Post Card Publishing Company in New York produced
their own linen aesthetic rather than imitating Teich's. While the California
printers developed washes of rich, unearthly colors, Manhattan turned black-
and-white sources into inked line drawings more like comic-book panels than
photos. Most of the firm's cards were bathed in lurid colors—in this case yellow,
orange, purple, and green. The credit line for this card, "photo by Ewing Galloway," provokes the question of how anyone could have regarded this scene as
having a basis in the obvious realism of photography.

Crude as it is, the image pulsates with the electrical sublime, presenting
Times Square as an intersection of currents of energy flowing in perpetual
motion along Broadway and Seventh Avenue. Surrounding buildings seem to
dematerialize. Neon billboards, incandescent bulbs spelling out names, and
display windows flood sidewalks with light. John A. Jakle has described major
urban intersections as "nodal points" that are as significant for conceptualiz-
ing cities as bird's-eye views or monuments.[6] Although this card is similar to
Teich's view of the Crocker Building in San Francisco in emphasizing lines of
sight beyond an angular divide, that image created a false nodal point where
none actually existed. This image, on the other hand, presents a view through
the northern end of Times Square, one of the nation's most famous urban locations, described as "the heart of New York" by the back caption.

Beyond an initial impression of flowing light, which would have attracted
a browsing tourist, the image contains a wealth of details, some more effective
than others but none photorealistic. Cars and buses are tiny bloated cartoon
shapes, emerging from side streets or changing lanes, with four clumsily inter-
rupting the flow of the image by cutting horizontally across at Forty-fifth Street.
Lettered signs proclaiming products and businesses are painstakingly outlined.
Rising above everything else is the skyline, an assemblage of abstracted buildings silhouetted against a sky shading from light blue into inky black. A similar
stylized backdrop might have crowned a comic book view of Metropolis, a parallel suggesting that perhaps Teich's competitors at Manhattan Post Card were
as young and eager as Jerry Siegel and Joe Schuster, both twenty-three when
their first Superman story appeared in *Action Comics* in 1938.

"WRIGLEY SIGN, TIMES SQUARE, NEW YORK"

TEICH 6A-H442, 1936

AN EQUALLY FANCIFUL TIMES SQUARE CARD PRODUCED IN 1936 by Teich for the Wrigley Company also relied on an artist's imagination to convey the electrical sublime. The "Great White Way," as electrified Broadway was known, is presented as mostly dark because the point was to showcase a massive illuminated sign, composed of thousands of shifting lights that advertised Wrigley's Spearmint gum. The sign ran the full length of the block-long facade of the Criterion theater and International Casino theater and supper club, both recently renovated in the streamline style. As the back caption boasts, the sign was "the largest of its kind in the world." Lighting consisted of 1,084 feet of neon tubing and 29,508 incandescent bulbs connected by 70 miles of wire. Tropical fish undulated across the 188-foot sign and bubbles rose up its 74-foot height in a precisely timed sequence of lights hard to imagine without a computer.[7]

The job file reveals that Wrigley provided a small painting with a head-on view of the sign as a source. The airbrush rendering was artist-generated rather than painted on a photo, with the street's details sketched freehand from reference photos. The finished card has flowing yellow pinstripe lines accentuating the sign's base, with a radiating glow that suggests indirect lighting. Vertical signs on the nearly darkened building fronts up Seventh Avenue announce the Loew's State, Palace, and Mayfair theaters, and a vaudeville marquee that is also visible in Manhattan Post Card's image of Times Square. A small, colorful advertisement for Sunkist oranges punctuates the Wrigley sign's horizontal sweep. While building facades are deep black against a smoky-gray patch of sky, a hazy yellow glow emanating from display windows along the sidewalk offers an energizing contrast. The toylike quality of vehicles inserted into many linen views is here mitigated by their indistinctness as silhouettes. The intensity of light bursting from sign and sidewalk is increased by the fact that the image bleeds to the edges of the borderless card. Teich seems to have rushed the card into production before the sign was completed—which would explain the use of artist-generated details rather than a photographic source. Wrigley specified that Teich's name not appear on the card and probably used the large order of 500,000 cards to publicize the sign's inaugural lighting.

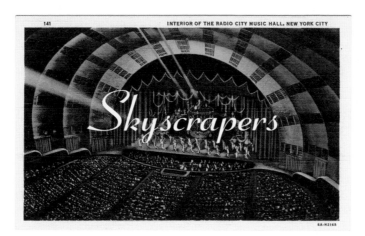

INTERIOR OF THE RADIO CITY MUSIC HALL, NEW YORK CITY

Skyscrapers

6A-H2165

117   PALMOLIVE BUILDING, BY NIGHT, CHICAGO

3A-H530

"PALMOLIVE BUILDING, BY NIGHT, CHICAGO"

TEICH 3A-H530, 1933

ALTHOUGH NEW YORK SET THE STANDARD FOR TALL BUILDINGS, perhaps the most dramatic of all skyscraper cards portrayed the Palmolive Building in Chicago. Whether or not local pride influenced the art department, the result suggests a desire to produce a compelling image for J. O. Stoll, a newsstand distributor who commissioned scores of cards from Teich. The night view is based on a slightly angled photo of the setback Art Deco office building completed in 1929 for the Colgate-Palmolive-Peet Company, formed by mergers of three soap and cosmetics companies. Located a dozen blocks north of the crowded Loop between Michigan Avenue (shown in the image) and Lake Shore Drive, the thirty-seven-story Palmolive Building stands in splendid isolation except for the Drake Tower, a thirty-story apartment building completed the same year, dimly visible to the right. The image is dynamic, full of motion. While the skyscraper draws the eye upward, three realistic autos move toward us and out of the frame, balancing the tower's visual thrust. Unlike the dull, uniform sky of the Times Square cards, this image presents the sky itself as actively in motion. Moonlight partially picks out three layers of wispy clouds. The Palmolive Building glows with intensity against the sky as columns of yellow light rise from hidden floodlights at the base of each setback.

Raymond Hood, the nation's most prominent skyscraper architect, had recently promised that "night illumination," so far only "barely . . . tested," would soon be "more fantastic than anything that has ever been accomplished on the stage." Here that promise seems fulfilled—and set off by pinpoints of window lights, by glowing white headlights and streetlamps, and above all by two beacons of light projecting at dynamic angles from a spire on the roof. A long caption is devoted exclusively to the Lindbergh Beacon, a technological marvel, with one lamp projecting a one billion–candlepower beam toward Midway Airport. The other lamp projected a revolving beam of two billion candlepower that was "visible to aviators . . . as far east as Cleveland, Ohio [300 miles away], and as far south as St. Louis, Missouri [265 miles away]." This view of the Palmolive Building portrays the compelling nature of the electrical sublime, the soaring beauty of tall buildings, the dynamism of the automobile, and the liberating promise of air travel. More than any other linen postcard, it celebrates modernity.[8]

4 CHRYSLER BUILDING, NEW YORK CITY

2A-H117

"CHRYSLER BUILDING,
NEW YORK CITY"

TEICH 2A-H117, 1932

UNLIKE TEICH'S VIEW OF THE PALMOLIVE BUILDING, WHICH includes three pedestrians, most linen cards portrayed skyscrapers in splendid isolation. Rather than situating a viewer on the ground, they looked across from neighboring buildings to which most people did not have access. The effect was to distance a viewer from the scene, transforming a building into a fetish object, miniaturized like a small metal souvenir model. The layout of most skyscraper cards paralleled this view of the Chrysler Building, which was completed in 1930. The building stands forth among an assemblage of lower buildings that provide a sense of scale but do not ground the viewer. Despite the typical composition, this rendering, which dates from 1932, differs aesthetically from most skyscraper views by sharing qualities of the earliest Teich linen cards. Minimal use of black opens up the image for subtle application of delicate color washes. Light sky tones of peach, yellow, green, and blue merge as if applied by watercolor. Deckle edges and the rare early texture of shallow embossed parallel waves add refinement by suggesting handmade paper. The Chrysler Building projects an airiness that seems to defy gravity. Lower buildings in the foreground, by contrast, are rendered in darker colors and blemished by rooftop excrescences—parapets, chimneys, and access points.

One can hardly imagine a more evanescent representation of this machine-age icon with its stainless steel crown. Even Hugh Ferriss, famous for dark, ponderous images, attempted to capture the Chrysler Building's lightness by portraying it under construction with a rising sun radiating through the open steel framing of the unfinished crown.[9] However, Ferriss's version lacked the utopian presence of this image. A year later Teich produced a new view based on the same source photo, as if this earlier card was simply too airy to convey a sense of reality. The replacement card has sharp, deep black details, saturated color tones in the surrounding buildings, and a cloudless blue sky whose clarity causes the bright whiteness of the highly defined Chrysler Building to pop out in visual contrast.[10] As different as these two views may seem, they share a sense of the modern city as a place of rational clarity. Teich's urban vision transcended both Ferriss's gloom and Weegee's sensational glimpses of life—and death—on the streets.

103:—EMPIRE STATE BUILDING BY MOONLIGHT. NEW YORK.

40786

"Empire State Building
by Moonlight. New York."

Manhattan 40786, n.d.

TOURISTS ENCOUNTERED A RANGE OF SKYSCRAPER REPRESEN-
tations. They would have seen Teich images of the Empire State Building nearly identical in form, line, and color palette to those of the Chrysler Building.
However, they might also have found this radically different image, printed by
Teich's local competitor. Although Manhattan Post Card typically relied on extensive line retouching that effaced an image's photographic origin and opened
up space for flat color fields (see pp. 310, 356), this atypical view of the Empire
State Building retains an illusion of heavy substance, partly owing to the sky's
inky blue-blackness and the neutral gray of surrounding buildings. The illusion
of three-dimensionality is enhanced if one turns the card at an angle in reflective light, revealing what appears to be heavily layered ink. The skyscraper's vertical lines, nearly obscuring the card stock's linen texture, project an illusion of
being raised on the surface by embossing, as do the outlines of lower buildings.

These qualities, unusual for a linen card, were employed in the service of a
romantic expressionist version of the technological sublime. The city appears
as a jumble of jagged architectural forms comprising a dense multidimensional
maze. Tiny dots of yellow light make little headway against a moody gloom.
Rising from that base, the shaft of the Empire State Building, organized around
the strong vertical of a silver-gray corner pier, rises muddily against a sky whose
swirling yellow-gray clouds suggest the romantic expressionist seascapes of the
late nineteenth-century painter Albert Pinkham Ryder. A standard linen yellow
moon serves as a foil to the image's most unexpected feature, an evanescent airship, glowing sickly yellow-green, moored to the building's mast. Although the
Empire State Building did have a mooring mast for dirigibles, none ever docked
there, and the back caption claims merely that if an airship did moor there, it
"would exert a greater pull than three locomotives." Portentous in mood, this
postcard promised romantic transcendence of the ordinary, if not through firmly grounded architecture, then through the miracle of lighter-than-air flight.
One detail remains to be noted. In the lower left corner is a cryptic notation—a
copyright symbol followed by the initials "I.U." These likely stand for the commercial photographer Irving Underhill but are obscurely rendered as if to disguise the image's photographic base. This is the realm of technological dream.[11]

R.C A BUILDING, ROCKEFELLER CENTER, AT NIGHT, NEW YORK CITY 67

PHOTO WENDELL MC RAE

"RCA Building, Rockefeller Center, at Night, New York City"

Teich 5A-H382, 1935

IT IS RARE FOR A SKYSCRAPER POSTCARD TO PRESENT A VIEW from ground level, looking up so obliquely that a building's lines converge as they rise. Most architectural photographers who documented buildings for developers and architects relied on the adjustments of a view camera to overcome parallax and maintain parallel lines, and postcard publishers generally followed that convention. This card, on the other hand, presents an image of the RCA Building similar to one that a tourist in Rockefeller Plaza might have snapped with a Kodak camera. A female tourist complained of having "a stiff neck from looking up at tall buildings," while another more generally declared, "This is certainly a great big world & I'm seeing it from all angles."[12]

Beyond the shared angle of vision, this image is unlike anything a tourist could have taken with a Kodak. For one thing, night views were beyond the capacity of a box camera or simple bellows camera. As in many night views, anything not essential was excluded. The card represents the RCA Building as if rising directly from the stone embrasure of the *Prometheus* sculpture and its fountain—and a viewer remains unaware that the plaza is depressed below ground level and separated from the tower by a busy street. The building itself resembles a telescoping artillery piece, with each section rising from an indented setback. The retouching artist scattered randomly lit windows up the facade—creating a variation that emphasizes the vertical lines of the building's piers. The image even obscures a polychromatic sculptural relief above the entrance, *Wisdom*, portrayed by a powerful figure of Zeus, merely suggested by a faint sketch so as not to interrupt the tower's flowing lines. Although a postcard border normally does nothing more than frame an image, here its strong yellow complements that of the tower. The result is a composition whose austere pseudo-realism is subordinated to a stylized formalism appropriate to the streamlined Art Deco skyscraper it represents. More than with most linen cards, the image's graphic style expresses the popular significance of the scene it portrays.

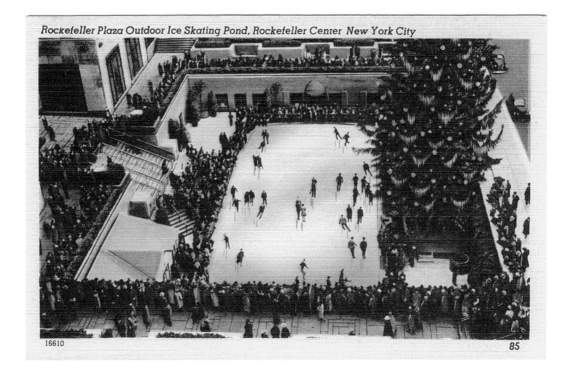

Rockefeller Plaza Outdoor Ice Skating Pond, Rockefeller Center New York City

16610

85

"ROCKEFELLER PLAZA OUTDOOR ICE SKATING POND, ROCKEFELLER CENTER NEW YORK CITY"

COLOURPICTURE 16610, N.D.

MOST LINEN POSTCARDS PORTRAYED SCENES WITH A DIRECT-
ness that left no uncertainty about their subjects, but this view of Rockefeller
Plaza might have momentarily confused some recipients. The location does
not fit usual categories but instead has a unique form not easily recognized.
The plaza's sunken level, an outdoor cafe during temperate weather, has been
turned into a skating rink each winter since the 1936 holiday season. The famous Christmas tree, here installed on the sunken level in front of the *Prometheus* sculpture, has instead for many decades been installed above, on the
sidewalk visible at the right side of the card. More than many linen images, the
card betrays its origin in black-and-white photography. The tree and the dense
masses of observers surrounding the rink on both upper and lower levels are
printed mostly in black. Occasional splashes of color—bright cloth coats scattered through the crowd, ornaments and loops of lights on the tree—barely suggest a colorized image.

However, these lackluster elements are more than balanced by a surreal
effect at the center of the image. Possibly having difficulty representing ice, a
colorist at Colourpicture seems to have decided to render the rink's surface by
means of a standard linen sky—as if a light blue sky were filled with cumulus
clouds. Though common on hundreds of linen postcards, this effect becomes
stunning when projected onto the surface of a sunken plaza. The skaters, rendered as insubstantial figures, thinner than the full-bodied members of the
crowd, are suspended, floating, with thin blue hash marks indicating faint shadows on ice that otherwise seems visually not to exist.

247 Grand Foyer of Radio City Music Hall, New York City

PHOTO BY WURTS BROS.

8A-H427

"GRAND FOYER OF RADIO CITY MUSIC HALL, NEW YORK CITY"

TEICH 8A-H427, 1938

THE PUBLIC WOULD HAVE EXPERIENCED THE FOYER OF RADIO City Music Hall, around the corner from Rockefeller Plaza, as bustling with theatergoers. Linen postcard interiors tended to be empty because they were based on images taken by architectural photographers, in this case probably Richard Wurts of the prominent Wurts Brothers studio. Since the point was to document a commission for architect and client, the presence of models would have distracted attention from the designed space. Wholesalers who ordered postcards from Teich may also have realized that including people in an interior was unwise because changing fashions would quickly date a card that otherwise could be reprinted and distributed for many years. Whatever the reason, most available source photos of interiors were unpopulated, and so were postcards made from them.

Today, as already noted, such interior images project an uncanny feeling that something is about to happen, but their effect would have been different for people who viewed them at the time of publication. This image's vertical orientation would have allowed a viewer to imagine moving unimpeded across the rich carpet's long vista to ascend the distant staircase, where a swirling mural, contrasting with the room's muted tones, promised a glorious revelation. Perhaps to enliven this dramatic effect, Teich's colorist misrepresented the mural, *Fountain of Youth*, by Ezra Winter. She replaced the sky's deep coppery tone with a more upbeat robin's-egg blue. This image invited viewers to imagine entering the space to participate in a grander reality. But the card might also have reinforced a feeling of exclusion for anyone standing on the outside, unable to afford the show, figuratively looking in through a seductive pasteboard window.

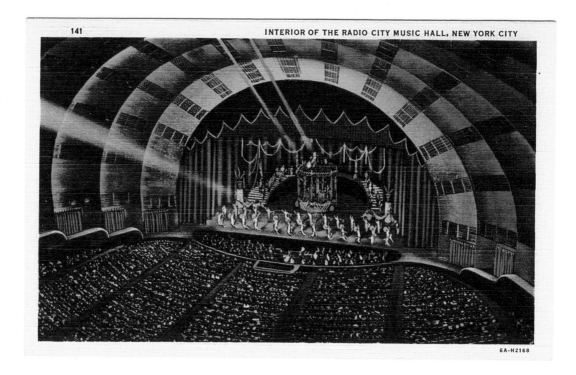

141   INTERIOR OF THE RADIO CITY MUSIC HALL, NEW YORK CITY

6A-H2168

"INTERIOR OF THE RADIO CITY MUSIC HALL, NEW YORK CITY"

TEICH 6A-H2168, 1936

THIS VIEW OF RADIO CITY MUSIC HALL'S AUDITORIUM SITU-
ates an observer above the crowd, looking down from the highest of three steep
mezzanines. Individuals on the main level are insignificant dots of color. Even
the dancers are not recognizable as individuals but instead are interchangeable
parts in the precision spectacle of the Rockettes troupe. All aspects of the building's design, from the wide, curving marquee over the entrance to the foyer's
long curve, promote a sense of smooth, elegant, unimpeded motion toward this
central visual experience.

In 1938, Curt Teich declared this image New York City's "most popular card."
Indeed, at least three other publishers printed cards with nearly identical images from the same angle. The job file for this Teich card contains a competing
card from Manhattan Post Card, a shiny non-linen lithograph whose image was
credited to the misspelled "Wurtz" agency.[13] A tear sheet from a souvenir booklet features the same image with a handwritten notation: "See attached card for
idea as to colors[,] doesn't make much difference what colors are used[,] any
rainbow effect[,] only use colors brighter than the ones on the attached card." In
fact the Teich card is not bright but instead composed of deep, rich colors. Both
Tichnor and Colourpicture offered the same image with the same stage set, a
carousel or birdcage with flanking staircases. While Tichnor used bright pastels
for the ceiling's sunburst bands, Colourpicture used a dull palette of blue-grays.
Manhattan Post Card offered at least two different views. One had the same arrangement of three spotlights but a different stage set with tiny nude stick figures high-kicking in front of red capes. The other, the crudest of all six images,
showed blurry dancers in front of a windmill and a cuckoo clock house.[14] At a
quick glance, nothing distinguishes one card from another. They merge into a
shifting rainbow pattern as colorful as the theater's sunburst ceiling. The sender
of the Teich card proclaimed Radio City Music Hall "a wonderful place" and told
a friend in Boston it was "a must when you come to N.Y."

MEDICAL ARTS BUILDING, HOT SPRINGS NATIONAL PARK, ARK.

"MEDICAL ARTS BUILDING, HOT SPRINGS NATIONAL PARK, ARK."

TEICH 5A-H1404, 1935

IT WAS A LONG WAY FROM ROCKEFELLER CENTER TO HOT Springs, Arkansas, a town of twenty thousand when the sixteen-story Medical Arts Building was completed in 1929. It remained the tallest building in Arkansas until 1960. Boasting stylized setbacks even though there was no danger of adjacent skyscrapers turning the streets into dark canyons, the Medical Arts Building offered evidence of the sophistication of a place known for medicinal spas and a wide-open gambling scene. Even a one-street town like Hot Springs, spread out along Central Avenue and surrounded by a canopy of trees, could take pride in possessing a single skyscraper, an elegant, locally proportioned gem.

Although Medical Arts was located across the street from the Arlington Hotel, a grand Spanish colonial revival structure, this card portrays the lone skyscraper in near isolation. A four-story business block to the left provides scale while also suggesting the tower's incongruity with its setting—a conclusion that would have seemed even more obvious if not for art department instructions to "remove shacks on right." The forested hillside behind the building integrates it into the natural realm. A cartoonlike car on an unreal street and sketchy figures of four pedestrians contribute nothing to realism. There is also little evidence of the signage normally associated with ground-floor retail shops. If the building's owner had commissioned the card, the retouching artist might have been asked to fade out the buildings to the left, thereby emphasizing the tower within the spa town's forested parkland. However, the distributor ordered many different local views over the years. The Medical Arts Building was a local monument and tourist attraction. At present, however, it is deserted except for first-floor merchants. Trespassing urban explorers have posted online photographs of empty rooms, peeling walls, and stacks of old medical journals. The former machine-age icon, still the tallest building in Hot Springs, has outlived its usefulness.[15]

TELEPHONE BUILDING AT NIGHT, BANGOR, MAINE

60298

"TELEPHONE BUILDING AT NIGHT, BANGOR, MAINE"

TICHNOR 60298, N.D.

MORE THAN MOST POSTCARDS, THIS NIGHT VIEW OF AN ART Deco office building in Bangor, Maine, invites an observer to imagine a scene from an ongoing narrative. The building's dark gray hulk looms up against a moonlit, cloud-swirled, blue-black sky. The yellow glow of electric light from every window casts a lurid gleam on the roofs of cars in the foreground and on the curb outlining a patch of grass. A similar light outlines the dark stone of the pilasters and door surround, the crenellation at the top, and the edges of setbacks. That illumination can only be from moonlight though the moon is located behind the building. Despite that error, the street, rendered in varied tones of reddish brown, represents an improvement over many foreground pavements in linen views. Unlike the automobiles illustrated on many linen cards, the expressive artist's renderings on this card do not appear two-dimensional or overly elongated.

Attention focuses not on these details but on the figure of a woman standing beside a car in the right foreground. Wearing a long red coat and dark hat, she stands half obscured in shadow, turned away from the viewer. Because she seems to look into the car, perhaps talking with someone inside, it is difficult to identify with her in the neutral way one does with foreground figures in many landscape paintings. Instead a viewer is free to wonder about her, to imagine plots in which she plays a role. This urban scene, portraying a romanticized Deco structure quite different from the blocky office building that still rises from a hillside in Bangor, suggests the dread of noir as much as the promise of electrical energy. The image may have expressed something of the loneliness at the edge of the American night to those who first viewed it.

PHOTO BY ELLISON

Main Streets

CONGRESS AVENUE LOOKING NORTH, AUSTIN, TEXAS

3A-H459

CONGRESS AVENUE LOOKING NORTH, AUSTIN, TEXAS

PHOTO BY ELLISON

3A-H459

"CONGRESS AVENUE LOOKING NORTH, AUSTIN, TEXAS"

TEICH 3A-H459, 1933

FRONTIER OPENNESS MARKS THIS VIEW OF CONGRESS AVENUE, the main business street of Austin, with the capitol of Texas visible in the distance. Although the street had long been paved by 1933, variegated pavement colors convey the feel of a dirt street despite streetcar tracks running up the middle (with overhead wires removed). The three-story building to the left of center, the Hotel Main with its iron balcony railings, suggests a classic western boomtown. That anachronistic impression comes through even though the image features several recent modern structures: the curved corner of the Littlefield Building (1910) to the right, the renovated Art Deco facade of Scarbrough's department store (1931) to the left, and the gleaming Gothic Deco tower of the Norwood Building (1929), the city's first skyscraper, rising behind the Hotel Main. This card, while typical of downtown street views in its diagonal perspective, in the clarity of color shifts from building to building, and in the sense of a clean sweep up the street, is unusual in the lack of any legible business signs—another detail affording the image a nearly mythical quality.

With architectural details marking this as a view of Austin, Texas, and no other place, it would make little sense to call it a generic downtown. However, the image's transcendence of everyday commerce transforms it into an utter idealization. Vaguely delineated parked cars join in nondescript lines along the sidewalks, and a few pedestrians emerge from the gloom below the shop fronts, with just a hint of people waiting for streetcars or buses under the Hotel Main's lower balcony if a viewer squints closely. All these understated, barely visible details are suffused in the haze of an early linen sky, with orange and peach hues along the horizon merging into a delicate watercolor blue. The overall impression of the idea of a main street rather than its reality characterizes this view as an example of urban picturesque.

1357—Third Avenue and Pike, Seattle, Wash.

2B-H347

"THIRD AVENUE AND PIKE, SEATTLE, WASH."

TEICH 2B-H347, 1942

THE ANGLE OF THIS VIEW OF DOWNTOWN SEATTLE, LOOKING north up Third Avenue, is nearly identical to that of Austin's Congress Avenue, but otherwise there are few similarities. Although Teich printed the card for a local distributor, it features two of the nation's leading dime store chains, Woolworth and Kress, whose signs immediately attract the eye. Presumably those stores offered the card for sale along with other Seattle views. Visible in the distance is a billboard advertising 76 gasoline, a brand of Union Oil. One can also make out other businesses—the Telenews and Eastern theaters, possibly another theater or a restaurant. Such commercial details lend an everyday specificity lacking in the Austin view. Also unlike the Austin card, this image of one of Seattle's busiest corners emphasizes crowds of pedestrians rendered in bright blotches of color, some suggesting recognizably full-bodied individuals when viewed from a distance, especially the three women on the right. Automobiles, both parked and in motion, fill the street. The stoplight that would have halted drivers waiting for people to cross Third Avenue seems to have been airbrushed out, but the triple-globed streetlight on the right frames the image much like a tree in the foreground of a picturesque landscape. Unlike the main street views described by Alison Isenberg as presenting a vista carefully streamlined so as to suggest the ease and comfort of downtown shopping, Third Avenue in Seattle appears here visually cluttered and physically clotted with cars and people—vibrant, perhaps, but certainly not efficient.

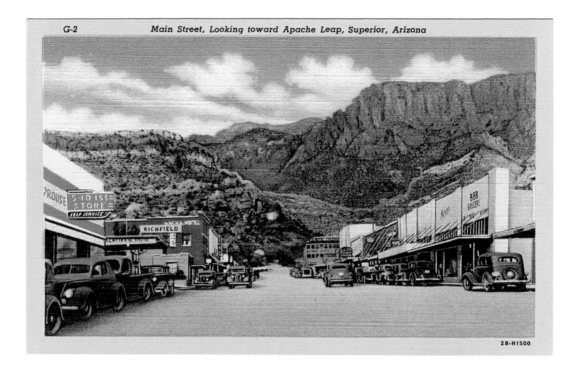

G-2   Main Street, Looking toward Apache Leap, Superior, Arizona

2B-H1500

"MAIN STREET, LOOKING TOWARD APACHE LEAP, SUPERIOR, ARIZONA"

TEICH 2B-H1500, 1942

Even the smallest places took on a degree of urbanity when portrayed on linen postcards. Superior, Arizona, a small town with a copper mine and smelter located thirty-five miles east of Scottsdale, appears here as a bustling commercial center. Its single thoroughfare, Main Street, is lined with retail establishments and full of parked cars. Anyone from the West would have recognized the paint scheme and letters "prouse" on the building to the left as signifying the Sprouse-Reitz dime store chain. The very phrase "self service" indicates modernity. At the far end of the row of substantial businesses on the right appears a higher building whose outline indicates a movie theater, essential to any self-respecting downtown as a source of up-to-date attitudes and fashions. Two hotels, one of brick, the other looking like a large resort, complete the picture of a self-sufficient, modern community whose citizens did not need to apologize for isolation in a desolate environment.

Indeed, the contrast between artificial and natural is this image's most striking characteristic. The street with buildings and cars seems superimposed over a typical linen view of mountain scenery, especially as the street ceases abruptly against the mountainside. More than other unreal street pavements in linen views, this one appears as a continuous sheet of some seamless artificial material. A real photo postcard from 1936 exhibits a similarly unreal contrast, as does a sun-faded portrayal by Google Maps Street View in 2008. In all three cases the effect is heightened by the lack of any vegetation to ease the transition. However, this postcard offers the most surreal of the views, perhaps owing to its bright colors and the lack of texturing on the street surface. Teich's retouching artist also heightened the disjunctive contrast by removing utility poles that the real photo postcard shows on the right side of the street. The streamlining of main streets described by Isenberg is clearly visible in this image, even exaggerated by the desolate surroundings—suggesting a degree of urban order that straggling Superior may not have projected in actuality, but that its inhabitants may have found appropriate.[16]

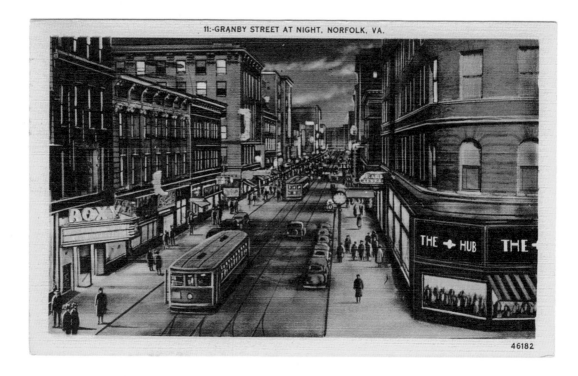

11:-GRANBY STREET AT NIGHT, NORFOLK, VA.

46182

"GRANBY STREET AT NIGHT, NORFOLK, VA."

METROCRAFT 46182, N.D.

AN ELECTRIC YELLOW LONELINESS SEEPS FROM SHOP WINDOWS in this night view looking north on Granby Street, the commercial thoroughfare of Norfolk, Virginia. Although scattered yellow lights also glow from behind windows of upper floors of buildings along the street, the overriding impression is of a gloomy darkness enhanced by the varied color tones and shadings of building fronts, street, sidewalks, and sky—more like the muted realism of the pre-linen aesthetic than the bolder tones of most linen cards. Not as careful as Teich or Manhattan to pick out lettering on commercial signs, Metrocraft's retouching artist emphasized only the Roxy theater, The Hub clothing store, and, just barely, Barr's jewelry shop, leaving neon glowing indistinctly up the street, communicating nothing.

Although Norfolk was a city of 130,000 inhabitants and home to a large naval base, the image suggests a sleepy place trying and failing to keep up with the modern tempo set by New York, Chicago, and Los Angeles. Two streetcars move toward the viewer and cars are scattered up the street, but there is none of the energy of a lively commercial district. Not even the bright clothing shop on the corner, probably a sleek, stylish application of New Deal storefront modernization funds, dispels the general gloom.[17] Gray pedestrians scattered along mostly empty sidewalks seem isolated. They are not window shopping, nor standing and talking with each other, nor walking with a leg extended forward. Instead they are frozen as if in complete alienation. At the risk of romanticizing this postcard, one might wonder about the people living out their lives in bleak apartments like those behind the yellow windows in the tall building whose side elevation is visible on the left-hand side of the street.

LA-46—Broadway, South from Sixth Street, Los Angeles, California

OB-H2586

"Broadway, South from Sixth Street, Los Angeles, California"

Teich OB-H2586, 1940

MORE ANIMATED IS THIS 1940 VIEW OF BROADWAY, THE HEART of the commercial and entertainment district of Los Angeles. Incisive lines of architectural details and signage convey an energy also reflected in the hurrying crowd, which is so fully rendered that one can make out fedoras, a shopping bag, a fur-trimmed coat, and the flash of legs. Rather than conveying loneliness, bright yellow here promises vibrant experience just beyond signs, marquees, and awnings that can barely contain the flowing stream of light. The caption describes "downtown Los Angeles" as "aglow with brilliant lights" and touts "attractive shops, theatres and cafes" that "afford great interest" to "visitors of the Southland"—a nickname that perhaps refers to the city's balmy climate.

Unlike the illegible names on Norfolk's Granby Street, those here reveal the care Teich's retouching artist took to emphasize such fashion emporia as Bullock's and Swelldom's department stores, Mullen & Bluett's menswear, Zukor's dress shop, and Le Roy's jewelry. An out-of-town visitor might have caught a movie at the Los Angeles, Palace, or Loew's State theater after registering at the Hotel Lankershim, picking up a few necessities at Kress's dime store, and seeking aspirin at the Owl drugstore. Lights in upper floors are rendered realistically in random patterns, and shadows and textures of buildings' piers, spandrels, and moldings simulate depth. Although perspective lines in some cards are so mechanically drawn as to suggest they were worked out at a drafting table, the two golden lines of street lights here converge at the end of the street with those of the shop windows in such a way as to create a subtle dynamism. What the view lacks is human diversity. A photo of the same intersection taken in 1940 by Ansel Adams reveals businessmen in suits, a woman in furs, others in cloth coats, a bareheaded worker in shirtsleeves, a man on a bicycle, and two workers who appear to be Latinos.[18] However successful a linen postcard might be at capturing the energy of modern times in a particular place, it also had to convey a comforting sense of the generic that any potential viewer could identify with.

Canal Street at Night, New Orleans, La.

"CANAL STREET AT NIGHT, NEW ORLEANS, LA."

COLOURPICTURE 18866, N.D.

THIS VIEW OF RAIN-SLICK CANAL STREET IN NEW ORLEANS, looking from the corner of Ramparts Street toward the Mississippi River, is one of the most compelling linen expressions of the electrical sublime. Produced by Colourpicture, the image exceeds that company's usual standards and would suggest an impressionist painting if its perspective were not aimed so straight down the trolley tracks. Some of the card's impact derives from the width of Canal Street, which historically separated the French Quarter from a section settled later by English speakers. This "neutral ground," as it is still known, was originally parkland running between two narrow roadways, but it had acquired streetcar tracks in the late nineteenth century. In 1929 the sidewalks and neutral ground were paved in white terrazzo, and ornamental light poles were installed on both sides of the tracks. Perhaps it was the reflective terrazzo and the lack of glaring headlights that enabled a source photo taken at night to be effectively retouched and colorized. The result is a fantasia of light, with reflections of buildings, neon signs, streetlights, and display windows shimmering in the pavement and diffused over its surface. Even overhead electric wires for the trolleys are faintly visible as two lines forming a V in the blue-black sky.

John A. Jakle has suggested this postcard may have been based on a color print, which could have been produced from a Kodachrome slide after 1936, two years before Colourpicture was founded. However, this image is in a consecutive series of about twenty New Orleans cards, many of which clearly derive from black-and-white source photos. It seems unlikely a company employing a pirated mass-production process would experiment so boldly—and with only one card in a series. The closer one looks at the card, the more awkward details one finds, despite its overall effectiveness. Retouching of the black lines of the lampposts and the streetcar's front window frame is clumsy, as are the stick-figure legs of a woman in the middle distance. Even so, this is a unique image.[19]

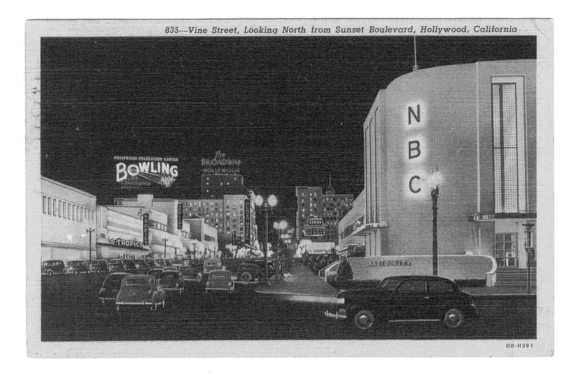

835—Vine Street, Looking North from Sunset Boulevard, Hollywood, California

OB-H391

"VINE STREET, LOOKING NORTH FROM SUNSET BOULEVARD, HOLLYWOOD, CALIFORNIA"

TEICH OB-H391, 1940

As a Los Angeles resident, G. I. Pitchford was attentive to the developing automotive cityscape there. He also held the art department to high standards. In general, the more manipulation an image required, the less realism the final postcard conveyed. In this case, however, retouching appears seamless. There is no loss of scale and none of the amateurish draftsmanship that often marred artist-generated automobiles. For this night view Pitchford provided his own daytime source photo. Pedestrians are scattered along the sidewalk in the source photo, the Hollywood Hills are visible in the distance, and a flag flies over NBC's streamlined Radio City Building, which housed the western offices of two radio networks. There is a line of parked cars in heavy shade on the west side of the street, and two large white blobs crudely mask out cars from the street. The job file contains another copy of the photo that has been retouched, nearly obscuring its photographic origin. Edges of buildings are heavily outlined, facades on the left are smoothed and simplified, signs are picked out in detail (including the iconic Brown Derby restaurant), hills are obliterated, pedestrians are removed, and the image is cropped to exclude the flag. The cars, all but one being products of freehand drawing, are correctly proportioned. The exception is the car in the lower right, which was cut and pasted from another photo.

Critical to the image's success is diversity of color, so unlike the uniform yellow of many urban night views. Pitchford issued precise color instructions, describing the Radio City Building as "a pale blue green" with "a pale green glow, not strong" coming from the vertical window. "Underneath the marquee," he continued, "the glow is pinkish amber," fading lower into "almost an orchid." He trusted the artists to "put color down the avenue," which they did, varying the yellow tones emanating from display windows of businesses and contrasting the brown and gray of tall buildings in the distance with a bright silvery gray along the west side of Vine. The art department followed Pitchford's command that they "fix autos." In 1940s Hollywood it was imperative to "not have the street without autos." Especially effective was the decision to remove pedestrians and emphasize the Southern California night as an automotive domain.[20]

Club Bingo, Las Vegas, Nevada

OC-H643

"CLUB BINGO, LAS VEGAS, NEVADA"

TEICH OC-H643, 1950

PITCHFORD WAS INVOLVED WITH DOZENS OF URBAN CARDS, both day and night views, including many representing Las Vegas. The town's growth from five thousand inhabitants in 1930, at the start of construction of Hoover Dam, to an expanding gambling resort with twenty-five thousand people in 1950 required frequent updates for the local distributor, Desert Souvenir Supply. Club Bingo was one of the earliest casinos south of downtown's Fremont Street on U.S. 91, later officially called Las Vegas Boulevard and known as the Strip. Opened in 1947, Club Bingo was demolished only five years later to make way for the Sahara. Equipped with a 300-seat bingo parlor and a supper club called the Bonanza Room, the establishment boasted a full range of casino games. According to the back caption, which emphasizes cosmopolitan urbanity, "here you can rub elbows with visitors . . . from all over the world."

Unlike most night views, this was based on a black-and-white photo taken at night. Pitchford's frisket indicated exact colors in colored pencil and in words (such as "pinkish orange" and "buff against green"). The art department followed instructions precisely while portraying the club as glowing with a rich golden hue that shamed most ordinary main street views. As in the card portraying Hollywood's Vine Street, automobiles received rich, subtly understated paint schemes, and an artist added a convincing freehand late-model convertible to the cars taken from the source photo. Although scraggly palm trees did line the highway at that time, none appeared in the source photo, so Pitchford provided a tracing-paper sketch indicating a single well-placed palm, thereby promoting Las Vegas as a desert oasis. The sophistication of this relatively late linen image ironically coincided in time with inroads being made on postcard racks by chromes. In fact, Pitchford sent the art department not only a Kodachrome slide he had taken of Club Bingo's vertical sign, to be used as a color guide, but also a competing chrome postcard portraying the entire club as a garish red-tinged building against a purple night sky. As gaudily unreal as that "Natural Color K Card" appeared, the apparent realism of shiny cards reproduced from color photos soon drove linen cards from the marketplace.

"THE BRIGHT LIGHTS OF LAS VEGAS, NEVADA"

TEICH 3B-H175, 1943

PITCHFORD TOOK PRIDE IN "MY LAYOUT FOR THE 'LIGHTS OF Las Vegas'"—a collage of fragments of twenty black-and-white photos of neon signs of casinos and hotels. The project had taken him more than a year to complete because he kept discovering "new and important signs" on "each trip over" to Las Vegas. Two years earlier he had submitted artwork for a similar Reno postcard, but he complained that the art department had "removed all evidence of backgrounds," leaving only a "dead black" surrounding the signs. This time he had devoted "considerable work" to the design—taking the photos, "making the subjects to proportion," and solving "the puzzle of re-arranging them," and he implored the artists to "do their best to make a good subject."[21]

Accompanying the paste-up was a large photographic copy of the montage. The copy had slightly less "strength of detail" and thus a resolution that was "about right" for a postcard. His design anchored a dramatically tilted array of glowing neon signs around the central outline of a diesel locomotive emblazoned with "Las Vegas Nevada, The Streamlined City." Although a streamlined locomotive might seem an odd icon for Vegas, that sign actually did project from the trackside of the town's railway station, welcoming everyone who arrived by train. Teich's artists produced an image exploding to the edges of the card with bright, colorful icons and signs. Secondary reflections onto the buildings' walls added a cubist effect to an otherwise black background.

Pitchford might have been inspired by a more artful image, an experimental photomontage of New York theater marquees and advertising signs by Walker Evans that appeared on the cover of the trade journal *Advertising & Selling* in 1931 (see below). But while Evans's tightly superimposed signs evoked sensory overload experienced by pedestrians walking up Broadway, Pitchford's more expansive spatial arrangement suggested the disorienting experience of driving

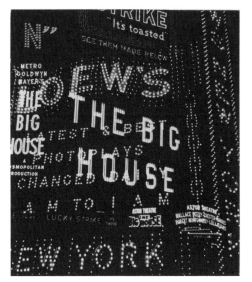

through Las Vegas. It was twenty-five years before the journalist Tom Wolfe heralded the city's "electro-graphic architecture." But Pitchford had already expressed its essence in this postcard and in his view of Club Bingo, whose neon lines rose into darkness apparently unsupported by any physical structure—a magically immaterial variant of the electrical sublime.[22]

WALKER EVANS, *TIMES SQUARE / BROADWAY COMPOSITION* (1931)

1 — STATUE OF LIBERTY, NEW YORK CITY

"Statue of Liberty, New York City"

Manhattan 1, n.d.

PUBLIC MONUMENTS PROVIDED A COMMON SUBJECT, AND THE Statue of Liberty was possibly the most frequently portrayed. Given its isolation in New York Harbor, publishers often resorted to atmospheric sky effects to distinguish one card from another. Although Teich produced an aerial view of Bedloe's Island with the statue rising in front of old military buildings, and Colourpicture offered a view of the island with New Jersey on the horizon, most cards represented the statue standing alone. Another Colourpicture image portrayed Liberty at sunrise, silhouetted against banked cumulus clouds glowing with yellows, pinks, reds, and purples. A night view from Teich presented eleven spotlights beaming onto the statue from the rampart at its base. Another night view by Manhattan Post Card reversed that effect with eight searchlights projecting from Liberty's torch out into threatening clouds.

Most unusual of all are a pair of day and night views that Manhattan Post Card based on a single source photo. The company considered the Statue of Liberty so important as to warrant numbers 1 and 2 in a series of more than seventy New York City scenes. On both cards the statue and its base fill a vertical frame. The company's typical line-drawing technique yields textured representations of the folds of Liberty's garment and the masonry base. Color fields are large and open, without any gradations in tone conveyed by black shading. In the night view a single spotlight shines diagonally upward from outside the frame, at too sharp an angle to be coming from any point on the island. The day view features

an airplane, one of the famous Clippers of Pan American Airways. Both views present an odd, tripod-like flagpole with guy wires and a tiny ladder in front of the rampart. This tripod appears to have been based on reality because it also figures, though less prominently, in Teich's aerial view. Even so, tripod and airplane together give this view of Liberty an unsettling quality. Why are these random details juxtaposed with an otherwise conventional view of the Statue of Liberty? There seems a subtle problem with scale as well and an implied narrative that defies understanding. Both these views, day and night, project a haunting quality reminiscent of the surrealist paintings of Giorgio de Chirico.[23]

"STATUE OF LIBERTY AT NIGHT, NEW YORK CITY," MANHATTAN 2, N.D.

10—Fountain Square, Cincinnati, Ohio

8A-H2420

"FOUNTAIN SQUARE, CINCINNATI, OHIO"

TEICH 8A-H2420, 1938

MANY CITIES ERECTED STATUES OR FOUNTAINS AT SIGNIFICANT points, and visitors regarded them as worth seeing and sharing with correspondents. Such monuments often commemorated native sons fallen in battle but sometimes indicated nothing more than attainment of a certain level of civic grandeur. Such was the case with a fountain erected in 1871 in Cincinnati at the intersection of Fifth and Vine Streets, which thereby became Fountain Square. Known as "The Genius of Water," the forty-three-foot-tall fountain encompassed a granite basin surmounted by four large, shallow bronze bowls into which water flowed from the outstretched hands of a nine-foot bronze figure of a woman in classical robes. Subsidiary figures and panels portrayed uses of water for life, industry, and pleasure. Donated to the city by the owner of Cincinnati's largest hardware store in memory of his late brother-in-law and business partner, the fountain transformed private grief into a public statement of the cultivated taste of the city's movers and shakers.

The Teich image portrays the fountain hemmed in by buildings, with those in red brick harking back to the era of the fountain. The Albee, which opened in 1927, was the city's most opulent movie palace, though its vertical sign, partially blocked by leaves, seems incongruously to announce "ALE." The modern structure visible to the left of the fountain is Carew Tower, a forty-nine-story Art Deco skyscraper completed in 1930—the only building in this view not subsequently demolished. The image is muddy compared to many Teich cards. Parked cars, a clock on the corner of the building to the right, and a person in front of the fountain are all rendered so indistinctly as to be nearly invisible. Even so, the dark buildings on the sides complement the relatively dark fountain, which visually pops out against the lighter buildings and sky of the background. The resulting image seems to emphasize contrasting historical eras, foregrounding the earlier for attention.

LA-15   FOUNTAIN, PERSHING SQUARE, LOS ANGELES, CALIFORNIA

6A-H2610

"FOUNTAIN, PERSHING SQUARE, LOS ANGELES, CALIFORNIA"

TEICH 6A-H2610, 1936

ALTHOUGH LOS ANGELES IS NOW A SPRAWLING AUTOMOTIVE city defined by freeways, during the 1930s it possessed a functioning streetcar system that had shaped outlying suburbs and an obvious downtown with Pershing Square at its heart. This view presents the square, which encompassed a full city block, as a lush oasis in the midst of a bustling city. Banana plant leaves, printed in a mottled green accentuated by shadows, frame the composition according to picturesque convention. Masses of banana plants extend back from both sides of the fountain, forming a sequestered space. Above them rise palm trees. The fountain itself, installed in 1910, represents four cherubs supporting a large vase from which water pours into a circular pool and then cascades below. Alternating lines of light blue and white convey a sense of the fountain's cooling effect, especially when contrasted with the almost oppressive enclosure of tropical vegetation.

Also countering the jungle effect is the continuously flowing pavement, which suggests easy circulation in and through the oasis. Although dimly visible figures of people sitting on benches to the right of the fountain, printed in a shaded green, merge into the natural realm, other men and women in a variety of carefully articulated outfits printed in bright artificial colors walk through the square with purposeful intent, as if absorbing the park's relaxing effects on the go while moving from one modern pursuit to the next. Despite the overwhelming vegetation, the postcard also emphasizes the square's urban environment. To the right is the solid mass of the Pershing Square Building, completed in 1924, which offers a dull foil to the gleaming Art Deco setbacks of the Title Guarantee Building, completed in 1931. The urban backdrop suggests Pershing Square offers only momentary respite, a conclusion confirmed by the low cream-colored building at the center of the image, whose vaguely represented facade serves mostly to indicate the existence of a clear path through the tropical vegetation.

126—United States Capitol by Night, Washington, D. C.

"United States Capitol by Night, Washington, D.C."

Teich 5A-H369, 1935

CURT TEICH TOLD A JOURNALIST IN 1938 THAT THE WHITE House was the most popular postcard subject, "photographed from every angle, by day and by night, in winter, spring, summer and autumn."[24] In fact, recent offerings of postcard dealers suggest that linen images of the U.S. Capitol were more numerous. All sorts of public buildings ranging from federal and state capitols to local courthouses, post offices, and city halls graced hundreds if not thousands of linen cards. Those portraying the U.S. Capitol set a standard for images of many of the state capitol buildings.

While most Capitol views conveyed panoramas of the entire building or situated it at the head of the Mall, this dramatic night image of the east front foregrounds the dome's reflection on a rainy sidewalk. The building blazes with light as if for a night session of Congress, and a flag flies at a jaunty angle from the base of the cupola—a detail not present in historical photographs and presumably imaginary. The back caption emphasizes not the Capitol as the seat of power but the image's mood—a product of "night and the magic of electricity" that together create a "chiaro-oscuro" whose "combination of darkness and light and reflection no artist's brush could create." In fact, however, the card owes much to interventions by Teich's art department. Solid color fields comprise most of the image, with its overall effectiveness carried by lines defining the building, the reflection, and a tracery of tree branches—all highlighted or fabricated by a retouching artist. Indeed, the Capitol's lines in particular seem far more the result of an artist's work than of any photographic process. The reflection is especially effective owing to the way the dome merges downward from a wavering sheen into relative clarity—as if the surface on which it appears shifts from wet pavement to a continuous puddle. The view must have been popular with tourists for Teich had earlier based at least two pre-linen cards on the same photo. When the local distributor switched the printing of some Washington cards from Teich to Metrocraft, the latter produced a nearly identical night view based on a different source photo taken at exactly the same spot. Though darker and muddier, with less care devoted to the dome's reflection, Metrocraft's imitation was still dramatically effective.[25]

Court House, Poughkeepsie, N. Y.   72

3B-H1273

"COURT HOUSE, POUGHKEEPSIE, N.Y."

TEICH 3B-H1273, 1943

UNLIKE STREET SCENES, WHICH OFTEN POSSESSED VITALITY stemming from an angle of vision through an intersection, or from pedestrians and vehicles in motion, or even from commercial signs, views of public buildings tended to be static and dull. At the least they possessed informational value, confirming the existence of institutions one would expect to find in any city or town no matter how small—and thus, ultimately, confirming the existence of civic order. Perhaps for that very reason local distributors ordered postcards of most prominent public structures. In the case of this view of the neoclassical Dutchess County, New York, Courthouse, built in 1903, the photographer responsible for the source image endowed a boxy structure with a dynamic visual quality by shooting from a perspective low enough to make the near corner loom upward. Gable windows jutting against the sky and a cornice with slotted dentition also added a sense of movement.

But the card's primary effect came from the art department's treatment of the building's polychromatic facade. The subtly varied gray of the marble base and pilasters contrasted with the brick's deep reddish brown—with further variety added by green inner window shades and by adjustable canvas awnings in a lively orange, some fully extended, others dropped down like shades, and still others pulled up all the way. While some images of public buildings are abstracted from their surroundings, here the street to the left fades into a leafy bower, with a car pulling out in the far distance. To the right is just a hint of a busy retail street, visually integrated with the courthouse by a line of brightly colored automobiles. Despite that nod to realism, the artists were instructed to remove a "police patrol truck," perhaps because it suggested a potential for civic disorder.

The image conveys a sense of local particularity—mostly owing to the building's unusual coloration. The generic features—a uniform street pavement awkwardly marked with lane and pedestrian crossing lines, a lackluster sky shifting from pale dirty yellow to light blue, and a flag sketched in by a retouching artist—served mostly, through familiarity and thus near invisibility, to emphasize the card's uniqueness by way of contrast. The less said, the better, about the figures of the pedestrians, though they appear credible when viewed from a distance.

Presbyterian Church, Marquette, Michigan

"PRESBYTERIAN CHURCH, MARQUETTE, MICHIGAN"

TEICH 1B-H1558, 1941

LEADING CHURCHES IN CITIES AND LARGE TOWNS OFTEN AP-
peared on linen postcards. Such cards were commissioned not by individual
congregations but by wholesale distributors as part of a full package of local
views. Churches were regarded both as important public institutions and as
prominent architectural landmarks. Just as images of government buildings
tended to project a static quality, so too did those of churches. This view of a
Norman-styled church on Michigan's Upper Peninsula, about a block from
Lake Superior, was typical in isolating the building from secular structures and
embedding it in a landscape of cultivated greenery. The three-quarter view fully
documented the church's exterior, including entrance, sanctuary, bell tower,
and meeting rooms and offices. The sky treatment—small wisps of cumulus in a
field of light blue—suggested a convention employed unobtrusively so as not to
distract attention from the solid granite building itself.

The image invokes a sense of the historical, whether by reference to English
cathedrals and parish churches or to similar large American churches. In fact,
however, the building, which was dedicated by the First Presbyterian Church
of Marquette in 1935 to replace an earlier structure destroyed by fire, was only
six years old when this card was produced. This portrayal of impressive bulk
would have indicated to local residents the sustaining presence of religion in the
modern age.[26] The generic quality of the representation is suggested by another
postcard featuring the Gothic Revival brick structure of the Central Methodist
Church of Knoxville, Tennessee. Its image is also based on a photo taken from
a three-quarter perspective and highlighting the same four architectural elements articulated in precisely the same order from left to right—the whole also
being embedded in greenery and portrayed against a humdrum sky. Unlike the
Marquette card, which has no caption on the back, the Knoxville card boasts
about the up-to-date modernity of the church, a new structure completed in
1927. Emphasizing the importance of the material church in the modern world,
the caption claims that the building's "massive equipment makes possible a program, meeting all the needs of the individual and the crowd."[27] The same might
have been written about First Presbyterian in Marquette—or indeed about hundreds of other religious landmarks.

LOWELL HOUSE. HARVARD UNIVERSITY. CAMBRIDGE. MASS.

61900

"Lowell House.
Harvard University.
Cambridge. Mass."

Tichnor 61900, N.D.

LIKE CHURCHES, EDUCATIONAL INSTITUTIONS OFTEN APPEARED in linen postcards without people, as if the physical buildings possessed integrity beyond the vagaries and imperfections of individual human beings. Views of downtowns and street scenes, on the other hand, required pedestrians and cars to enliven them and confirm the success of commercial establishments. But for a church, a school, or a university, whether public or private, it was enough to project a solid presence. Lowell House, a residential hall at Harvard, was another wholly modern structure designed in a revival style to take advantage of the cultural capital of historical associations. Completed in 1930 and covering two city blocks, the immense brick complex consisted of two quadrangles built in a Georgian style complementing the eighteenth- and early nineteenth-century dormitories of Harvard Yard several blocks to the north. This view of Lowell House emphasizes its bell tower, the only vertical feature, viewed from inside the larger of the two courtyards.

The image follows a predictable aesthetic, with a leafy frame along the left, but also reveals slipshod cropping in the half-split chimney on the right edge. Even the card's coloring was poorly executed. The actual bricks of Lowell House are not the fire-engine red used for the tower and right-hand wall in the postcard but are instead a dark reddish brown, similar even in bright sunlight to the hue of the shaded left-hand wall as depicted in the card. Despite a varying pattern of open and closed windows, the overriding impression is of an ill-proportioned, over-large tower rising over regimented blocks of rooms. The building might just as easily have been a hospital or asylum as a college residence hall.

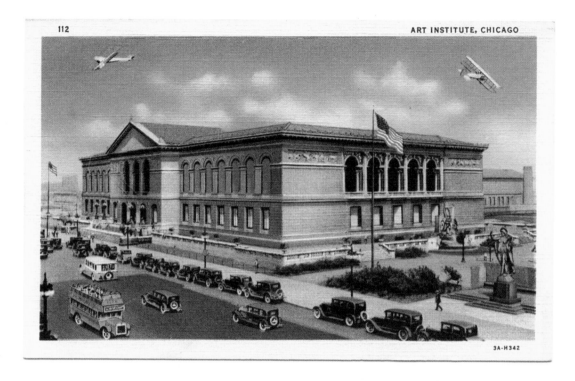

"Art Institute, Chicago"

Teich 3A-H342, 1933

Whatever the case with many public buildings, this image of the Art Institute of Chicago is certainly not dull. Cars and buses, including a double-decker, navigate Michigan Avenue, which is lined with parked cars. A pedestrian walks past a recognizable rendering of Albin Polasek's sculpture *The Spirit of Music* and may be glancing at Lorado Taft's *Fountain of the Great Lakes* at the end of the building. Two flags fly in patriotic display. And two airplanes, one a biplane, soar over the art museum toward opposite edges of the frame. Repeating arches along the neoclassical facades also contribute a sense of kinetic motion. This view indicated that a monumental public building did not have to be stodgy even if its visual appeal was unrelated to its function, which in this case, according to the back caption, was to serve as "a great storehouse of treasures."

Earlier postcards of the Art Institute, from 1907 onward, lacked this card's dynamism, instead portraying the structure, which had opened in 1893, as marooned in a sea of straggling grass sometimes bordered by scrawny saplings. The landscaping on the south side did not exist in cards from the 1910s, and Michigan Avenue's vast width dwarfed horse-drawn buggies and early cars. Even a Teich pre-linen card from 1914 looked desolate despite sidewalks dotted with stick-figure pedestrians. By contrast, the art department seems to have entered a celebratory mode for this card, which belonged to a separately numbered series with more than a hundred views of Chicago released in 1933 for the Century of Progress International Exposition.

At some later time the card was reprinted with deeper, more vivid colors, a change so rare that it is noteworthy, and that reprint is illustrated here. Teich strived to make reprintings identical in hue to the originals and retained multiple copies of each card for that purpose. A new distributor, N. Shure, who took over the series from J. O. Stoll, may have demanded more vibrant colors. But the very details that yielded such a lively image in the first place—Model T Fords, a double-decker bus from the 1920s, and a biplane—eventually grew outdated. To avoid radical retouching, the company printed an entirely new view in 1941, one whose source photo yielded an image devoid of extraneous detail. The Art Institute was once again monumental, static, and dull.[28]

PALACE OF FINE ARTS, SAN FRANCISCO, CALIF. 27

© STANLEY A. PILTZ 2B-H321

"PALACE OF FINE ARTS, SAN FRANCISCO, CALIF."

TEICH 2B-H321, 1942

JUST AS CHICAGO'S ART INSTITUTE WAS ORIGINALLY CON-
structed for the World's Columbian Exposition of 1893, San Francisco's Palace
of Fine Arts was built for the Panama-Pacific Exposition of 1915. Designed as
an open-air Greco-Roman temple mostly surrounded by a lagoon with a semicircular pergola extending eleven hundred feet at its back, the complex masked
an exhibit hall forming a semicircular ring. The palace was so popular that it
was retained at the close of the fair. Progressive high-culture parks like this,
intended to provide aesthetic and moral uplift to citizens of all classes, were
frequent subjects for urban postcard views. According to this card's back caption, the palace was then "one of the world's finest examples of architecture."
Even so, there was room for improvement as revealed by two nearly identical
cards Teich printed ten years apart for the photographer and distributor Stanley
A. Piltz. The first appeared in 1932, soon after the linen process was adopted.
Based on a photo taken by Piltz from the left-hand shore of the lagoon, with a
small fountain as a framing device, the original card displayed the delicacy of
early linens. A light cerulean sky with wisps of cloud served as backdrop to the
palace's open-air dome. Considerable artistry went into the reflections on the
lagoon's surface, interrupted by ripples from the fountain.[29]

Ten years later Pitchford sent the home office a copy of the original card on
which he had roughly sketched in two swans in the foreground. "Competition
brought out a card that had swans in the picture, and it sells," he wrote, "hence
the change in this subject." He advised the art department to retain "colors like
the old subject, as they were very good." The job file for the 1942 card contains a
source photo onto which cutouts of two photos of swans have been collaged, but
the swans on the new card seem instead to be the products of freehand drawing,
not of a camera lens. The soft-focus foreground haziness of the swans does not
fit with the sharp focus of the palace in the distance. But few purchasers likely
noticed that discrepancy, and Pitchford's contribution revived a tired view of a
popular tourist attraction.

64 *Municipal Auditorium by Night, Kansas City, Mo.*

8A-H2371

"MUNICIPAL AUDITORIUM BY NIGHT, KANSAS CITY, MO."

TEICH 8A-H2371, 1938

THIS NIGHT VIEW OF KANSAS CITY'S MUNICIPAL AUDITORIUM portrays the power of urban electrification to turn night into day. The stream-lined Art Deco structure was completed in the mid-1930s as part of a ten-year city plan promoted by Democratic political boss Thomas Pendergast and fund-ed by local bonds and federal grants. With three halls—the Arena, seating fif-teen thousand people, the Music Hall for orchestra and opera, and the Little Theatre—the complex served as evidence of government's role in promoting cultural expression. The postcard's visual effect depends on the inky blue-black of the night sky (relieved by a few squiggles of cumulus clouds), which contrasts with the illuminated building and its surroundings. Although the sky extends an illusion of depth to the entire image, if one ignores the sky and focuses only on the auditorium, the degree to which it is actually defined by minimal line drawing becomes obvious. Black lines economically define edges, corners, win-dows and doors, decorative incisions, medallions, and bas-reliefs. Almost no black is used in surface texturing. The only surface variation comes from a ton-ally shifting light blue wash bathing limestone that, in reality, possesses a honey color. Elements outside the building reinforce a perception of its unreality. The hazy yellow auras of the street lamps are unconvincing, and the automobiles discredit the image in the opposite way, seeming so solid, so photorealistic with their distinctive body styles, that they reflect badly on the building's sketchy two-dimensionality. One final detail, the person on the sidewalk at the frame's lower edge, seems photographically defined, no matter how faintly, and thus also highlights, by contrast, the building's lack of realism. Even so, the sky's dramatic illusion of depth may have proved convincing to purchasers and recipients.

"THE ORCHESTRA PROMENADE, MUNICIPAL
AUDITORIUM, KANSAS CITY, MO."

TEICH 7A-H745, 1937

IN 1937 A NEWS DISTRIBUTOR IN KANSAS CITY ORDERED A series of ten postcards of the new Municipal Auditorium, mostly richly colored views emphasizing the civic building's expensive streamlined Deco interiors. Teich artists deployed a complex medley of accurate colors whose vibrant fields nearly obscure the visually necessary black lines. This image of a long promenade accompanied nuanced views of the Music Hall auditorium's curving, dark red walls and the octagonal Little Theatre's complex decorative scheme. The promenade opens through doors on the right into the Music Hall's orchestra seats, while a central balcony and two side staircases (one visible in the far distance) overlook a lower lobby on the left.

Particularly effective are representations of four large murals portraying the four seasons of life's progression, painted by Walter Alexander Bailey, who had studied with the Regionalist painter Thomas Hart Benton at the Kansas City Art Institute. The postcard captures the murals' contrasting forms and colors and its decorative expressionist style. The image also economically suggests the visual complexity of the circular Deco lighting fixtures (echoed by corresponding mosaic patterns in the floor), the marble veneers, and the bronze grillwork, all of which contributed, according to the back caption, to "a quality of magnificence and distinction." Teich's achievement is especially impressive given the lack of contrast in the Commercial Photo Company's washed-out source photo. As in the view of Radio City Music Hall's foyer (see p. 326), the empty stillness belies the buzzing energy of well-dressed people during the intermission of a performance. A tourist is invited to contemplate the elegant appointments as if awarded a glimpse of an unattainable realm. However, the off-center perspective view, taken from the eye level of someone standing at the end of the promenade, also invites a viewer to imagine walking possessively through this luxurious realm. The auditorium was the democratic possession of all Kansas City's citizens, as announced by Teich in a series of commercial images even more democratically available.

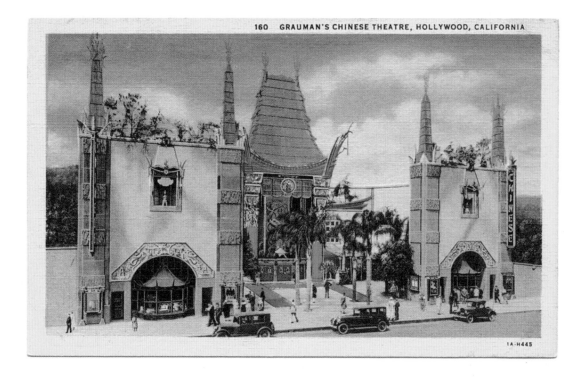

160   GRAUMAN'S CHINESE THEATRE, HOLLYWOOD, CALIFORNIA

1A-H445

"Grauman's Chinese Theatre, Hollywood, California"

Teich 1A-H445, 1931

WHILE TEICH'S VIEWS OF MUNICIPAL AUDITORIUM IN KANSAS City conveyed a sense of local participation in the urbanity of places like New York or Chicago, an earlier view of Grauman's Chinese Theatre in Hollywood portrayed it as an exotic oasis in a sea of trees fronted by a street so devoid of traffic as to seem almost provincial. First printed in 1931 for Western Publishing & Novelty, the card did not mention Teich & Co. Only a serial number identified it as a Teich card. The art department relied heavily on gray photographic details. Except for generic greenery substituting for adjacent buildings, the card reads as a poorly reproduced halftone black-and-white photo splashed here and there with color. Scattered pedestrians are represented in monotone—with only two highlighted in yellow. Three cars at the curb are equally dull. Even the trunks of four palm trees in the theater's forecourt are rendered in dull black-and-white halftone. Perhaps the artist intended to emphasize the contrast of an explosion of color in the stylized entrance pagoda at the back of the court and in red carpets rolled out to the sidewalk. Whatever the case, the image is lackluster, especially since it appeared during the first year of the linen process, when artists were mostly creating delicate watercolor effects.

The company redesigned the postcard sometime during the late 1930s after Grauman's placed a freestanding ticket booth near the sidewalk. In addition to adding that detail to the old retouched source photo, the artists boosted contrasting colors on the side wings, deepened the central pagoda's colors, improved a generic sky, enriched pedestrians through multicolored clothes, removed the dull black cars, and rendered the street surface as a deep chocolate brown. Such a complete transformation between printings without a new serial number may be unique in the run of Teich linens. No doubt the presence of obsolete cars in an iconic view prompted the change, but the shift also produced a card more in line with company standards.

160 Grauman's Chinese Theatre, Hollywood, California

"World Premier. Grauman's
Chinese / Hollywood,
California"

Tichnor 63799, n.d.

EVEN TEICH'S IMPROVED VERSION OF GRAUMAN'S THEATRE IS dull compared with this extravagant representation of a crowd awaiting the arrival of movie stars for a premiere while pastel-colored searchlights sweep the sky. Produced by Tichnor's short-lived Los Angeles branch, the fantastic scene gives an impression that it was based not on photography but on an artist's imaginative rendering. Owing to multiple angles of light, the image appears tilted, perhaps fractured. Close examination suggests a source photo could have been taken from a vantage point across the street, in a building not much taller than the theater. As printed, the pagoda, the obelisks, and the figures of hundreds of people in the crowd reveal a density of detail in black that extends beyond what the image requires. In other words, considerable photographic detail is submerged or obliterated by being wholly overprinted with saturated colors. After reaching a conclusion regarding the image's photographic origin, one then notices that lines marking the vertical edges of the theater's two side wings are not parallel. Those on the left rise straight up, but those on the right tilt as if inserted freehand by an artist to intensify the carnival spirit.[30]

A dramatic sense of motion unusual for linen postcards pervades the scene—not only searchlights whose multiple starting points create a staccato rhythm but also cars gliding toward the forecourt to disgorge celebrities, crowds whose multicolored pointillist heads surge toward the theater, and bursts of light suggesting the quick passing of a single instant. The inky blackness obliterates all surroundings and isolates Grauman's in a dreamlike realm that surpasses fantasies of world's fairs and anticipates the total environments of later theme parks like Disneyland. This image moves beyond the modern electrical sublime to anticipate—by half a century—the disorienting, euphoric hedonism of postmodern urbanity.

84 Atlantic City Auditorium and Convention Hall by Night, Atlantic City, N. J.

Recreation

Largest Convention Hall in the World, Seating Capacity 40,000, Ball Room 3,000

7A-H3506

51   PICNIC GROUNDS, EUCLID BEACH PARK, CLEVELAND, OHIO

5A-H2696

"PICNIC GROUNDS, EUCLID BEACH PARK, CLEVELAND, OHIO"

TEICH 5A-H2696, 1935

WHILE A NINETEENTH-CENTURY UPPER-CLASS TRADITION EN-couraged city dwellers to seek renewal among picturesque urban retreats like New York's Central Park, which was landscaped to appear as a natural environment, the working class often preferred more active leisure pursuits. Coney Island, the iconic amusement park with mechanical rides, games of chance, and other stimulating pleasures, was imitated in cities across the nation. Euclid Beach Park, which opened in 1895 several miles east of Cleveland on the shore of Lake Erie, became popular by combining lake bathing with rides and other amusements.

Although picnickers in this view are relaxing under leafy trees, warmed by sunlight and presumably cooled by a breeze from the lake, they are also crowded together at long, closely packed tables. A crowd also surrounds two pavilions in the distance and extends back on the right to infinity. Despite the wooded surroundings, rendered in a palette of varied shades, textures, and receding degrees of precision, these people mostly seem to be enjoying the proximity of others. At least the image invites us to view them that way. Black shading defines outlines and facial details of the people whose likenesses fill the lower third of the frame. They are also dappled with bright colors that, along with the white shirts of many of the men, contrast with the usual linen effects of trees and sky.[31] Retouching of faces to render specific individuals unrecognizable seems haphazard. The faces of people seated in a group to the left of the tree dividing the frame are mostly unretouched. They probably would have recognized themselves as easily as in a photo. By contrast, the faces of the large group in the lower right corner—two women, two teenage girls, and five younger children—are heavily retouched, rendering them unrecognizable. But their faces, and the collars, folds, and other details of their clothes, have been rendered so broadly as to suggest a casual sensuality—exactly what upper-class critics earlier in the century would have disparaged in such a promiscuous gathering of people.

49:—SUNSET ON LAKE ERIE. EUCLID BEACH PARK, CLEVELAND, OHIO

1407

"Sunset on Lake Erie. Euclid Beach Park. Cleveland. Ohio"

[Metrocraft] 1407, n.d.

THE MOST POPULAR GENERIC SUBJECT FOR LINEN POSTCARDS was a sunset over water—an opportunity for impressive color effects. Many such views were based on stock photos of unknown locations and were imprinted with names of multiple places—wherever they were sold. However, this view seems based on an actual photo of the lakeshore at Euclid Beach Park. The water's calm surface suggests a freshwater lake rather than the ocean, and the park boasted a pier like that portrayed here. The lack of bathers also offers evidence for Euclid Beach because many visitors, content to enjoy rides and other amusements, would not have indulged in swimming.

Like the previous card, this one invites a viewer to identify with particular individuals, and a tree trunk divides each image at about the same point. Otherwise there are no similarities. One can imagine a day-tripper selecting one or the other based on whether she had enjoyed a boisterous family picnic or a contemplative walk along the shore. This sunset by Metrocraft is startling because it diverges from the standard sunset aesthetic and instead exhibits somewhat dull colors. Even so, the merging upward of red at the horizon into irregular, muddy bands of orange, green, rust, and blue creates a richness reinforced by the tree leaves, the strip of grass, and the path, whose dark green and gray emerge slowly from what at first seems an overall silhouette against the muted fire of sky and lake.

However, it is the human figures that give this image its interest. Each individual is carefully delineated through the medium of the silhouette—a young man in a worker's cap on the right, and then, moving left, an older man in a jacket and hat, a stocky woman whose hat, skirt, and chunky oxfords are economically suggested, and a couple walking with a little boy as the setting sun reflects from their calves. The quiet intensity of this view conveys the immediacy of a particular moment, which is unusual for such mass-produced images, and also an unreal, even surreal, quality. On the other hand, the woman who sent this card in August 1940 observed prosaically that it was "nickel day over at Park so they are expecting big crowd this P.M."

L-85   BATHING IN THE LAGOON, LOOKING EAST FROM AUDITORIUM, LONG BEACH, CALIFORNIA

3A-H1327

"BATHING IN THE LAGOON, LOOKING EAST FROM AUDITORIUM, LONG BEACH, CALIFORNIA"

TEICH 3A-H1327, 1933

ALTHOUGH SOME OCEAN SCENES PORTRAYED EMPTY BEACHES, perhaps with a couple strolling along the water's edge, most emphasized the human factor. Beyond the basics of sand, sea, and sky, most beach scenes encompassed people spread over sand and water, umbrellas and scattered belongings, buildings and artificially planted vegetation skirting the beach, and sometimes automobiles parked behind in long rows—almost as if to make the point that nature abhors a vacuum. A series of seven cards published by Teich in 1933 for Western Publishing & Novelty in Los Angeles offered various perspectives on the beach and cityscape surrounding Long Beach's new Municipal Auditorium, a structure completed the previous year on landfill projecting into the harbor, surrounded by a semicircular breakwater and its lagoon.[32]

This particular view, looking from the auditorium along the shore and across the lagoon to the breakwater's eastern terminus, emphasizes a surreal riot of artificial colors. A seething mass of people and umbrellas pulses with pointillist vitality. Even the alternating yellow, white, and brick red swatches of buildings that otherwise form a geometric frame for the kaleidoscopic display contribute to the image's shimmering, eye-popping quality. A pale generic sky, robin's-egg blue with horizontal wisps of cloud, seems like a dull painted backdrop. By contrast, the foreground vegetation, heavily reliant on black ink derived from the source photo, lends a balancing note of reality—or what passed for the more mundane aspects of reality in linen postcards.

LB-84— BATHING IN THE LAGOON, SHOWING MUNICIPAL AUDITORIUM, LONG BEACH, CALIFORNIA

3A-H1326

"BATHING IN THE LAGOON, SHOWING MUNICIPAL AUDITORIUM, LONG BEACH, CALIFORNIA"

TEICH 3A-H1326, 1933

THIS COMPANION POSTCARD, LOOKING UP THE SAME BEACH IN
the opposite direction, toward the auditorium at the upper left, poses a more
complex clashing of the photorealistic and the visionary. Bathers appear in intricate photographic detail, while the beach umbrellas still radiate an artificial
intensity and the background buildings shimmer in a variety of shades and
textures. The backdrop seems unreal, an enticing scrim compared to the foreground's messy reality of towels, caps, and awkward poses. Certain details—the
greenish sheen of the shallow water to the lower left and the reflections in the
viscous sand just above the water line—are skillfully rendered, but the overall
effect is of haunting unreality. Compared to the vibrant umbrellas and shimmering buildings, the human figures in the foreground seem dull, their forms
mostly conveyed by the black plate. Figures farther back, such as people in the
middle ground who are wading in the water, appear as stick figures owing to
heavily retouched black outlines. Even people viewed up close look deformed—
as Ralph Teich recalled, the artists had to do "a little bit of etching or faking on
the face" for anyone recognizable who had not signed a model's release.[33]

Teich's cards reveal no uniform solution to the challenge of arriving at an
acceptable colorized impression of a bathing beach. In 1933 alone, styles ranged
from a promiscuous heap of voluptuous bathers floating in the Great Salt Lake,
rendered as if under the influence of Reginald Marsh's lush paintings of Coney
Island, to a bird's-eye view of hundreds of gaunt semi-stick figures on the sand
at Wildwood-by-the-Sea, New Jersey, an image prefiguring Alberto Giacometti's emaciated postwar sculptures. Even so, these postcards seemed to represent
the experiences of those who sent them to friends with such sentiments as those
expressed separately by card purchasers Frank and Anita in the late 1930s. Both
reported they were "having a swell time" at beaches on the Gulf Coast. While
Frank told Bill there were "millions of bathing beauties and I have met a lot of
them o boy," Anita teased Joyce by exclaiming, "boy the moonlight on the sea
was really *Romantic* looking last night & did I wish for someone."[34]

L-4—A Daily Scene on the Pike, Long Beach, California

OB-H898

"A DAILY SCENE ON THE PIKE, LONG BEACH, CALIFORNIA"

TEICH OB-H898, 1940

WEST OF MUNICIPAL AUDITORIUM IN LONG BEACH, A ROLLER-coaster extended several hundred feet over the water on pilings. One block inland from its entrance, an amusement district called "the Pike" paralleled the shore. Originally a boardwalk, it was paved and lined with midway attractions. Until Knott's Berry Farm and Disneyland opened in the 1950s, the Pike functioned as Los Angeles's amusement park. Based on Pitchford's source photo, this view looks westward. Long shadows and a clock reading nearly 2:00 suggest a bright, sunny winter afternoon. Some people stroll along in winter coats, while others have shed their coats and carry them over their arms. A daring woman in a white bathing suit passes George's refreshment stand on the right, and three young women with blouses over shorts or bathing suits walk toward the viewer. Although patriotic bunting and a giant arrow leading to an indoor freshwater swimming pool known as the Plunge suggest amusements that seemed tawdry by the end of the twentieth century, this crowd reflects solid respectability.

Most of the pedestrians, besides the young women and a boy with an ice cream cone, would have looked no different on a street in downtown Los Angeles. However, this image is quite different from most scenes for which Pitchford took source photos. In this case he included his family. The woman in a blue coat in the left foreground is his wife, Star. Beside her walks a girl in a burgundy dress with a white collar, his daughter, Marilyn, nicknamed Marnie, then about fifteen. Walking alone to the right of his mother is Bob, then about twelve. More than seventy years later Marnie and Bob talked about their father posing them in photos that later became postcards. Marnie spontaneously mentioned this image, and Bob described a postcard showing the two of them eight years later lounging with others around a swimming pool at the Palm Springs Tennis Club. According to Bob, that image was "an iconic photo . . . the most popular picture of Palm Springs." Though Pitchford's family appears casual as they stroll on the Pike, it must have been tedious waiting as he disappeared under his view camera's black cloth hood and waited for the right composition of random passersby. Neither Marnie nor Bob recalled having had any special feelings about appearing on a postcard sold by the thousands.[35]

Noah's Ark at Night, Old Orchard Beach, Me.

"NOAH'S ARK AT NIGHT, OLD ORCHARD BEACH, ME."

TICHNOR 85883, N.D.

RATHER THAN MERELY OFFERING REJUVENATION THROUGH open-air saltwater bathing, beach resorts intensified the mixing of people from different economic classes and ethnic groups that was already occurring in major cities with large department stores and popular entertainment venues such as movie theaters, dance halls, and penny arcades. As the historian John F. Kasson first suggested, mechanical amusement park rides exaggerated and intensified the effects of modern transportation and manufacturing machines, as if visitors desired continuous artificial stimulation even during moments of supposed relaxation.[36] Other than a glowing full moon and wispy clouds, nothing from the natural realm enters this view of an attraction at Old Orchard Beach, Maine, which can be dated by automotive styling to about 1950. Looming behind the prominent forms of three cars is Noah's Ark, a funhouse of traditional amusements. Such thrills as a large rolling barrel to walk through, a shaking and vibrating floor, a maze of dark passageways, and random blasts of air lifting women's skirts were housed in a wooden ship mechanically rocking forward and back. Part of a franchise begun in 1919, the Noah's Ark at Old Orchard Beach was constructed in 1929 and destroyed by fire forty years later.[37]

The image is a fantastic assemblage of complex shapes, phosphorescent colors, and neon signs that draw the eye in opposite directions, to the right with the forms of the ark and a purplish wave shape over the entrance, and to the left with the flowing streamlines of the cars. The postcard presents a dream world grounded only by the pavement along the lower margin. Purchasers most likely ignored the presence of two human figures, one standing beyond the hood of the green car, the other represented by a head and shoulder visible through the red car's front windows, probably someone standing behind the car and not sitting in it. Diminished but not airbrushed out, and printed in gray tones, these vaguely delineated figures add a dull element of the ordinary to an otherwise phantasmagoric image.

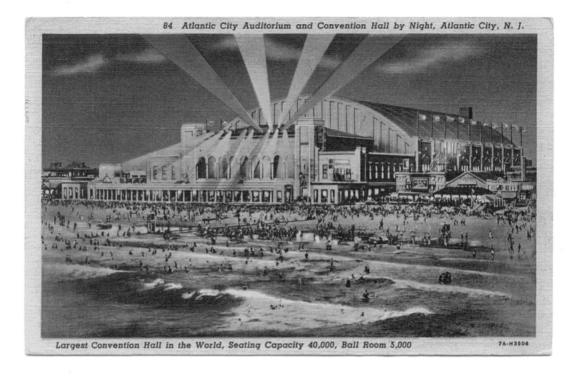

"Atlantic City Auditorium and Convention Hall by Night, Atlantic City, N.J."

Teich 7A-H3506, 1937

"Atlantic City Auditorium and Convention Hall, Atlantic City, N.J.," Teich 3A-H1235, 1933

A SENSE OF FEVERISH ACTIVITY EXTENDING INTO THE NIGHT IS also conveyed by this 1949 card of the Atlantic City Auditorium, which was reportedly the largest clear-span structure in the world when it opened in 1929, with a barrel vault based on the steel-truss engineering of large train stations. Teich had used the same source photo for a daytime view in 1933—a card revealing more of the structure's Romanesque detailing than is visible in this night view. Examining the two cards side by side, an observant tourist might have questioned their realism, a frequent problem with parallel day/night views. Waves break identically in both images, while the same bathers, whether alone or in clumps, appear as if frozen in place for hours. Not everything stays the same, however. While U.S. flags continue to fly along the side of the structure after day turns to night, three clumps of flags across the front of the building have disappeared, possibly so as not to compete with garish colored searchlights. In the daytime view, the arches over the entrance and the spaces between columns at the base are in shadow. In the night view, bright yellow light pierces out from many of these spaces as the whole structure pulsates with electric energy, including a glowing red advertising sign for Gulf Oil. This night view proved so successful that Tichnor directly imitated it—possibly without a source photo—by presenting an artist's stylized rendering of Teich's version of the building, dotting in dozens of minute stick figures along the beach and the Boardwalk (but not in the water), feathering waves over the water like icing on a cake, and crowning the whole with an even less convincing plume of colored searchlights. If the Teich postcard referenced reality while exaggerating its impact, then Tichnor's card moved even further from reality by offering an abstraction of the Teich image.[38]

20   CROWD ON BOARDWALK, SHOWING STEEL PIER, ATLANTIC CITY, N. J.

"Crowd on Boardwalk, Showing Steel Pier, Atlantic City, N.J."

Teich 4A-H1628, 1934

ONE HOUR BY TRAIN FROM PHILADELPHIA, THREE HOURS FROM New York, and easily accessible by car, Atlantic City attracted urban dwellers from all the mid-Atlantic states. According to the back caption for this view of the entrance to the Steel Pier on the Boardwalk, sixteen million visitors annually promenaded past this spot. They came from all classes and occupations, encompassing, according to the caption's rare literary reference, both "the Colonel's Lady and Judy O'Grady." Although the ocean is perhaps distantly visible as a line of dark blue at the end of the street, all attention is on the marquees inviting visitors to make their evening plans or to slip inside for a "photoplay." The Steel Pier extended over the ocean to the right some 1,780 feet, offering every conceivable entertainment, from ballroom dancing and vaudeville by the Modern Minstrels to a diving horse that plunged forty feet with a female rider into a tank of water twelve feet deep.[39]

Nearly every line of text in this image is legible, no matter how tiny, a testament to the skill of Teich's retouching artist. Oddly, given the need to secure repeat orders to make a profit with a particular card, titles of movies on the marquee, including Cecil B. DeMille's *Cleopatra* with Claudette Colbert and just a hint of *Bulldog Drummond Strikes Back* with Ronald Colman, dated this card to 1934 and made it almost instantly obsolete. Although a few people on the far right seem to be lounging on the rail separating the Boardwalk from the beach, most people represented in the image are firmly in and of the crowd, both seeing and being seen. Today a viewer of this card is reminded of the behavior of masses of people in any festival marketplace, though the dresses, suits, and straw hats create a sense of formality not actually felt by participants in the scene who were, after all, dressing normally for the time. The card's pastel colors evoke the sensation of balmy sea air, while the two push cars, only one of which is wholly visible, remind us this is a resort, however stridently urban it might seem.

WF-41 NIGHT VIEW OF WORLD'S FAIR GROUNDS FROM OBSERVATION PLATFORM OF SKY RIDE,

CHICAGO WORLD'S FAIR 3A-H580

"Night View of World's Fair Grounds from Observation Platform of Sky Ride, / Chicago World's Fair"

Teich 3A-H580, 1933

MACHINE-AGE AMERICA'S UTOPIAN SIDE WAS ON DISPLAY AT the Chicago Century of Progress International Exposition, which opened in May 1933, near the low point of the Depression. Although organized to mark Chicago's centennial, the fair's major purpose was recognizing and promoting science's contributions to modern life. Given the turn toward totalitarianism in Europe, some observers might have balked at the official theme: "Science Finds—Industry Applies—Man Conforms."[40] But the slogan also suggested that artificial environments and experiences were shaping existence. While the typical city of linen postcards epitomized modernity, the Century of Progress forecast a world even further transformed by science and industry. Given Teich's location in Chicago, it was not surprising that the company received orders for dozens of views of the exposition.

This night view was based on a photo looking south along the spine of the exposition and the shore of Lake Michigan. It conveys a sense of total artificiality, with nothing in the image traceable to natural origins. Unlike most urban night views, and defying instructions to "put clouds in sky," this overview contains neither clouds nor moonlight. An unvarying deep black that lightens into gray near the horizon replaces the rich, complex blue sky of many night views. Illuminated roadways, bridges, and promenades; stark angular buildings floodlit to highlight bright synthetic colors; and searchlight beams fanning out from a point at the end of the fairground—everything floats in an inky black medium disconnected from Chicago's everyday reality. Scattered dim lines in the upper right are so schematic as to deny reality to the preexisting city they are meant to represent. The only reminders of the natural world are a tiny reflection on the lake on the far left and two obscure areas of vegetation—which by their minimal presence reinforce the artificial contrivance of both the image and the scene it represents. Dozens of tiny vertical lines on the pedestrian mall and the foreground bridge suggest human figures dwarfed by long bands of intense colored light that dematerialize the structures they illuminate. More than almost any other linen image, this one projects its viewer into a realm of utter artifice and unreality.

WF-50

AVENUE OF FLAGS, CHICAGO WORLD'S FAIR

3A-H650

"Avenue of Flags, Chicago World's Fair"

Teich 3A-H650, 1933

TEICH'S VIEWS OF THE CENTURY OF PROGRESS WERE PREPARED with greater care than many other cards, perhaps owing to the local connection, perhaps to a desire to expose millions of visitors—some of them potential wholesale customers—to a colorful new format then produced only by Teich. Or maybe the heightened precision of line and delicacy of color was owing to the fact that they were printed only two years into the Art-Colortone process— before linen images began shifting toward darker, more saturated, sometimes muddled hues. As already noted, Teich's in-house newsletter expressed pride that it was possible "to perfect this latest color process just in time" for the Chicago fair. An anonymous client described Teich's linen postcards as "true reproductions" of the "wonderful color harmony" that was the exposition's "revelation" and "most striking feature."[41] Whatever the case, this view of the fair's entrance promenade revealed the linen process as a unique, hybrid form of representation.

The card shows a crowd flowing toward the observer from the exposition's north entrance eastward along the Avenue of Flags. In the distance outside the gate is the Shedd Aquarium's octagonal dome. Among the structures along the promenade, only the Sears Roebuck Building, on the left, is visible. The image's schematic quality derives from strong lines taken from the source photo, against which the colorful realism of the mass of people offers a strong contrast. Receding rows of flag stanchions with triangular plates and horizontal fins, and visitors' outlines and facial features, are precisely but minimally defined by the black plate, leaving plenty of open space for patches of color. More than most crowds on linen cards, this one is composed of well-delineated individuals. Unless a viewer focuses abnormally closely, the human figures exhibit both precision of outline from the source photo and festive diversity from an array of applied colors for dresses, hats, and jackets. This skillful hybrid of photographic detail and imagined color produces in the foreground a vivid hyperrealism that projects toward the viewer from the unconvincing flatness of red flags and robin's-egg blue sky. The image conveys a message that the Century of Progress belonged to the people—though that insight might have been lost on a correspondent who reported having "put on about 20# [pounds] from all the Beer & Eats."

WF-37

GENERAL MOTORS BUILDING, CHICAGO WORLD'S FAIR

3A-H659

"GENERAL MOTORS BUILDING,
CHICAGO WORLD'S FAIR"

TEICH 3A-H659, 1933

WORLD'S FAIR VIEWS DISTILLED STANDARD TROPES OF URBAN postcards—for example, the mini-genre of day and night views based on a single source photo. The card with the Avenue of Flags discussed above has an unconvincing nighttime double.[42] While the daytime crowd conveys heightened realism, the night crowd has little color and resembles an underexposed black-and-white photo. More effective as a night scene is this portrayal of the General Motors Building at the Century of Progress—a view focusing not on the crowd but on a futuristic structure whose bold color scheme lent itself to dramatic lighting.

Central to this image is the strong vertical form of the 177-foot tower, whose zigzag setbacks recalled New York's Art Deco skyscrapers. The curvilinear lower section, emblazoned with names of GM cars and the Frigidaire line of appliances, appears to be a horizontal projection from the tower. In fact, the building's footprint was a rectangle with rounded corners, and the tower was set into one of the long sides. The impossibility of visually encompassing the entire structure from the ground gave the mini-skyscraper exaggerated prominence. Both the tower and the zigzag pylons at intervals along the curving facade were painted in a burnt orange whose night illumination afforded a rich contrast to the blue-black sky.

Viewed against a threatening night sky, the building conveys a mood of triumphant modernity, and a retouching artist added an inspired touch, a Goodyear blimp overhead. Although a short ride on the blimp cost as much as a night in a first-class hotel, the image implied that such travel would soon become commonplace. This card was ordered two weeks after the view of the Miami Beach causeway to which a blimp was also added (see p. 272). Someone in the art department must have been enthusiastic about airship travel, but most fairgoers were limited to more prosaic transportation. At the bottom of the scene is a chain-link fence that could easily have been deleted. However, that detail signified what the guidebook called the "fenced-in speed lane" of the streamlined Greyhound "auto-liners" that whisked people from end to end of the fair.[43] The fence, but not the blimp, also appeared on two different daytime cards that were based on the same source photo and shared the same serial number. One featured the burnt orange of 1933; the other was updated with the muted white of the GM Building's 1934 incarnation.[44]

36A44

DUTCH VILLAGE, CHICAGO WORLD'S FAIR

KAUFMANN-FABRY PHOTO

4A-H1019

"DUTCH VILLAGE, CHICAGO WORLD'S FAIR"

TEICH 4A-H1019, 1934

NOT ALL CENTURY OF PROGRESS ATTRACTIONS FORECAST TECH-
nological utopia. Some appealed to nostalgia or wanderlust by portraying what
purported to be traditional scenes from around the world. That these were commercial concessions not sponsored by foreign governments or major corpora-
tions suggests that they had wide appeal. Indeed, the number of foreign-themed
"villages" tripled during the exposition's second year. In 1933 visitors wandered
the streets of the Belgian Village or the Moroccan Village and enjoyed Sally
Rand's risqué fan dance at the Streets of Paris. The 1934 season witnessed new
villages devoted to England, Ireland, Italy, Mexico, Switzerland, and Tunisia,
among others. This view of the Dutch Village is based on a photo by Kaufmann
& Fabry, the fair's official photographers, who published real photo postcards
and souvenir picture books.

As seen from outside, the Dutch Village is a chaotic hodgepodge, perhaps
owing to fencing and turnstiles, a huge sign, and two large lighting fixtures enclosing dozens of incandescent bulbs within a circular ring of neon. Inside the
gate, greater coherence prevailed. Narrow streets wound around a canal; next
to the windmill was a square in which traditionally dressed young people demonstrated folk dances. According to a 1952 account, "Edam cheese was manufactured" on site and "marketed by villagers' boats floating on the canals."[45] As
in the fair's other villages, each presenting a pastiche of architectural details,
restaurants, shops, artisans, street vendors, and costumed staff, fairgoers could
lose themselves in a tiny maze promoting momentary escape from the great
vistas and large modern buildings dominating the exposition. The size of the
two women in the foreground indicates the small scale of the buildings—an
architectural deception used later by Walt Disney for his Main Street USA at
Disneyland. These themed enclosures domesticated a complex, increasingly
dangerous foreign world and granted fairgoers a comforting sense of possession. As always, that sense was multiplied when a scene was reduced to the size
of a postcard.

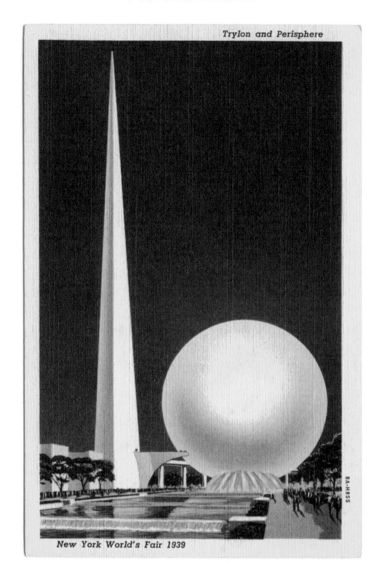

Trylon and Perisphere

New York World's Fair 1939

"TRYLON AND PERISPHERE / NEW YORK WORLD'S FAIR 1939"

TEICH 8A-H955, 1938

FEW STRUCTURES SYMBOLIZED A WORLD'S FAIR AS SUCCESSFUL-ly as the Trylon and Perisphere, the so-called theme center at the New York World's Fair of 1939. The paired shapes of needle and globe comprised a perfect trademark, instantly recognizable in any format or size. This card was ordered in April 1938, a year before the opening ceremonies, part of a series portraying the fair before construction and landscaping were anywhere near completion. Instructions to the art department declared, "This is the most important subject out of the entire set and should be the best seller." The image was based not on a photo but on a rendering made in 1937 by John C. Wenrich, an architectural illustrator employed by the New York World's Fair Corporation. Although the job file copy of Wenrich's rendering is lost, there is a copy in the fair's official records; a comparison shows that the card has identical proportions, identical buildings and trees flanking a reflecting pool, identical bands of low waterfalls, and pedestrians in identical positions. Not surprisingly there were errors in this image of the Trylon and Perisphere because the plans were changed during construction. For example, the low waterfalls were never realized. And the fountains that on the card form a base for the Perisphere came not from Wenrich's rendering, which had a line of much lower fountains, but from a different rendering, by Hugh Ferriss—which survives in the job file. Finally, the theme center as actually constructed had yet a third fountain arrangement.

The only other difference between Wenrich's rendering and the postcard— besides the latter's colorizing—is the omission of a Goodyear blimp Wenrich had included. Although blimps were common in images of the world's fair in

Chicago in 1933, they were notable for their absence from the one in New York in 1939—perhaps owing to the fire that destroyed the German airship *Hindenburg*. The disaster occurred in New Jersey two weeks after this card was ordered, while the image was moving through the art department, and it likely prompted the blimp's removal. As it was, a blimp would only have distracted from the card's eye-popping symbolism. Despite precise, tiny details, the card displays a dramatic abstraction of the fair's icon, one so obvious that it can be recognized even from forty feet away if someone holds up the postcard.

JOHN C. WENRICH, *THEME CENTER— TRYLON AND PERISPHERE—SKETCH*, 1937

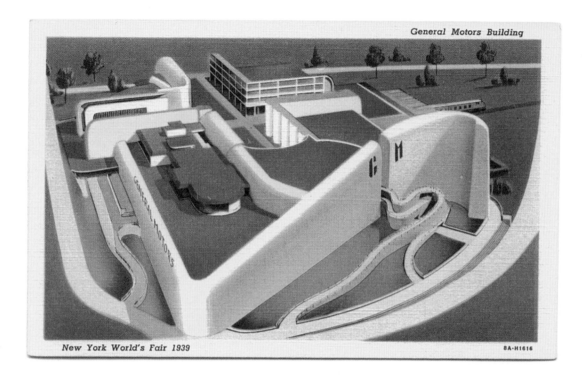

General Motors Building

General Motors

G M

New York World's Fair 1939

8A-H1616

"GENERAL MOTORS BUILDING /
NEW YORK WORLD'S FAIR 1939"

TEICH 8A-H1616, 1938

MORE THAN OTHER EXPOSITIONS DURING THE 1930S (SUCH AS San Diego 1935, Dallas 1936, and San Francisco 1939), the New York World's Fair provoked postcard companies to prepare series of cards featuring individual buildings long before the fair opened. Based on models and renderings, such cards appeared frankly as airbrushed "artist's conceptions." To compare this fanciful image of the General Motors Building with Teich's image of its predecessor at Chicago (see p. 406) is to grasp the rapid shift in architectural visions of modernity as angular Art Deco yielded to streamlining. Rather than conveying a sense of dynamic urban energy, this image suggests a stylized pastoral scene by placing the building's complex form in a field of green and partly surrounding it with pools of water. The image is based on a retouched photo of a model of the building, both of which were prepared in the office of Norman Bel Geddes, the structure's designer. At least two other printers, Grinnell Litho and Miller Art, issued advance cards based on the same model.

Around the time the fair opened, Teich released a new card with a version of this image more accurately reflecting the site's layout, with ramps and lower roadway revised, generic trees added along the roadways, and grass replacing water.[46] A long caption went unchanged except that the future tense used in 1938 to indicate the upcoming "World of Tomorrow" yielded to the present tense. But the building remained unreal, an assemblage of smooth organic forms, with trees and dots of people added to indicate scale, inserted into a pastoral setting divorced from other fair buildings and from the wider urban fabric. Even the revised image shows what appears to be a country lane running along the background. An aerial photo would have revealed, just outside the left border of the image, the wide four lanes and grassy median of the Grand Central Parkway—a real-life version of the dioramas of future superhighways that GM displayed inside the building. As with so many linen cards that defy realism, we must wonder whether consumers perceived any incongruity. Perhaps the image's unreality actually reinforced the validity of the fair's projection of a perfect streamlined future. As one historian has observed, "The fair was the city's perfected dream of itself."[47]

PHOTOGRAPH BY R. KENDALL WILLIAMS

Accommodations

TRAMOR CAFETERIA   The Finest Cafeteria in the South   ST. PETERSBURG, FLA.

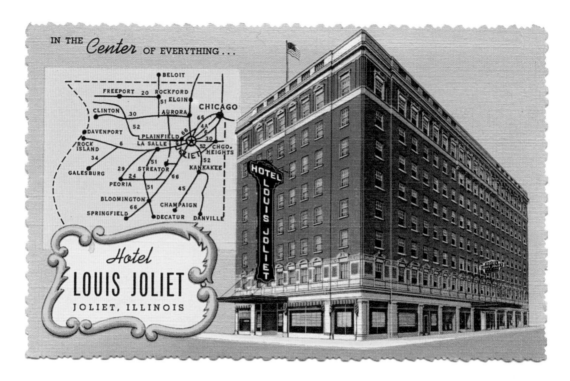

"In the Center of Everything . . . /
Hotel / Louis Joliet / Joliet, Illinois"

Teich 1B-H148, 1941

BUSINESS WAS BOOMING IN THE PRE-DEPRESSION 1920S, AS was auto traffic, and salesmen increasingly traveled by car rather than train. The Hotel Louis Joliet, completed in 1927 as the largest and most luxurious in Joliet, billed itself on the back of this postcard as "a modern commercial and tourist hotel." Commercial travelers probably made up the majority of guests, but the hotel would have attracted wealthier tourists who did not have to make do with a cabin, court, or municipal camp. The Louis Joliet was typical of hundreds of red-brick hotels located in every city or town large enough to sustain the patronage. In addition to a two-story lobby, the Louis Joliet offered three air-conditioned restaurants, a cocktail lounge, ground-floor shops, a parking garage, and proximity to the Rialto Square Theater, constructed on the same block by the investors who funded the hotel.

Some proprietors who ordered postcards chose to feature their hotels as situated in active commercial landscapes. Others downplayed their surroundings by asking that the structures on either side be faded into hazy insubstantiality.[48] Still other hotels, such as the Louis Joliet, were removed entirely from their surroundings and portrayed as if the images were based on photographs of models—a form of miniaturization emphasizing the grand hotel as a self-contained world. In this case, however, the U.S. flag above the hotel implied a wider patriotic allegiance.

While some hoteliers requested cards with two small interior views illustrating a restaurant, lounge, or bedroom stacked beside a vertical view of the exterior (see fig. 3.9), others wanted a map locating a hotel in its region. Proclaiming Joliet "in the center of everything," this map marks the city with a star and indicates that all roads in northern Illinois, even those from Chicago, converge on the small manufacturing city. The woman who slipped this card into an envelope for a friend or relative wrote on the back that she was sending it "for the little map which indicates where we are." The proprietor likely intended to use the card for promotional mailings demonstrating the hotel's central location to potential guests, especially commercial travelers. The ornamental cartouche surrounding the hotel's name and the card's elegant deckle edge promised luxurious accommodations.

HOTEL
LOUIS
JOLIET
COCKTAIL
LOUNGE
•
JOLIET, ILL.

7A-H356

"Hotel Louis Joliet Cocktail Lounge / Joliet, Ill."

Teich 7A-H356, 1937

ALTHOUGH THIS VIEW OF THE HOTEL LOUIS JOLIET'S COCKTAIL lounge preceded the exterior view by four years, they appear designed to work together. Each image is offset to one side, with an angle of vision slanting away from the text. The lime green used for the background on the exterior view is identical to that on the lower part of the cocktail lounge card's sidebar, which merges upward into a light yellow green similar to the hue inside the exterior view's cartouche. These cards made a jaunty contrast when displayed at the front desk, with their differing frames and irregular picture dimensions. The cocktail lounge's image possesses an energy that is frequently found in commercial interiors on linen cards. Whether in large cities or small, such spaces typically reflected current design idioms. Commercial photographers hired at the completion of an architectural project strived to portray an interior at its most impressive, and their work was later used as source photos for postcards.

An interior view demanded careful work from a retouching artist—with more detail than was required for a landscape or street view. The rendering itself seems a work of art, with little obviously derived from the source photo, which is entirely hidden beneath varying tones of gray paint. Every line in the complex rendering is outlined or highlighted depending on its relation to the photo's light source. Ghostly reflections of tableware in polished black Formica are rendered with illusionistic perfection. Burnished highlights gleam from curved glass ashtrays. Individual bottles behind the bar glow with reflected light. The clock is legible in the rendering, as are two signs above the bar announcing a pork tenderloin sandwich for thirty-five cents and a steak sandwich for forty cents—their words picked out in letters less than a millimeter high. One can even discern buttons on the cash register and stacks of dishes to the left of the kitchen door. What might seem overkill in the retouched photo yielded a finished postcard with an enhanced realism. Although the words in the signs above the bar cannot be read from the postcard, there is a feeling that, as in real life, the information is actually there and could be read if one could move in a bit closer. That awareness is enhanced by the immediacy of bright contrasting colors, which suggest a realm paradoxically more vibrant than everyday life, a place where the night is always still young.

"ADAMS HOTEL / TULSA, OKLA."

TEICH 1B-H391, 1941

REGARDLESS OF LAYOUT OR BACKGROUND, MOST LINEN CARDS of hotel exteriors emphasized red-brick solidity in a commercial scene otherwise subject to impermanence. Few cards indulged the playfulness animating this night view of the Adams Hotel in Tulsa. Although the caption describes the hotel as "modern as tomorrow," the Adams projected an architectural eclecticism later described as "an imaginative combination of Gothic, Italian Renaissance and Baroque."[49] Here the hotel appears as a fluidly gleaming white confection—with lower stories dripping with ornament, bold piers projecting upward, decorative medallions along the spandrels, honey-yellow illuminated windows alternating with purplish-blue darkened rooms, and fairy-tale crenellations piercing a deep night sky. The surroundings might be described as urban mythological, with a golden glow emanating from street-level windows and highlighting pedestrians in reflections from a mirror-smooth sidewalk. The soft, rounded forms of late-model sedans and a backdrop of jagged, black silhouettes recall children's book illustrations. Above it all is the Adams logo in a Deco font borrowed from the hotel's letterhead at the proprietor's insistence after he had rejected a handmade color proof.

Although the hotel opened in 1928, its architecture was typical of the turn of the century. Recent color photos reveal a facade encrusted with molded terra cotta ornament in fantastic shapes—bosses, coats of arms, curlicues, sconces, crosses, and gargoyles—creating a delicate tracery around generously sized windows. Photos also reveal that the building's piers, gleaming so purely white in the card, are actually faced with red brick, dark enough to create a sharp contrast with the terra cotta. Given that the proprietor, a Mr. Wasson, was harder to work with than most clients, this fantasy must have reflected his own idealized sense of the hotel. The author of a Teich in-house memo traced a long history of problems with Wasson and addressed the initial color proof's poor rendering of the terra cotta, finally lamenting, "I don't know what we are going to do." Somehow they managed, creating this nearly unique image of a hotel standing in majestically surreal isolation.

LOBBY — HOTEL ATLANTIC — CLARK ST. NEAR JACKSON BOULEVARD — CHICAGO

"LOBBY—HOTEL ATLANTIC—CLARK ST. NEAR JACKSON BOULEVARD—CHICAGO"

TEICH 7A-H1938, 1937

MANY HOTEL GUESTS INSCRIBED MESSAGES WHILE SITTING IN the very lobbies portrayed by the cards they wrote on. The typical hotel lobby, regarded as an extension of the domestic parlor since the early nineteenth century, was more fully used in the early twentieth century than similar spaces in twenty-first-century hotels. The Hotel Wyoming was about ten years old when Curt Teich's brother Max purchased it in 1902 in partnership with a brother-in-law. They renamed the eight-story structure the Hotel Kaiserhof and gave its public rooms a lavish Old World ambience. In 1915 they expanded, doubling the number of rooms to 450 by adding an eighteen-story tower. As late as 1965, shortly after Max's death, a restaurant critic lauded a tradition of excellent German cuisine under continuous family management since 1903. However, confronted by anti-German hysteria during the First World War, the owners had renamed the establishment the Hotel Atlantic. It was demolished in 1971.[50]

Over the years Teich provided postcards for the hotel in every style for which the company was known. The first card, imported from Germany soon after Max bought the hotel, was an exterior in the firm's monotone lithograph series of Chicago views. One of the final cards was an exterior from the late 1950s, incongruously based on artwork done originally for a crude pre-linen card just after the hotel's 1915 expansion. That early card had presented the old hotel and new tower as if drawn in perspective by an art student, with fanciful renderings of tiny Model T Fords and streetcars on an absurdly wide street. The same artwork had been used in 1933 for a linen card with streamlined cars and with the sign changed from Kaiserhof to Atlantic. The 1950s image boasted cars with tail fins but was otherwise unchanged. That card's glossy surface attempted to suggest that the wholly unreal image was just like any other contemporary chrome card based on color photography. Given the hundreds of acceptable hotel exteriors printed by Teich, it is hard to imagine why the company did so poorly for so long with exterior views of Max Teich's hotel.[51] However, that was not the case for interiors, as this detailed lobby rendering from 1937 reveals. A comparison with similar views from 1917 and 1933 indicates many minor changes in rugs, chair design, and upholstery—all aimed at reducing overstuffed clutter and creating a spacious, modern feeling.

MIRROR ROOM -- HOTEL BENTLEY — ALEXANDRIA, LA.

"Mirror Room—Hotel Bentley— Alexandria, La."

Mid-West Map A-1865, n.d.

FEW LINEN INTERIORS RADIATE THE INTENSITY OF THIS VIEW of the Mirror Room, an Art Deco cocktail lounge on the ground floor of the Hotel Bentley, a neo-Renaissance structure from 1908. Dominating Alexandria, Louisiana, the hotel was the unofficial headquarters for U.S. Army officers leading 400,000 troops in war games in 1941 as the nation faced the threat of war. As in most other interior views of restaurants and nightclubs, a diagonal aisle divides the room, leading toward distant doors much as a street leads toward an urban skyline or a stream toward a wilderness horizon. Sharply retouched lines define the image by accenting chairs, tables, wall and ceiling panels, and fluted pillars. That schematic representation is transformed by sophisticated texturing through color, producing unprecedented depth. Modulated shadows from furniture on a two-tone floor create a shifting pattern instead of the dull uniformity common to many linen aisles and streets. Backs of chairs facing the viewer are subtly lighter than those grouped around tables on the left. Above all, reflections in the mirrored ceiling give this image its uniqueness. A shimmering intensity marks the ceiling's far reaches, while reflections of tables and chairs are sharper than their real counterparts. While the image probably owes as much to an effective source photo as to skilled artist manipulations, the resulting card carries visual impact, promising vibrant nightlife for visitors to the provinces—including such future military leaders as Omar Bradley, Dwight D. Eisenhower, and George S. Patton.

At least three companies published images of the Mirror Room using the same source photo. One of them, undated, with an idiosyncratic serial number of a type shared by several midwestern distributors, recalled comic-strip art, with strong lines filled by light color fields. The second, an offering by Teich from 1938, was similarly cartoonlike, though more subtly colored. Artistically most impressive is the card illustrated here, undated but found online postmarked in July 1941. Its nearly unprecedented intensity derives to a great extent from the contrast of its rich, dark tones. The distributor of this card was Mid-West Map Company of Aurora, Missouri. It is not known whether MWM, a regional printer of road maps, actually printed this card or merely ordered it from another printer, but there is a certain satisfaction in the notion that a small competitor took on an image already issued by the industry giant and utterly transformed it.[52]

SOMERSET HOTEL   MIAMI BEACH, FLORIDA

DIRECTLY on the Atlantic Ocean

9A-H1747

"Somerset Hotel / Miami Beach, Florida / Directly on the Atlantic Ocean"

Teich 9A-H1747, 1939

MOST LINEN HOTEL VIEWS PRESENTED REALISTIC EXTERIORS, but those from Miami Beach were so different as to constitute a separate genre. As the resort city emerged from the Depression, investors built dozens of small Art Deco hotels. From 1935 to 1950 most of Teich's Miami Beach hotel cards conformed to a model exemplified by this image of the Somerset Hotel. Illustrations exhibited a playful style with little evidence of photographic input. Storybook palms, colorful beach umbrellas, lawns flat as carpets, and cartoon-like people surrounded blinding white buildings with bold lines and smooth surfaces. Most images indicated street access with elongated automobiles and beach access even for hotels not actually on the ocean. Delicate atmospherics completed a format suggesting Miami Beach was literally out of this world.

The genre evolved through competition among new hotels. Proprietors submitted orders before construction was complete so postcards would be available before the opening day. Fanciful artwork resulted from having no photo to form the "skeleton" of a realistic black plate. The Somerset's job file contains a construction photo showing walls of undressed concrete block and a facade still in scaffolding. Plans, renderings, and construction photos can also be found in job files for other Miami Beach hotels.[53] As owners of newer hotels demanded similar cards, a local style emerged, with a single artist probably specializing in the aesthetic.

Sales agent George Heunisch, a German immigrant who arrived in Florida from Chicago in 1936, promoted this Miami Beach style.[54] For a card based on a "full colored architect's drawing," Heunisch told artists to "work up patio at right by furnishing a few round tables surmounted [by] umbrellas," "couples walking along hotel sidewalk," and a "beach with crowd of bathers." Another card's image required a "bathing beach, waterfront, sunset in distance and ocean liner coming from left [to] right." Other requests included "wherever desirable streamlined automobiles" and a "great deal of sunset effect." In his instructions Heunisch used cross-references, such as "coconut trees, foliage and trunks, exactly same as those on card 4A-H562." His operative word was "illusion," as in "illusion [of] bathers on beaches," "illusion of attractiveness of Ocean immediately back of hotel," and ultimately "the illusion of beach life."[55] The genre's success prompted proprietors of resort hotels outside Florida to demand it, and Teich's competitor Colourpicture copied it.[56] But this illusionary aesthetic did not survive in ordinary places.

ONE OF THE KENTS RESTAURANTS IN ATLANTIC CITY

1700-02 PACIFIC AVENUE — AT ILLINOIS AVENUE CORNER — OPPOSITE POST OFFICE

"One of the Kents Restaurants in Atlantic City / 1700-02 Pacific Avenue— At Illinois Avenue Corner— Opposite Post Office"

Teich 9A-H1773, 1939

WHILE NEW YORKERS WHO COULD AFFORD A WINTER BEACH holiday traveled to Miami Beach, those in Philadelphia who sought relief from summer heat went to Atlantic City. This tourist-oriented restaurant chain had three outlets in the city and a candy shop on the Boardwalk. Former visitors and residents waxed nostalgic about Kents on a website devoted to memories of Atlantic City, offering praise for its upscale menu (they "even had lobster") and for the bakery renowned for "crispy" donuts and "twice-iced chocolate cakes."[57] During the late 1930s and early 1940s, Kents Restaurant & Baking Company ordered a postcard of each restaurant from Teich. This Pacific Corner location had recently opened across the street from the central post office and two blocks from the ocean.

The night view emphasizes dramatic, all-encompassing darkness that isolates the restaurant from other retail businesses. Kents appears as a bright, inviting oasis with expanses of plate glass accentuated by subtly shaded white stucco, jaunty awnings with green and yellow stripes, and a black base, probably of glass veneer, whose representation satisfies the instruction to show its "'Marble-ish' effect." Although the restaurant's interior is rendered faintly, suggested rather than delineated by light patches of color, some details are still clear. One can make out bakery display cases on the left and tables and chairs on the right. This linen view is somewhat reminiscent of Edward Hopper's iconic *Nighthawks*, completed three years later, which portrays the interior of a brightly lit diner with three customers and a counterman. However, while Hopper provokes a viewer to ponder facial expressions and imagine relationships, the empty interior of Kents enables one to imagine personally entering the restaurant. While Hopper's light is unforgiving, that of Kents is warm and inviting. And while Hopper rendered the diner's nondescript, seedy surroundings, the total darkness beyond Kents proclaims it as the only attraction in town—a destination, not a way station.

THE LOTUS — 727 14TH ST., N. W. — WASHINGTON, D. C.   6A-H1019

"THE LOTUS—727 14TH ST., N.W.— WASHINGTON, D.C."

TEICH 6A-H1019, 1936

RETOUCHED SOURCE PHOTO, INTERIOR OF THE LOTUS, 1936

DICK G. LAM, THE CHINESE AMERICAN OWNER OF THE LOTUS restaurant and nightclub in Washington, DC, kept its interior decor updated. Postcards from about 1926 to 1950 portray five different interiors for the popular nightspot. In the earliest incarnation, the pillars had a bark-like covering and sprouted leafy branches that merged with the ceiling. A Teich pre-linen from 1928 indicates a restrained "Oriental" design, which by 1936 had yielded to this bolder one. In 1944, under the influence of streamlining, chrome surfaces reigned supreme, but a Teich linen from 1950 shows rich, dark colors arrayed in bold planes. Throughout the period, the Lotus, promoted as the city's largest Chinese American restaurant, received top billing in the *Washington Post*'s entertainment column for flamboyant variety shows with choreographed dancers, comedians, fan dancers, tap dancers, and acrobats—all of them mainstream performers of European ethnicity.[58]

Like many restaurant and nightclub proprietors, Lam proved to be an exacting client. Various cards he ordered from Teich all portrayed this "Chinese-American Restaurant of Distinction" in utterly realistic detail. Although there is no evidence that Lam submitted swatches of carpeting, upholstery, wallpaper, or paint chips for precise color matching, the sales agent for this card prepared sketches indicating colors for the tiniest parts of the image. For example, a half-page sketch of the panel on the nearest pillar specified fourteen different colors, defining such indistinct details as green ferns and pink flowers. Even more superfluous was a full-page sketch of a circular mural behind the orchestra, barely visible in the card's upper left quadrant, where eleven colors were intended to portray a pagoda surrounded by mountains. Typed instructions described the chairs as "covered with slip covers" of "white material with red flowers" and "little yellow and green trimmings to divide the flowers." The retouched photo, approved by Lam after revisions, is one of the most detailed in Teich's records. Lam later returned the color proof for the card, requesting that a sprinkling of

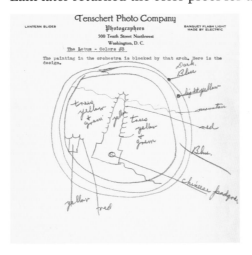

white stars be removed from the ceiling. The caption describes the Lotus as "the first Cabaret Restaurant established in Washington," with "three Stupendous Revues daily," "superb cuisine," and "fascinating music." The delicacy of this image was no doubt perceived as appropriate for an "Oriental" retreat.

SALES AGENT'S SKETCH OF PAGODA MURAL WITH INSTRUCTIONS FOR COLOR, 1936

PHOTOGRAPH BY R. KENDALL WILLIAMS

9A-H511

TRAMOR CAFETERIA   *The Finest Cafeteria in the South*   ST. PETERSBURG, FLA.

"Tramor Cafeteria / The Finest Cafeteria in the South / St. Petersburg, Fla."

Teich 9A-H511, 1939

THE CAPTION ON THE BACK OF THIS CARD BOASTS THAT THE
Tramor Cafeteria was Florida's largest, serving "over 5,000 meals daily . . . in
a tropical Spanish atmosphere with orchestral music and entertainment." An
architectural landmark of St. Petersburg even now, the building was a regular
destination for winter visitors into the late twentieth century. After opening as
Bob's Cafeteria in 1930, the business was renamed in 1939, an event that may
have occasioned this postcard. There is a refreshing frankness to the image,
with details—colorful mosaic floor tiles, ceramic water pitchers, and folds in the
tablecloths—carefully rendered. Identical rows of tables, differing only in the
color of the pitchers, suggest mass production, or more accurately democratic
mass consumption. The caption's wording, emphasizing both cosmopolitanism
and high-volume production, is echoed in the image. Although the decor evokes
the traditional courtyard of a Spanish hacienda, the modern efficiency of the
gleaming stainless steel serving line is represented on the right side.

However, the Tramor's most unusual feature is a slightly curved ceiling mural representing a delicate light blue Mediterranean sky scattered with cirrus
clouds. Recent color photos suggest an effect strikingly similar to that of the
faux sky over the arcaded indoor Forum Shops that opened at Caesars Palace in
Las Vegas in 1992. Teich's artists were unable to capture such a direct simulation. Instead they fell back on what they knew best—a generic linen representation of sky and clouds. In that sense, they rendered the illusion perfectly. Anyone familiar with linen postcards who glanced at this image would have thought
they were looking at an outdoor square filled with tables. The patently artificial
sky paradoxically conveys the realism of the image within the parameters of the
linen postcard aesthetic. The illusion was so perfect that the card was revised
during World War II to include several military planes flying over the Tramor's
Spanish square, against its painted sky, under the legend "Keep 'Em Flying!"[59]

The Longest Lunch Counter in the World. F. W. Woolworth Co.—431 So. Broadway, Los Angeles, California

7A-H3065

"THE LONGEST LUNCH COUNTER IN THE WORLD. F. W. WOOLWORTH CO.—431 SO. BROADWAY, LOS ANGELES, CALIFORNIA"

TEICH 7A-H3065, 1937

ALTHOUGH WOOLWORTH WAS AN EARLY TEICH CUSTOMER whose 1912 orders enabled the company to expand its business, this card illustrating a lunch counter in Los Angeles was ordered not by Woolworth but by Western Publishing & Novelty—suggesting that the store's 100-yard counter was a tourist attraction. A black-and-white real photo card from the same time, taken at a slightly different angle, reveals harsh reflections from wall tiles, counters, seat backs, linoleum flooring, and ceiling, but Teich's image has a softening effect.[60] Sharp foreground details yield to delicate shadows on the floor and a hazy vanishing point. Sales agent Pitchford directed the art department to "bring out" the items on the right side—"lip sticks, rouge, nail polish," all in "attractive containers, in bright colors, most of them mounted on small display cards." He asked the retouching artist to create order by "follow[ing] out the idea, that they are in uniform displays, that is, so much space allotted to each item, small squares and panels on the counter." Most striking about this image, however, is the empty corridor extending to infinity between a row of gradually diminishing stools and an equally diminishing display of retail goods.

The absence of people creates a unique interior aesthetic. Without people, and thus without the sense of scale that human figures provide, a typical interior, such as those of this Woolworth's lunch counter or the Buckhorn Curio Store (see p. 162), opens from a generous wide-angle perspective and narrows into a diagonal vista of exaggerated depth. The characteristic form of such interior images parallels the presentation of city streets in many urban postcard images, such as the view of Market and Post Streets in San Francisco (see p. 308).[61] Whether an interior depicts a hotel lobby, a nightclub, a restaurant, or a lunch counter, its major elements—tables, chairs, counters, and aisles—assume nearly architectural qualities, mirroring images of buildings arrayed in the typical grid pattern of city streets, viewed at an angle. Reversing the parallel's direction, one might also regard many of Teich's urban views as formally resembling interiors. By removing people from the picture and reducing the largest city to postcard size, Teich's artists miniaturized public space for individual possession. The resulting stylized approximations of the American scene—empty, airbrushed, and streamlined—catered to a desire for a world cleansed of uncertainty and risk.

Corey's Fine Foods
— 4th and Fremont Sts.
Las Vegas, Nevada
Phone: 3088

"COREY'S FINE FOODS / —4TH AND FREMONT
STS. / LAS VEGAS, NEVADA / PHONE: 3088"

COLOURPICTURE K1853, N.D.

LINEN POSTCARDS OFFERED REASSURANCE ABOUT THE AMERI-
can scene's promise in the face of economic depression and global war. Even
so, some images embodied ambiguity—a quality that encourages projection by
viewers. The last two images in this section transport us to a particular time
and place, immediate postwar Las Vegas, and raise concerns about the limits of
interpretation. Corey's Cafe possesses a facade typical of any modernizing main
street—in this case evidence of expansion triggered by Hoover Dam and by the
emergence of a gambling resort for Southern California. A rectangular front
dominated by bold modern patterns and a streamlined stainless steel overhang
boasts a sign with a caricature of a chef bursting from the capital C in "Corey's" and projecting against the sky. Scores of day and night photos taken by
Pitchford reveal the cafe's bustling surroundings on Fremont Street, lined with
overgrown storefront casinos like the Pioneer and the Monte Carlo as well as
ordinary businesses like those found in any town. Pitchford's camera captured
scenes of young men loitering on street corners and in doorways, suggesting an
unfocused energy permeating the scene.

Although Corey's was surrounded by honky-tonk establishments, this Colourpicture card makes the cafe appear as if located in any ordinary commercial
district, with shade trees extending toward a residential neighborhood. Unlike
most linen cards with restaurant exteriors, this image provokes an observer not
to think of entering the restaurant but to wonder about ongoing street life. A
mother and child are about to walk out of the left frame, and two women are
walking up the side street in shadow toward indistinct male figures. Are the
women friends, or perhaps mother and grown daughter? Have they just met
for breakfast on a cold winter morning? The dynamic presence of a late-model
car on the lower right, extending from outside the frame, invites a viewer to
regard the image not as self-contained but as part of a borderless reality whose
unknown narratives extend beyond what is shown. Something quite real, and
therefore potentially unsettling, may be happening here. Or such a conclusion
may be unwarranted, a product of projection backward from the present.

Lobby
El Patio Hotel

"LOBBY / EL PATIO HOTEL"

FULLCOLOR F10630, N.D.

EL PATIO HOTEL WAS LOCATED IN LAS VEGAS HALF A BLOCK
north of Fremont, just up Second Street from the luxurious Hotel Apache. It
is hard to imagine a more unpromising postcard interior than El Patio's lobby.
Much of the image is filled by an expanse of faded, dirty beige carpet flecked
with yellow and green—its pattern vaguely revealed beneath the chair at lower
left. Mismatched furniture and utilitarian equipment line the sides of the room.
The overwhelming impression is of a depressing brown, somewhat relieved
by dark green curtains and couch and by a matching set of red armchairs and
couch. A cream-colored plastic radio sits on a glass-topped table, and a utilitarian water cooler with a wall-mounted paper-cup dispenser stands at the center of the scene. A beige wall facing the observer lacks any decorative feature.
The front desk projects into the frame on the lower right. Toward the back is
a half flight of stairs, covered with bilious-green carpeting, turning to the left
and leading to rooms whose decor one assumes to be as minimal as the lobby's.
While the caption boasts of air conditioning, four freestanding ashtrays suggest
a perpetual odor of stale smoke. El Patio is described as "proud of its refined
accommodations," but it comes across as a dead end, the end of the line, a place
inhabited by those who have scraped together a final stake for fortune's wheel—
or by those who have already lost everything. Few linen postcards are less likely
to be inscribed with a casual "wish you were here." For once an image represents
a scene congruent with bleak social reality. To imagine it as the setting for a noir
narrative is to invest it with more energy than it possesses.

6

From a Rearview Mirror

CONTEMPORARY REFLECTIONS

SHORTLY AFTER THE TURN OF THIS CENTURY, around the time my interest in linen postcards was shifting from a collector's to a cultural historian's, a casual Sunday visit to an art museum brought an unexpected surprise. The gift shop presented a predictable mix of art books, notepaper, framed prints, overpriced educational toys, and jewelry. Among the latter were several bracelets, necklaces, pendants, and earrings that caught my attention because they featured tiny fragments of linen postcards embedded in simple Deco-styled silver settings. A large bracelet consisted of six linked trapezoids, each enclosing a different bit from a single postcard representing the New York skyline (fig. 6.1). A pendant in the shape of a slightly flattened pentagram framed a tight view of one of the piers of the Brooklyn Bridge against a peach and turquoise sky. Most haunting was a small bracelet, a thin silver hoop connecting to a bezel less than an inch in diameter surrounding a section of red-brick wall with several windows and pull-down shades. A clear epoxy sealant protected these tiny views and gave them a reflective surface with a hint of amber.

Although fabricated by a contemporary artisan, Stephanie Lindsey, these evocative pieces of jewelry with their fragmentary images

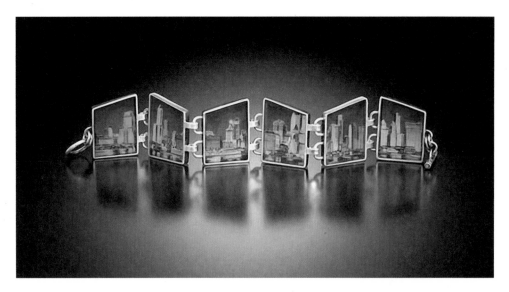

FIG. 6.1. Stephanie Lindsey, bracelet, *Baby Jane* jewelry, 1997-2008

seemed to be artifacts from a vanished world, perhaps talismans granting momentary access. Lindsey explained her use of "vintage" linen postcards by referring to the "vibrancy, color, and nostalgia" of their portrayal of "tourist destinations and attractions across America." *Baby Jane*, the name she gave the series, came from a nickname by which her mother, then recently deceased, was known as a little girl.[1] Although that information was not available to a casual shopper, the jewelry evoked Lindsey's desire to connect with an irrevocably lost time preceding her own existence. Most women who adorned themselves with these pieces were too young to have directly experienced linen postcards or the American scene they portrayed. A free-floating nostalgia suffused these simple but resonant pieces. For some people they might have expressed a vogue for retro fashion, but depending on the depth of one's attraction, they might also have functioned as fetish objects.

Whether or not Lindsey knew the connection, her appropriation of linen postcards echoed an assemblage by the artist Joseph Cornell, who employed fragments of New York skyscraper postcards in an untitled "penny arcade portrait" of Lauren Bacall (fig. 6.2). Completed in about 1946 as an homage to the young actress, who had recently starred in the film *To Have and Have Not*, Cornell's shadow box took the form of a stylized pinball machine framed in dark-stained wood, just over twenty inches high, sixteen inches wide, and nearly four inches deep. A series of smaller wooden frames within the larger frame enclose a movie magazine portrait of a sultry Bacall at the center, several passport-size versions of the same portrait, portraits of the actress as a child, and photos of a dog arranged vertically to the left and right, and near the bottom, two squares with indistinct dark blue portraits of Bacall on either side of a vaguely disturbing blank square.

A wooden ball released at the top right of the box will zigzag downward from side to side, its progress occasionally visible as it passes behind circular holes in a dark blue wooden panel, then twice in front of the recessed central portrait of Bacall, and finally along a bottom row enclosed in transparent glass to an exit flap in the side. Near the top of the box is a long horizontal frame surrounding five squares, one of which is empty, the other four containing urban scenes constructed from bits and pieces of linen postcards of the Empire State Building, Rockefeller Center, and the Chrysler Building. The latter's distinctive tower is presented in the middle of a square section, complete with surrounding sky, that Cornell cut from a Colourpicture card. Another of the five positions in the frame is filled with a square cut from a card displaying a dark night view of skyscrapers. Two other vignettes contain imaginary scenes constructed from

FIG. 6.2. Joseph Cornell, *Untitled* [Penny Arcade Portrait of Lauren Bacall], ca. 1945-1946

zigzag bits of individual buildings cut from various linen cards and recombined, some directly overlapping, others arranged with considerable intervening space from front to back, like bits of stage scenery, to yield an illusion of great depth.[2]

Many of Cornell's shadow-box assemblages serve as associational portraits of desirable but unattainable actresses and dancers. These fetish objects are composed of small three-dimensional objects and two-dimensional printed pictures and texts appropriated from the detritus of everyday life and recombined according to systems of meaning probably clear to Cornell but hauntingly just out of reach for outside observers. Even when he worked with a contemporary subject, most of his raw materials, especially those taken from printed sources, came from secondhand dealers. Often thirty to fifty years old and more, these artifacts already possessed an aura of nostalgia. It is not so common in his work to find materials like these cutouts from linen postcards that came directly from his contemporary moment. Unlike Lindsey's jewelry, which evokes the past even for people who do not know what they are looking at, nothing of Cornell's assemblage directly evokes the past. Despite the distressed look of the box's wooden frame, the postcards and the machine-age skyscrapers they represent were as contemporary in the 1940s as the young actress or the penny arcade machine in which Cornell encapsulated her. Even so, the downward path of the ball toward the obscurely threatening dark blue images seemed even then to imply that the attractive young woman was already trapped in time's corrupting influence. That sense of loss, here experienced before the fact, evokes the nostalgia of so many of Cornell's pieces. Despite his tender awareness of the fragility of innocence, there is a creepy side to the appropriation of Bacall's images and their juxtaposition with phallic skyscraper forms. Cornell's art suggests an intensely private person abstracting bits and pieces from the flow of mass culture, sorting and arranging them, and eventually combining them to construct fetish objects as a means of expressing otherwise inchoate desires. In that sense, Cornell's motivation for making art may overlap in some ways with the motives of more ordinary collectors of linen postcards.

The Collecting Impulse

Collectors who have written about linen postcards describe an element of compulsion in their collecting habit. Few people consciously set out to begin a collection, whatever its contents, other than children following a parent's promptings or millionaires advised to invest in art. The first object to be acquired in any series is arbitrary. The next few are acquired randomly, by gift, accident, or impulsive whim. Only gradually does the person acquiring those first few objects realize that a collection is emerging. The collecting impulse seems to arise from unconscious emotional satisfactions obtained from the first few acquisitions in a series. The painter John Baeder, for example, began collecting linen postcards by accident. During the late 1960s, when he was in his early thirties, he happened upon some cards offered by a junk dealer and acquired a few "that appealed to me for reasons I wasn't aware of at the time." He recalled that "a pattern started to emerge" as "particular images . . . touch[ed] me somewhere in my psyche." Scattered purchases became a collection. Obsessed with the cards, he spent hours with an engraver's magnifying glass "studying the buried information in these images." And when he turned to painting what he saw, reproducing enlarged versions of linen postcards of roadside diners complete down to the captions, he did so because, as he wrote, "I had to get them out of my system."[3]

A similar sequence of events motivated another linen postcard collector, a graphic designer the same age as Baeder. Barry Zaid was hooked when he discovered an album of miscellaneous postcards inside a wooden toolbox acquired at an auction. Although that find led to a collection of early British lithographic cards while he was living briefly in England, he was drawn to linen postcards after returning home to Toronto. As he recalled, "I kept noticing these American cards, which reminded me of those I remembered seeing at the general store near the summer cottage . . . my family rented when I was young." He realized there was "something magical" about linens, with their "perfect" skyscrapers, bridges, beaches, and, above all, "those skies!"—"gorgeous robin's-egg blues gently fading into pale peach." Like Baeder he became a "linen-card junkie" and examined his cards with a magnifying glass to understand their attraction. As Zaid sorted his cards and grouped them for display, "certain cards seemed to want to go together" as if gifted with agency. Taken as a whole, the collection portrayed "a world frozen in time, a world that in many cases no longer exists," but also, in something of a contradiction, "a world even better than reality." Perhaps more than Baeder, who did admit to a psychological compulsion, Zaid recognized that his obsession derived from nostalgia for childhood, from a deep-seated sense of contemporary loss and imperfection.[4]

An essay on collecting by the French postmodern theorist Jean Baudrillard put such activity in an unattractive light. After observing that collecting allows children to exert control over the world "by laying things out, grouping them, handling them," he suggested there is something unwholesome about adult collectors. Although he found that the urge to collect usually subsides after puberty, it sometimes reappears in middle-aged men, who are "most prone to the passion." Wrapped up in the "perversion" of fetishism, many such collectors "maintain about their collection an aura of the clandestine, of confinement, secrecy and dissimulation, all of which give rise to the unmistakable impression of a guilty relationship." Similar thoughts about collecting have occurred to John

Tagg, a historian of photographic representation. "There is something morbid about looking at pictures, something frigid, and something furtive," he claims while lamenting that "we shuffle from one image to the next like the buyers of old books."[5]

More measured in her assessment of the psychology of collecting, the literary critic Susan Stewart has described how objects in a collection are taken out of their natural or historical contexts and placed in a new context that the collector finds satisfying. A collector is "not simply a consumer" of objects but "generates a fantasy" in which the self "becomes producer of those objects, a producer by arrangement and manipulation." Wrenched out of original environments and purposes, the objects of a collection are rearranged to become parts of a "scenario of the personal." A certain controlling restraint on the part of the collector, parallel to the painstaking craftsmanship exhibited by Cornell in his assemblages, prevents a complete surrender to underlying psychological desires. "The boundary between collection and fetishism," according to Stewart, "is mediated by classification and display in tension with accumulation and secrecy."[6]

Although few collectors would accept such interpretations, they do sometimes seem to wish to redeem practices that might otherwise seem frivolous or somehow dubious. Classifying or displaying a collection may serve to rescue it from apparent disrepute. Baeder, for example, transmuted his obsession with linen postcards into the production of art. After completing his series of enlarged paintings of postcards, he turned to the reality behind the images and began photographing diners and other roadside attractions throughout the Northeast. His photos then inspired a new series of paintings that brought him a reputation as a photorealist. As for Zaid, who focused on cards portraying hotel exteriors and interiors, he "dream[ed] of doing a book" making use of his collection, perhaps a "mystery" that "would use the hotel cards as a background as the subject traveled across the country." Eventually he abandoned that idea and instead published an "album" of hotel cards titled with the generic but evocative phrase "wish you were here."[7] It seems significant that Zaid fantasized about his collection in terms of detective fiction and film. Linen cityscapes and interiors evoke auras of place and setting that are prominent in those genres. Indeed, linen cards date from the classic noir era. Zaid's birth, his personal point of origin, also dates back to that era. For him linen cards seem suffused with the nostalgia and loss of early childhood.

Anyone who seeks an accurate understanding of these historical artifacts must confront the fact that they seem to easily engage personal nostalgia. Even the geographer John A. Jakle, whose approach to linen postcards is often less speculative than mine, opens his book about nighttime views of American cities by recalling a train ride across Kansas as a young boy.[8] The historical fallacy of projection (reading back into the past from a contemporary viewpoint) becomes especially seductive when dealing with emotionally charged material. About all one can do is remain vigilant for signs of present personal concerns mingling with interpretations of the past. I have tried to suggest how the images on linen postcards, though artificially constructed and often visually unreliable, did exemplify realities of the time when they were published, purchased, and used. All the same, these images now appeal to collectors for personal reasons and contribute to the contemporary imagescape in ways that complicate their authenticity as historical artifacts. Old postcards are wanderers through time, arriving in the present, whether through inheritance or secondhand purchase, from a past they once truly inhabited. They represent and reveal much about that past, but their visual images also misrepresent the realities that inspired them. We in the present who attend to linen cards cannot help being influenced by visual artifacts whose images originally portrayed not the reality of America but an idealized national self-portrait at a particular moment in history. In a sense linen postcards are as real as any historical artifacts can be, but they are also utterly unreal. The actual past they survive from was not the one portrayed on their vivid surfaces, but those past visions, however superficial or ideologically slanted, continue to influence the present.[9]

The Anatomy of Melancholy: Messages from the Past

The apparent unreality of linen postcards may be reinforced by the fact that cards in a contemporary collection have been removed from a multitude of individual contexts and artificially gathered together much later in time. A collector views them not individually, as did the person who originally purchased a card or received it in the mail, but as an unnatural grouping. A single view card's hyperbolic relationship to the scene it claimed to represent may not have seemed so extravagant to someone who experienced it in isolation from other exaggerated images. Naomi Schor described how the postcards in her collection evoked responses quite different from those experienced by their original owners. Even as she sought to reconstruct everyday early twentieth-century life in Paris from her cards, she admitted that "time is not recaptured" through them. They do not "produce memories" for anyone who did not inhabit their era. According to Schor, "A collection is composed of objects wrenched out of their contexts of origins and reconfigured into the self-contained, self-referential context of the collection itself."[10]

To focus on the individual images conveyed by postcards, as in much of this book, is to ignore the original contexts of many cards as vehicles of communication between sender and recipient, or as souvenirs of personal travels. The actuality of human connections adheres to every single old postcard except for those relative few found in bulk in abandoned warehouses or inventories of defunct stores. That historical fact serves as a cautionary note to anyone inclined to dismiss mass-produced images as inauthentic. In discussing a quite different area of material culture, that of Native American craft techniques applied to producing tourist souvenirs, the anthropologist Ruth Phillips has argued that to disparage the resulting artifacts for lack of authenticity is "to silence not just the producers of these objects but also their consumers by failing to recognize the historical significance of the patronage of ordinary people."[11] But beyond recognizing that the postcards in one's collection have, as a group, been touched by thousands of hands, mostly those of individuals now deceased, how is one to give voice to the consumers, owners, and users?

So far this discussion of linen postcards has been devoted mostly to interpreting representative but simultaneously extraordinary images. The attempt has been to discern what meanings these images might reasonably have conveyed to viewers or what meanings viewers might have brought to them from their own cultural experience. Now it is time to turn, relatively briefly, to consider how people made use of these cards in their daily lives. What sorts of messages did they inscribe on them and for what purposes? Anyone who accumulates more than a few old postcards is quickly drawn to the elliptical, often tantalizing messages inscribed on the backs of those that were sent through the mail. Some are humorous, some dripping with pathos, while others are informative or merely formulaic. Even the latter—especially when one examines postmarks and addresses as well as variations in handwriting, spelling, and grammar—provoke curiosity and speculation.

The British artist and postcard collector Tom Phillips (unrelated to the anthropologist) has described the seductive experience of reading postcard messages by strangers. At the turn of this century he compiled a coffee table book with miniature color reproductions of two thousand cards of all varieties from what he referred to as "the postcard century" (the 1900s). All the cards had been sent through the mail, and Phillips embedded the message from each card in a commentary that loosely associated it to the next card. Although he characterized a somewhat dull message as "typical of many," he recalled how "the mere act of copying them out yields more information than at first sight appears to be there." Even in telegraphic inscriptions he discerned "telltale signs of character and mood" and "ripples of disquiet beneath the surface, hints of the larger life of which they are the mere shards."[12] Phillips's careful phrasing suggests that the appeal of postcards extends beyond the images. Often a collector is tempted to act as detective, gleaning scraps of information from individual messages and imagining scenarios and narratives to make provisional sense of them. Susan Pearce has gone so far as to propose that collections of historical artifacts "provide a doubtful excitement for their possessors," offering "a kind of pornography of the past."[13]

Before turning to examine some of the fragments of lives uncovered in my own collection of linen postcards, we need a sense of the limits of the artificial universe under consideration. Somewhat less than a third (1,857) of the roughly 6,000 linen postcards in my collection were sent through the mail between 1931 and 1967, the final year represented. The distribution of postmarked cards over time forms a bell curve rising steadily each year from 1931 to 1942, remaining level from 1942 until 1950, and then falling away sharply, with a mere handful of cards postmarked each year after 1959. By then, chromes had wholly replaced linens as newly printed cards, and retail stocks of older cards were used up or discarded. Because I collected my cards based on their images with no regard for whether or not they had been written on or mailed, I have tended to assume my collection represents a cross section of types of messages conveyed by linen postcards. However, it might be more accurate to claim they comprise a cross section of those cards that were eventually saved by recipients, rather than a cross section of all those that were mailed.

As nearly as I can determine, some 62 percent of the cards in my collection were written by women, with a fifth of those being sent in the name of a married couple but with handwriting or phrasing that suggests a wife's agency. And 57 percent of the cards were addressed to women, with another 17 percent addressed to a married couple. In addition, about one in every forty cards with messages was sent from one collector to another. Mostly women, these collectors obtained the names and addresses of fellow hobbyists from specialized collectors' magazines or columns in general magazines and then exchanged cards through the mail. Given that the vast majority of messages concern personal and family matters, and that only 30 cards out of 1,857 fulfilled a business function, it may be that women tended more than men to save the postcards they received. Whatever the case, the fact that linen cards sold for a penny or two or were given away by businesses suggests that a high proportion must have been discarded immediately after use or after a short period of display. But all one can conclude is that my collection seems to encompass a cross section of post-marked cards that happened to be saved—whether for their messages, for their images, or both, and whether by women, by men, or by children attracted to the pictures.

Most messages ignore the scene on the front of a card in order to focus on unrelated personal matters.[14] Exceptions to that rule can be striking, as in the case of a view of Harvard Square in Cambridge, Massachusetts, onto which a doting father in 1951 sketched a humorous stick figure of "baldy" running from the square's newsstand to a row of shops across the street (fig. 6.3). "Daddy's thinking about you," he wrote, telling "Sugar," "this place in this picture is where

Fɪɢ. 6.3. Inscribed copy of "Harvard Square. Cambridge. Mass.," Tichnor 61909, n.d.

I am when I mailed this." Even cards sent by obvious tourists and vacationers, making up about a third of those with messages, usually do not refer to a card's subject at all. About a tenth of tourist cards offer a brief sightseeing description. Most mention only that a vacation or trip is under way, with a few even employing the generic phrase "Having a wonderful time, wish you were here"—in one instance set off by self-conscious quotation marks. Most vacationing tourists listed a few sights they had seen, recorded extremes of weather, toted up miles traveled, greeted individual family members by name, or noted the estimated time of arrival back home.

Some travelers went further than that. A family in California mentioned that they "drove through the Redwoods for hours yesterday" and "took pictures of our car in the tree you drive through," while a tourist in Rocky Mountain National Park passed "a snow capped mountain and threw snowballs"—in mid-August—"and it wasn't very cold where the snow was either." Occasionally a message waxes rhapsodic, as in the case of a woman called Betty who wrote from Yosemite National Park to tell Margaret and John in Los Angeles, "It would do you both a world of good to come up here." Betty was camping in "a beautiful spot—and a wonderful place for a vacation," with "no airplanes—street cars or trains—no sirens (except in skirts)." She and her companions were not exactly roughing it. They had an "electric grill" and "make our breakfast & lunch & we eat dinner out." With their two tents it was "a picnic to see who sleeps where." The humor of this card allows us to discern what Tom Phillips refers to as "tell-tale signs of character and mood," while its details offer "hints of the larger life" beyond the "shards." However, we are left to ponder whether Betty is a married woman with several children, part of an extended family reunion, or one of a group of college girls. There is simply no way of knowing. The message offers enough information to provoke curiosity but not enough to guarantee certainty.

From travel cards one can glean a sense of what it must have been like to drive on American highways before postwar construction of the interstate highway system. Most reports of total mileage driven seem today literally nothing to write home about. Someone who had just arrived in Minneapolis reported having "made the trip in 13 hrs (600 miles)" and bragged that "only a Chevy could do it." Many messages referred to flat tires as a routine fact of life. A man arriving in Del Rio, Texas, told his father they "had a flat just as we drove into town," but soon afterward they "ate a Mexican supper" and were "having [a] swell time." Finding acceptable places to eat along the way was not easy. Nor could everyone afford to eat at roadside restaurants, with Depression economies influencing even people who had the disposable income to travel. A woman on a trip to Texas wrote her mother in Anna, Illinois, that the "ham you fixed sure was good, and did it come in handy."

With new tourist courts springing up, accommodations were available for those who were not auto camping or who wanted a break from camping. Indeed, the relative luxury of a court or cabin could be a tourist attraction in itself. A woman writing from New Hampshire enthused about the "cute cabins" at the English Village West in Franconia Notch: "We've just had a shower up here. Ever hear of any thing like that?" While she was amused at finding such a modern amenity in a cabin, other travelers, from a more modest background, might have been genuinely impressed. The major complaint of motorists was the boredom of driving, as in the case of a family from Atlanta who were finally "back in the South and so glad to be out of Texas," with its "miles of tumbleweed." Underlying many messages, especially those reporting safe arrival at a final destination, was the ever-present concern about the risk of injury or death. Travelers in Louisiana reported seeing "one car up side down in a ditch, and a dead mule . . . some one had hit," while a couple in Arkansas "ran into a Dust-Storm" and had "seen two wrecks already." Such brief, uninflected comments indicate not only that such events were worth mentioning but also that it was necessary to neutralize them by presenting them as matter-of-factly as possible.

Not all travel was for pleasure. Many messages document separations—of sweethearts, of married couples, of parents and children, of individuals from their roots. Some of the most poignant cards are written to children, with a message intended as much for the other parent as for the child. "How is little

Toad Frog eye?" asked a father who was halfway across the country from his son. "Daddy sure misses his little Baby boy," he continued, telling him, "Be a good boy Take care of Moma and say your Prayers every night." A Latino father somewhere in Texas sent a labored greeting to his two sons in Silver City, New Mexico: "Helo Boys How are you two doing thies dayes Hope you two are studing hard so you can make another grad fore Next year so work Hard this last few dayes of school so you can Pass And Write to me your Dad." Whether their long-term separation arose from the father's employment, from divorce, or perhaps from a family crisis requiring his presence elsewhere remains unclear. At the opposite end of the socioeconomic spectrum, a girl attending a summer camp on Nonesuch Pond in Wellesley, Massachusetts, was exhorted to "have a grand time" but also told to "work industriously for that brings accomplishment," with the writer's final wish being, "Hope you get Swimmer" (presumably a badge or rank). All these messages display momentary heartache—an awareness of the promise of childhood but also its uncertainties. We ponder the situations of senders and recipients. We gain just enough sense of individuality from the writers' concerns and phrasings to imagine their situations and those of their children, but otherwise the past eludes us.

Some correspondents referred to travel and relocation for employment—but few enough to suggest that tourist cards tended to be saved while those serving everyday message functions were discarded. During this period, companies in every industry depended on traveling sales agents. The era was also one of forced mobility as uprooted people traveled in search of work. In 1939, for example, a young man called Walter was living in a modest three-story apartment building just south of downtown Los Angeles, according to the return address on a card mailed to his friend Cliff back in Escanaba, Michigan. Walter had been offered a job as a "dishwasher for $35.00 a mo. R&Board," but he was holding out for "a Waiter, or Bus Boy job before that." Another card seven months later found him living "among the Danes in a very nice valley," the Santa Ynez, about fifty miles northwest of Santa Barbara, where he had "a good job at $60.00 a mo. and room & board." He was working at Andersen's Valley Inn, pictured on the card, which is today still known for its split pea soup. Living thriftily, Walter was saving fifty dollars a month and planned to have enough funds in two years' time to "take a trip to Detroit & Esky [Escanaba]."

Others reported greater success. Muriel wrote to "Uncle Lester" in Scituate, Massachusetts, that her husband, Francis, had become "foreman in a cabinet shop" in Baldwin Park, California, east of Los Angeles, with "loads of carpenter work & good pay," enough that they had "bought a house." Edna wrote back home to Smithville, Texas, on a postcard of the interior of the Forum Cafeteria inside the Chicago Loop, reporting that her sister's husband "runs this place" and was able to provide "a beautiful apartment." The rural Texan was probably impressed by the streamlined splendor of the Forum, part of a small national chain. Professional travelers at the time included women as well as men. A woman in the furniture business told her aunt in New Hampshire about a trip to the wholesale "furniture markets" of Grand Rapids, Michigan. Another woman whose independence provokes curiosity wrote from on the road in Kansas to inform a daughter in Fort Worth that she would be returning home to Chicago after "taking 122 men to work in the beet harvest."

But for every apparent success story, other messages indicate the unlucky and desperate, drifting farther from their origins, relying on dwindling funds, and seeking cheaper lodgings—like the woman in San Francisco who was reduced to "moving in with an elderly lady." One wonders how seriously to take Roland's upbeat report that he had "finally settled down permanently" in Detroit, where the people were "ever so nice." Addressing an unmarried high school teacher in Refugio by first name, he concluded, "Texas seems so far away from here, almost like a foreign country." That final comment, whether or not intended with regret, recalls the French philosopher Jacques Derrida's observation that "if you want to understand what an 'anatomy' of the post card might be, think of the *Anatomy of Melancholy*."[15]

Often postcard messages reveal infirmities and illnesses of people whose mortal struggles ended long ago. They or their loved ones writing about them seem not to have cared that dozens of people, including postal clerks and letter carriers, could scan their words along the way. A man in Pueblo, Colorado, was said to be "doing fine" after a "bone infection" forced him to have "his right leg amputated." Another, in Mineral Wells, Texas, was also "doing fine" after a doctor removed a "skin eruption" that otherwise "could have run into cancer." A woman in Houston was said to be "feeling some better today" after receiving a blood transfusion "cause she was so weak." Less fortunate was a woman in Casa Grande, Arizona, who was "in great pain," with "her face and body . . . all bruised and scarred up." A friend was "grieving my self to death" over the woman's condition because, as she reported, "[I] don't think she has one chance." Others made it through. A woman in Biloxi, Mississippi, shared the "wonderful news" that "I am out of that awful Bondage." Although she was "still very tender" and would "have to be very careful for a long time," she felt "so Luckie that it was no worse than it was." A few people faced illness and adversity with a sense of humor, such as a San Antonio man who complained to a male correspondent that he was "laid up" under the care of a doctor, who told him he could not "work, drink, ride the car or anything," and who, adding insult to injury, was "trying to make a vegetarian out of me."

Even deaths were announced by postcard, though only five in my entire collection. A woman in Baltimore matter-of-factly told a friend in Berkeley, "I lost my brother," and then immediately changed the subject, wondering, "What is the trouble with Sadie," who was "cutting off her nose to spite her face." And then there was a woman in Silsbee, Texas, who acknowledged receiving a card from a female correspondent in Hinsdale, Illinois, and was "sorry to hear that you lost your little boy." Although it was "a hard task to have to give them up," it seemed that "God knows best" and "needed him in Heaven more than you all did."

The major problem with this collage of individual voices, not quite a cacophony, is similar to the problem already discussed with regard to this book's selection of a few specific visual images from a collection of 6,000 linen postcards. Although I have arranged quotations from messages to demonstrate typical subjects addressed by postcard correspondents, the ones I selected are, frankly, unusually vivid or revealing. Unlike hundreds of relatively more ordinary messages, each has some quality—whether of phrasing, pacing, or situation—that marks it as noteworthy. They provoke curiosity and invite speculation. Some seem to erupt from out of nowhere. That is the case with the most unusual message in my possession, a rant from a woman living in Los Angeles to a sister in Waco, Texas.

Written in 1936 on the back of a view of the Mount Lowe Scenic Railway north of Pasadena, the message is an inarticulate cry of grief, rage, and betrayal that one can hardly imagine being sent without the privacy of an envelope even if a letter did cost twice as much to mail. It is worth quoting in full:

> *Dear Sis.*
> *Received your card & sure am surprised to hear from you not a sister to me more like a perfect stranger I don't see why you my only sister should acted toward me the way you did I have been terribly hurt more heartbroken the way I have been treated by all my home—broke up. I am crying I would like to see you. I have 2 lovely girls. Write me a big letter soon*
> *Love to all, from [illegible]*

One cannot help wondering what had happened to this woman. She seems to have been irreparably separated from her extended family in Waco and stranded in Los Angeles with two daughters. She expresses a feeling of being utterly alone, and there is no mention of a husband. We have no idea how she came to be alienated from her family, whether she flaunted local morality, entered into a bad marriage, or said something in a split second that could never be taken back or forgiven. Or perhaps her sister or the entire family made her a scapegoat and drove her away. Or perhaps the writer was afflicted by mental illness and sent this plea to a sister who would receive it with a familiar sinking dismay—powerless yet again to salve and rescue a lost loved one. For whatever reason, the postcard survived. One cannot imagine it being given to the recipient's daughter or to a neighbor boy for a postcard collection. Instead it was tucked away as a bitter family memento, eventually reaching an impersonal estate sale or flea market.

Although messages on postcards form a reasonably convincing impressionistic collage of everyday hopes and fears, they can also provoke voyeurism. This provocative fragment invites one to imagine a scenario that would illuminate or explain, defuse or even ultimately extend, its unsettling raw emotion.[16] However representative a collection might be, in terms of both images and messages, there remains the issue of whether a collector/historian can move beyond the desire to project, to narrate and explain on the basis of evidence that is actually not quite there. Perhaps interest in a single unusual fragment, such as the Los Angeles woman's emotional plea, cannot extend beyond gratuitous curiosity. But does the larger collection of messages reward more responsible historical inquiry? Is it possible to project intelligently onto these remains without violating their actual historicity, their status as artifacts left behind by historical actors who remain largely unknown?

History and Nostalgia

Despite my argument for an objective, representative cross section in the postcard messages of my collection, there is actually a slight artificial imbalance. On three occasions I acquired a series of cards written during a relatively brief period of time by a single sender to a single recipient. In each case I violated my practice of selecting postcards only for their images. Most likely I became aware of each series by flipping consecutive cards in a dealer's box and realizing the same person wrote all of them. After skimming a few messages, I wanted them for my collection despite mostly lackluster images.

All three series of cards share several characteristics. In each case, a man was writing to a woman. Second, the correspondence occurred during or just after World War II. And finally, each series is relatively small, ranging from fifteen to twenty-one cards. It is possible that there is a meaningful pattern to my purchase of these three series, or the similarities may be coincidental. My parents met about two years after the war, and I was born in 1949 shortly before the most recent postmark among these cards. Even so, I believe I would have acquired such a series from any decade during the linen postcard era—and with correspondents whose ages and situations were not at all parallel to those of my parents. However, like the images on individual cards, these sets somehow "spoke" to me almost with the force of Roland Barthes's *punctum*. The gathered fragments in these three cases seem to promise more than Phillips's individual "shards," though obviously much less than would be provided by a complete archive of one person's correspondence.

It may not be accidental that these three sets of cards date from the 1940s. Mobilization of soldiers and sailors during the war set a significant part of the American population in motion, and civilians from farms and small towns added to the upheaval by migrating long distances to take jobs in defense plants. Hundreds of thousands of people, many away from home for the first time, wrote to parents, sweethearts, spouses, family, and friends, who in turn wrote back to them. Presumably the volume of postcards sent through the mail rose precipitously. At first glance, the Teich Postcard Archives might suggest otherwise. In 1942, the first full year of U.S. involvement in the war, Teich's annual production of new designs dropped by 40 percent to about 1,600, a level maintained until 1946, a year in which the number of new designs returned to that of 1941. During the war the Teich plant in Chicago was engaged in defense work, printing over three million maps for the invasions of Europe and Japan. Even so, Teich continued producing reprints of existing cards, though no record of the volume has survived. In 1944 an incredulous Curt Teich Jr. praised western representative G. I. Pitchford for the previous year's "almost unbelievable" sales.[17]

Wartime messages ran the gamut from humorous to heartbroken. An army private stationed in Florida warned a buddy in Michigan who was about to be drafted that he might "run into you one of these days as I'm an M.P. so be careful." Another wrote a pal back in Texas that he was "in the army and in Mississippi at that," reporting further that "they think they are going to make a mechanic out of me." Lucille teased a male friend in Peoria that she was "doing all right with the sailors and solders in Frisco" and that they were all "having a lot of fun." The situation for married women was obviously different. A woman in New Jersey informed an acquaintance in Kansas that "several married men with children have been called," that is, drafted, and she had her "fingers crossed for my hubby." Another wife who had followed her husband from Wisconsin out to Morro Bay, California, mentioned she was "a lonely widow again" because Clarence was "in camp" and soon leaving for "desert maneuvers." Some mothers were so distraught, their emotions spilled out in messages to complete strangers. Irene, a postcard collector in Illinois, wrote to Enid in Missouri, complaining, "My Son left for the Navy 5 wks ago, and I have been so upset." And a woman in Omaha told a pen pal in South Bend that she "had a nervous breakdown partly due to my 2 boys going to the Navy." A Marine named Vernon captured existential reality while waiting to be shipped out to the Pacific from Camp Elliott in San Diego. Writing his family on a card with a glittering nighttime view of Wilshire Boulevard, the "Miracle Mile" of Los Angeles, he told them not to reply to his message. He would "be sailing for the next twenty days" to an un-

FIG. 6.4. Inscription from "Sgt" on "A Message from / Cincinnati / Ohio / 'The Queen City of the West,'" Teich 2B-H304, 1942

known destination. "But wish me luck," he closed, "because this time I'm playing for keeps."

Of the three sets of postcards mailed during and just after the war, only two are discussed here. The omitted series comprises fifteen cards sent by a mechanical engineer who, after serving in the army, was traveling on business in the upper Midwest and writing to the woman he was soon to marry. The most immediately compelling of the other two series contains seventeen cards sent between April 1944 and September 1945 by a man who signed himself with a flourish as "Sgt" in quotation marks. His correspondent was a young woman who lived on a rural postal route outside McGregor, Texas, a small town just north of the infantry training center at Camp Hood. Sgt wrote in a florid hand with a wide-nibbed pen, usually sprawling his telegraphic phrases diagonally across the message section (fig. 6.4). We learn nothing about his correspondent, whose address always appears with the title "Miss" written above the musical lilt of her three short names.

The only certainty in this story is that Sgt traveled frequently. Every card is a large-letter card, with locations ranging from New York and Washington, DC, to Hollywood and Salt Lake City, from Minneapolis to Miami Beach, with more than one visit to Lowry Field (a training center for bomber crews in Denver). Sgt's messages skated over the surface of his life, each no more than a phrase or two, reporting Salt Lake City a "really beautiful spot," Houston a "busy little place," Minneapolis a "cold Lil Bohemia" at fifty below, and Miami Beach "just too hot to really enjoy." Sgt liked his entertainment. In Hollywood he attended a couple of NBC radio shows, *Maxwell House Coffee Time* and *The Abbott and Costello Show*. Early in 1945 he watched Judy Garland in the musical film *Meet Me in St. Louis*, which was playing in—where else?—St. Louis, and eight months later he was back again, attending a baseball game and the opera. Was he a veteran, on active duty, a defense contractor, a traveling salesman, a restless wanderer? Was she his wife, a girlfriend, a daughter, a granddaughter, a favorite niece, a sister, a high school student, a grown woman, a casual acquaintance, perhaps a waitress in a diner outside Camp Hood? Two cards mailed on consecutive days from different places in Florida only complicate matters. The first had him "trying to find a rich young war widow who is spending the winter here," while the next day he was "still shopping for that widow but who knows what to-morrow may bring." As for Cincinnati, that wild town elicited a suggestive "Woo! Woo! Woo!—" Despite the apparent details in these messages, the actuality of Sgt's life eludes us as much as the nature of his relationship with his female correspondent. We are left with only his humor's effervescent froth.

The remaining series of cards seems to promise greater understanding of the people involved. There are twenty-one postcards, three written in October 1943 and the rest during March and April 1944. Charlie, an ensign in the U.S. Naval Reserve stationed at Fort Pierce, Florida, was writing to Elizabeth (or "Lib") in Houston. Mention of an "8th anniversary" might suggest they were married, but the title "Miss," the different last names, and the general tone indicate they were childhood sweethearts. Like Sgt, Charlie possessed irrepressible high spirits. He often underlined humorous points two or three times. He was also something of an artist, making amusing cartoon sketches, including one of a rural hayseed with weeds sticking from his ears and mouth (fig. 6.5) and one of himself with his naval cap at a jaunty angle. From the messages we learn the military had taken over the barrier island at Fort Pierce,[18] and that Charlie lived in a tent a stone's throw from the Atlantic, attended frequent training classes, and tried to write Lib a daily letter and even more frequent postcards. His idea of a good time on an evening's "liberty" in town included wandering into a rehearsal of the junior play at the high school and "struggling through 3 acts of pure corn."

Charlie seems to have written postcards to Lib almost as an excuse for doodling. With the exception of a dark, densely printed image titled "A Hungry Alligator in Florida," which prompted him to admit that he "gave up trying to write on the front," he embroidered the cards' images with sketches and humor-

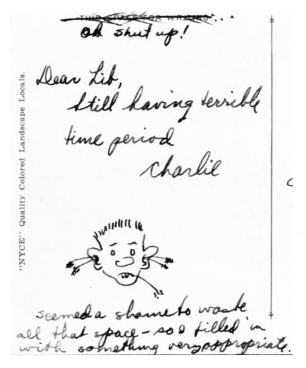

FIG. 6.5. Sketch sent by Charlie to Lib on an untitled generic landscape card, NYCE 46943, n.d., which the distributor had overprinted with the phrase "Greetings from West Columbia, Texas"

ous captions. A generic view of a palm-lined drive, titled "Beautiful Estate in Florida," received stick figures of a boy and girl walking hand in hand with their heads inclined toward each other, and a caption: "Guess who I wish this were." A view called "A Coconut Palm Fringed Beach in South Florida" is transformed by five stick figures sitting on the horizontal trunk of a palm tree ("All the little ensigns learning knot tying, etc.") and a stick figure in an officer's cap standing in the foreground ("Blah, Blah"). An arrow is drawn to one ensign ("Me, thinking of you"), above which a thought balloon reads "LIB." Three of the cards feature cartoon sketches of the large landing craft Charlie was learning to command, and one has a sketch of four boats lined up "like a string of little ducks on a pond" along the pink horizon of an image of a fisherman fighting a tarpon (fig. 6.6); another has "my romantic little LCV" superimposed on an aerial view of Fort Pierce's yacht club.

Even with all the joking, Charlie was not afraid of expressing his feelings for Lib through the relatively public medium of postcards. He told her she was "the very first thing I think of on awakening." The two-hour break every noon was "the *best* time of the day" for him because he "reserve[d] it to read all my

"LANDING A BIG ONE" OFF THE COAST OF FLORIDA—F137
"TO CATCH A TARPON IS THE THRILL OF A LIFETIME"

& here go the landing boats, like a string of little ducks on a pond—

FIG. 6.6. Inscribed copy of "'Landing a Big One' off the Coast of Florida," E. C. Kropp 8952N, n.d.

mail from you." Occasionally they talked by phone, and he was especially happy one morning because, as he wrote, "just think—I talked to my honey chile last night—sigh—." Frequently he mentioned attending church services, and he reported on one occasion that he was writing a postcard to her as he sat in signaling class at 9:30 in the morning—precisely "because you told me *not* to in class, & I feel mean," but, more to the point, "because I'm thinking of you." In ten minutes he would be released from class to attend church. It was a "perfectly *lovely* [triple underscoring] Sunday morning," and he closed the card by saying, "sho' do wish I were going to church with *you*." Charlie's feelings for Lib seem sweet and innocent. Occasionally we sense his loneliness and uncertainty about the future. There is pathos in his reworking of the standard postcard cliché as he writes, "Wish *you* were *here*. Wish *we* were here, for awhile" (double underscoring). Like the Marine waiting to be shipped out from San Diego, Charlie no doubt often contemplated his fate, so entwined with his feelings for Lib.

From this extended series of messages sent by a young naval officer to his girlfriend it is possible to construct a more multidimensional sense of their personal situation than one could ever extrapolate from the shard of a single postcard message. Anyone looking through these cards wants to know how it all turned out. Did Charlie make it through the war? Did he and Lib build a life together? Until a few years ago, such questions necessarily went unanswered.

Now, on the other hand, with Google providing access to huge but quirkily random databases, and with a bit of luck in the specifics inscribed on postcards, it is sometimes possible to augment the story. Because soldiers and sailors could send mail for free, without stamps, they had to provide full names and official return addresses. Charlie's surname was unusual and his online traces are easily located. He was born in 1924, the son of a retail merchant, and spent at least some of his childhood in the small town of Brazoria, near Houston. His postcards to Lib were delivered to a two-story brick house, possibly a duplex, in the Montrose district of Houston, a building that now houses a neighborhood bar sandwiched between modest houses with equally modest businesses. Charlie shipped out for the Pacific in September 1944. He was one of four officers assigned to a "Landing Craft Infantry (Large)," a small vessel constructed for landing troops during invasions but not ordinarily intended for ocean voyages. More than a thousand such craft were employed on both fronts during the war. He may have assisted in landing troops on Leyte Island in the Philippines in late November, during the final days of the battle for that island. He survived the war, and he and Lib married in 1946. She earned a bachelor's degree that same year and a master's in architecture the following year. Charlie worked as a petroleum engineer, some of the time with Exxon, in a career that took the couple from Houston to Corpus Christi, then to New Orleans, and finally again to Corpus Christi. Elizabeth and Charlie had two sons and a daughter and remained married forty-one years, until Charlie's death in 1987 at sixty-two. Elizabeth followed in 1997 at sixty-nine.

Some of these details may be inaccurate. However, web searches do reveal probable descendants who might verify or complicate the story. But to contact them in hopes of finding further correspondence, photographs, other documents, and family memories would take this inquiry beyond postcards—at worst into idle curiosity and at best into social history, which considers people in the aggregate, making use of individual stories like Lib and Charlie's as a means of dramatizing the situations of groups of similar people. If, on the other hand, we regard these twenty-one postcards and accompanying facts as a multidimensional variant of the "mere shards" described by Phillips, we find ourselves drawn into the narrative they suggest in precisely the same way we might meditate on the woman who believed her family had abandoned her, or even on the woman whose brother-in-law managed a cafeteria in Chicago. That we seem to know more about Charlie is an illusion. The life history in the previous paragraph is too smooth, too lacking in incident, crisis, success, failure, happiness, joy, or despair. For all its details, it reads too much like one of those accounts at the end of some movies that inform the audience what happened later to wholly fictional characters embodied by actors. The story is, in its way, too predictable, even too generic. We are pleased that Charlie survived the war and married Lib, and that they apparently had a rewarding life together, though we may feel disappointment at their relatively early deaths.

Although Charlie's messages and cartoons offer "telltale signs of character and mood" (in Phillips's phrase), an outsider looking over these postcards is mostly seeking a convincing narrative. Because the cards are physical remnants of two lives—material artifacts that both Charlie and Lib actually touched, inscribed, and kept for several decades—there is a tendency to invest them with a factual aura. But true knowledge eludes the collector, who is left constructing a narrative that might make sense in terms of the fictional conventions of books and movies but offers little in the way of knowledge and understanding.

Perhaps my meaning will become clearer if we move away from Charlie and Lib's seemingly multidimensional postcards and focus instead on a single card taken from among those already discussed in this book, the card portraying the shuffleboard courts of St. Petersburg, Florida (see p. 166). Google Maps Street View reveals that the female recipient of this card, postmarked February 6, 1944, in St. Petersburg, lived on a wide boulevard in South Weymouth, Massachusetts, in a medium-sized, two-story frame house built sometime in the mid- to late nineteenth century. From the correspondent's spidery handwriting, her long account of a game played largely by retirees, and the fact that she addressed the recipient as "Miss," one might conclude, based on little or no evidence, that the recipient was an older unmarried woman. The exterior and surroundings of her house seem promising at first glance, but in fact we learn nothing from them. Almost any situation can be imagined, from that of a live-in maiden aunt secure in her sister's family, to a desperate widow renting a small upstairs bedroom. There is simply no way of knowing, though this shard of authentic reality invites speculation. Even augmented by digital data, most postcards offer only fragments whose banality is occasionally tempered by an odd turn of phrase or a situation that provokes curiosity about individuals for whom there is little historical documentation.

The operative mode of the postcard collection may indeed be nostalgia, which Susan Stewart has described as "sadness without an object, a sadness which creates a longing that of necessity is inauthentic because it does not take part in lived experience." She further defines this free-floating nostalgia in terms appropriate to a collection of two-dimensional visual images that formerly passed through the hands of unknown persons and presumably entered, however briefly, into their awareness. The nostalgic longing arises, she writes, from "the inability of the sign [that is, the postcard] to 'capture' its signified [that is, the reality it purports to represent], [the inability] of narrative to be one with its object, and of the genres of mechanical reproduction to approximate the time of face-to-face communication."[19]

The artist and critic Svetlana Boym has also interpreted nostalgia in a way that particularly speaks to a collection of postcards—material artifacts with visual images of places, whose dates of manufacture and consumption situate them in the flow of historical time, both real and imagined. Starting with the original medical definition of nostalgia as a physical manifestation of homesickness, Boym argues, "At first glance, nostalgia is a longing for a place, but actually it is a yearning for a different time." That time, in her assessment, is "the time of our childhood" and of "the slower rhythms of our dreams." Even more, nostalgia encompasses "rebellion against the modern idea of time, the time of history and progress." A nostalgic person "desires to obliterate history and turn it into private or collective mythology," and in that way "to revisit time like space."[20]

Linen postcards, whether or not they contain messages, represent places from the past in graphic styles of the past. Their acquisition today enables collectors to imagine traveling into a past that is fundamentally represented as composed of space, not time. The American scene of Curt Teich and other producers of linen cards portrays a vision of the past that, despite its setting during a period of economic hardship and global warfare, radiates a comforting certainty. Natural scenes and rural landscapes conform to a mythical sense of the land. Urban views and those of major engineering projects radiate a sense of technological competence, even assurance. As for those more problematic cards that suggest a noir sensibility, such images, perhaps because they are so closely similar to the scenes of scripted novels and movies, also contain the promise that secrets will eventually be revealed and tensions resolved.

The America imaged by Curt Teich was already vanishing even as the ink dried on the final linen cards printed in Chicago. Although preparation of new linen images continued into the mid-1950s, with only a few hundred ordered in 1954 compared with nearly 4,000 at the high point in 1937, the dwindling output of linen cards consisted mostly of occasional reprints of images from past decades. Holiday Inn and Howard Johnson's, space-age coffee shops and Disney-inspired theme parks, and even local news agencies had embraced shiny chromes based on true color photography. Only businesses like small-town drug stores and mom-and-pop motels were still depleting stockpiles of linen cards acquired a decade or two earlier. The landscapes such cards portrayed had long since vanished as interstate highways bypassed scenic roads and main streets, and shopping centers eroded the localism that linen views had promoted. Even western mountains and deserts appeared different on chrome cards—brighter, harsher, less forgiving. The visionary America of linen postcards, which had combined a traditional belief in nature's redemptive quality with a simple faith in technological progress, no longer represented a world confronting nuclear weapons, global polarization, corporatism, consumerism, racial strife, and youth culture. Nostalgia for linen cards reflects a longing for that lost America as much as anything else.

FIG. 6.7. Walker Evans, *Postcard Display*, 1941

In the final analysis, linen postcards perform two different, nearly opposite, functions. On the one hand, they expose to historical inquiry some of the ways in which Americans between the early 1930s and the late 1940s popularly regarded the landscapes and cityscapes in which they lived and traveled. But on the other hand, they afford collectors and unwary historians with a nostalgic vision of spaces that may seem more desirable than those they now inhabit, spaces that can be acquired, sorted, and manipulated in miniature form. In both cases, whether viewed in their past or viewed from the present, linen postcards, which are genuine historical artifacts, tend to obscure reality and its history. Original users of the cards indulged a collective imaginary reflecting an optimistic view of a vibrant, expansive national scene. And today's collectors, with varying motives, construct individual private imaginaries from these time-traveling images. To close with an ironic aphorism from Stewart, "The past lends authenticity to the collection."[21]

1. "They Do Say It's Real": An Introduction to Linen Postcards

1. All postcards described or quoted from are in my collection unless otherwise noted.

2. *Sales Pointers* (Chicago: Curt Teich & Co., 1935), 9–10, box 1, folder 1, Curt Teich Company Papers, Curt Teich Postcard Archives, Lake County Discovery Museum, Wauconda, IL; and *Jobbers Profits* (Chicago: Curt Teich & Co., 1935), 2, box 1, folder 2, Teich Company Papers.

3. Caren Kaplan, *Questions of Travel: Postmodern Discourses of Displacement* (Durham: Duke University Press, 1996), 61.

4. To calculate the total number of linen views printed, one might begin by totaling Teich's production of individual linen cards, about 49,000, as revealed by annual serial numbers of a complete set in the Teich Postcard Archives. One would then subtract the approximate number of nonview advertising and comic cards (4,000). The Print Department of the Boston Public Library holds proofs of about 25,000 linen cards printed by Tichnor Brothers. Serial numbers on cards printed by Colourpicture suggest a total of about 20,000. After again adjusting downward for nonview cards and upward for production by smaller companies, one reaches a minimum of 100,000 and easily as many as 125,000 different linen views. Following a similar logic, Mark Werther and Lorenzo Mott suggest an upper limit of 150,000 individual views in their guide for collectors, *Linen Postcards: Images of the American Dream* (Wayne, PA: Sentinel, 2002), 36–37. However, competing companies sometimes printed nearly identical views, whether owing to reliance on similar or identical source photographs or on pirating of images. Records in the Teich Postcard Archives indicate 6,000 was a typical print run for a single postcard, though popular subjects were printed in runs of 12,500 or 25,000 and occasionally 50,000. Small printers presumably had smaller runs. One way of reaching an estimate of at least one billion cards is to assume 100,000 individual views, each with a print run of 10,000.

5. John Baeder, *Gas, Food, and Lodging* (New York: Abbeville, 1982), 20.

6. The front cover of Springsteen's debut album, *Greetings from Asbury Park, N.J.*, Columbia KC 31903, 1973, 33^{1}/$_{3}$ rpm, consists of a reproduction of a shiny chrome postcard from the 1950s, "Greetings from Asbury Park, N.J.," Tichnor GB5913, n.d., which was derived from an earlier linen card, Tichnor 68159, n.d., probably from the 1940s.

7. "The Legend of the Dogwood," Tichnor, n.d.

8. The best account of a contemporary postcard show is by Daniel D. Arreola, *Postcards from the Rio Bravo Border: Picturing the Place, Placing the Picture* (Austin: University of Texas Press, 2013), xiii–xiv.

2. Curt Teich and the Early History of Postcards

1. Frank Staff, *The Picture Postcard & Its Origins* (London: Lutterworth, 1966), 46–66.

2. J. R. Burdick, *Pioneer Postcards: The Story of Mailing Cards to 1898* (New York: Nostalgia, n.d.), 20–30.

3. Julian Ralph, "The Postal-Card Craze," *Cosmopolitan*, February 1902, 421; and "New Post-Card Regulations," *Harper's Weekly*, March 30, 1907, 481.

4. On this period in general, see Dorothy B. Ryan, *Picture Postcards in the United States, 1893–1918* (New York: Clarkson N. Potter, 1982); its earlier version, George Miller and Dorothy Miller, *Picture Postcards in the United States, 1893–1918* (New York: Clarkson N. Potter, 1976); and Howard Woody, "International Postcards: Their History, Production, and Distribution (Circa 1895 to 1915)," in *Delivering Views: Distant Cultures in Early Postcards*, ed. Christraud M. Geary and Virginia-Lee Webb (Washington, DC: Smithsonian Institution Press, 1998), 13–45. On the Detroit Photo-

graphic Co., see Jeff R. Burdick, *The Handbook of Detroit Publishing Co. Postcards* (Essington, PA: Hobby Publications, 1955); Miller and Miller, *Picture Postcards in the United States*, 149–152; and Thomas W. Southall, "'In the Colors of Nature': Detroit Publishing Company Photochroms," in *Intersections: Lithography, Photography, and the Traditions of Printmaking*, ed. Kathleen Stewart Howe (Albuquerque: University of New Mexico Press, 1998), 67–75. On Joyce Hall, see Barry Shank, *A Token of My Affection: Greeting Cards and American Business Culture* (New York: Columbia University Press, 2004), 130–131.

5. "The Pernicious Picture Post Card," *Atlantic Monthly*, August 1906, 288; and "The Fortieth Birthday of the Post Card," *Scientific American*, November 13, 1909, 363.

6. *Tariff Hearings Before the Committee on Ways and Means of the House of Representatives*, 60th Cong., 6:6194 (statement of James Artman, December 17, 1908), 6:6199 (statement of H. M. Rose, December 17, 1908); and appendix to *Tariff Hearings*, 60th Cong., 8:8326 (petition of Post Card Manufacturers' and Allied Trades' Protective Association, February 15, 1909). The full petition is on 8326–8342, but in general see 8259–8354.

7. Julius Gugler, "The Duty on Picture Post-Cards," *The Nation*, July 15, 1909, 51; and appendix to *Tariff Hearings*, 8:8290 (letter from C. A. Kendrick, Kendrick Book and Stationery Co., Denver).

8. As quoted by Ryan, *Picture Postcards in the United States*, 29; see also 28–32; and George Miller, "Buy American: Tariff Protection for Postcards 1897–1909," *Postcard Collector* 6 (May 1988): 42–44.

9. Most biographical details are from Curt Teich Sr., *The Teich's [sic] Family Tree and History* (Chicago: privately printed, 1958), box 1, folder 1, Teich Family Papers, Curt Teich Postcard Archives; supplemented by *90 Jahre 1857–1947* (Lobenstein, Germany: Arthur Goehring, 1947), box 3, folder 4, Teich Family Papers; and Ralph Teich, "A Son Remembers Curt Otto Teich, Sr.," *Postcard Journal* 1, no. 1 (Summer 1984): n.p. Curt Teich's birth certificate, Greiz, March 26, 1877, is in box 1, folder 3, Teich Family Papers. See also E. G. Thoman, "A Million Dollars a Year in Penny Postcards,"*American Business*, May 1938, 24–

25, 56, 57; and Katherine O'Brien, "An Offset Pioneer," *American Printer*, October 1, 2006, http://www.americanprinter.com/special-interests/digital-presses/an-offset-pioneer. I also relied on "Das Wirken von Friedrich und Christian Teich für die Heimatstadt," an article from Bad Lobenstein's official newsletter, *Stadt Bad Lobenstein Amts- und Mitteilungsblatt*, no. 20 (2007): 1, 4 (no longer available on the town's website). Dates during the period 1890–1910 given in *Teich's Family Tree* sometimes conflict by a year with those in U.S. Census records and ships' passenger manifests, to which I defer. Curt Teich semi-Anglicized his grandfather's name as "Friederich," but Friedrich used the usual German spelling in his own publications. A useful summary of Teich's career is provided by Heather Johnson, "The Postcard Factory: Curt Teich and the Golden Age of Postcards," *Image File* 18, nos. 3–4 (2012): 4–9.

10. On the arrivals of Christian and Max, see passenger manifest, SS *Saale*, October 25, 1892, frame 109, line 213, and passenger manifest, SS *Chester*, February 27, 1893, frame 305, line 95, both on http://www.libertyellisfoundation.org.

11. Curt Teich's report cards and "leaving certificate" from the Annenschule (Realgymnasium) in Dresden are in box 1, folder 4, Teich Family Papers. Passenger manifest, SS *Saale*, April 12, 1895, frame 282, ticket 6234, on http://www.libertyellisfoundation.org, gives Teich's first name as "Kurt," a spelling that conflicts with his birth certificate. Certificate of naturalization, Cook County, IL, November 24, 1899, box 1, folder 5, Teich Family Papers.

12. I am indebted to Axel Plank, a collector in Blankenstein, Germany, for photocopies of five such postcards printed by Verlag von Christian Teich bearing postmarks from 1898 and 1901. According to Plank's letter of December 28, 2008, he and fellow collectors estimate that Verlag von Teich printed about ten cards illustrating Lobenstein (with one to two hundred of each printed) and about thirty cards illustrating surrounding towns (with fifty to a hundred of each printed).

13. Teich, *Teich's Family Tree*, 28, Teich Family Papers.

14. The address side bears the German printer's serial number, 37421. Identical in form, technique, and paper stock are three

other cards: "Chicago / Court House," Curt Teich & Co., Printers, Chicago, No. 3 (Röder no. 30465); "Chicago / Old Colony Building," Curt Teich & Co., Chicago and St. Louis, No. 58 (Röder no. 37609), postmarked June 29, 1905; and "Chicago / Stock Exchange Building," Curt Teich & Co., Printers, Chicago and St. Louis, Teich number illegible (Röder no. 37602), postmarked November 14, 1905. On Röder and the connection with Teich, see Woody, "International Postcards," 25; and Christine Pyle, "Donation Fills in Missing Pieces," *Image File* 13, no. 2 (2003): 3–5.

15. Documents pertaining to incorporation (applied for on March 15, 1904, granted on May 4, 1904) and the subsequent name change (December 31, 1906) are in box 7, folder 1, Teich Company Papers. Ralph Teich, in "A Son Remembers," recalled the date of incorporation as 1898, but the documents suggest otherwise. Teich departed Hamburg on June 4, 1904, "Hamburg Passenger Lists, 1850–1934," Hamburg State Archives, vol. 373–71 VIII A 1, part 156, p. 1076, on http://www.ancestry.com.

16. On real photo postcards, see Rosamond B. Vaule, *As We Were: American Photographic Postcards, 1905–1930* (Boston: David R. Godine, 2004); Robert Bodgan and Todd Weseloh, *Real Photo Postcard Guide: The People's Photography* (Syracuse: Syracuse University Press, 2006); and Luc Sante, *Folk Photography: The American Real Photo Postcard, 1905–1930* (Portland: Yeti, 2009). Although regional in coverage, John Miller Morris, *Taming the Land: The Lost Postcard Photographs of the Texas High Plains* (College Station: Texas A&M University Press, 2009), and Arreola, *Postcards from the Rio Bravo Border*, are particularly useful. More idiosyncratic are Hal Morgan and Andreas Brown, *Prairie Fires and Paper Moons: The American Photographic Postcard, 1900–1920* (Boston: David R. Godine, 1981); and Laetitia Wolff, *Real Photo Postcards: Unbelievable Images from the Collection of Harvey Tulcensky* (New York: Princeton Architectural Press, 2005).

17. On postcards of lynchings, see James Allen, ed., *Without Sanctuary: Lynching Photography in America* (Santa Fe: Twin Palms, 2000); and Dora Apel, *Imagery of Lynching: Black Men, White Women, and the Mob* (New Brunswick: Rutgers University Press, 2004).

Most lynching cards were real photos, produced within a day or two of the occurrence, though a few were mass-produced in halftone and at least two color lithographs exist. See Allen, afterword to *Without Sanctuary*, 204–205.

18. On exaggeration cards, produced not only as real photos but also as lithographs, thereby ironically negating their claim to photographic verisimilitude, see Roger L. Welsch, *Tall-Tale Postcards: A Pictorial History* (South Brunswick, NJ: A. S. Barnes, 1976); and Hal Morgan, *Big Time: American Tall-Tale Postcards* (New York: St. Martin's Press, 1981).

19. Patricia C. Albers and William R. James, "Utah's Indians and Popular Photography in the American West: A View from the Picture Post Card," *Utah Historical Quarterly* 52 (Winter 1984): 84; and Bogdan and Weseloh, *Real Photo Postcard Guide*, 39–40.

20. Curt Foerster, "American Photographic Postcards," *Photo-Era Magazine*, February 1929, 84.

21. An excellent description is in *Encyclopædia Britannica*, 11th ed., s.v. "process" (a major article on photomechanical reproduction, which in 1911 was known as "process" printing), characterizing collotype as "largely used for postcards." See also Robert Taft, *Photography and the American Scene: A Social History, 1839–1889* (New York: Macmillan, 1942), 431–435; and Helmut Gernsheim in collaboration with Alison Gernsheim, *The History of Photography: From the Camera Obscura to the Beginning of the Modern Era* (New York: McGraw-Hill, 1969), 547–549.

22. On halftone, see Taft, *Photography and the American Scene*, 434–447; Gernsheim, *The History of Photography*, 549–552; Neil Harris, "Iconography and Intellectual History: The Halftone Effect," in his *Cultural Excursions: Marketing Appetites and Cultural Tastes in Modern America* (Chicago: University of Chicago Press, 1990), 304–317; David Clayton Phillips, "Art for Industry's Sake: Halftone Technology, Mass Photography and the Social Transformation of American Print Culture, 1880–1920" (Ph.D. diss., Yale University, 1996); and Richard Benson, *The Printed Picture* (New York: Museum of Modern Art, 2008), 222–223. Benson provides visually compelling explications of various techniques

for printing images. Two works by William M. Ivins Jr., who might be considered the Marshall McLuhan of visuality, remain essential for anyone seeking to blend technological and cultural perspectives while interpreting printed images: *How Prints Look: Photographs with a Commentary* (Boston: Beacon, 1958; orig. 1943); and *Prints and Visual Communication* (New York: Da Capo Press, 1969; orig. 1953).

23. On chromolithography, see Peter C. Marzio, *The Democratic Art: Chromolithography 1840-1900: Pictures for a 19th-Century America* (Boston: David R. Godine, 1979); and Shank, *A Token of My Affection*, 65-118.

24. Southall, "'In the Colors of Nature,'" 69-70. Enlarged digital scans of two Detroit postcards, one from 1899 and the other from 1910, reveal random collotype-like graining for each of the multiple color inks.

25. All descriptions of printing characteristics of cards are based on 2400-dpi digital scans enlarged in Photoshop to seventeen times actual size.

26. "Wayne County Building, Detroit, Mich.," Teich A-17399, ca. 1910. On the labor required to design and print view cards, see the petition of the Post Card Manufacturers' and Allied Trades' Protective Association, appendix to *Tariff Hearings*, 8:8339. My understanding of pre-linen and linen postcard printing processes is indebted to two veterans of the industry. Walter A. Harles, who began working for Teich in 1937, provided a written description of three successive lithographic techniques after we spoke by phone on August 19, 2008. Lawrence F. Tichnor, who entered his family's firm, Colourpicture, as a sales agent in the late 1930s, spoke with me by phone for several hours on August 20 and 22, 2008, about many aspects of the postcard business, including printing. Neither is responsible for any errors in my treatment of this complex topic.

27. Walker Evans, "Main Street Looking North from Courthouse Square: A Portfolio of American Picture Postcards from the Trolley-Car Period," *Fortune*, May 1948, 102. On Evans's collection, see Jeff L. Rosenheim and Douglas Eklund, *Unclassified: A Walker Evans Anthology* (Zurich: Scalo, 2000), 200-207; and Jeff L. Rosenheim, *Walker Evans and the Picture Postcard* (Göttingen: Steidl/Metropolitan Museum of Art, 2009), 13-19. The latter

reproduces nearly five hundred cards from Evans's collection.

28. Teich, *Teich's Family Tree*, 29, Teich Family Papers. On pre-linen postcard production through 1930, see 29-33.

29. Teich as quoted by Thoman, "A Million Dollars a Year in Penny Postcards," 25. Characterization of Teich's early Chicago cards is based on five examples in my collection with serial numbers ranging from 69 to 285, two mailed in 1906 and two in 1908. Buettner, whose name appears as "Büttner" on the passenger manifest, SS *Kaiser Wilhelm der Grosse*, February 2, 1905, frame 394, line 19, on http://www.libertyellisfoundation.org, stated upon arrival that he intended to join his friend Curt Teich in Chicago. Buettner was listed as a lithographic artist in Chicago in the U.S. Census 1910, Illinois, series T624, roll 272, 143, and in the U.S. Census 1920, Illinois, series T625, roll 337, 143, both found on http://www.heritagequestonline.com. Hochegger was listed as a pressman in Chicago in the U.S. Census 1910, Illinois, series T624, roll 264, 153, on http://www.heritagequestonline.com. Although the census enumerator recorded Germany as Hochegger's birthplace, Teich described him as an Austrian.

30. Information on the Leighton order comes from Teich, *Teich's Family Tree*, 32, Teich Family Papers; Lawrence F. Tichnor, telephone conversations, August 20 and 22, 2008; and Debra Gust, staff researcher, Teich Postcard Archives, telephone conversation, October 29, 2008. Gust provided a printout list of all cards printed by Teich for Leighton.

31. Woody, "International Postcards," 17-18; Burdick, *The Handbook of Detroit Publishing Co. Postcards*, 5, 7; and Southall, "'In the Colors of Nature,'" 70.

32. A review of twenty-five printing handbooks published between 1910 and 1940 yielded Charles W. Hackleman, *Commercial Engraving and Printing* (Indianapolis: Commercial Engraving, 1921), as authoritative, exhaustively detailed, and clearly written. I have relied on it throughout this chapter. On offset lithography, see 503-519. See also Frank O. Sullivan, "The Inland Offset Lithographer," *The Inland Printer* 74 (January 1925): 537-544; Warren C. Brown, *Offset Lithography* (New York: National Lithographer, 1927); Boyd

R. Alvord, *Engraving and Printing Methods* (Scranton: International Textbook, 1949), 86–88; and Benson, *The Printed Picture*, 254–256.

33. Thoman, "A Million Dollars a Year in Penny Postcards," 56. See also Teich, *Teich's Family Tree*, 30, Teich Family Papers. Theodore Regensteiner, another early Chicago postcard publisher, described a parallel process in his autobiography, *My First Seventy-Five Years* (Chicago: Regensteiner, 1943), 137–139.

34. "Carnegie Library, Marion, O.," Teich A-8244, n.d., postmarked July 31, 1913, has 133 lines per inch; "Bird's Eye View of Toledo, Ohio," Teich 12048, n.d., dated by hand September 23, 1914, has 110 lines per inch.

35. Teich, *Teich's Family Tree*, 30, Teich Family Papers.

36. Ralph Teich interview by Dan Cochrane, typed transcript, ca. 1986, box 7, folder 4, Teich Company Papers.

37. Miller and Miller, *Picture Postcards in the United States*, 152.

38. On the new plant, see Christine A. Pyle, "For Rent," *Image File* 6, no. 4 (1991): 9–11. Teich described himself as a "manufacturer" in his response to the U.S. Census 1920, Illinois, series T625, roll 342, 224, on http://www.heri tagequestonline.com. Descriptions of Teich's printing plant and houses are based on photographs from Google Maps Street View. In 1990 the plant at 1733–1755 West Irving Park Road became the sixty-seven-unit Post Card Place Lofts, with conversion supervised by architect Patrick FitzGerald. Luc Van Malderen, in a brief text accompanying his *American Architecture: A Vintage Postcard Collection* (Mulgrave, Australia: Images, 2000), 15, wrongly states that "the now silent factory houses archives and a museum." Ron Richman (born Reichmann) reported an anecdote about household economy told by his mother, Julia Gerweck, in conversation with Katherine Hamilton Smith after a meeting of the Edgewater Historical Society, Chicago, March 26, 1994, according to a memo by Smith, April 7, 1994, box 12, folder 1, Teich Family Papers.

39. General industry details are from Miller and Miller, *Picture Postcards in the United States*, 29–31; and Ryan, *Picture Postcards in the United States*, 32.

40. A legend on the back reads, "Published Expressly for F. W. Woolworth Co." To complicate the story, it should be noted that Woolworth absorbed Kirby in 1912.

3. The Linen Postcard: Innovation and Aesthetics

1. Quotations are from John Baeder, *Diners* (New York: Harry N. Abrams, 1978), 97; Allen F. Davis, *Postcards from Vermont: A Social History, 1905-1945* (Hanover: University Press of New England, 2002), 314; Werther and Mott, *Linen Postcards*, 11; John A. Jakle, *Postcards of the Night: Views of American Cities* (Santa Fe: Museum of New Mexico Press, 2003), 27; and Katherine Hamilton Smith as quoted by Kim Keister, "'Wish You Were Here!,'" *Historic Preservation* 44 (March/April 1992): 55.

2. See Teich, *Teich's Family Tree*, 36, Teich Family Papers. On July 23, 1935, the U.S. Patent Office issued trademark 326,438 to Curt Teich & Company for the term "C. T. Art-Colortone." The company asserted in its application of February 27, 1935, that the phrase had been in continuous use since January 1931. See http://tsdr.uspto.gov/documentviewer?caseId=sn60 326438&docId=ORC20051029173950#docIn dex=0&page=1. Despite frequent claims, both recent and historical, that the company held invention patents for the new printing process, a search of patent records suggests that that was not the case, and that the process remained proprietary. Teich & Co. established a new numbering system for C. T. Art-Colortone cards, running from 1931 to 1954, with each card's serial number (for example, 5A-H312 or 0B-H128) indicating its date of first printing. The first letter indicates the decade (A = 1930s, B = 1940s, C = 1950s). The preceding numeral indicates the year within that decade (in these two examples 1935 and 1940). The letter H indicates the Art-Colortone process, and the concluding numbers indicate a card's chronological order within a given year. The serial number usually appears on the front of a card, within the border to the lower right. However, some appear in various locations on the backs of cards, even within the rectangle indicating where a postage stamp is to be placed. Many

cards were given second numbers to indicate their positions within a series established by a client (for example, see fig. 1.1) or in one of Teich's own thematic series (see fig. 4.2).

3. Various comments quoted by Carl Richard Greer, *Advertising and Its Mechanical Production* (New York: Tudor, 1936), 259–260. In general see Greer, 252–263; and John Cameron Aspley, ed., *The Sales Promotion Handbook* (Chicago: Darnell, 1957), 318. I am indebted to Alan Petrulis for a convincing presentation of this difficult topic in "Linen Cards 1931–1959" on the website Metropolitan Postcard Club of New York City, http://www.metropostcard .com/card11linen.html, and for his subsequent e-mail messages, July 19 and 21, 2008.

4. Greer, *Advertising and Its Mechanical Production*, 252.

5. One must evaluate carefully what little has been written about linen cards. The mistaken claim that the texture came from rag content in the paper is repeated by Helen Chantal-Pike, *Greetings from New Jersey: A Postcard Tour of the Garden State* (New Brunswick: Rutgers University Press, 2001), 213; Davis, *Postcards from Vermont*, 314; Michael G. Bushnell, *Historic Postcards from Old Kansas City* (Leawood, KS: Leathers, 2003), 1; and John A. Jakle and Keith A. Sculle, *Picturing Illinois: Twentieth-Century Postcard Art from Chicago to Cairo* (Urbana: University of Illinois Press, 2012), xiii. Moira F. Harris wrongly states that the cards were embossed after printing; see her article "Small Format, Big View: Curt Teich Postcards of Minnesota," *Minnesota History* 54 (Fall 1995): 307. And David Prochaska misleadingly refers to them as "airbrushed by hand in pastel colors" in his article "Exhibiting the Museum," in *Postcards: Ephemeral Histories of Modernity*, ed. David Prochaska and Jordana Mendelson (University Park: Pennsylvania State University Press, 2010), 119.

6. *Sales Pointers*, 8, Teich Company Papers.

7. Sources on CMYK halftone printing include Hackleman, *Commercial Engraving and Printing*, 276–300; David Cumming, *Handbook of Lithography* (London: A. & C. Black, 1932), 274–310; Greer, *Advertising and Its Mechanical Production*, 226–229; and C. Mason Willy, *Practical Photo-Lithography* (London: Sir Isaac Pitman & Sons, 1940), 124–177.

8. Thoman, "A Million Dollars a Year in Penny Postcards," 56. On color in magazine advertising, see Greer, *Advertising and Its Mechanical Production*, 212. See also generally Michelle H. Bogart, *Artists, Advertising, and the Borders of Art* (Chicago: University of Chicago Press, 1995), and on color in particular, Roland Marchand, *Advertising the American Dream: Making Way for Modernity* (Berkeley and Los Angeles: University of California Press, 1985), 120–127; Regina Lee Blaszczyk, *Imagining Consumers: Design and Innovation from Wedgwood to Corning* (Baltimore: Johns Hopkins University Press, 2002), 146–150, 194–207; and Regina Lee Blaszczyk, *The Color Revolution* (Cambridge: MIT Press, 2012), 45–70.

9. "Arrows That Found Their Marks," *Curteich News* 4, no. 12 (December 1935): 12; only scattered issues are available in box 1, folder 12, Teich Company Papers. See also Thoman, "A Million Dollars a Year in Penny Postcards," 56; and "Curt Teich & Company Incorporated: Auditors Report for Year 1939," typescript, n.p., box 1, folder 20, Teich Company Papers.

10. A letter from Curt Teich Jr. to G. I. Pitchford, May 16, 1966, noted the date of Pitchford's first order fifty-three years earlier and exclaimed, "Let's go on and make this 60 years—what say?" The letter is part of a substantial collection of business correspondence, documents, photographs, negatives, cameras, and personal effects of Garnet Irving Pitchford (he went by his initials), here called the Pitchford Archive, in the possession of his son, Robert Pitchford, of Palm Desert, California. Unless otherwise noted, biographical information is based on those materials, on a telephone interview with Bob Pitchford on April 23, 2012, and on personal interviews conducted June 4–5, 2012, with Bob Pitchford, his sister, the late Marilyn June Maurer, and his wife, Vera Pitchford. Further mention of the Pitchford Archive is provided only in the case of direct quotation or specific reference. Bob and Vera's daughter Ginny Pitchford maintains a selection of her grandfather's photographs at www.pitchfordphotos.com.

11. Carbon copy of a letter from Pitchford to a Mr. Whiston, June 21, 1915, Pitchford Archive.

12. Facsimile of a letter from Hamilton W.

Wright Jr., director, Miami News Service, City of Miami, to Frank Hochegger, vice president, Teich & Co., n.d., in *Jobbers Profits*, 14, Teich Company Papers.

13. Ralph Teich interview by Cochrane; pep talk from *Jobbers Profits*, 15, 3; both in Teich Company Papers.

14. *Sales Pointers*, 35, Teich Company Papers.

15. Ibid., 3, 7.

16. General letter from Teich & Co., "To our representatives," January 2, 1914, Pitchford Archive. Surviving correspondence in both directions seems complete for this period, but after 1918 only particularly significant or occasionally random letters remain. According to Bob Pitchford, an assistant employed for his father by the company during his final years destroyed many business papers after his death.

17. Quotations from an interview with Marilyn June Maurer by the author, June 5, 2012. Other quotations are from customer index cards in Pitchford's handwriting, Pitchford Archive.

18. Although numbered as a linen card, the color chart was printed on smooth card stock without linen embossing, presumably so as not to complicate color selection. I am indebted to Bob Pitchford for an example of this card.

19. Marzio, *The Democratic Art*, 108, 309.

20. Job file, "Great Salt Lake Cut-off at Sunset, Great Salt Lake, Utah," Teich 6A-H2493, 1936. Job files are a separate category in the Teich Postcard Archives, organized by serial numbers of cards.

21. Job file, "Typical Southern Sidewalk Colonnades, Main Street, Yuma, Arizona," Teich 0C-H814, 1950, Teich Postcard Archives.

22. The job file for the Lycoming Hotel postcard contains a copy of "Hotel Ponce de Leon / Roanoke, Va.," Teich 5A-H2004, 1935, printed on thin paper as a sales sample with a price list on the back. The Lycoming card had to be redone only nine months later owing to the hotel's renovation. The remake (7A-H2124) retained the aviation layout, which ironically seems out of step with the cocktail lounge's new warmer, wood-based interior.

23. In 1930, the first year for which financial records survive, Pitchford received $11,336 in sales commissions from Teich (ten percent of his total sales), out of which

he covered travel expenses. In 1943, the only year for which expense records survive, travel expenses totaled $2,146. Similar expenses in 1930 would have left a net income of over $9,000. Pitchford grossed $4,083 in 1932 and only $2,995 in 1933, but rising commissions reached $12,962 in 1937 and $14,191 in 1939. In 1943, Teich & Co. issued a W-2 form listing an income of $30,438. Relative placement of Pitchford's income is based on two statistical tables: "Percent Distribution of Families and Unattached Individuals, by Income Levels: 1929–1964" and "Family Personal Income Received by Each Fifth and Top 5 Percent of Families and Unattached Individuals: 1929–1964" (years are incomplete in both tables), in Bureau of the Census, U.S. Department of Commerce, *Historical Statistics of the United States, Colonial Times to 1970, Bicentennial Edition* (Washington, DC: U.S. Government Printing Office, 1975), pt. 1, 299, 301. Also pertinent are Pitchford's only surviving contract with Teich, for the period February 1, 1945, to January 31, 1946, and a letter of conveyance of that contract from Curt Teich Jr., December 20, 1944, Pitchford Archive. See also the U.S. Census 1940, California, series T627, roll 254, 143, on http://www.heritagequestonline.com.

24. Timothy B. Spears, *100 Years on the Road: The Traveling Salesman in American Culture* (New Haven: Yale University Press, 1995), 79.

25. *Sales Pointers*, 85, Teich Company Papers, stated in 1935 that the company employed 275 men and women in twelve departments (not counting sales agents, who worked on commission). Three years later the firm reported 310 employees (60 office workers and 250 technical and printing workers, including 100 artists); see Thoman, "A Million Dollars a Year in Penny Postcards," 56. The following account of the production of a linen postcard is based mostly on the job file for "City Hall, Sioux Falls, S.D.," Teich 7A-H1798, 1937, Teich Postcard Archives; and on general information from *Sales Pointers*, 58–63, from Ralph Teich interview by Cochrane, and from Ralph Teich's handwritten notes, 5 pp., box 7, folder 3, Teich Company Papers. The retouching process is discussed and illustrated by Keister, "'Wish You Were Here!,'" 59; and Werther and Mott, *Linen Postcards*, 15–17.

26. Curt Teich Jr. is identified as "general plant superintendent" in "Another Two-Color Harris Offset Press," *Curteich News* 2, no. 6 (September 1933): n.p., Teich Company Papers.

27. Dealers and collectors who write handbooks and articles about postcards regard the company or individual who commissioned and distributed a card as its "publisher," while Teich was a "printer" filling a job order. The distinction is probably legally accurate. However, given that Teich created an aesthetic genre, processed thousands of images, and sometimes sold a single image to multiple distributors, I have decided mostly to ignore it.

28. Roger Gilmore, ed., *Over a Century: A History of the School of the Art Institute of Chicago, 1866–1981* (Chicago: School of the Art Institute of Chicago, 1982), 80–85; and Susan F. Rossen, ed., *Inland Printers: The Fine-Press Movement in Chicago, 1920–45* (Chicago: Caxton Club of Chicago, 2003), 22.

29. On photo retouching, see Hackleman, *Commercial Engraving and Printing*, 75–109. On use of the airbrush in retouching, see Frank J. Knaus, *How to Paint with Air* (Chicago: Paasche Airbrush Co., 1947), 64–68.

30. Hackleman, *Commercial Engraving and Printing*, 281; and Ralph Teich interview by Cochrane, Teich Company Papers.

31. Hackleman, *Commercial Engraving and Printing*, 281. Quotations are from *Sales Pointers*, 6, Teich Company Papers.

32. Brenda Warner Rotzoll, "Vera Berdich, 88, Artist Who Was Major Influence on Imagists," *Chicago Sun-Times*, October 17, 2003. John Baeder characterized retouching and colorizing as gendered processes in *Gas, Food, and Lodging*, 21. He stated in an e-mail to the author, December 8, 2008, that the information must have come from a conversation with someone at the Teich Postcard Archives. My understanding of Teich's proprietary colorizing process has benefited from phone conversations with Lawrence F. Tichnor and Walter A. Harles; from Harles's two-page written account; and from Ralph Teich's handwritten notes. The topic is difficult, particularly owing to my failure to locate any artists who worked on Teich linen postcards, and my summary is hardly definitive.

33. Approximate intensity numbers are based on a comparison of an enlarged digital scan of that portion of the printed postcard with a chart of relative intensities for cyan, yellow, and magenta, ranging from 1 (lowest) to 10 (highest), that is located at http://english .iro-color.com/colorchart/color/brightest-color-chart.html.

34. *Sales Pointers*, 88, Teich Company Papers.

35. *Curteich News* 4, no. 12 (December 1935): 11, Teich Company Papers.

36. Acquisition of the second two-color Harris offset press was announced in "Another Two-Color Harris Offset Press"; see also *Sales Pointers*, 85, both in Teich Company Papers.

37. The following discussion of prices is based on *Price List for Jobbers of Local View Post Cards, Folders, Miniatures, Books* (Chicago: Curt Teich, July 1, 1936); and *The "A" Line Price List* (Chicago: Curt Teich, June 1, 1936); both in box 1, folder 4, Teich Company Papers. "A" stands for "advertising."

38. Ralph Teich interview by Cochrane, Teich Company Papers.

39. The cost of plate preparation is from *Jobbers Profits*, 22, Teich Company Papers. The Teich Postcard Archives reveal the print run in the initial order for each postcard but contain no record of how many times a particular card was reordered, nor in what volume.

40. "Auditors Report for Year 1939," Teich Company Papers.

41. Leah Dilworth, *Imagining Indians in the Southwest: Persistent Visions of a Primitive Past* (Washington, DC: Smithsonian Institution Press, 1996), 111; Baeder, *Diners*, 98; Baeder, *Gas, Food, and Lodging*, 20, 32; Peter Bacon Hales, "American Views and the Romance of Modernization," in Martha A. Sandweiss, ed., *Photography in Nineteenth-Century America* (New York: Harry N. Abrams, 1991), 241; and Tom Phillips, *The Postcard Century: 2000 Cards and Their Messages* (London: Thames & Hudson, 2000), 10–11, 6.

42. Richard Morphet, introduction to *Wish You Were Here: The History of the Picture Postcard*, exhibition catalog (Hempstead, NY: Emily Lowe Gallery, Hofstra University, 1974), n.p. The exhibition, organized by Jill Kornblee and Harold Jones, was ahead of its time in consid-

ering postcards as cultural artifacts. See "Now It's Art: Postcard Show Hits the Road," *Modern Photography*, January 1975, 41.

43. Ralph Teich interview by Cochrane, Teich Company Papers.

44. Letter from Curt Teich to G. I. Pitchford, April 6, 1933, Pitchford Archive.

45. "The C. T. Art-Colortone Process," *Curteich News* 2, no. 6 (September 1933): n.p., Teich Company Papers. On Urban's color scheme, see Lisa D. Schrenk, *Building a Century of Progress: The Architecture of Chicago's 1933-34 World's Fair* (Minneapolis: University of Minnesota Press, 2007), 98–106, plate 16 (between 136 and 137); and Blaszczyk, *The Color Revolution*, 203–211.

46. "What Shall I Say" and "Go to the Movies for Fun, Ideas, and Business," *Curteich*

News 4, no. 7 (July 1935): 3–4, Teich Company Papers; and "Arrows That Found Their Marks," 12.

47. Werther and Mott, *Linen Postcards*, 11; and Mike Davis, *Ecology of Fear: Los Angeles and the Imagination of Disaster* (New York: Vintage, 1998), 61. Werther and Mott place so much emphasis on "stunners" that they underline their definition of the term.

48. Mark Pascale as quoted by Keister, "'Wish You Were Here!,'" 60; and Hales, "American Views and the Romance of Modernization," 241.

49. Ralph Teich interview by Cochrane, Teich Company Papers. On Thomas Dexter of Dexter Press, see "The King of the Postcards," *American Magazine*, March 1950, 114.

4. Landscapes in Linen Postcards: A National Imaginary

1. Woody Guthrie, "This Land Is Your Land" (1940), http://www.woodyguthrie.org/Lyrics/This_Land.htm.

2. Not all of the photographs produced by the FSA's Historical Section and its successor agency at the Office of War Information were monotone. The Library of Congress, which holds about 171,000 such black-and-white images, also holds 1,600 color transparencies (slides) made after the introduction of 35 mm Kodachrome roll film in 1936. See Paul Henderson, "The Color of Memory," in *Bound for Glory: America in Color, 1939–43* (New York: Harry N. Abrams, 2004), 7–8. On FSA photography, see F. Jack Hurley, *Portrait of a Decade: Roy Stryker and the Development of Documentary Photography in the Thirties* (Baton Rouge: Louisiana State University Press, 1972); William Stott, *Documentary Expression and Thirties America* (New York: Oxford University Press, 1973); James Curtis, *Mind's Eye, Mind's Truth: FSA Photography Reconsidered* (Philadelphia: Temple University Press, 1989); and John Raeburn, *A Staggering Revolution: A Cultural History of Thirties Photography* (Urbana: University of Illinois Press, 2006), 143–193.

3. Lewis Mumford as quoted by Jerrold Hirsch, *Portrait of America: A Cultural Histo-*

ry of the Federal Writers' Project (Chapel Hill: University of North Carolina Press, 2003), 39. On WPA guidebooks, see also Christine Bold, *The WPA Guides: Mapping America* (Jackson: University Press of Mississippi, 1999). An earlier project of representing the nation to itself was *Picturesque America*, a collection of 900 landscape engravings embedded in regional essays issued in installments by the publisher D. Appleton in the early 1870s. When collected in two leather-bound volumes, the set offered an illusion of completeness that postcards lacked. Its inclusion of scenes of cities, railroads, and manufacturing plants among predominantly natural landscapes promoted a national ideology of progressive uplift. See Sue Rainey, *Creating "Picturesque America": Monument to the Natural and Cultural Landscape* (Nashville: Vanderbilt University Press, 1994).

4. On uses of FSA photographs, see Cara A. Finnegan, *Picturing Poverty: Print Culture and FSA Photographs* (Washington, DC: Smithsonian Books, 2003).

5. Evans, "Main Street Looking North," 102; and "A Glimpse of Bryce Canyon," Teich 2A-H216 (1932), postmarked Bryce Canyon, UT, July 21, 1939.

6. Hoffman Birney, *Roads to Roam* (Philadelphia: Penn, 1930), 59; W. J. T. Mitchell,

"Imperial Landscape," in *Landscape and Power*, ed. W. J. T. Mitchell (Chicago: University of Chicago Press, 1994), 15; and Daniel Boorstin, *The Image: A Guide to Pseudo-Events in America* (New York: Atheneum, 1971; orig. 1962), 14. Mitchell may have based his unacknowledged paraphrasing of Birney's question on a reference in John A. Jakle, *The Tourist: Travel in Twentieth-Century North America* (Lincoln: University of Nebraska Press, 1985), 66. It is possible to approximate a provisional answer to Birney's question. Teich & Co. kept a series of thick binders known as the Geographical Index (now in the Teich Postcard Archives), arranged by state and then location, into which a clerk entered each individual card by subject, production number, customer name, and (from the linen postcard era onward) initial print run. Between 1932 and 1951, the company produced 208 individual views of the Grand Canyon, with initial orders totaling 1,788,500 cards. Working from a measurement of 145 linen postcards to a tightly packed 2-inch stack, one can roughly calculate that all those cards would yield a single stack 2,056 feet high. However, if compressed into a tightly packed cube, they would encompass 275 cubic feet. The cube would measure only 6.5 feet on a side and would fill about 10 percent of a standard 40-foot shipping container. Even with reprints, linen cards from other printers, and all the pre- and post-linen postcards of the canyon combined, the grand total would be immediately lost if lowered into the Grand Canyon's immensity.

7. A key source on artists envisioning the West is still William H. Goetzmann, *Exploration and Empire: The Explorer and the Scientist in the Winning of the American West* (New York: Alfred A. Knopf, 1966). See also William H. Goetzmann and William N. Goetzmann, *The West of the Imagination* (New York: W. W. Norton, 1986). An early treatment of photography in the West is Taft, *Photography and the American Scene*, 248–310. For revisionist interpretations emphasizing the imperialist ideology of the visual culture of westward expansion, see essays in William H. Truettner, ed., *The West as America: Reinterpreting Images of the Frontier, 1820-1920* (Washington, DC: Smithsonian Institution Press, 1991). Martha A. Sandweiss, *Print the Legend: Photography*

and the American West (New Haven: Yale University Press, 2002), is both exhaustive and compelling.

8. See Harvey Green, "'Pasteboard Masks': The Stereograph in American Culture, 1865–1910," in *Points of View: The Stereograph in America—A Cultural History*, ed. Edward W. Earle (Rochester, NY: Visual Studies Workshop Press, 1979), 109–115; Richard N. Masteller, "Western Views in Eastern Parlors: The Contribution of the Stereograph Photographer to the Conquest of the West," in *Prospects 6*, ed. Jack Salzman (New York: Burt Franklin, 1981), 56; and Peter B. Hales, *William Henry Jackson and the Transformation of the American Landscape* (Philadelphia: Temple University Press, 1988), 48.

9. Job file, "Palace of Fine Arts, San Francisco, Calif.," Teich 2B-H321, 1942, Teich Company Papers.

10. Marttila & Kiley, Inc., *American Public Attitudes towards the Visual Arts: Summary Report and Tabular Report* (New York: Nation Institute, 1994); and "Painting by Numbers: The Search for a People's Art," *The Nation*, March 14, 1994, 334–348. See also "United States: Most Wanted Painting," http://awp.diaart.org/km/usa/most.html.

11. Teich often reused specific cards in different situations without changing their serial numbers. My collection contains two variants of this card, one with no location indicated, the other with "Greetings from St. Charles, Michigan" later overprinted on the lower border. However, this linen card was originally produced for a Boston distributor, the American Art Post Card Company, in a series of twenty-seven views of Maine (5A-H2268 to 5A-H2294), only two of whose subjects could be regarded as generic. The Holstein cattle card was in fact recycled. Its job file contains a pre-linen American Art postcard (118607) based on the same photograph and entitled "Greetings from Maine / Homeward Bound," printed in 1928 for H. A. Dickerman & Son of Taunton, Massachusetts.

12. Roland Barthes, *Camera Lucida: Reflections on Photography*, trans. Richard Howard (New York: Hill and Wang, 1981; orig. 1980), 25–27, 55, 59.

13. Paul Vanderbilt, *Between the Landscape and Its Other* (Baltimore: Johns Hopkins Uni-

versity Press, 1993), 7; Walker Evans, "'Lyric Documentary': An Illustrated Transcript of a Lecture by Walker Evans Presented at Yale University, March 11, 1964," in Rosenheim, *Walker Evans and the Picture Postcard*, 103; and Edward Weston as quoted by Miles Orvell, *The Real Thing: Imitation and Authenticity in American Culture, 1880–1940* (Chapel Hill: University of North Carolina Press, 1989), 220.

14. Naomi Schor, "*Cartes Postales*: Representing Paris 1900," *Critical Inquiry* 18 (Winter 1992): 225 (reprinted, slightly revised and compressed, as "Collecting Paris," in *The Cultures of Collecting*, ed. John Elsner and Roger Cardinal [Cambridge: Harvard University Press, 1994], 269); Baeder, *Diners*, 77; and Werther and Mott, *Linen Postcards*, 11.

Portfolio 1: Landscapes

1. The concept of juxtaposing paired images and texts, one set after another, with meaning accumulating by multidimensional association, was inspired by the format of a pioneering work of documentary photography and history by David Wharton, *The Soul of a Small Texas Town: Photographs, Memories, and History from McDade* (Norman: University of Oklahoma Press, 2000).

2. Tichnor's untitled imitative card bears neither the company's name nor a serial number but employs a distinctive decorative font for the words "Post Card" above the address section; "Greetings from McVeytown, Pa." is overprinted on my copy in red. The later Teich card is untitled, 5A-H2494, 1935, and was published in a series of generic views titled "River Scenes." Because Teich's earlier card was not published in a named series, I have interpreted its image as the lake it appears to be. The later Teich linen was in fact based on the same source photo as a pre-linen American Art card, "Greetings from Maine / River Road," 1A3040, 1931, which shows a line of crooked utility poles running just outside the fence on the right side of the road—airbrushed out for the two linen views. Statistics are from U.S. Bureau of the Census, *Historical Statistics of the United States, 1789–1945* (Washington, DC: U.S. Government Printing Office, 1949), 220, 223. Journalists John J. McCarthy and Robert Littel are quoted by Warren James Belasco, *Americans on the Road: From Autocamp to Motel, 1910–1945* (Cambridge: MIT Press, 1979), 131.

3. William P. Sanborn was a Denver photographer whose real photo views of business districts and narrow-gauge railways in Colorado and Wyoming bore "Sanborn" as a stylized signature. Although his company commissioned Teich to produce scores of linen views of the two states, those portraying Rocky Mountain National Park received the most careful attention. See "Cheyenne Photos," From Wyoming Tales and Trails, http://www.wyomingtalesandtrails.com/cheyenne3.html; and "The William P. Sanborn Colorado Narrow Gauge Album," Vintage Railroad Postcards, http://railroadpostcards.blogspot.com/2010/10/william-p-sanborn-colorado-narrow-gauge.html.

4. Miles Orvell, an outside reader of this book's manuscript whose questions helped clarify this issue, maintains in his classic study *The Real Thing* (1989), 73–102, that nineteenth-century commentators on photography valued the new medium precisely because it both mimicked reality and offered an artificially constructed simulacrum of it.

5. The source photo is T. J. Hileman, *Glacier National Park: Grinnell Glacier*, James W. Schultz Photographs Collection, Montana State University Libraries, http://arc.lib.montana.edu/schultz-0010/item/243. See also Alfred Runte, *National Parks: The American Experience*, 2nd ed. (Lincoln: University of Nebraska Press, 1987), 92–94; and "T. J. Hileman: 1882–1945," Hockaday Museum of Art, Kalispell, MT, http://www.hockadaymuseum.org/index.cfm?inc=page&page=240&page_content=The%2DHockaday%2DMuseum%2Dof%2DArt%2DCollection.

6. Reyner Banham, *Scenes in America Deserta* (Cambridge: MIT Press, 1989; orig. 1982), 92.

7. Angela Miller, *The Empire of the Eye: Landscape Representation and American Cultural Politics, 1825–1875* (Ithaca: Cornell University Press, 1993), 247, 243, 275, 243;

in general, see pp. 243–288. Miller avoids the term "Luminism," but for its introduction as a defined style, see essays in John Wilmerding, ed., *American Light: The Luminist Movement, 1850-1875: Paintings, Drawings, Photographs* (New York: Harper & Row, 1980).

8. Thoman, "A Million Dollars a Year in Penny Postcards," 56. Teich's observation seems questionable. According to the company's Geographical Index, the company produced sixty-four individual linen views of Niagara Falls, with initial orders totaling 1,550,000 postcards, but only nine individual linen views of the White House, totaling initial orders of 212,000. Statistics on repeat orders of individual cards are not available.

9. "American Falls, Illuminated, from Canadian Side, Niagara Falls, Ont.," Teich 2A-H167, 1932; "American Falls, Illuminated, Niagara Falls, N.Y.," Teich 4A-H1112, 1934; and "American Falls, Illuminated, from Canadian Side, Niagara Falls, Ont.," Teich 0C-H309, 1950.

10. David E. Nye, *Electrifying America: Social Meanings of a New Technology, 1880-1940* (Cambridge: MIT Press, 1990), 58; on the illumination in general, see 58–62. See also David E. Nye, *American Technological Sublime* (Cambridge: MIT Press, 1994), 171–172.

11. On Lamar Campbell Le Compte, founder of Asheville Post Card Company, see the finding aid for the "L. C. Le Compte Postcard Collection," D. H. Ramsey Library and Special Collections, University of North Carolina, Asheville, http://toto.lib.unca.edu/findingaids /photo/lecompte/lecompte.html. Asheville cards are often found unused in mint condition. After Le Compte's death in 1977, according to anecdote, the company's inventory of several million cards extending back to the 1930s was dumped on the collectors' market.

12. Jakle, *Postcards of the Night*, especially 27–29.

13. Job file, "The Moss Hung Cliffs of Witches Gulch, / Dells of the Wisconsin River," Teich 4A-H1935, 1934, Teich Postcard Archives. On Bennett's career, see Steven D. Hoelscher, *Picturing Indians: Photographic Encounters and Tourist Fantasies in H. H. Bennett's Wisconsin Dells* (Madison: University of Wisconsin Press, 2008).

14. In 1939, income generated for Teich in each of the southern states (excluding Florida and Texas) was below the national average. Some of the smaller or less populous states (for example, Connecticut, Montana, and Vermont) generated less income than individual southern states, but overall sales were dominated by New York, California, Illinois, Florida, Ohio, and Texas, in that order. See "Auditors Report for Year 1939," Teich Company Papers.

15. "Beautiful Scenery along the Banks of a River in Dixieland," Teich 21298, n.d., written but not addressed or mailed.

16. That card, "Bathing in the Surf," Teich 4A-H815, 1934, was mailed from Seymour, Indiana, May 19, 1941, by a correspondent who made no reference to its absurdity.

17. Robert Frost, "The Oven Bird," in *The Oxford Book of American Verse*, ed. F. O. Matthiessen (New York: Oxford University Press, 1950), 559; the poem was originally published in 1916.

18. "Auditors Report for Year 1939," Teich Company Papers.

19. Job file, "Smoke Trees on the Desert in California," Teich 7A-H3624, 1937, Teich Postcard Archives.

20. Travelers' comments were inscribed on "The Lookout, Grand Canyon National Park, Arizona," Teich 8A-H1520, 1938, postmarked Delhi, CA, May 31, 1939; "Natives of the Desert," Teich 4A-H52, 1934, postmarked Phoenix, AZ, July 9, 1936; and "Rotunda Internacional, Mission Inn, Riverside, Calif.," Teich 2A-H133, 1932, postmarked Las Vegas, NV, February 21, 1951.

21. See Roger G. Hatheway and Russell L. Keller, *Lake Arrowhead* (Charleston, SC: Arcadia, 2006), 9–20.

22. On the possessive landscape view, see Albert Boime, *The Magisterial Gaze: Manifest Destiny and American Landscape Painting, c. 1830-1865* (Washington, DC: Smithsonian Institution Press, 1991), 75, 21; Miller, *Empire of the Eye*, 149; and, defining the "panoptic sublime," Alan Wallach, "Making a Picture of the View from Mount Holyoke," in *American Iconology: New Approaches to Nineteenth-Century Art and Literature*, ed. David C. Miller (New Haven: Yale University Press, 1993), 80–91.

23. Marta Weigle and Barbara A. Babcock, introduction to *The Great Southwest of the Fred Harvey Company and the Santa Fe Railway,*

ed. Marta Weigle and Barbara A. Babcock (Phoenix: Heard Museum, 1996), 5; and Hal K. Rothman, *Devil's Bargains: Tourism in the Twentieth-Century American West* (Lawrence: University Press of Kansas, 1998), 70. On Colter and the Watchtower, see Matilda McQuaid with Karen Bartlett, "Building an Image of the Southwest: Mary Colter, Fred Harvey Company Architect," in Weigle and Babcock, *The Great Southwest*, 24–35; and Arnold Berke, *Mary Colter: Architect of the Southwest* (New York: Princeton Architectural Press, 2002), 186–207.

24. Nicholas Scrattish, "Historic Resource Study: Bryce Canyon," September 1985, http://www.cr.nps.gov/history/online_books/brca/hrs5b.htm.

25. Job file, "Mt. San Gorgonio and Palm Springs as Seen from near the Smoke Tree Forest," Teich 9A-H892, 1939, Teich Postcard Archives. Information on Willard comes from WorthPoint, http://www.worthpoint.com/worthopedia/stephen-h-willard-vintage-photo-rock-creek. The Palm Springs Art Museum houses Willard's archive.

26. For the postcards mentioned, see Morgan, *Big Time*, 18, 10, 54.

27. On construction of Mt. Lemmon Road, see U.S. Department of Agriculture, Forest Service, "Coronado National Forest," http://www.fs.usda.gov/recarea/coronado/recreation/scenicdrivinginfo/recarea/?recid=25628&actid=105.

28. Pitchford's instructions are from the frisket overlay for this postcard, found in the job file for a new version of the image from ten years later, updated to show asphalt paving on the former gravel road: "Mt. Lemmon Road, near Tucson," Teich 0C-H1571, 1950, Teich Postcard Archives. Pitchford always bought Buicks, a new one every two years.

29. Thoman, "A Million Dollars a Year in Penny Postcards," 56. On Old Faithful and Yellowstone geysers in general portrayed in terms of modern industry, see the chapter "Pittsburgh at Yellowstone: Old Faithful and the Pulse of Industrial America," in Cecelia Tichi, *Embodiment of a Nation: Human Form in American Places* (Cambridge: Harvard University Press, 2001), 99–125. For a similar interpretation of a postcard representation of a constructed place from which one may view a sublime natural phenomenon, this time at the Grand Canyon, see David E. Nye, "Visualizing Eternity: Photographic Constructions of the Grand Canyon," in *Picturing Place: Photography and the Geographical Imagination*, ed. Joan M. Schwartz and James R. Ryan (London: I. B. Taurus, 2003), 85.

30. Henry David Thoreau, *Walden; or, Life in the Woods* (Boston: Houghton Mifflin, 1893; orig. 1854), 377; and Runte, *National Parks*, 41. Echoing Runte's comment, Barbara Novak, in *Nature and Culture: American Landscape and Painting, 1825–1875* (New York: Oxford University Press, 2007; orig. 1980), 18, observes of the painter Thomas Cole that his "career coincided with the discovery of the American landscape as an effective substitute for a missing national tradition."

31. "Alligator Farm, St. Augustine, Fla.," Teich 8A-H1232, 1938; "Rattle Snake Swallowing a Rabbit," Teich 2A-H862, 1932; "Gila Monster," Teich 8A-H1955, 1938; "Horned Toad and Young," Teich 4A-H928, 1934; and "Brahman Bull in Florida Pastures," Teich 9B-H993, 1949.

32. *Adirondack Record Post* as quoted by Steven Engelhart, a consultant to Friends of the North Country, in a successful application to have the bridge included on the National Register of Historic Places, February 1998; http://www.oprhp.state.ny.us/hpimaging/hp_view.asp?GroupView=1230; and http://www.oprhp.state.ny.us/hpimaging/hp_view.asp?GroupView=1229. The text of the application dates the article September 21, 1933, while footnote and bibliography date it June 8, 1933.

33. "Auditors Report for Year 1939," Teich Company Papers.

34. Every known postcard by Ray Walters (including thirty-one designed for E. C. Kropp, Milwaukee) is illustrated in Courtney Mack and Stephen Mack, *Walters' World: His Comic Postcards, His Art* (Marana, AZ: Whispering Dove Design, 2003); for a brief biography, see 8–15. On trailers and auto camping in general, see Belasco, *Americans on the Road*, especially chapters 3–5.

35. The four photographs taken by Gerald Cleveland, which have negative numbers Env16_066, Env16_070, AI-29, and BBN, are in the Ulysses Samuel (U. S.) Cleveland Collection, Charlotte County Historical Center,

Charlotte Harbor, FL, searchable at http://ccflhistory.contentdm.oclc.org/cdm/landingpage/collection/p15007coll1. The halftone postcard, viewed on eBay, was mailed from Punta Gorda with an illegible postmark and was inscribed "Ans. Feb 19—36" by its recipient.

36. Micheal Bergstrom, "Tin Can Camp: Trailer Park Beginnings," *Sarasota Herald-Tribune*, July 10, 1996, 45, http://news.google.com/newspapers?nid=1755&dat=19960710&id=vm4fAAAAIBAJ&sjid=BH0EAAAAIBAJ&pg=5003,5786886; Belasco, *Americans on the Road*, 109.

37. Belasco, *Americans on the Road*, 129. See also Jakle, *The Tourist*, 166.

38. Four non-Teich linen postcards viewed on eBay illustrate the house and demonstrate frequent modifications to the courts, including the painting of the brick cabins white around 1950. George Rose, son of the couple who built and ran the Oaks Tourist Court, briefly sketched its history in "The Westender Newsletter," September 19, 2008, http://joebrownhigh.org/WestEnder/2008-09-19.html. See also "Stewart Avenue," April 11, 2006, http://postpessimist.blogspot.com/2006/04/stewart-avenue.html.

39. Duncan Hines, *Lodging for a Night*, 4th ed. (Bowling Green, KY: Adventures in Good Eating, 1941), 168. On the Nelson Dream Village, see "Arthur Nelson's Dream Village and Nelson Tavern," *Laclede County, Missouri: History and Families* (Nashville: Turner, 2000), 62; and William Kaszynski, *Route 66: Images of America's Main Street* (Jefferson, NC: McFarland, 2003), 45–47. Photographs and postcards of various phases of Nelson's establishment are available at http://www.66postcards.com/postcards/index.html, with many of them credited to the Lebanon-Laclede County Library.

40. Google Maps Street View for 301 Avenue F, NW, Childress, Texas. Searches in a computerized subject index maintained by the Lake County Discovery Museum indicate only sixty-five linen postcards under the heading "Advertising—Mechanical Services, Gas Stations, Parking" and thirteen under "Industry, Oil—Gas Station," as compared to 2,760 under "Advertising—Hotels," 1,810 under "Hotels," and 962 under "Advertising Restaurants and Bars—Restaurant Interior."

41. As quoted by sociologist Norman Hayner, "Auto Camps in the Evergreen Playground," *Social Forces* 9 (December 1930): 257.

42. Donald E. Everett, "Buckhorn Saloon," *Handbook of Texas Online*, http://www.tshaonline.org/handbook/online/articles/dub01.

43. Federal Writers' Project, *Florida: A Guide to the Southernmost State* (New York: Oxford University Press, 1956; orig. 1939), 260–261. See also A. Wynelle Deese, *St. Petersburg, Florida: A Visual History* (Charleston, SC: History Press, 2006), 34–37; and Phil Beard, "Green Benches," from a blog, *Notes on the Arts and Visual Culture*, April 30, 2009, http://buttes-chaumont.blogspot.com/2009/04/green-benches.html.

44. Federal Writers' Project, *Florida*, 261. The daytime view is "World's Largest Shuffleboard Club, St. Petersburg, Fla.," Teich 9A-H1015, 1939.

45. "The Hall of Waters," RoadsideAmerica.com, http://www.roadsideamerica.com/story/16236. See also "The Hall of Waters & Cultural Museum," Excelsior Springs Area Chamber of Commerce, http://www.exspgschamber.com/hallofwaters.html.

46. "Orton Plantation," http://www.ortonplantation.com/orton_history.htm.

47. Thoman, "A Million Dollars a Year in Penny Postcards," 57.

48. See for example John Denis Mercier, "The Evolution of the Black Image in White Consciousness, 1876–1954: A Popular Culture Perspective" (Ph.D. diss., University of Pennsylvania, 1984), 303–307; and Wayne Martin Mellinger, "Toward a Critical Analysis of Tourism Representations," *Annals of Tourism Research* 21 (1994): 756–779. Mercier's encyclopedic unpublished study of visual and material representations of African Americans is indispensable. I am also indebted to Wayne Martin Mellinger, "Postcards from the Edge of the Color Line: Images of African Americans in Popular Culture, 1893–1917," *Symbolic Interaction* 15 (1992): 413–433; and Kenneth W. Goings, *Mammy and Uncle Mose: Black Collectibles and American Stereotyping* (Bloomington: Indiana University Press, 1994). Joseph Boskin, *Sambo: The Rise & Demise of an American Jester* (New York: Oxford University Press, 1986), 130–135, briefly describes typical postcard images of blacks. Brooke Baldwin,

"On the Verso: Postcard Messages as a Key to Popular Prejudices," *Journal of Popular Culture* 22 (Winter 1988): 15–28, analyzes messages written on the backs of postcards portraying African Americans.

49. "Uncle Tom," Teich 6A-H443, 1936. Teich printed several earlier versions of "Uncle Tom" going back to about 1910, with each subsequent version looking less like the photographic original (which is unlocated). Sometime during the 1940s, Asheville Post Card Company published a version cropped to show only the figure's head and shoulders (E-5412).

50. All discussed by Mercier, "Evolution of the Black Image," 295–311, 385–395, 406–409. Mercier discusses postcard images, mostly by Raphael Tuck and by Teich, on 312–338.

51. "'Old Folks at Home,'" Asheville E-5409, n.d. Images from Tuck Series 2421 are available on an excellent website, Tuck DB Postcards, http://tuckdb.org/sets/19797?set_tab =medium. Pre-linen variants of "My Old Log Cabin" were viewed on eBay and CardCow. com. The job file for Teich's linen card contains copies of both Tuck's original card and a Teich pre-linen. The title "My Old Log Cabin" appears next to four different Teich serial numbers in the "Southern Scenes" category of the company's Geographical Index. Unlike entries for cities and states, which were maintained until the company's demise, entries under "Southern Scenes" ceased in 1928, just before the linen era began.

52. "Solid Comfort," Hugh C. Leighton L413, n.d. Two variants of a Teich pre-linen with a partially illegible serial number low enough to place it in 1911 were viewed on eBay.

53. "Aunt Venus Hunting," Teich 6A-H446, 1936. The stereograph card is Image ID 1649512, Schomburg Center for Research in Black Culture, New York Public Library, http:// digitalcollections.nypl.org/items/5e66b3e9-1227-d471-e040-e00a180654d7. The Detroit Photographic card was offered on eBay. The inscribed linen card was viewed on Flickr but is no longer available. See also Psyche Williams-Forson, "Hidden in the Picture: Visualizing African American Material Life and Culture," *Image File* 15, no. 4 (2008): 5.

54. "Dinnertime," Teich 6A-H456, 1936; "'Give Us De Rine?' 'Ain't Goin' Be No Rine,'" Teich 6A-H450, 1936; "Seben Come Eleben," Teich 6A-H452, 1936; and "A 'Lasses Party," Teich 6A-H458, 1936. The photo from 1901 was by Fred L. Howe, a commercial photographer active in Atlanta until his death in 1903; see http://album.atlantahistorycenter.com/store /Category/437-fred-l-howe-1895-cotton-states-and-international-exposition-photo graphs.aspx.

55. For example, see "I Is Busy / 'Scuse de View," Teich 0B-H1403, 1940.

56. Sol Eytinge Jr., "A Blackville Serenade," *Harper's Weekly*, June 16, 1883, 372. Teich had used "The Blackville Serenade" as the title for a different image on a pre-linen card, A-31435, ca. 1912, showing three twelve-year-old boys sitting on a stile singing while one of them plays a homemade guitar; the image was based on a photo by one Havens, copyrighted 1891. On Eytinge's Blackville series and Thomas Worth's dehumanizing Darktown series for Currier & Ives, see Michael D. Harris, *Colored Pictures: Race and Visual Representation* (Chapel Hill: University of North Carolina Press, 2003), 57–67; and Shawn Michelle Smith, *Photography on the Color Line: W. E. B. Du Bois, Race, and Visual Culture* (Durham: Duke University Press, 2004), 80–86.

57. Many cards portraying Mexican American women emphasize picturesque traditional garb. Two señoritas in embroidered white peasant blouses and long skirts, one with a stylishly tilted sombrero, the other with huge hoops dangling from her ears, sit decoratively on the side of a well in "The Wishing Well, Agua Caliente, Mexico," Teich 3A-H1337, 1933, distributed by Western Publishing & Novelty, Los Angeles. Another young woman, dressed similarly, dances with a male companion in "Dance of the 'Sombrero,'" Teich 7A-H1305, 1937, one of ten cards in "General Texas Scenes," an image Teich regarded so highly that the company copyrighted it—an infrequent move.

58. Ten real photo views of the main street of Agua Prieta are reproduced in Daniel D. Arreola and Nick Burkhart, "Photographic Postcards and Visual Urban Landscape," *Urban Geography* 31 (2010): 885–904, an article that uses postcards as evidence in tracing changes in urban landscapes.

59. Cards were viewed on eBay and CardCow.com. On La Ballena, see Lawrence D. Taylor, "The Wild Frontier Moves South: U.S.

Entrepreneurs and the Growth of Tijuana's Vice Industry, 1908–1935," *Journal of San Diego History* 48 (Summer 2002): 209; and Paul J. Vanderwood, *Satan's Playground: Mobsters and Movie Stars at America's Greatest Gaming Resort* (Durham: Duke University Press, 2010), 108.

60. African Americans were also erased from two paired day and night images: "Boardwalk at Music Pier, Ocean City, N.J.," Teich 8A-H2260, 1938, and "Boardwalk at Music Pier at Night, Ocean City, N.J.," Teich 8A-H2261, 1938. The job file's unretouched source photo shows a black couple walking up the boardwalk at the center of the image. In the postcards they are rendered as white.

61. Phil Pasquini, "Dragon Street Lamps," philpasquini.com/Pasquini_Site/Dragon _Street_Lamps.html. The shift in perceptions of Chinatown was recognized as early as 1914 by Clarence E. Edwords, *Bohemian San Francisco: Its Restaurants and Their Most Famous Recipes—The Elegant Art of Dining* (San Francisco: Paul Elder, 1914), 54–55. See also Lisa L. Hsia, "Eating the Exotic: The Growing Accessibility of Chinese Cuisine in San Francisco, 1848–1915," *Clio's Scroll* 5 (Fall 2003): 5–6, 11–14; Robert W. Bowen and Brenda Young Bowen, *San Francisco's Chinatown* (Charleston, SC: Arcadia, 2008), 83, 87, 89; and Madeline Y. Hsu, "From Chop Suey to Mandarin Cuisine: Fine Dining and the Refashioning of Chinese Ethnicity during the Cold War Era," in *Chinese Americans and the Politics of Race and Culture*, ed. Sucheng Chan and Madeline Y. Hsu (Philadelphia: Temple University Press, 2008), 173–193.

62. "Street Scene at Night, Chinatown / San Francisco, Calif.," Teich 4A-H850, 1934; and "Grant Avenue in Chinatown," Longshaw S.F. 4, n.d.

63. "Picturesque Costumes, Chinatown, San Francisco, Calif.," Teich 2A-H795, 1932.

64. Genthe published his photos in *Pictures of Old Chinatown* (New York: Moffat, Yard, 1908) and *Old Chinatown: A Book of Pictures by Arnold Genthe* (New York: Mitchell Kennerly, 1913), both with texts by Will Irwin. John Kuo Wei Tchen reassesses Genthe's work using new prints from glass negatives and lantern slides in *Genthe's Photographs of San Francis-*

co's *Old Chinatown* (New York: Dover, 1984). I am indebted to Wendy Rouse Jorae, *The Children of Chinatown: Growing Up Chinese American in San Francisco, 1850–1920* (Chapel Hill: University of North Carolina Press, 2009); on postcards, see 188–197. Compare "The Soothsayer, Chinatown, San Francisco, Calif.," Teich 0B-H2764, 1940, with the photograph *The Fortune Teller* in Genthe, *Old Chinatown*, 201. Two photos of a scene similar to that of "Bulletin of Latest News, Chinatown, / San Francisco, Calif.," Teich 2A-H794, 1932, appear in Genthe, *Old Chinatown*, 105; and Tchen, *Genthe's Photographs*, 32. On deleting queues, see job file, "Reading the Bulletin Boards, Chinatown, San Francisco, Calif.," Teich 5A-H2622, 1935, Teich Postcard Archives.

65. "Parade 'Golden Dragon' of Good Luck, Chinatown, San Francisco, Calif.," Teich 8A-H2833, 1938.

66. Biographical information is from Susan Marie Sullivan, "Many Brushes: Elbridge Ayer Burbank, Painter of Indian Portraits" (master's thesis, University of San Diego, 1983), which is available on a comprehensive website maintained by the public library in Burbank's hometown, Harvard, Illinois: http://www. harvard-diggins.org/Burbank/Years/1983 /Thesis_Susan_Marie_Sullivan_final_indexed .htm. Among hundreds of images on the site are three sketches of Chinatown: a new lamppost in front of a hardware store from 1927, a bazaar from 1940, and a published sketch of golden dragon dancers from 1936, more fully realized than his lion dance sketch.

67. See, for examples, "The Painted Desert," Teich 3A-H34, 1933; "Cliff Dwellings in Canyon del Muerto," Teich 4A-H1130, 1934; "The Grand Canyon of Arizona," Teich 7A-H572, 1937; and "Hopi Indians (Orlin and Zellah) on the Edge of the Painted Desert," C. T. Art-Colortone, no number, n.d.

68. Emily Post, *By Motor to the Golden Gate* (1916), as quoted by Jakle, *The Tourist*, 236.

69. On the Indian Building, see Dilworth, *Imagining Indians in the Southwest*, 84–87; and Kathleen L. Howard, "'A Most Remarkable Success': Herman Schweiger and the Fred Harvey Indian Department," in Weigle and Babcock, *The Great Southwest*, 87–101. Only one card in my collection represents someone

taking a photo: "Middle Fountain Pool, Cascades, Sparks Foundation, Jackson, Mich.," Teich 2A-H635 (1932).

70. "Indian Workroom, Fred Harvey Indian Building, Albuquerque, New Mexico," Teich 6A-H1025, 1936; "Whirling Log (Good Luck) Sand Painting of the Navajo Indians," Teich 9A-H805, 1939; and "Pueblo Indian Turquoise Driller," Teich 7A-H2238, 1937. On Fred Harvey's representation of southwestern Indians, see Hales, *William Henry Jackson*, 266; and Dilworth, *Imagining Indians in the Southwest*, 3, 95–98. In general, see James C. Faris, *Navajo and Photography: A Critical History of the Representation of an American People* (Albuquerque: University of New Mexico Press, 1996).

71. On J. R. Willis, see William E. Tydeman, "New Mexico Tourist Images," in *Essays in Twentieth-Century New Mexico History*, ed. Judith Boyce DeMark (Albuquerque: University of New Mexico Press, 1994), 199–212; and Adobe Gallery, Santa Fe, NM, http://www.adobegallery.com/artist.php?artist_id=212.

72. Patricia C. Albers and William R. James make these points in a series of interrelated coauthored articles based on a personal collection of 25,000 postcards depicting Native Americans; see especially "Tourism and the Changing Photographic Image of the Great Lakes Indians," *Annals of Tourism Research* 10 (1983): 123–148; "Images and Reality: Post Cards of Minnesota's Ojibway People, 1900–80," *Minnesota History* 49 (Summer 1985): 229–240; and "Travel Photography: A Methodological Approach," *Annals of Tourism Research* 15 (1988): 134–158. Edward McAndrews, *The American Indian Photo Post Card Book* (Los Angeles: Big Heart, 2002), reproduces real photo postcards by eighty photographers.

73. The classic text tracing the concept of the vanishing Indian is Robert F. Berkhofer Jr., *The White Man's Indian: Images of the American Indian from Columbus to the Present* (New York: Alfred A. Knopf, 1978), esp. 88–90. For similar treatments of the concept of the American Indian existing outside time and history, see Mick Gidley, "Edward S. Curtis' Indian Photographs: A National Enterprise," in *Representing Others: White Views of Indigenous Peoples*, ed. Mick Gidley (Exeter: University of

Exeter Press, 1992), 117; and Patricia C. Albers, "Symbols, Souvenirs, and Sentiments: Postcard Imagery of Plains Indians, 1898–1918," in Geary and Webb, *Delivering Views*, 77.

74. Henry Wadsworth Longfellow, *The Song of Hiawatha* (Boston: Ticknor and Fields, 1856; orig. 1855), 39.

75. On the Miccosukee Seminoles, see Patsy West, *The Enduring Seminoles: From Alligator Wrestling to Ecotourism* (Gainesville: University Press of Florida, 1998); and Brent Richard Weisman, *Unconquered People: Florida's Seminole and Miccosukee Indians* (Gainesville: University Press of Florida, 1999).

76. Source photos for several uncredited cards in my collection were found on a website maintained by Ebbets's daughter, http://www.ebbetsphoto-graphics.com. Ebbets is best known for *Lunchtime atop a Skyscraper* (1932), a photograph of eleven construction workers sitting on a girder suspended over Manhattan.

77. "'Seminole Nation' Holds 'Mother's Day,'" Florida," Tichnor 69514, n.d.

78. On the source photo, see Richard Melzer, *New Mexico: A Celebration of the Land of Enchantment* (Layton, UT: Gibbs Smith, 2011), 282–283.

79. Tichnor's imitation is "Black Rock Beach, Great Salt Lake, Utah," Carpenter Paper Co. 69279, n.d. Although the Tichnor name does not appear on the card, the numbering system and fonts identify the printer. Other cards mentioned are "Scenes at Wrightsville Beach, N.C.," Teich 9A-H1688, 1939; "Greetings from Asbury Park, N.J.," Teich 9A-H1688, 1939; "Greetings from Hampton Beach, N.H.," Teich 9A-H1688, 1939; and "Greetings from Carolina Beach / N.C. / Carolina's Playground," Teich 1B-H677, 1941.

80. "A 'Tug of War' on a Beach," Teich 5A-H1298, 1935; "Aqua Maids of Florida," Teich 8B-H868, 1948; and "Study in Knees at Cypress Gardens in Beautiful Florida," Tichnor 63104, n.d.

81. Examples include "Last Picture of Frank James, 'The Outlaw', Taken at His Farm near Excelsior Springs, Mo.," Teich 8A-H1278, 1938; "Old Cowhand's Home," Colourpicture 16526, n.d.; "Handicrafts of the Southern Appalachian Mountains," Teich 43904-N (non-

linen 1930s–1940s reprint of a 1913 card); and "Mennonite and Amish People of Lancaster County, Pa.," Teich 33756-C-N (despite its uncharacteristic serial number, a 1930s–1940s linen reprint of a 1913 card).

82. For examples, see "Soldiers of A.A.F.T.T.C. On Parade—Lincoln Road / Miami Beach, Florida," Tichnor 74471, n.d.; "Cadet Graduation at U.S. Naval Air Station, Corpus Christi, Texas," Teich 3B-H500, 1943; "Mess Line, Fort Leonard Wood, Missouri," Teich 1B-H812, 1941; "Interior, Emmanuel Chapel, Camp Grant, Illinois," Teich 3B-H789, 1943; and "Library, Camp Livingston, Louisiana," Teich 3B-H792, 1943. On Teich's wartime production of military-themed cards, see the superb treatment by Anne Bress, "An Air-Brushed War: An Analysis of American Picture Postcards of World War II from the Curt Teich Postcard Archives" (master's thesis, University of Chicago, 1996); copy in Teich Postcard Archives.

83. The earlier, pre-linen card was Teich R-91646 (ordered January 23, 1924), which was published with at least two different captions, the original being "Picking Cherries in Large Orchard Just outside the City, Sturgeon Bay, Wisconsin." Instructions for that card had included a poorly printed color lithographic view of a different scene of cherry picking from another publisher, accompanied by the statement that the earlier card "better represents an orange tree" than a cherry tree and warning, *"you can't make them* [the cherries] *too small."*

84. Donald Worster, "Dust Bowl," *Handbook of Texas Online*, http://www.tshaonline .org/handbook/online/articles/ydd01; and Clinton P. Hartmann, "Wheat Culture," *Handbook of Texas Online*, http://www.tshaonline .org/handbook/online/articles/afw01.

85. On meatpacking tours, see Roland Marchand, *Creating the Corporate Soul: The Rise of Public Relations and Corporate Imagery in American Big Business* (Berkeley: University of California Press, 1998), 258–260. On *Harper's Weekly* process illustrations, see Vanessa Meikle Schulman, *Work Sights: The Visual Culture of Industry in Nineteenth-Century America* (Amherst: University of Massachusetts Press, 2015), chap. 5.

86. "Oil Field," Teich 5A-H1011, 1935, is such an "Oil Field Scene." Oklahoma City views include "Governor's Mansion and State Owned Wells in Oklahoma City, Oklahoma," Teich 6A-H1394, 1936; "Oklahoma State Capitol and Grounds, Oklahoma City, Okla.," Teich 8B-H413, 1948; and "View of Capitol Grounds from the Steps of the State Capitol, Oklahoma City, Okla.," Colourpicture K9312, n.d. Single wells are portrayed generically on "Oil Gushers [*sic*] in Oklahoma," Teich 4A-H321, 1934; and "Instead of a Gusher—Fire! / Oil Well Explosion in West Texas," Teich 4A-H296, 1934.

87. For other views, see Russell Lee, *Sacramento Pit, Now Abandoned*, May 1940, LC-USF34-036441-D, Prints and Photographs Division, Library of Congress, Washington, DC, http://www.loc.gov/pictures/resource/fsa .8b25036; and Burton Frasher Sr., "The Famous Sacramento Pit at Bisbee, Arizona" (1939), F859, Frasher Foto Postcard Collection, Pomona Public Library, Pomona, CA, http://content.ci.pomona.ca.us/cdm4/item_ viewer.php?CISOROOT=/Frasher&CISOPTR =3562&CISOBOX=1&REC=2. Bob Pitchford mentioned his father's friendship with Holger Lollesgard in an interview with the author, June 4, 2012. On Frasher, see Jeremy Rowe, "Have Camera, Will Travel: Arizona Roadside Images by Burton Frasher," *Arizona History* 51 (Winter 2010): 337–366.

88. John Warner and Walter Mueller, "Mesabi Miracle: Is It Coming to an End?," *The Wisconsin Engineer* 52 (May 1948): 12, http://digicoll.library.wisc.edu/cgi-bin/UW /UW-idx?type=turn&entity=UW.WIEv52no8 .p0014&id=UW.WIEv52no8&isize=text.

89. Diana J. Kleiner, "Sulfur Industry," *Handbook of Texas Online*, http://www.tsha online.org/handbook/online/articles/dks04; and Edward Coyle Sealy, "Galveston Wharves," *Handbook of Texas Online*, http://www.tsha online.org/handbook/online/articles/etg01.

90. Many of the 129 images returned in a search for the terms "Russell Lee Houston" in the Library of Congress Prints & Photographs Online Catalog portray the unloading, compressing, and loading of cotton in October 1939; perhaps the most pertinent is *Stevedores Loading Cotton on to the Freighter. Port of Houston, Texas*, LC-USF34- 034565-D [P&P], http:// www.loc.gov/pictures/item/fsa2000015811/

PP. See also James C. Maroney, "International Longshoremen's Association," *Handbook of Texas Online*, http://www.tshaonline.org /handbook/online/articles/oci01, and "Galveston Longshoremen's Strike of 1920," *Handbook of Texas Online*, http://www.tshaonline.org /handbook/online/articles/oeg02.

91. Federal Writers' Project, *New Orleans City Guide* (Boston: Houghton Mifflin, 1938), 275; on the docks in general, see 270–285. Characterizations of other postcards and the general process are based on images on sale and auction websites.

92. On the utopian concept of New England mills, see John F. Kasson, *Civilizing the Machine: Technology and Republican Values in America, 1776–1900* (New York: Grossman, 1976), 53–106.

93. Handwritten comment on an unmailed copy of "Night View of Carnegie Illinois Steel Mill on Monongahela River, Clairton Works," Teich 7A-H1808, 1937. For other industrial views, see "General View of Youngstown Sheet and Tube Company, Night View, Campbell Works / Youngstown, Ohio," Teich 1B-H2588, 1941; and "One of the Many Steel Mills near Warren, and Niles, Ohio," Teich 6A-H143, 1936. On violence during the Little Steel strike, see "Youngstown Joins in Drive for Jobs," *New York Times*, June 24, 1937, 4; and "Witnesses Recall Little Steel Strike Riots of 1937," YWTV News, Youngstown, OH, May 22, 2012, http://www .clipsyndicate.com/video/play/3511061/witness es_recall_little_steel_strike_riots_of_1937.

94. On the history of the American Zinc and Tin plant, later part of Carnegie-Illinois Steel Company, see Michael E. Workman with Cassandra Vivian, addendum to "Monessen Steel Works (Pittsburgh Steel Company, Monessen Works)," HAER No. PA-253, n.d., Historic American Engineering Record, National Park Service, http://lcweb2.loc.gov/master/pnp/hab shaer/pa/pa2700/pa2744/data/pa2744data .pdf; and Cassandra Vivian, *Monessen: A Typical Steel Country Town* (Charleston, SC: Arcadia, 2002), 17, 40, 80–81. There is at least one pre-linen postcard, probably by Teich, that shows the rolling mill in daylight based on a source photo taken from almost the same position.

95. Kenneth Warren, *Big Steel: The First Century of the United States Steel Corporation, 1901–2001* (Pittsburgh: University of Pittsburgh Press, 2001), 269. *The Drama of Steel*, a documentary film with footage of a hot strip mill, was released during the late 1930s by the Bureau of Mines, Department of the Interior; it can be viewed at http://archive.org/details /gov.archives.arc.12505. Bob Pitchford recalled his grandfather's steelmaking background in an interview with the author, June 4, 2012.

96. With one exception, all copies of this card I have seen in dealers' stocks or reproduced on the Internet are identical to the one illustrated here. However, in my possession is a variant with cool tones based mostly on blue. The serial number is the same. That card is probably from a late printing, in the early 1950s.

97. *Jobbers Profits*, 2, Teich Company Papers.

98. "The Pennsylvania Turnpike: A History," http://users.zoominternet.net/~jamieo /Turnpike_Page.htm. Travelers' messages are from "Fort Snelling–Mendota Bridge," Teich 5A-H1890, 1935, postmarked Minneapolis, MN, September 20, 1939; "Greetings from America's Main Street / U.S. 66 / Scenic Missouri," Teich number obscured, postmarked Amarillo, TX, July [illegible], 1951.

99. For recent photos, see "Old US 80, Winterhaven, CA to Yuma, AZ: Ocean to Ocean Bridge," on Steve Alpert's website, Alps' Roads, http://www.alpsroads.net/roads/az/old_80. The history of the Yuma crossing is well summarized by Chris McDaniel, "Ocean-to-Ocean Bridge Critical Link between Shores," *Yuma Sun*, May 29, 2011, http://www.yumasun.com /ocean-to-ocean-bridge-critical-link-between- shores/article_fa9d146f-f725-53cf-bce4- a99a45908e7c.html.

100. General information is from Joseph E. Stevens, *Hoover Dam: An American Adventure* (Norman: University of Oklahoma Press, 1988). Visitor quotations are from "Wild Flowers (Verbenas) on the Desert in Winter," Teich 3A-H992 (1933), postmarked Los Angeles, CA, July 12, 1948; and a travel journal kept by Anna McLean Meikle from July 28 to August 17, 1936, entry for August 5 (in my possession). For real photo views of Hoover Dam's construction, see Donald C. Jackson, *Pastoral*

and *Monumental: Dams, Postcards, and the American Landscape* (Pittsburgh: University of Pittsburgh Press, 2013), 221–230.

101. "Upstream Face and Intake Towers, Boulder Dam," Teich 6A-H1180, 1936; "Racing Yacht on Lake Mead, Boulder Dam / Boulder Dam Recreational Area," Teich 8A-H2611, 1938; and "Grand Canyon and Lake Mead from Rampart Cave / Boulder Dam Recreational Area," Teich 8A-H2612, 1938.

102. Robert Frank refused permission to reproduce the image. On his *Hoover Dam, Nevada*, 1955, see Sarah Greenough, "Fragments That Make a Whole Meaning in Photographic Sequences," in *Robert Frank: Moving Out*, ed. Sarah Greenough and Philip Brookman (Washington, DC: National Gallery of Art, 1994), 96–97, 168; and John O'Brian, "Postcard to Moscow," in Prochaska and Mendelson, *Postcards*, 183–186, 190, 222n11.

103. "Coney Island Steamer 'Island Queen', Cincinnati, Ohio," Teich 8A-H2424, 1938, postmarked Cincinnati, OH, August 17, 1943. On ridership, see U.S. Bureau of the Census, *Historical Statistics of the United States, 1789–1945* (Washington, DC: U.S. Government Printing Office, 1949), 202.

104. John Gruber, "Illinois Central Art and Photography," *RailNews*, December 1998, 46–49; Mary Beth Klatt, "Double Exposure: Photo Collection Captures the Growth of Railroads and Film," *Chicago Tribune*, September 15, 2002, http://articles.chicagotribune.com/2002-09-15/travel/0209150526_1_railroads-locomotives-conrail-train; Brian Solomon and John Gruber, *Railway Photography* (Iola, WI: Krause, 2003), 21; and Harlan R. Hardie, "My Career on the Illinois Central Railroad in Chicago from 1960 to 1967," http://personalweb.donet.com/~harlan/Illinois_Central/Part_I_Congress_Street.html (on the Congress Street Yard).

105. The card was postmarked at the Burlington Station, Omaha, NE, December 14, 1941. For examples of more typically populated images of terminals, see "Grand Lobby, the Union Station, Kansas City, Mo.," Teich 7A-H2916, 1937; and "Ticket Concourse, Union Station, Los Angeles, California," Teich 9A-H917, 1939. On the Union Pacific's staffing innovation, see Eunice Peterson Hoevet, "Nurse-Stewardesses: Nursing Takes to the Railroad," *American Journal of Nursing* 37 (January 1937): 18–20; and Shirley Burman, "American Railroad Women: Research Project 1981–Present," http://www.americanrailroadwomen.com/RR%20Nurses%20Pg.html.

106. Anna Meikle listed expenses of $149.03 in her travel journal. The family mostly camped, with an occasional stay in a tourist court.

107. Two of the cars are in the collection of the Museum of the American Railroad, Frisco, TX. See http://www.museumoftheamericanrailroad.org/Exhibits/CollectionOverview/tabid/62/agentType/View/PropertyID/32/Default.aspx.

108. On Lamb's Greyhound terminals, see Christopher Gray, "A Bus Terminal, Overshadowed and Unmourned," *New York Times*, November 3, 2011, http://www.nytimes.com/2011/11/06/realestate/the-west-30s-streetscapes-a-bus-terminal-overshadowed-and-unmourned.html; and Frank E. Wrenick, *The Streamline Era Greyhound Terminals: The Architecture of W. S. Arrasmith* (Jefferson, NC: McFarland, 2007), 55–56. Arrasmith, after winning a bid in 1937 to design a terminal in Washington, DC, designed at least fifty more Greyhound bus terminals over the next two decades. The bus in the postcard may be a Model 743 from 1937—with such innovations as a body of aluminum alloy, a rear diesel engine (yielding a flat front), a passenger deck raised above a luggage compartment accessed from outside, air conditioning, and Loewy's paint scheme. See Raymond Loewy, Design for a Motor Coach, U.S. Design Patent 113,009, issued January 24, 1939; and Larry Plachno, "Greyhound Buses through the Years, Part I," *National Bus Trader*, September 2002, 20–22.

109. Visitation figures are from a detailed historical summary in "Pan American Seaplane Base and Terminal Building: Designation Report," City of Miami, 1993, a feasibility study for expanding the site's historical designation from the terminal building, which has housed the Miami City Hall since 1954, to include associated hangar buildings, http://www.historicpreservationmiami.com/pdfs/Pan%20American%20Seaplane%20Base%20and%20Terminal%20Building.pdf.

110. The County Causeway, along which

oceangoing ships left Miami's harbor, is now the MacArthur Causeway. I am indebted to John Shipley, Miami-Dade Public Library, for providing a photocopy of the source photo, *447f Steamships at Docks, Miami. Arandora Star and Causeway. 2-13-32*, taken February 13, 1932, Gleason Waite Romer Collection, Miami-Dade Public Library. On Romer's career, see Gary Monroe, *Romer's Miami: Gleason Waite Romer (1887–1971)*, exhibition catalog (Miami: Miami-Dade Public Library System, 1985). The source photo was included in the exhibition but does not appear in the catalog. On the *Arandora Star*, see "Blue Star's S.S. 'Arandora Star': One of the Luxury Five,"

http://www.bluestarline.org/arandora.html. Someone, possibly the distributor, must have objected to this postcard's apocalyptic mood. The original order for the card was recorded on June 6, 1933, and my example was postmarked on October 11, 1933. However, there is a variant, postmarked on March 21, 1934, observed on CardCow.com. The dull redesign, bearing the same serial number, exhibits a light-colored, smokeless sky—with a pale salmon hue at the horizon merging upward through scattered white cirrus clouds into a washed-out blue. Even the ocean and the sand along the shore are more muted in hue.

5. Cityscapes in Linen Postcards: Images of Modernity

1. Thoman, "A Million Dollars a Year in Penny Postcards," 56.

2. Berenice Abbott as quoted by Bonnie Yochelson, *Berenice Abbott: Changing New York* (New York: Museum of the City of New York, 1997), 12. See also Raeburn, *A Staggering Revolution*, 114–142.

3. Thoman, "A Million Dollars a Year in Penny Postcards," 57.

4. Berenice Abbott, *Changing New York: Photographs by Berenice Abbott* (New York: E. P. Dutton, 1939), 19. Abbott is quoted by Miles Orvell in his introduction to John Vachon, *John Vachon's America: Photographs and Letters from the Depression to World War II*, ed. Miles Orvell (Berkeley: University of California Press, 2003), 318n39, 29.

5. On Chicago's early explosive growth through continuing destruction and reconstruction, see Daniel M. Bluestone, *Constructing Chicago* (New Haven: Yale University Press, 1991).

6. John W. Reps, *Views and Viewmakers of Urban America: Lithographs of Towns and Cities in the United States and Canada, Notes on the Artists and Publishers, and a Union Catalog of Their Work, 1825–1925* (Columbia: University of Missouri Press, 1984), 3–4, 28–31.

7. On this point, see Peter Bacon Hales, *Silver Cities: Photographing American Urbanization, 1839–1939*, revised and expanded (Albuquerque: University of New Mexico Press,

2005), 32. On daguerreotype panoramas, see 30–58.

8. Ibid., 123–211 (the phrase is the chapter title).

9. Ibid., 203.

10. M. G. Van Rensselaer and Joseph Pennell as quoted by Merrill Schleier, *The Skyscraper in American Art, 1890–1931* (Ann Arbor: UMI Research Press, 1986), 29; and Montgomery Schuyler as quoted by William R. Taylor, *In Pursuit of Gotham: Culture and Commerce in New York* (New York: Oxford University Press, 1992), 28. On the skyline in general, see Schleier, 28–31; Taylor, 23–33; Nye, *American Technological Sublime*, 91; and William Chapman Sharpe, *New York Nocturne: The City after Dark in Literature, Painting, and Photography* (Princeton: Princeton University Press, 2008), 219.

11. Nye, *American Technological Sublime*, 77, 192. See also Nye, *Electrifying America*, 60.

12. Dietrich Neumann, ed., *Architecture of the Night: The Illuminated Building* (Munich: Prestel, 2002); Sharpe, *New York Nocturne*, 10; John A. Jakle, *City Lights: Illuminating the American Night* (Baltimore: Johns Hopkins University Press, 2001); and Jakle, *Postcards of the Night*, 29–30.

13. Sharpe, *New York Nocturne*, 255–256.

14. Ibid., 256, 247.

15. Miller, *Empire of the Eye*, 281–282.

16. Samuel H. Gottscho, *Night View, North, from RCA Building*, LC-G612-20946,

Gottscho-Schleisner Collection, Prints and Photographs Division, Library of Congress, Washington, DC, http://lcweb2.loc.gov/master /pnp/gsc/5a17000/5a17700/5a17746u.tif. On Gottscho, whose work was often used for postcard source photos, see Donald Albrecht, *The Mythic City: Photographs of New York by Samuel H. Gottscho, 1925-1940* (New York: Princeton Architectural Press, 2005). On the downward urban gaze, see also Nye, *Electrifying America*, 76–77.

17. The fact that women seem to have made greater use of postcards than men is addressed in the final chapter.

18. Hales, *Silver Cities*, 460. On the noir city, see also Mary Woods, "Photography of the Night: Skyscraper Nocturne and Skyscraper Noir in New York," in Neumann, *Architecture of the Night*, 68–76; and Sharpe, *New York Nocturne*, 266–318.

19. On Jacob Riis, see Hales, *Silver Cities*, 271–347; on Weegee (Arthur Fellig), see Colin Westerbeck and Joel Meyerowitz, *Bystander: A History of Street Photography* (Boston: Little, Brown, 2001), 335–342.

20. M. Christine Boyer, *The City of Collective Memory: Its Historical Imaging and Architectural Entertainments* (Cambridge: MIT Press, 1994), 41.

21. J. B. Priestley as quoted by Jakle, *City Lights*, 236–237.

22. Jay Ruby, "Images of Rural America: View Photographs and Picture Postcards," *History of Photography* 12 (October–December 1988): 338, 340.

23. Alison Isenberg, *Downtown America: A History of the Place and the People Who Made It* (Chicago: University of Chicago Press, 2004), 42, 45.

24. Isenberg, "Fixing an Image of Commercial Dignity: Postcards and the Business of Planning Main Street," in *Downtown America*, 42–77; quotations from 43–44, 67, 70. Isenberg's interpretation is generally accurate but falters in the details. Most pre-linen lithographic cards were minimally retouched and maintained a representational integrity that seems photorealistic when compared to linen cards. Indeed, four of the five postcards for which she compares source photos with Teich's retouched photos were linens from the late 1930s or early 1940s, by which time the urban reform movements she discusses had ended. Even so, Isenberg's observation about the streamlining of main streets is essential for understanding urban images on post-1931 linen cards.

25. Evans, "Main Street Looking North," 102. See also Evans's significantly titled "When 'Downtown' Was a Beautiful Mess," *Fortune*, January 1962, 100–106; and Evans, "Come on Down," *Architectural Forum*, July 1962, 96–100. All three articles are reproduced in facsimile in Rosenheim, *Walker Evans and the Picture Postcard*, 80–100. Among the more than five hundred nearly all pre-linen postcards reproduced from Evans's collection by Rosenheim are many that feature utility poles, wires, muddy streets, and shoddy pavement. Evans reproduced no linen cards in the three articles; nor did his personal collection contain more than a small number sent him by friends who did not realize the difference between pre-linens and linens. Rosenheim also seems unaware of the distinction.

26. "Sample Items from a Small Town Shooting Script," reprinted in Vachon, *John Vachon's America*, 292.

Portfolio 11: Cityscapes

1. "Just Arrived in New York / The Wonder City," Teich 4B-H73, 1944. The 1932 card was based on a source photo taken at the same spot as a photo also from 1932 by Samuel H. Gottscho. The same trees frame both images, though they were taken at different times from slightly different positions. See Gottscho, *Lower Manhattan from Governor's Island, 5 p.m.*, LC-G622-T-18150, Gottscho-Schleisner Collection, Prints and Photographs Division, Library of Congress, Washington, DC, http://www.loc.gov/pictures/resource/gsc.5a18518. Two large-format books present color reproductions of hundreds of U.S. urban view cards. Van Malderen, *American Architecture*, emphasizes individual structures from various cities from 1900 through the linen era. Thomas Kramer, ed., *New York in Postcards, 1880–*

1980: The Andreas Adam Collection (Zurich: Scheidegger & Spiess, 2010), is a more ambitious volume organized by functional types of public spaces and buildings.

2. The recipient's approximate age can be reconstructed through a Google search for her distinctive three names.

3. Leo Marx, *The Machine in the Garden: Technology and the Pastoral Ideal in America* (New York: Oxford University Press, 2000; orig. 1964), 220–222.

4. See "Baltimore Bridges," Kilduffs, http://www.kilduffs.com/Bridges.html.

5. Architectural photos of New York distributed by the large picture agency Peyser & Patzig sometimes portrayed as many as five to ten U.S. flags in scenes of a scope similar to that on this postcard. For examples, see David Stravitz, *New York, Empire City: 1920–1945* (New York: Harry N. Abrams, 2004), 32, 50–51. However, Teich often added flags when source photos lacked them.

6. Jakle, *The Tourist*, 271–272. On Times Square at night, see Nye, *Electrifying America*, 69–73.

7. Jakle, *City Lights*, 204–205.

8. Raymond Hood as quoted by Dietrich Neumann, "'Architecture of the Night' in the U.S.A.," in Neumann, *Architecture of the Night*, 58. On the Lindbergh Beacon, see Jakle, *City Lights*, 188–189.

9. Hugh Ferriss, *The Metropolis of Tomorrow* (New York: Ives Washburn, 1929), 53.

10. "Chrysler Building, New York City," Teich 3A-H93, 1933. Teich produced four different linen views of the Chrysler Building between 1932 and 1951, according to the company's Geographical Index.

11. Teich issued a view of the Empire State Building based on an uncredited photo taken from exactly the same spot. The Teich image projected a wholly different mood, all clarity and light against a limpid blue sky ("Empire State Building, New York City," Teich 3A-H91, 1933). All in all, Teich produced fourteen different linen views of the Empire State Building between 1932 and 1951, totaling 262,500 cards in initial orders (not including reprints).

12. "George Washington Bridge, Fort Tryon Park, Riverside Drive / Hudson River and Jersey Palisades, New York City," Tichnor 64253, n.d., postmarked Church Street Annex, NY,

February 24, 1939; and "Statue of Liberty, New York City," Manhattan 1, n.d., postmarked Washington, DC, February 23, 1941.

13. The competing card was "Radio City Music Hall, World's Largest Theatre, New York City," Manhattan 39080, n.d. For Teich's reported comment, see Thoman, "A Million Dollars a Year in Penny Postcards," 57.

14. "Radio City Music Hall, New York City," [Tichnor] 62302, n.d., published by Acacia Card Company but with Tichnor fonts; "Interior Radio City Music Hall. Rockefeller Center New York," [Colourpicture] 14855, n.d., published by Alfred Mainzer but with Colourpicture fonts; "Radio City Music Hall, New York City," Manhattan 61, n.d.; and "Stage—Radio City Music Hall, N.Y.C.," Manhattan 68, n.d.

15. For examples, see Fonzi, "Medical Arts II—Hot Springs," *Urban Exploration*, February 11, 2008, http://fonziurbex.blogspot.com/2008/02/medical-arts-building-ii-hot-springs.html; and Karina Koji, "Medical Arts Building," http://www.flickr.com/photos/faeriecat/sets/72157613452244698.

16. Linen views of main streets typically embraced modernity, but Miles Orvell argues convincingly that in general most forms of cultural expression during the 1930s presented main streets with nostalgia as embodying American values regarded as at risk during a period of rapid change. See Orvell, *The Death and Life of Main Street: Small Towns in American Memory, Space, and Community* (Chapel Hill: University of North Carolina Press, 2012), 100–129.

17. Postcards of this corner in 1904 and 1911 reveal an arched stone entrance, later walled off inside and out, with the display window extended in front. On federal loans for downtown modernization, see Gabrielle Esperdy, *Modernizing Main Street: Architecture and Consumer Culture in the New Deal* (Chicago: University of Chicago Press, 2008), 49–93.

18. Ansel Adams, *Sixth Street and Broadway, Los Angeles* (ca. 1940), Los Angeles Public Library, on http://photos.lapl.org.

19. Jakle, *Postcards of the Night*, 84. On the history of the Canal Street trolleys, see H. George Friedman Jr.'s superb website, Canal Street: A Street Railway Spectacular, http://www.cs.uiuc.edu/homes/friedman/canal/Canal.htm.

20. Pitchford's typed and hand-annotated instructions were prepared for a similar image, "Radio Center, Sunset Boulevard, Hollywood, California," Teich 0B-H392, 1940, but were applied to both cards.

21. For the earlier card, "The Bright Lights of Reno, Nevada," Teich 1B-H969, 1941, Pitchford's instructions had observed, "This subject might work up better full face," that is, with no border.

22. Evans's photo, often entitled *Times Square / Broadway Composition*, was published on June 24, 1931; see James R. Mellow, *Walker Evans* (New York: Basic Books, 1999), 129–130, 146–147. Pitchford's occupation made him a possible reader of *Advertising & Selling*. See also Tom Wolfe, "The New Life Out There: Electro-graphic Architecture," *New York*, December 9, 1968, 47–50. Robert Venturi, Denise Scott Brown, and Steven Izenour extended Wolfe's observations in *Learning from Las Vegas* (Cambridge: MIT Press, 1972).

23. Other postcards mentioned include "Statue of Liberty on Bedloe's Island in New York Harbor, New York City," Teich 6A-H2561, 1936; "Statue of Liberty on Bedloe's Island in New York Harbor[,] New York City," [Colourpicture] 14803, n.d., published by Alfred Mainzer but with Colourpicture fonts; "The Statue of Liberty at Sunrise, New York City," Colourpicture K1218, n.d.; "Statue of Liberty as Illuminated at Night, New York City," Teich 6A-H2562, 1936; and "Statue of Liberty by Night, New York City," Manhattan 519, n.d.

24. Thoman, "A Million Dollars a Year in Penny Postcards," 56.

25. "U.S. Capitol at Night, Washington, D.C.," Metrocraft 41918, n.d. Instructions in the job file for the Teich card directed artists to use the photo from a pre-linen card numbered D-24, printed in 1928, and the job file for that card in turn points to the photo from an earlier pre-linen card, numbered 82955, printed in 1920. Such recycling was common with popular views that did not change over time.

26. *The First Presbyterian Church, Marquette, Michigan: Ninetieth Anniversary, June 14–15, 1947* (Marquette: Guelff Printing Co., 1947), 13–14, Hathi Trust Digital Library, http://catalog.hathitrust.org/Record /003267819.

27. "Central Methodist Church, Knoxville, Tenn.," Teich 9A-H2113, 1939.

28. "Art Institute, Chicago," Teich 1B-H1471 (1941). For a range of earlier views from roughly the same vantage point, see "The Art Institute of Chicago: Inside-Out," Chicago Postcard Museum, http://www.chicagopostcardmuseum .org/special_exhibits_hall_art_institute_of _chicago.html.

29. The earlier card is "Palace of Fine Arts, San Francisco, Calif.," Teich 2A-H781, 1932.

30. The card is indeed based on a dramatic nighttime source photo, a copy of which was in the possession of G. I. Pitchford. The horizontal photo was cropped to yield the card's vertical image. Searchlight beams do not appear in the photo, which does, inexplicably, indicate the same lack of parallelism between the two side wings.

31. The sales representative's instructions in the job file for this card specified "grass in open space, sky bright blue, dresses of bright colors and white."

32. For ocean views with ranks of cars in the foreground overwhelming tiny bathers in the distance, see "Atlantic Ocean and the Most Wonderful Beach in the World, Daytona Beach, Fla.," Teich 3A-H859, 1933; and "Savannah Beach on Tybee Island, Savannah, Ga.," Teich 6A-H1881, 1936. A brief history of the Municipal Auditorium at Long Beach (demolished in 1975), illustrated with twenty useful black-and-white photographs, is available at the website of Scotty Moore, Elvis Presley's former lead guitarist, http://scottymoore.net /longbeach.html.

33. Ralph Teich interview by Cochrane, Teich Company Papers.

34. The cards referred to are "Saltair Pavilion, Great Salt Lake, Utah," Teich 3A-H212, 1933; and "Bathing Beach Looking South from Ocean Pier, Wildwood-by-the-Sea, N.J.," Teich 3A-H979, 1933. Quotations are from "Bascule Bridge, Corpus Christi, Texas," Teich 3A-H1501, 1933, postmarked Corpus Christi, TX, August 18, 1938; and "Gulf Pier Cafe—Galveston, Tex.," Teich 5A-H2616, 1935, postmarked Galveston, TX, May 4, 1939.

35. Quotation from an interview with Bob Pitchford by the author, June 4, 2012. Bob and Marnie recalled this scene in an interview the

following day. For an illustrated history of the Pike, see http://www.millikanalumni.com/Pike/Pike.html.

36. John F. Kasson, *Amusing the Million: Coney Island at the Turn of the Century* (New York: Hill & Wang, 1978), 75–78.

37. Joel Styer, "The Noah's Ark," *Laff in the Dark*, http://www.laffinthedark.com/articles/noahsark/noah.htm.

38. "Night View of Atlantic City Auditorium and Convention Hall, Atlantic City, N.J.," Tichnor 60941, n.d. For a history of the auditorium and a series of photos, see James H. Charleton, "National Register of Historic Places, Inventory—Nomination Form, June 17, 1985": http://pdfhost.focus.nps.gov/docs/NHLS/Text/87000814.pdf, and http://pdfhost.focus.nps.gov/docs/NHLS/Photos/87000814.pdf.

39. James D. Ristine, *Atlantic City* (Charleston, SC: Arcadia, 2008), 88, 91. Rudyard Kipling's poem "The Ladies" related its military narrator's experience with a variety of women, mostly of color, by concluding, "They're like as a row of pins — / For the Colonel's Lady an' Judy O'Grady / Are sisters under their skins!," Kipling, *Collected Verse* (New York: Doubleday, Page, 1907), 317.

40. *Official Guide Book of the Fair 1933* (Chicago: A Century of Progress, 1933), 11.

41. "The C. T. Art-Colortone Process," n.p.

42. "Avenue of Flags, Chicago World's Fair," Teich 3A-H652, 1933.

43. *Official Guide Book of the Fair 1933*, 140.

44. "General Motors Building, Chicago World's Fair," Teich 3A-H634. The card from 1933 was published by Max Rigot; the following year's was by N. Shure, which replaced Rigot as Teich's major distributor for the Century of Progress.

45. Lenox R. Lohr, *Fair Management: The Story of a Century of Progress: A Guide for Future Fairs* (Chicago: Cuneo, 1952), 176.

46. "General Motors Building at New York World's Fair," Teich 9A-H529, 1939.

47. Peter Conrad, *The Art of the City: Views and Versions of New York* (New York: Oxford University Press, 1984), 248.

48. Examples of these two types are "The Berkshire Hotel / Chicago, Illinois," Teich 2B-H695, 1942; and "Dixon Hotel—12th and Baltimore—Kansas City, Mo.," Teich 8A-H3140, 1938.

49. Mincks-Adams Hotel, "National Register of Historic Places—Nomination Form," June 1978, http://pdfhost.focus.nps.gov/docs/NRHP/Text/78002273.pdf.

50. Based on conflicting information collated from "Enlarging the Kaiserhof," *The National Provisioner*, January 21, 1905, 37; Teich, *Teich's Family Tree*, 27, Teich Family Papers; Frank A. Randall and John D. Randall, *History of the Development of Building Construction in Chicago*, 2nd ed. (Urbana: University of Illinois Press, 1999), 145; William R. Host and Brooke Ahne Portmann, *Early Chicago Hotels* (Charleston, SC: Arcadia, 2006), 54–56; David G. Clark, *Route 66 in Chicago* (Charleston, SC: Arcadia, 2007), 95; and "Down They Forgot as Up They Grew: Hotel Kaiserhof" (a blog entry by a guide with the Chicago Architecture Foundation), March 7, 2011, http://www.connectingthewindycity.com/2011/03/down-they-forgot-as-up-they-grew-hotel.html. Construction of the original Hotel Wyoming, possibly earlier known as the Hotel Gore, which was purchased by Max Teich and Carl C. Roessler, is variously given as 1889 and 1892. With the 1915 addition, the Kaiserhof/Atlantic stretched along 314–328 South Clark Street.

51. Perhaps Max Teich preferred his hotel exteriors rendered as simple colorized line drawings. A hotel he purchased in St. Louis appeared as such in "New Hotel Jefferson / The Aristocrat of St. Louis," Teich 3A-H332, 1933.

52. The job file for "Mirror Room—Hotel Bentley—Alexandria, La.," Teich 8A-H798, 1938, Teich Postcard Archives, includes a retouched photo of the interior and a warning from the client: "In reference to eliminating the reflections in the mirror ceiling so there will not be any confusion in the view, I am under the impression that if this is done it will detract from the advertising value of our mirror room." Although the client decided to "leave it to you to work out the scheme . . . as making post cards is your business," the fact that the hotel had transferred its patronage to MWM three years later indicates displeasure with Teich's rendition. The Teich card and a version by Beals in Des Moines, IA, were viewed on eBay.

53. See for example job files for "Kenmore

Hotel / Miami Beach, Florida," Teich 6A-H2367, 1936; "The Norman / Directly on the Ocean," Teich 7A-H2254, 1937; and "Allen Apartment Hotel," Teich 0B-H1580, 1940; all in Teich Postcard Archives.

54. A brief obituary of Heunisch appeared in the *Orlando Sentinel*, January 6, 1991, http://articles.orlandosentinel.com/1991-01-06/news/9101060212_1_born-in-germany-orlando-george-g. He was sales representative for Florida in 1939 according to "Auditors Report for Year 1939," Teich Company Papers.

55. Quotations are from the following job files, located in the Teich Postcard Archives: "The Norman / Miami Beach, Florida / Directly on the Ocean," Teich 7A-H2254, 1937; "Normandy Plaza Hotel / Miami Beach, Florida," Teich 7A-H1376, 1937; "Kenmore Hotel / Miami Beach, Florida," Teich 6A-H2367, 1936; "Hotel Biarritz / 1435 Collins Ave. / Miami Beach, Florida / Half Block from Ocean," Teich 6A-H1866, 1936; "Hotel Helene / Miami Beach, Florida," Teich 7A-H1433, 1937; "Normandy Plaza Hotel"; "Hotel Biarritz"; and "Hotel Good / Collins Ave. at 43rd St. / Miami Beach, Florida," Teich 7A-H1878, 1937.

56. An example of the former is "New Patricia Hotel on the Ocean Front, Myrtle Beach S.C., 'America's Finest Strand' / 670 Miles South of New York, 735 Miles North of Miami," Teich 2B-H728, 1942; of the latter, "The Patrician / Directly on the Ocean / Miami Beach, Florida," Colourpicture 14527, n.d.

57. Quotations are from the now defunct "Memory Lane" section of the website I Love Atlantic City Online, http://iloveac.com. See also Karen L. Schnitzspahn, *Jersey Shore Food History: Victorian Feasts to Boardwalk Treats* (Charleston, SC: American Palate, 2012), 41.

58. Other cards described were viewed on eBay and CardCow.com: "The Lotus Restaurant—727 14th St., N.W.—Washington, D.C.," ca. 1926; "The Lotus Restaurant, 727 14th St. N.W., Washington, D.C.," Teich 120273, 1928; "The Lotus / 727—14th, N.W. / Washington, D.C.," Teich 4B-H620, 1944; and "The Lotus—727 14th St., N.W.—Washington, D.C.," Teich 0C-H810, 1950. Information is from facsimiles of *Washington Post* articles obtained through ProQuest Historical Newspapers.

59. The revised card retained the original serial number. On the Tramor's history, see Waveney Ann Moore, "Tampa Bay Times Lists Historic Tramor Cafeteria for Lease or Sale," *Tampa Bay Times*, June 13, 2012, http://www.tampabay.com/news/business/real estate/tampa-bay-times-lists-historic-tramor-cafeteria-for-lease-or-sale/1234951; and Katherine Snow Smith, "Hofbrauhaus St. Petersburg Hopes for June Opening at Former Tramor Cafeteria," *Tampa Bay Times*, February 19, 2015, http://www.tampabay.com/news/business/hofbrauhaus-st-petersburg-hopes-for-june-opening-at-former-tramor-cafeteria/2218305.

60. The real photo card was observed on eBay.

61. For other examples, see "Main Street, Salt Lake City, Utah," Teich 8A-H2740, 1938; and "Essex Street, Main Business Section, Lawrence, Mass. / The Queen City of the Merrimac Valley," Teich 5B-H955.

6. From a Rearview Mirror: Contemporary Reflections

1. I relied on Stephanie Lindsey's website, www.babyjane.us, no longer in existence.

2. This description is based in part on a brief video prepared to promote the piece's auction by Christie's in 2014: http://www.christies.com/features/joseph-cornell-untitled-penny-arcade-portrait-4587-3.aspx. The card used by Cornell was "Chrysler Building, New York City," Colourpicture K4844, n.d. See Adam Gopnik, "Sparkings: Joseph Cornell and the Art of Nostalgia," *New Yorker*, February 17, 2003, http://www.newyorker.com/archive/2003/02/17/030217crat_atlarge; and Lynda Roscoe Hartigan, *Joseph Cornell: Navigating the Imagination* (New Haven: Yale University Press, 2007), 200, 181.

3. Baeder, *Diners*, 77, 98, 96. On the initial collecting impulse, see Mieke Bal, "Telling Objects: A Narrative Perspective on Collecting," in Elsner and Cardinal, *The Cultures of Collecting*, 101.

4. Barry Zaid, *Wish You Were Here: A Tour*

of America's Great Hotels during the Golden Age of the Picture Post Card (New York: Crown, 1990), 6–7.

5. Jean Baudrillard, "The System of Collecting," in Elsner and Cardinal, *The Cultures of Collecting*, 9; and John Tagg, *The Burden of Representation: Essays on Photographies and Histories* (Amherst: University of Massachusetts Press, 1988), 206.

6. Susan Stewart, *On Longing: Narratives of the Miniature, the Gigantic, the Souvenir, the Collection* (Durham: Duke University Press, 1993; orig. 1984), 158, 162, 163.

7. Zaid, *Wish You Were Here*, 7.

8. Jakle, *Postcards of the Night*, 7.

9. For parallel discussions of nostalgia experienced through genuine historical artifacts, in this case photographs, whose claims to represent historical authenticity are problematic, see Sandweiss, *Print the Legend*, 215–216, 326–343.

10. Schor, *"Cartes Postales,"* 199–200 (reprinted as "Collecting Paris" in Elsner and Cardinal, *The Cultures of Collecting*, 255–256).

11. Ruth B. Phillips, *Trading Identities: The Souvenir in Native North American Art from the Northeast, 1700–1900* (Seattle: University of Washington Press, 1998), x.

12. Phillips, *The Postcard Century*, 12. The generous humanity of Phillips's expansive presentation of both image and message can be contrasted with the snide approach of another British artist, the photographer Martin Parr, in two short, bleak collections entitled *Boring Postcards* (London: Phaidon, 1999) and *Boring Postcards USA* (London: Phaidon, 2000).

13. Susan M. Pearce, *On Collecting: An Investigation into Collecting in the European Tradition* (London: Routledge, 1995), 248.

14. Quotations in the following paragraphs are from postcards in my collection, with original grammar, spelling, capitalization, and punctuation retained.

15. Jacques Derrida, *The Post Card: From Socrates to Freud and Beyond*, trans. Alan Bass (Chicago: University of Chicago Press, 1987; orig. 1980), 245.

16. On the concept of a surviving fragment and its presumed larger whole, see Celeste Olalquiaga, *The Artificial Kingdom: A Treasury of the Kitsch Experience* (New York: Pantheon, 1998), 221.

17. Letter from Curt Teich Jr. to G. I. Pitchford, January 21, 1944, Pitchford Archive. On Teich's war work, see letters from Col. L. B. Chambers, Corps of Engineers, Army Map Service, to "Curt Teich and Sons," August 22, 1945; and Lt. Col. Frederick W. Mast, Corps of Engineers, Army Map Service, to Curt Teich Jr., September 12, 1945; both in box 1, folder 13, Teich Company Papers. On wartime production in general, see Pyle, "For Rent," 9–11; and Bress, "An Air-Brushed War."

18. For an account of Fort Pierce's transformation from resort town to naval training center, see Robert A. Taylor, *World War II in Fort Pierce* (Charleston, SC: Arcadia, 2003; orig. 1999).

19. Stewart, *On Longing*, 23–24.

20. Svetlana Boym, *The Future of Nostalgia* (New York: Basic Books, 2001), xv–xvi.

21. Stewart, *On Longing*, 151.

ILLUSTRATION CREDITS

Fig. 2.1. Lake County (IL) Discovery Museum, Curt Teich Postcard Archives

Fig. 2.10. Lake County (IL) Discovery Museum, Curt Teich Postcard Archives

Fig. 3.1. Lake County (IL) Discovery Museum, Curt Teich Postcard Archives

Fig. 3.5. Photo courtesy of Robert I. Pitchford

Fig. 3.7. Lake County (IL) Discovery Museum, Curt Teich Postcard Archives

Fig. 3.8. Courtesy of Robert I. Pitchford

Fig. 3.10. Lake County (IL) Discovery Museum, Curt Teich Postcard Archives

Fig. 3.11. Lake County (IL) Discovery Museum, Curt Teich Postcard Archives

Fig. 3.12. Lake County (IL) Discovery Museum, Curt Teich Postcard Archives

Fig. 3.13. Lake County (IL) Discovery Museum, Curt Teich Postcard Archives

Fig. 3.17. Lake County (IL) Discovery Museum, Curt Teich Postcard Archives

Fig. 4.1. © Komar & Melamid and Nation Institute

(p. 108) Wisconsin Historical Society WHi-111700

(p. 132) © Palm Springs Art Museum

(p. 141) Photo courtesy of Robert I. Pitchford

(p. 142) © Haynes Studios, courtesy of Montana Historical Society Research Center

(p. 144) © Haynes Studios, courtesy of Montana Historical Society Research Center

(p. 152) Photo courtesy of Charlotte County Historical Center, 22959 Bayshore Road, Charlotte Harbor, Florida

(p. 186) Photo courtesy of Robert I. Pitchford

(p. 196, top) © J. R. Willis. Courtesy of Scott L. Peeler Jr.

(p. 196, bottom) © J. R. Willis. Courtesy of Scott L. Peeler Jr.

(p. 202) Photo by Charles C. Ebbets/Copyright Ebbets Photo-Graphics, 2014

(p. 214) © McCormick Company. Courtesy of McCormick Company

(p. 257) Photo courtesy of Robert I. Pitchford

(p. 272) Courtesy of the Gleason Waite Romer Collection at the Miami-Dade Public Library System

Fig. 5.1. Photo by Berenice Abbott/Getty Images

Fig. 5.2. Library of Congress, Map Collections, http://www.loc.gov/item/75694940

Fig. 5.3. Reprinted from Hugh Ferriss, *The Metropolis of Tomorrow* (New York: Ives Washburn, 1929)

Fig. 5.4. © 2014 Georgia O'Keeffe Museum / Artists Rights Society (ARS), New York; Oil on canvas / $40^1/_8 \times 19^3/_{16}$ in. (101.918 × 48.736 cm) / Sheldon Museum of Art, University of Nebraska–Lincoln, NAA—Thomas C. Woods Memorial / N-107 / Photo © Sheldon Museum of Art

Fig. 5.5. Gelatin silver print, Minneapolis Institute of Arts, Gift of the William R. Hibbs Family 86.108.37/Photo by Berenice Abbott/Getty Images

Fig. 5.7. Indianapolis Museum of Art, William Ray Adams Memorial Collection, 47.4 © Edward Hopper

(p. 304) Courtesy National Gallery of Art, Washington, DC

(p. 318) Lake County (IL) Discovery Museum, Curt Teich Postcard Archives

(p. 336) Color postcard reproduction of image #C01146, Russell Chalberg Collection, Austin History Center, Austin Public Library

(p. 353) © Walker Evans Archive, The Metropolitan Museum of Art / The J. Paul Getty Museum, Los Angeles

(p. 411) New York World's Fair 1939–1940 records, Manuscripts and Archives Division, The New York Public Library, Astor, Lenox and Tilden Foundations

(p. 430, bottom) Lake County (IL) Discovery Museum, Curt Teich Postcard Archives

(p. 431) Lake County (IL) Discovery Museum, Curt Teich Postcard Archives

Fig. 6.2. Art © The Joseph and Robert Cornell Memorial Foundation / Licensed by VAGA, New York, NY; Private Collection / Photo © Christie's Images / Bridgeman Images

Fig. 6.7. Metropolitan Museum of Art, Walker Evans Archive, Gift of Arnold Crane, 2003 (2003.564.18); © Walker Evans Archive, The Metropolitan Museum of Art

Abbott, Berenice, 6, 275–277, 283–285, 288, 301

Abbott and Costello Show, The (radio program), 458

accordion folders, 44–45, 223

Acoma Pueblo, NM, 8

Action Comics, 311

Adams, Ansel, 345

Adams Hotel, Tulsa, OK, 420–421

Adirondack Mountains, NY, 148–149

Advertising & Selling, 353

advertising industry, 24, 41

advertising postcards, 45–46, 57–58, 154–155

advertising signs, 160–161, 184–185, 188–189, 310–313, 338–353, 396–399

Aerial Lift Bridge, Duluth, MN, 244–245

aesthetic, linen: authenticity of, 8; discussion of, 58–68; generic aspects of, 48; hyper-real aspects of, 59; of individual publishers, 311; introduction of, 5; optimism of, 71–72; sources of, 40–41; surreal aspects of, 9–10, 59; uniqueness of, 5, 10, 252–253, 404–405

African Americans, 6, 86, 173–181, 186–187, 227–229, 264–265

agriculture, 62–66, 174–175, 212–217

Agua Prieta, Mexico, 184–185

airbrushing, 51–53.

airships, 9, 272–273, 320–321, 406–407, 411

Albuquerque, NM, 125, 194–195, 197, 204–205

Albuquerque Municipal Airport, Albuquerque, NM, 204–205

Alexandria, LA, 424–425, 489n52

Alice's Adventures in Wonderland (Carroll), 145

Allegheny Mountain Tunnel, Pennsylvania Turnpike, PA, 249

Alvarado Hotel, Albuquerque, NM, 195

Amarillo, TX, 215

America, national imaginary of, 3, 35, 69–77, 79–80, 463–464, 473n3. *See also* United States of America

American Business, 42, 173, 275

American Guide Series, 70, 71

American Indians. *See* Native Americans

American Landscape (Sheeler), 237

American Medical Association, 169

American Photochrom Company, 19

Americans, The (Frank), 259

American scene: automobile as central to, 140–141, 246–247; coherent vision of, 12, 70, 77, 80; iconography of, 5; mass-produced quality of, 11; middle-class quality of, 6; modern aspect of, 259, 275; nostalgia for, 290, 442; optimistic portrayal of, 3, 37, 58, 71, 437, 463–464; Southwest and West as central to,

121; streamlining of, 435; as subject of postcards, 4, 15, 64, 70; tariff on images of, 16; as Teich's subject, 46, 63, 70, 80, 125, 151; and "This Land Is Your Land," 70

America's Most Wanted (Komar and Melamid), 75–77

amusement parks, 384–387, 392–395

Anatomy of Melancholy (Burton), 453

Andersen's Valley Inn, Buellton, CA, 452

Anglo-Americans, 183, 185, 187. *See also* whiteness

animals, 10, 76, 146–147, 180–181, 372–373, 460

Apache tribe, 197

Appalachian mountaineers, 6

Arandora Star (ship), 272–273

Arc de Triomphe, Paris, France, 309

Architecture of the Night (Neumann), 281

Arizona, 121. *See also specific cities and places*

Arlington Hotel, Hot Springs, AR, 331

Armour & Company, 217

Armour Star Frankfurters, 46

Arrasmith, W. S., 484n107

Arrowhead, Lake, CA, 50, 122–123

art: and the city, 275–277, 281–285, 286–288; inscribed on postcards, 449–450, 458–560; landscape tradition of, 5–6, 72–75; postcards compared to, 91, 103, 113; postcards promoted as, 3, 34, 91; postcards regarded as, 59–60

Art-Colortone. *See* C. T. Art-Colortone

Art Deco: and commercial architecture, 6, 9, 424–427; demise of, 413; and graphic art, 154–155, 420–421; modernity proclaimed by, 281; and public architecture, 374–377; and railway terminals, 262–263; and skyscrapers, daytime views of, 318–319, 330–331, 336–337, 358–361, 406–407; and skyscrapers, night views of, 281–282, 284, 295, 316–317, 320–323, 332–333

artificiality: versus the natural, 236–237, 256–257, 306–307, 340–341; versus the real, 21–22; of world's fairs, 296, 402–403

Art Institute of Chicago, Chicago, IL, 51, 55, 64, 113, 370–371

Arts and Crafts movement, 125, 197

Asbury Park, NJ, 9, 207

Asheville Post Card Company, 105, 117, 177

Atchison, Topeka & Santa Fe Railway. *See* Santa Fe Railroad

Atlanta, GA, 154–155

Atlantic City, NJ, 396–399, 428–429

Atlantic City Auditorium, Atlantic City, NJ, 396–397

Atlantic Monthly, 15

atomic bomb, 259

auditoriums, 374–377, 390–391, 396–397
Ausable Chasm, NY, 148–149
Austin, TX, 336–337, 339
automobile: fantastic images of, 306–307, 310–313, 330–331, 420–421; as icon of modernity, 316–317, 348–351; in the landscape, 64, 138–141; point of view from, 64, 88–89, 140–141, 291, 299; as protective cocoon, 146–147; and railroads, 261; and tourism, 125, 143, 148–149, 247
Avenue of Flags, Century of Progress International Exposition, Chicago, IL, 404–405, 407
aviation, 204–205, 268–273, 356–357, 370–371, 406–407

Baby Jane jewelry, 441–442, 444
Bacall, Lauren, 442–444
Badlands, SD, 138–139, 141
Bad Lobenstein, Germany. *See* Lobenstein, Germany
Baeder, John, 6, 35, 59, 79, 445, 446
Bailey, Walter Alexander, 377
Baltimore, MD, 306–307, 309
Baltimore Trust Company Building, Baltimore, MD, 307
Bangor, ME, 332–333
Banham, Reyner, 95
Bank of Manhattan Trust Building, New York, NY, 298–299
Barthes, Roland, 78–80, 455
Bassani device, 56–57
Bates Mill, Lewiston, ME, 232–233
Bath Street Viaduct, Baltimore, MD, 306–307, 309
Baton Rouge, LA, 243
Baudrillard, Jean, 445
Bausch and Lomb, 15
beaches, 206–207, 386–391, 396–397, 426–427
Bear Lake, CO, 90–91, 105
Beaux-Arts neoclassicism, 263
Becky Sharp (film), 62
Belasco, Warren, 153, 155
Bel Geddes, Norman. *See* Geddes, Norman Bel
Bell, Frank, 207
Ben Day dots, 27
Bennett, H. H., 6, 44, 74, 109
Benton, Thomas Hart, 377
Berdich, Vera, 55
Berlin, Irving, 71
Bernstein, Max, 217
Berté, Jean, 37
Between the Landscape and Its Other (Vanderbilt), 78
Bierstadt, Albert, 5, 73, 91, 99
Bingo, Club, Las Vegas, NV, 350–351, 353
bird's-eye views, 277–278, 280, 285, 291, 294, 304–305
Birney, Hoffman, 72

Bisbee, AZ, 220–221
Blackfeet tribe, 93
Black Rock Beach, UT, 206–207
Blue Ridge Lines, 266–267
Boardwalk, Atlantic City, NJ, 396–399
Bob's Cafeteria, St. Petersburg, FL. *See* Tramor Cafeteria
Boime, Albert, 123
Boorstin, Daniel, 72
Boston, MA, 38, 39
Boulder City, NV, 44
Boulder Dam. *See* Hoover Dam
Boulder Dam Service Bureau, 253
Boyer, Christine, 288
Boym, Svetlana, 462–463
Bradley, Omar, 425
bridges, 3, 39, 148–149, 232–233, 242–247, 250–251, 302–303, 304–307
Bridgton, ME, 116–117
Broadway, Los Angeles, CA, 344–345
Brothers, Earl, 44, 253
Brown Derby restaurant, Hollywood, CA, 348–349
Bryce Canyon National Park, UT, 72, 130–131
Buckhorn Curio Store, San Antonio, TX, 162–163, 435
Buckley's Texaco Service, Childress, TX, 158–159
Buettner, Otto, 28
Bulldog Drummond Strikes Back (film), 399
Burbank, E. A., 193
Burke, Edmund, 281
Burlington Railroad, 263
Butler Airphotos, 305

California, 121. *See also specific cities and places*
Cambridge, MA, 368–369, 449–450
Camden, NJ, 3, 39
Camera Craft Shop, Hilo, HI, 101
canals, 232–233, 244–245
Canal Street, New Orleans, LA, 346–347
Canyon Lodge Lounge, Yellowstone National Park, WY, 144–145
canyons, 108–109, 128–131, 138–139, 252–253
Capitol Building, Austin, TX, 336–337
Carceri d'invenzione (Piranesi), 111
Cardinell-Vincent Company, 42
Carew Tower, Cincinnati, OH, 242–243, 358–359
Carlin Post Card Company, 42–43
Carnegie-Illinois Steel Company, Irvin Works, PA, 238–239
Carnegie-Illinois Steel Company, tin mill, Monessen, PA, 236–237
Carolina Beach, NC, 207
Carroll, Lewis, 145
Catalina Highway, Tucson, AZ. *See* Mt. Lemmon Road
Catalina Island, CA, 10, 64
caves, 110–111

Center Street, Marion, OH, 32–33

Central Methodist Church, Knoxville, TN, 367

Central Park, New York, NY, 385

Central Trust Bank Building, Cincinnati, OH, 242–243

Century of Progress International Exposition, Chicago, IL, 9, 60–62, 296, 371, 402–409

Changing New York (Abbott), 276, 277

Charlie (postcard correspondent), 458–462

Chattanooga, TN, 106–107

Cheoah River, 105

Cherokee, NC, 160–161

Cherokee tribe, 161

Chicago, Burlington & Quincy Railroad, 263

Chicago, IL: development of, 277, 280, 403; early photographs of, 279; and Heunisch, 427; and Hileman, 93; modernity of, 68, 294, 343; as railway center, 63, 64, 68, 93, 260–261, 265; as regional center, 417; as subject of early Teich postcards, 28, 29, 423; as Teich & Company's location, 2, 5, 32, 41, 43, 50, 67, 157, 403, 456, 463; as Teich art department's location, 47, 48, 50, 65, 129, 193, 221, 286, 289, 290; as Teich home, 13, 17, 18, 28. *See also specific buildings and places*

Chicago Art Portfolio (Frank), 279

Chicago World's Fair, 1893. *See* World's Columbian Exposition

Chicago World's Fair, 1933. *See* Century of Progress International Exposition

children, 174–175, 180–181, 184–185, 190–193

Childress, TX, 158–159

Chinatown, San Francisco, CA, 188–193, 303

Chinese Americans, 6, 86, 188–193, 209

chrome postcards: as color guide, 351; style of, contrasted to linen postcards, 463; as subjects of photo by Frank, 259; as successors to linen postcards, 2, 9, 55, 67, 99, 133, 159, 423, 449

chromos, 24

Chrysler Building, New York, NY, 281, 318–319, 321, 443

Church, Frederic Edwin, 73, 91, 99

churches, 366–367

Cincinnati, OH, 242–243, 278, 358–359

city, the: bird's-eye views of, 277–278, 280, 285, 291; comparison of, to interior views, 425, 435; comparison of, to natural landscape, 280; domestication of, 284–285; gendered views of, 282–285; generic representations of, 288–291; images of (1800s), 277–280; images of (1900s), 6, 280–285; images of, overviews, 298–311; and noir sensibility, 165, 285–288; panoramas of, 278–279; skyline views of, 280, 285; world's fair parallels to, 407

City Hall, Baltimore, MD, 306–307

City Lights (Jakle), 282

cityscape, defined, 294–296

Civil War, 107, 117

Clarksdale, MS, 267

Classic Landscape (Sheeler), 237

Cleopatra (film), 398–399

Cleveland, Gerald, 152–153

Cleveland, OH, 7, 304–305, 384–387

CMYK printing, 25, 40, 56–57

Coca-Cola, 160–161, 184–185

Cocteau, Jean, 275

Colbert, Claudette, 399

Cold Water Canyon, Wisconsin Dells, WI, 108–109

Cole, Thomas, 73

Colgate-Palmolive-Peet Company, 317

collage. *See* photo collage

collecting: motives for, 444–447; in the 1930s and '40s, 449

collectors: author as, 9–11; disdain of, for linen postcards, 4; disdain of, for pre-linen Teich postcards, 33; Evans as, 27

collotype printing, 18, 22, 23, 279. *See also* Photochrom

Colman, Ronald, 399

Colonial Williamsburg, VA, 113

color, 60–62. *See also* colorizing

Colorado River, 250–253

color chart, of Teich & Co., 47–48, 49

colorizing, 24–28, 47–48, 53–57, 109, 129

Colourpicture: Cornell's use of postcard by, 443; generic coloring by, 324–325; Native American portrait by, 198–199; and southern culture, awareness of, 107; Statue of Liberty views by, 357; as Teich competitor, 5, 55, 67, 329, 427; unique work by, 346–347, 436–437

Colter, Mary, 125, 127

comic books, 311

comic postcards, 45, 150–151, 181, 196–197

"comics," 151

Commercial Photo Company, 377

Coney Island, New York, NY, 385, 391

Congress Avenue, Austin, TX, 336–337, 339

control: of the city, 279, 284–285, 289–291, 303; through collecting, 445; of industrial process, 217, 235, 237, 239, 259; of nature, 103, 139, 143. *See also* order

Coos Bay Bridge, North Bend, OR, 243

Corey's Fine Foods, Las Vegas, NV, 436–437

Cornell, Joseph, 442–444, 446

correspondents. *See* messages, postcard

correspondents, series of: Charlie, 458–462; Sgt, 457–458

crafts, 196–197, 202–203

Crater Lake National Park, OR, 94–97

Crocker Building, San Francisco, CA, 308–309, 311

C. T. American Art, 34, 60, 66

C. T. Art-Colortone, dates of serial numbers of, 469n2. *See also* linen postcards

C. T. Art-Colortone De Luxe, 113
C. T. Photochrom, 34
Currier & Ives, 24, 73, 177
Curteich C. T. Art-Colortone. *See* C. T. Art-Colortone
Curteich News, 42, 60–62
Curt Teich & Company. *See* Teich, Curt, & Company
Curt Teich Postcard Archives. *See* Teich Postcard Archives
Cuyahoga Valley, Cleveland, OH, 304–305

daguerreotypes, 278–279
Dakota News Agency, 50, 51, 54, 57
dams, 252–259
Dance of the Magnificent Lion, Chinatown, San Francisco, CA, 192–193
Dante, 111
Davis, Allen F., 35
Davis, Mike, 63
DC-3 airliners, 204–205, 268–269
Death Valley, CA, 134–135
De Chirico, Giorgio, 357
Deco. *See* Art Deco
Delaware River Bridge, Philadelphia, PA, 3, 39
Del Rio, TX, 451
DeMille, Cecil B., 399
democratization: of images, 377; of landscape tradition, 73–75; of lithography, 24; of real photo postcards, 20; of urban views, 279
Department of Docks and Police Station, Pier A, North River, Manhattan; May 5, 1936 (Abbott), 276–277
Depression: auto camping during, 150–153; construction during, 281, 427; home canning during, 213; and linen postcards, 3, 35–37, 41, 57, 437; and a national imaginary, 3, 69–71; national park usage during, 131; and public works, 253; and railroads, 261; and storefront modernization, 343; travel during, 111, 451; and world's fairs, 6, 403
Deseret Book Company, 131, 207
desert scenes, 1–2, 120–121, 132–135, 140–141
Desert Souvenir Supply, 351
Desert View, Grand Canyon National Park, AZ, 124–127
design, 48–50, 62–66
Detroit, MI, 23, 27
Detroit Photographic Company, 14–15, 74, 179
Detroit Publishing Company, 25, 29, 32, 74, 243
Dexter Press, 67
Dilworth, Leah, 59
Disney, Walt, 409
Disneyland, CA, 381, 393, 409
Divine Comedy (Dante/Doré), 111
domestication: of the city, 284–285; of images, 74, 285; of the sublime, 123, 127
Door County, WI, 212–213

Doré, Gustave, 111
Dowler Brothers Pianos, Marion, OH, 23
Drake Tower, Chicago, IL, 316–317
Dubois & Son, 46
Duluth, MN, 43, 231, 244–245
Dust Bowl, 70, 215
Dutchess County Courthouse, Poughkeepsie, NY, 364–365
Dutch Village, Century of Progress International Exposition, Chicago, IL, 408–409

Eastern Photo Litho Company, 117
Eastman Kodak Company, 20, 133. *See also* Kodachrome film; Kodak cameras
Ebbets, Charles C., 203
Echo River, Mammoth Cave, KY, 110–111
E. C. Kropp, 229. *See also* Kropp, Emil C.
Eiffel Tower, Paris, France, 245
Eisenhower, Dwight D., 425
El Capitan train, 264–265
electrical sublime: and Canal Street, New Orleans, LA, 346–347; in the city, 281, 285, 300–301, 380–381; in Las Vegas, NV, 352–353; and the Palmolive Building, Chicago IL, 316–317; in Times Square, New York, NY, 310–313
Elizabeth (postcard recipient), 458–462
El Paseo de Los Angeles, Los Angeles, CA, 183
El Patio Hotel, Las Vegas, NV, 438–439
El Tovar Hotel, Grand Canyon National Park, AZ, 125
embossing, 37–41
Emerson, Helen Lowley, 205
Emily Lowe Gallery, Hofstra University, Hempstead, NY, 60
Empire State Building, New York, NY, 276, 281, 283, 300–301, 303, 320–321, 443
Encyclopédie, ou dictionnaire raisonné des sciences, des arts et des métiers, 217
ethnic representation, 85–86, 172–205
Euclid Beach Park, Cleveland, OH, 384–387
Evans, Walker: as documentary photographer, 3, 70; linen postcards disdained by, 72, 97, 290; on "lyric" photography, 78–79; photographs by, 353, 464; as postcard collector, 27, 486n25; on pre-linen street views, 27–28, 33, 290–291
Evansville, IN, 267
Everglades, FL, 202–203
exaggeration postcards, 20, 135
Excelsior Springs, MO, 168–169
exoticism, 86, 177, 183, 189–193, 197, 209, 430–431
expositions, international. *See* world's fairs
expressionism: Bailey and, 377; Ferriss and, 281; Longshaw image and, 135; Manhattan image and, 321; Metrocraft images and, 103, 105; Ryder and, 321; Teich images and, 113, 219
Eytinge, Sol, 181

Fardon, G. R., 279

Farm Security Administration, 70–71, 221, 227, 473n2

Federal Art Project, 276

Federal Writers' Project, 70, 71

Fellig, Arthur. *See* Weegee

Ferriss, Hugh, 281, 282, 283, 319, 411

fetishism, 442–446, 448–449

First Presbyterian Church, Marquette, MI, 366–367

Fitchburg, MA, 29

Five Titans (Presler), 261

Florida, 112–113. *See also specific cities and places*

folders, accordion, 44–45, 223

food, 46

forests, 88–89, 98–99

Fort Pierce, FL, 458

Fortune, 27

Fort Wayne, IN, 288

Forum Cafeteria, Chicago, IL, 452–453, 461

Forum Shops, Caesars Palace, Las Vegas, NV, 433

Fountain of the Great Lakes (Taft), 370–371

Fountain of Youth (Winter), 326–327

fountains, 156–157, 358–361, 372–373, 410–411

Fountain Square, Cincinnati, OH, 358–359

Franconia Notch, NH, 451

Frank, Robert, 259

Frank, S. B., 279

Frasher, Burton, 221

Fred Harvey Company, 44, 125, 195, 205, 265

Fred Harvey Indian Building, Albuquerque, NM, 194–195, 197

Fremont Street, Las Vegas, NV, 64

Friedrich, Albert, 163

Frost, Robert, 117

FSA. *See* Farm Security Administration

Galion, OH, 21

Galloway, Ewing, 311

Galveston, TX, 224–225, 227

Galveston Wholesale News Company, 225

Garland, Judy, 458

Geddes, Norman Bel, 413

gender: and postcard use, 285, 449; and representations of the city, 282–285. *See also* men, images of; women, images of

General Motors Building, Century of Progress International Exposition, Chicago, IL, 9, 61, 406–407, 413

General Motors Building, New York World's Fair of 1939, New York, NY, 412–413

generic scenes: with African Americans, 174–181; characterized, 44–45; with Chinese Americans, 190–193; of landscapes, 76–77, 88–89, 474n11; with Native Americans, 196–201; of the ocean, 114–115, 207; of sunset, 112–113

generic series: "Bathing Scenes," 115; "Chocolate Drop Comics," 181; "Cotton Picking Scenes," 175; "Happy South Scenes," 175, 177, 179, 181;

"Ocean Scenes," 115; "Oil Field Scenes," 219; "Rural Scenes," 76; "Southern Pickaninny Scenes," 175, 181; "Surf Scenes," 115; "Trailer Comics," 151; "Water Scenes," 115

generic versus unique: in comparison of Longshaw and Teich postcards, 67–68; in images, 5–6, 50, 77–80, 84, 288–291, 365; in messages on postcards, 454

generic visual effects: characterized, 48, 99, 107; used on specific images, 66, 324–325, 364–365, 388–389, 426–427, 432–433

genre painting, 173, 177

Genthe, Arnold, 191

geometrical sublime, 281

George Washington Bridge, New York, NY, 243

Germany: as supplier of postcards, 15–16, 21, 25, 27, 28–29, 32, 177

Geronimo, 197

Giacometti, Alberto, 391

Gifford, Sanford, 99, 283–284

Gilpin, William, 73

Glacier Gorge, CO, 90–91

Glacier National Park, MT, 92–93

Glacier Park Hotel, Glacier National Park, MT, 93

glaciers, 92–93

"God Bless America" (Berlin), 71

Golden Gate Bridge, San Francisco, CA, 243

"Goldilocks and the Three Bears," 145

Gone with the Wind (Mitchell), 173

Goodyear blimps, 9, 205, 272–273, 406–407, 411

Google, 461

Google Maps Street View, 341, 462

Gothic Deco, 336–337

Gottscho, Samuel H., 284

government buildings, 50–58, 219, 362–365

Governor's Island, New York, NY, 298–299, 301

Granby Street, Norfolk, VA, 342–343, 345

Grand Canyon National Park, AZ: mediated experience of, 72; as subject of landscape painting, 73; as subject of postcard views, 103, 124–129, 255, 259; and the sublime, 233; as tourist destination, 253; volume of postcard views of, 72, 474n6

Grand Central Parkway, New York, NY, 413

grand-style urban photography: defined, 279; echoed by interior views, 425, 435; human figures in, 285; influence of, on linen postcards, 280, 308–309; noir style contrasted with, 286

Grant Avenue, San Francisco, CA, 188–189, 193

Grauman's Chinese Theatre, Hollywood, CA, 9, 378–381

Great Depression. *See* Depression

Great Lakes, IL, 208–209

Great Northern Railway, 93

Great Salt Lake, UT, 206–207, 391

Great Smoky Mountains National Park, TN, 113, 161

greeting cards, 13, 15, 33

"Greetings from" postcards, 9, 18, 76–77, 115, 459. *See also* large-letter postcards

Greyhound auto-liners, 407

Greyhound Bus Terminal, Pittsburgh, PA, 266–267

Grinnell Glacier, MT, 92–93

Grinnell Litho Company, 413

Guthrie, Woody, 69, 71, 275

Hales, Peter Bacon, 59, 64, 97, 279, 285

halftone-lithographic postcards, 25–31, 33–34, 37. *See also* pre-linen postcards

halftone printing, 22–23, 38–40, 279

Hall, Joyce, 15

Hallmark, 15

Hall of Science, Century of Progress International Exposition, Chicago, IL, 61

Hall of Waters, Excelsior Springs, MO, 168–169

Hampton Beach, NH, 207

Harper's Weekly, 177, 181, 217

Harris Company, 31

Hartman Litho Sales Company, 117

Harvard Square, Cambridge, MA, 449–450

Harvard University, Cambridge, MA, 368–369

Harvey, Fred. *See* Fred Harvey Company

Harvey, H. J., 229

Haussmann, Georges-Eugène (Baron), 309

Hawaii National Park, HI, 100–101

Haynes Studios, 44

health care, 168–169, 330–331

Herz, Harry, 125

Heunisch, George, 427

Hibbing, MN, 222–223

Hibbing Daily Tribune, 223

high-angle street views. *See* grand-style urban photography

High Gear Road, CA, 122–123, 127

highways, 88–89, 138–141, 246–251, 254–255, 272–273

Hileman, T. J., 74, 93

Hilo, HI, 101

Hindenburg airship, 411

Hines, Duncan, 157

Hochegger, Frank, 28, 31

Hofstra University, Hempstead, NY, 60

Hollywood, CA, 348–349, 378–381

Homer, Winslow, 115

Hood, Raymond, 317

Hoover Dam, 252–259, 269, 351, 437

Hoover Dam (Pitchford), 257

Hopi tribe, 199

Hopper, Edward, 286–288, 429

Hotel Atlantic, Chicago, IL, 422–423

Hotel Bentley, Alexandria, LA, 424–425, 489n52

Hotel Fensgate, Boston, MA, 38–41

Hotel Hollenden, Cleveland, OH, 7

Hotel Kaiserhof, Chicago, IL. *See* Hotel Atlantic

Hotel Lobby (Hopper), 286–288

Hotel Louis Joliet, Joliet, IL, 416–419

Hotel Main, Austin, TX, 336–337

Hotel Ponce de Leon, Roanoke, VA, 48

hotels, 7, 38–41, 48–50, 142–145, 287, 416–427, 438–439

Hotel Wyoming, Chicago, IL. *See* Hotel Atlantic

Hot Springs, AR, 294, 330–331

Houston, TX, 226–227

Hudson River School, 5, 73

Huey P. Long Bridge, Baton Rouge, LA, 243

Hull-Rust mine, Hibbing MN, 222–223

iconography, 4–6, 8, 41, 60, 68, 71

Illinois Central Railroad, 261

illumination: of the city, 281–285, 300–303, 310–313, 332–333, 342–353; of individual buildings, 362–363, 374–375, 396–397, 428–429; of Mammoth Cave, 110–111; of Niagara Falls, 102–103, 111; of St. Petersburg Shuffleboard Club, 166–167; of steel mills, 236–237

images: artificiality of, 21–22; democratization of, 73–75, 279, 377; domestication of, 74, 285; manipulation of, for ethnic scenes, 192–193; manipulation of, general processes of, 53; manipulation of, by photo collage, 64–66, 122–123, 186–187, 206–207, 306–307, 372–373; manipulation of, by photographers, 20; manipulation of, for postcards, characterized, 8; manipulation of, for street scenes, 48, 306–307, 348–351; piracy of, 21, 67–68, 89, 207, 363, 397; realism of, 1–2, 4–5, 8, 21–22; recycling of, for African American subjects, 177, 179, 181; recycling of, for Chinese American subjects, 191, 193; recycling of, from linen postcards, 193, 207, 299, 319, 329, 379; recycling of, for nonmainstream white subjects, 209; recycling of, from older photos, 74, 229; recycling of, from pre-linen postcards, 213, 263, 363, 474n11

Indian Model 340 motorcycle, 46

Indians. *See* Native Americans

Industrial Trust Tower, Providence, RI, 288

Inness, George, 304–305

Interior, La Ballena, Tijuana, Mexico (Pitchford), 186

interior views: characterized, 6; of hotels, 49, 144–145, 287, 422–425, 438–439; of industrial sites, 258–259; of public buildings, 126–127, 168–169, 262–263, 270–271, 326–329, 376–377; of railway trains, 264–265; of restaurants and bars, 186–187, 418–419, 430–435; of tourist attractions, 162–163

Irving Trust Company Building, New York, NY, 298–299

Irvin Works, Carnegie-Illinois Steel Company, PA, 238–239

Isenberg, Alison, 289–290, 339, 341

Ives, Frederick, 22

Jackson, William Henry, 6, 15, 64, 73, 74
Jakle, John A., 35, 282, 311, 347, 446
Jamestown, NY, 7
Jersey Supply Company, 115
Joliet, IL, 416–419
Joshua Tree National Monument, CA, 133
Joyce, James, 275
Jubb, William, 117
Jungle, The (Sinclair), 217
Juniata County, PA, 289

Kansas City, MO, 216–217, 263, 374–377, 379
Kansas City, MO, stockyards, 216–217
Kansas City Art Institute, Kansas City, MO, 377
Kaplan, Caren, 5
Kasson, John F. 395
Kaufmann & Fabry, 261, 409
Kauterskill Clove (Gifford), 283–284
Kennebec River, Waterville, ME, 25–27
Kensett, John Frederick, 99
Kents Restaurant, Atlantic City, NJ, 428–429
Kiva, the, Desert View, Grand Canyon National
    Park, AZ, 126–127
Knott's Berry Farm, CA, 393
Knoxville, TN, 367
Kodachrome film, 2, 55, 66, 72, 133, 347, 351,
    473n2
Kodak cameras, 20, 111, 147, 323
Komar, Vitaly, 75–77
Kress, S. H., & Company, 47
Kropp, Emil C., 14. *See also* E. C. Kropp

La Ballena, Tijuana, Mexico, 186–187
labor, images of, 174–177, 226–229
labor movement, 221, 235
Lackawanna Valley, The (Inness), 304–305
Lagoon, the, Long Beach, CA, 388–391
La Guardia Airport, New York, NY, 268–269
Laguna, NM, 8
Lake County Discovery Museum, Wauconda, IL,
    11–12
lakes: eastern, 88–89, 104–105, 112–113, 386–387;
    midwestern, 230–231, 244–245; western,
    90–91, 94–97, 120–121, 206–207, 252–255
Lam, Dick G., 431
Lamb, Thomas W., 267
landscape: defined, 84; and a national imaginary,
    72–77. *See also* picturesque, the
Lange, Dorothea, 3, 70
large-letter postcards, 44–45, 207, 223, 457–458
Las Vegas, NV, 64, 350–353, 433, 436–439
Latinos, 187, 345, 452. *See also* Mexican Americans
Lebanon, MO, 156–157
Lee, Russell, 70, 221, 227
Leighton, Hugh C., 25–26, 28–29, 31, 32, 41, 179
Lewiston, ME, 232–233

Lib (postcard recipient), 458–462
Life, 3
Lincoln Tower, Fort Wayne, IN, 288
Lindbergh Beacon, Chicago, IL, 316–317
Lindsey, Stephanie, 441–442, 444
linen postcards: accordion folders based on,
    44–45, 223; authenticity of, 447, 464; col-
    lectors of, 3–4, 444–447, 449; colorizing of,
    47–48, 405; demise of, 66–67, 133, 351, 449,
    463; and the Depression, 35–37, 41; de-
    scribed, 2–3; design of, 48–50; development
    of, 37–41; economics of, 38, 40–41, 57–58;
    as fantasy, 10, 67–68, 380–381, 410–413,
    420–421, 426–427; and halftone, 38–40; and
    historians, 3–4, 446–447; as hyperreal, 59,
    405, 419; iconography of, 4–8; as a national
    imaginary, 3, 35–37, 70–72, 79–80, 463–464;
    and nostalgia, 462–464; number of, printed,
    5, 465n4 (chap. 1); preserved, 3–4, 121; pro-
    duction process of, 50–58; and sales agents,
    41–50; as surreal, 102–105, 134–135, 214–
    215, 310–311, 386–391, 394–395. *See also*
    aesthetic, linen; messages, postcard
lithography, 15–16, 24–28, 73, 277–278. *See also*
    offset lithography
Littlefield Building, Austin, TX, 336–337
Little Steel companies, 235
Lobenstein, Germany, 16–18, 28
lodges, park, 142–145
Loewy, Raymond, 267
Lollesgard, Holger, 221, 251
Lollesgard Specialty Company, 125
Long Beach, CA, 218–219, 388–393
Longfellow, Henry Wadsworth, 201
Longshaw Card Company, 67, 135, 311
Lookout Mountain, TN, 106–107, 113
Lorrain, Claude, 73, 280
Los Angeles, CA: Long Beach in environs of,
    219; and Longshaw Card Company, 135; as
    machine-age exemplar, 68, 294, 343; union
    railway station in, 263; views of, 182–183,
    344–345, 360–361, 434–435. *See also* Hol-
    lywood, CA
Lotus, The, Washington, DC, 430–431
Louisiana Purchase Exposition, St. Louis, MO, 18
Lowe, Mount, Scenic Railway, CA, 454
Lowell House, Harvard University, Cambridge,
    MA, 368–369
Lowley, Mike, 205
Luminism, 99, 283–284
Lycoming Hotel, Williamsport, PA, 48–50
lynchings, 20, 467n17
"lyric, the," 78–79

machine age: and the city, 68, 280–285; and fur-
    niture design, 265; the Old South contrasted
    to, 173; as self-conscious concept, 4, 86, 275;
    and the skyscraper, 280–285, 288, 318–319,

330–331, 444; and transportation, 267; and world's fairs, 403

Maehara, K., 101

magisterial gaze. *See* possessive gaze

Maid of the Mist (boat), 103

Main Building, University of Texas, Austin, TX, 9

Main Street, Superior, AZ, 340–341

Main Street, Yuma, AZ, 48

Main Street USA, Disneyland, CA, 409

Mammoth Cave, KY, 110–111

Manhattan, New York, NY: Lower, 298–299; Midtown, 300–301

Manhattan Post Card Publishing Company, 311, 313, 321, 329, 343, 357

manipulation, of images: for ethnic scenes, 192–193; general processes of, 53; by photo collage, 64–66, 122–123, 186–187, 206–207, 306–307, 372–373; by photographers, 20; for postcards, characterized, 8; for street scenes, 48, 306–307, 348–351

Marion, OH, 23, 32–33

Market Street, San Francisco, CA, 308–309, 435

Marquette, MI, 366–367

Marsh, Reginald, 391

Marttila & Kiley, 75, 76

Marx, Leo, 305

Maryland Casualty Company Building, Baltimore, MD, 306–307

Massachusetts, 121. *See also specific cites and places*

Maurer, Marilyn June, 393

Maxwell House Coffee Time (radio program), 458

Mead, Lake, 252–255

mechanization: of agriculture, 215–217; of printing, 29–31; of shipping, 224–225, 227–229

Medical Arts Building, Hot Springs, AR, 330–331

Meet Me in St. Louis (film), 458

Melamid, Alex, 75–77

men, images of, 150–151, 189, 198–199, 208–209

Mesabi Iron Range, MN, 223, 231

messages, postcard: about Century of Progress International Exposition, 405; about death, 453–454; demographics of, 449; about despair, 454–455; discussed, 447–462; about employment, 452–453; about illness, 453; about personal loss, 453; about postcard images, 1, 10, 72, 91, 113, 127, 167, 235, 301, 417; about race, 179; about separation, 449–450, 451–452; series of, 455–462; about tourist sites, 93, 153, 253, 271, 323, 387, 391, 450–451; about travel conditions, 121, 161, 247, 261, 451; about World War II, 253, 456–460

Mesta Machine Company, 239

Metrocraft, 5, 103, 105, 117, 225, 343, 363, 387

Metropolis of Tomorrow, The (Ferriss), 281–282

"Mexicali" beer hall, Tijuana, Mexico, 186–187

Mexican Americans, 6, 86, 182–187. *See also* Latinos

Mexico, 42, 163, 184–187

Miami, FL, 44, 270–273

Miami Beach, FL, 206–207, 273, 407, 426–427

Miami Daily News, 207

Miccosukee tribe, 203

Mid Continent News, 199

middle class, 4, 6, 213

Mid-West Map Company, 425

military life, 208–209

Miller, Angela, 99, 283–284

Miller Art Company, 413

miniaturization: and domestication, 123, 285; of fetishes, 318–319; of hotel images, 416–417; by Luminist painters, 99; and reduction to essentials, 66, 160–161, 434–435; of world's fair architecture, 408–411

mining, 220–225, 230–231

Minnehaha, 201

Minnesota, 121. *See also specific cities and places*

Minsky Brothers, 239

Mirror Room, Hotel Bentley, Alexandria, LA, 424–425, 489n52

Mitchell, Margaret, 173

Mitchell, W. J. T., 72

Moccasin Bend, NC, 106–107

modernity: of agriculture, 214–215; of the automobile, 139, 143, 146–147; of aviation, 268–269; of a bridge, 232–233; of a church building, 366–367; of the city, 86, 275–291, 294–295, 316–317, 413; contrasted to nature, 256–257; contrasted to traditional minorities, 6, 8, 179, 196–197; of design styles, 270–271; doubts about, 273; idealized by postcards, 244–245, 291, 316–317; of industry, 225; of a service station, 158–159; as urban characteristic, 294, 341; and world's fairs, 6, 402–403, 406–407

monuments, 356–361

Moran, Thomas, 5, 24, 48, 73, 91, 129

Moran Point, Grand Canyon National Park, AZ, 128–129

Morphet, Richard, 59–60

Mott, Lorenzo, 35, 63, 79

mountains, 90–93, 122–123, 140–141, 340–341

Mt. Lemmon Road, Tucson, AZ, 140–141

Mt. Lemmon Road, Tucson, AZ (Pitchford), 141

Mumford, Lewis, 70

Municipal Auditorium, Kansas City, MO, 374–377, 379

Municipal Auditorium, Long Beach, CA, 390–391, 393

Municipal Courts Building, Detroit, MI, 23, 27

Municipal Tourist Camp, Punta Gorda, FL, 152–153

Museum of the City of New York, New York, NY, 276

museums, 276, 370–371

musicians, 180–181

Nation, The, 75
National Association of Post Card Manufacturers, 33
national parks, 1–2, 90–97, 100–101, 124–131, 142–147
Nation Institute, 75
Nationwide Post Card Company, 159
Native Americans, 8, 44, 72, 86, 125, 127, 193, 194–205, 448. *See also specific tribes*
Navajo tribe, 125, 196–199
Nelson, Arthur, 157
Nelson Dream Village, Lebanon, MO, 156–157
Neumann, Dietrich, 281
New Deal, 37, 343. *See also* American Guide Series; Farm Security Administration; Federal Art Project; Federal Writers' Project; Works Progress Administration
New England, 117, 232–233
New Orleans, LA, 113, 228–229, 231, 346–347
news agencies, 43–44
New York, NY: Abbott's view of, 275–277, 301; Evans's view of, 353; images of, in Cornell's work, 442–444; images of, in Lindsey's jewelry, 441–442; Manhattan Post Card Company's views of, 357; modernity of, 68, 288, 294, 343; noir images of, 286; O'Keeffe's view of, 282–283, 285; overviews of, 298–301; skyline of, 280, 298–299, 301; skyscrapers of, 281–284, 317, 407. *See also specific buildings and places*
New York at Night (Abbott), 283, 284, 285, 301
New York Night (O'Keeffe), 282, 283, 285
New York Nocturne (Sharpe), 282–285
New York World's Fair Corporation, 411
New York World's Fair of 1939, New York, NY, 296, 410–413
Niagara Falls, NY, 73, 102–103, 105, 476n8
nightclubs, 7, 186–187, 350–351, 418–419, 424–425, 430–431
Nighthawks (Hopper), 286, 429
Night View, North, from RCA Building (Gottscho), 284
night views: of cities, 166–167, 244–245, 300–303, 310–313; of city streets, 342–353; of highways, 246–249; of hotels, 420–421; of industry, 234–239; of landscapes, 100–101, 106–107; of restaurants, 428–429; of skyscrapers, 316–317, 320–323, 332–333; of specific buildings, 357, 362–363, 374–375, 380–381, 394–397; of world's fairs, 402–403, 406–407, 410–411
Noah's Ark, Old Orchard Beach, ME, 394–395
noir: and the city, 285–288, 333, 439; and postcard collecting, 446
Norfolk, VA, 294, 342–343, 345
Norwood Building, Austin, TX, 336–337
nostalgia: through artifacts, 441–444; of the author, 9; at Century of Progress International Exposition, 408–409; and collecting, 4, 445, 446; of Evans, 290, 291; and linen postcards, 462–464; for main streets, 487n16; in the 1930s, 243, 487n16; for the Old South, 173; and real photo postcards, 20
Nye, David E., 103, 281

Oaks Tourist Court, Atlanta, GA, 154–155
Oasis of Mara, CA, 132–133
ocean scenes, 10, 114–115, 460
Ocean-to-Ocean Highway Bridge, Yuma, AZ, 250–251
Office at Night (Hopper), 286
offset lithography, 29–32
oil wells, 218–219
O'Keeffe, Georgia, 282, 283, 285
Oklahoma, 219. *See also specific cities and places*
Oklahoma City, OK, 219
Old Faithful geyser, Yellowstone National Park, WY, 103, 142–143
Old Faithful Inn, Yellowstone National Park, WY, 142–143, 145
Old Orchard Beach, ME, 394–395
Oliver Iron Mining Company, 223
Olvera Street market, Los Angeles, CA, 182–183
Omaha, NE, 262–263
order: applied to the highway, 159; applied to interiors, 435; of the possessive gaze, 123; urban, 70, 188–189, 288–289, 299, 305, 341, 365. *See also* control
Orleans Street Viaduct, Baltimore, MD, 306–307, 309
Orton Plantation, Wilmington, NC, 172–173
Orvell, Miles, 487n16
overlooks, scenic, 106–107, 122–127
overviews, urban, 298–311

Padilla Studios, 183
paintings, as postcard subjects, 326–327, 376–377
Palace of Fine Arts, San Francisco, CA, 372–373
Palmolive Building, Chicago, IL, 316–317, 319
Palm Springs, CA, 133, 393
Palm Springs Tennis Club, Palm Springs, CA, 393
Panama-Pacific Exposition, San Francisco, CA, 373
Pan American Airways Terminal, Miami, FL, 270–271
Pan American Clipper seaplanes, 205, 271, 356–357
panoramas: daguerreotypes, 278–279; paintings, 73
parks, public, 166–167, 372–373
Parr, Martin, 491n12
Pascale, Mark, 64
pastoral, 76–77, 106–107, 174–175, 232–233, 304–305, 413
Patton, George S., 425
Payne-Aldrich tariff, 15–16, 28, 32

Peale, Charles Willson, 163

Pearce, Susan, 448–449

Pendergast, Thomas, 375

Pennell, Joseph, 280

Pennsylvania Turnpike, PA, 246–249

Penny Arcade Portrait of Lauren Bacall (Cornell), 442–444

Pensacola, FL, 287

Pershing Square, Los Angeles, CA, 360–361

Pershing Square Building, Los Angeles, CA, 360–361

Phantom Ship, Crater Lake National Park, OR, 94–97

Phelps Dodge Corporation, 221

Philadelphia, PA, 3, 39

Phillips, Ruth, 448

Phillips, Tom, 59, 448, 451, 455, 456, 461, 462

Phoenix, AZ, 125

Phostint, 25

Photochrom, 14–15, 25, 32

photo collage, 64–66, 122–123, 186–187, 206–207, 306–307, 352–353, 372–373

photographers: of cityscapes, 278–279; of landscapes, 5–6, 73–75; as postcard subjects, 194–197, 480n69; and real photo postcards, 20–21; sales agents as, 42–43, 47, 64, 65; as Teich clients, 109, 133

photography: color, 473n2; documentary, 290–291; by Farm Security Administration, 70–71, 290–291, 473n2; of interiors, 286; interpretation of, 78–79; reproduction methods for, 20–28; and stereograph cards, 74; urban, 278–279

picturesque, the: and the city, 277–279, 280, 299, 305, 336–337; conventions of, applied to interiors, 424–425; conventions of, applied to painting, 72–77; conventions of, applied to postcards, 5–6, 101, 116–117, 130–131; and Native Americans, 195; Pitchford's use of, 64–66; and technology, 138–139, 230–231, 304–305; and urban parks, 385. *See also* pastoral

Picturesque America, 473n3

Pike, the, Long Beach, CA, 392–393

Pike Street, Seattle, WA, 338–339

Piltz, Stanley A., 309, 373

piracy, of images, 21, 67–68, 89, 207, 363, 397

Piranesi, Giovanni Battista, 111

Pitchford, Garnet Irving (G. I.): and automotive landscapes, 348–353; background of, 42–43; as caption writer, 239; designs by, 64–66, 140–141, 186–187, 352–353, 372–373; disagreements of, with Teich art department, 221, 251, 253, 353; family of, as photographic models, 392–393; financial success of, 50; instructions of, on color, 48, 65–66, 95, 121, 207, 257, 349, 351; instructions of, on photo collage, 353; instructions of, on representing

race, 193, 197; instructions of, on retouching, 48, 65–66, 141, 239, 255, 303, 349, 351, 373, 435; photo collages by, 64–66, 122–123, 186–187, 206–207, 265, 352–353; photographic procedures of, 43, 47, 64, 257; photographs by, 141, 186–187, 207, 257, 349, 351, 353, 392–393, 437; professional responsibilities of, 46–47; and Teich, Curt, 60; during World War II, 456

Pitchford, George, 239

Pitchford, Marilyn. *See* Maurer, Marilyn June

Pitchford, Robert (Bob), 392–393

Pitchford, Star, 50, 392–393

Pittsburgh, PA, 235, 237, 239, 266–267

Polasek, Albin, 371

possessive gaze: and African Americans, 175; and cityscape, 279, 283–284; and landscape, 5, 6, 107, 123, 127; and Mexican Americans, 183

Post, Emily, 195

Postcard Display (Evans), 464

postcards: early history of, 13–16; early printing methods of, 20–28; economics of, 15–16, 28; exhibitions of, 59–60; functions of, 1, 4–5; German printers of, 15–16, 21, 28–29; halftone-lithographic, 25–31; publishers of, defined, 472n27; real photo, 20–22. *See also* linen postcards

post-impressionism, 113

postmodernity, 381

Post Street, San Francisco, CA, 308–309, 435

Poughkeepsie, NY, 364–365

Prang, Louis, 24, 48

pre-linen postcards: Carlin Post Card Company and, 42; color palette of, 41, 74; Evans's admiration for, 290–291; as historical sources, 229, 431; linen postcards compared to, 97, 99, 117, 343, 371; referred to, 113; as sources of linen postcard images, 175, 177, 191, 213, 221, 251, 363, 423; Teich & Company and, 60, 109. *See also* halftone-lithographic postcards

Presler, Adolph, 261

Price, Uvedale, 73

Priestley, J. B., 288

printing: by CMYK process, 25, 40; of early postcards, 20–28; of linen postcards, 53, 55, 57; mechanization of, 31–32

progressive reform, 289–290

projection, when interpreting images, 286, 333, 342, 437, 446–447, 455

Prometheus, Rockefeller Center, New York, NY, 322–323, 325

Prospect Street, Fitchburg, MA, 29

Providence, RI, 288

publisher, defined for postcards, 472n27

Pueblo tribe, 125, 195

punctum, 78–80, 455

Punta Gorda, FL, 152–153

Qualla Park Shop, Cherokee, NC, 160–161
Queen's Court, Bryce Canyon National Park, UT, 130–131

racial representation, 85–86, 172–205
Radio City Building, Hollywood, CA, 348–349
Radio City Music Hall, New York, NY, 326–329, 377
railroad trains, 62–68, 194–195, 222–223, 236–237, 260–261, 264–265
Raleigh, NC, 290
Rand, Sally, 409
Raphael Tuck & Sons, 177
RCA Building, New York, NY, 322–323
realism: client desire for, 54; of halftone-lithographic postcards, 27–28, 290; photographic, 20–28; of postcard views, 1–2, 4–5, 8, 21–22; versus artifice, 91, 419
real photo postcards, 20–22, 199, 221, 237, 409, 435
recreation, 164–167, 206–207, 212–213, 324–325, 383–399, 460
Redwood Highway, CA, 98–99, 109, 450
reformers, progressive, 289–290
Reno, NV, 353
Republic Steel Corporation plant, Youngstown, OH, 234–235
residential scenes, 8, 29, 172–173, 176–177
resorts, 396–399
restaurants, 428–437
retirees, 164–167
retouching: of human faces, 208–209, 212–213, 226–227, 384–385, 390–391; of human faces, ignored, 164–165, 168–169, 186–187, 190–191, 264–265, 384–385; of interiors, 418–419, 430–431; process of, 51–53; of urban scenes, 290–291
Rialto Square Theater, Joliet, IL, 417
Riis, Jacob, 286
Rim of the World Highway, CA, 123
rivers: bridged, 242–243, 250–251, 304–305; dammed, 252–255; as energy source, 25–27, 253–254; scenic, 76, 106–107; underground, 110–111; urban, 116–117, 234–235, 242–243, 304–305
Roanoke, VA, 48
Roberts, Mike, 259
Rockefeller Center, New York, NY, 276, 281, 322–329, 331, 377, 443
Rockettes, 329
Rocky Mountain National Park, CO, 90–91, 105, 450, 475n3
Röder, C. G., 18
Roebling, John A., 243
Roebling Suspension Bridge, Cincinnati, OH, 242–243
Romer, G. W., 272–273
Rosa, Salvator, 73, 139

Route 66, 156–157, 247, 251
Ruby, Jay, 289
Runte, Alfred, 145
Russ Building, San Francisco, CA, 302–303
Ryder, Albert Pinkham, 321

Sacramento Pit, Bisbee, AZ, 220–221
Saguaro National Park, AZ. See Sahuaro National Monument
Sahuaro National Monument, AZ, 1–2
Salem, OR, 278
sales agents: as designers, 47–50, 62–66, 75, 427, 431; as photographers, 42, 43, 47, 64, 65; role of, 41–50, 60–63. See also Pitchford, Garnet Irving
Sales Pointers, 45
Salton Sea, CA, 120–121
San Antonio, TX, 162–163, 435
San Bernardino Mountains, CA, 50, 122–123
San Bernardino Valley, CA, 283
Sanborn, William P., 475n3
Sanborn Souvenir Company, 91
San Carlos Hotel, Pensacola, FL, 287
San Diego, CA, 125, 187
San Francisco, CA: Chinatown views of, 188–193; early photographs of, 278–279; as Golden Gate Bridge site, 243; and Longshaw Card Company, 135; views of, 302–303, 308–309, 311, 372–373, 435
San Francisco Album (Fardon), 279
San Francisco Ferry Terminal, San Francisco, CA, 303
San Francisco-Oakland Bay Bridge, San Francisco, CA, 302–303
Santa Catalina Island, CA, 10, 64
Santa Fe Railroad, 44, 62–68, 125, 195, 261, 264–265
Santa Fe Railroad station, Albuquerque, NM, 194–195
Santeetlah, Lake, NC, 104–105
Saturday Evening Post, 41
Scarbrough's department store, Austin, TX, 336–337
"scenics," 151
Schor, Naomi, 79, 447
Schuster, Joe, 311
Schuyler, Montgomery, 280
Scientific American, 15
sculpture, 322–323, 356–361, 370–371
searchlights, 302–303, 316–317, 357, 380–381, 396–397, 402–403
Sears Roebuck Building, Century of Progress International Exposition, Chicago, IL, 404–405
Seattle, WA, 338–339
Seminole tribe, 202–203, 205
series. See generic series
service stations, 158–159
Seymour, IN, 115

Sgt (postcard correspondent), 457–458
Sharpe, William Chapman, 282–285
Shedd Aquarium, Chicago, IL, 405
Sheeler, Charles, 237
Shelton Hotel, New York, NY, 283
shipping, 224–231
ships, 272–273
S. H. Kress & Company, 47
Shure, N., 371
Siegel, Jerry, 311
Signal Hill, Long Beach, CA, 218–219
Sinclair, Upton, 217
Sioux Falls, SD, 50–58
skylines, 280, 285, 294, 298–299, 301, 306–307
skyscrapers: as cultural icons, 280–285; as early postcard subject, 19; as linen postcard subject, 295, 298–299, 315–323, 330–333; represented at Century of Progress International Exposition, 406–407
slavery, 173
Smith, Kate, 71
Smith, Katherine Hamilton, 35
Sohmer, Theodore, 44
Somerset Hotel, Miami Beach, FL, 426–427
Song of Hiawatha, The (Longfellow), 201
South, the, 113, 172–181
Southern Pacific Railroad, 251
Southwest, the, 85, 119–135, 163
Spirit of Music, The (Polasek), 371
Springsteen, Bruce, 9
Statue of Liberty, New York, NY, 356–357
St. Charles, MI, 76–77
steel mills, 234–239
Steel Pier, Atlantic City, NJ, 398–399
stereograph cards, 74, 177, 179, 197, 279
stereopticon, 74, 109
Stevens Brook, Bridgton, ME, 116–117
Stewart, Susan, 446, 462, 464
stockyards, 216–217
Stoll, J. O., 317, 371
Stowe, Harriet Beecher, 177
St. Petersburg, FL, 164–167, 432–433, 462
St. Petersburg Shuffleboard Club, FL, 166–167, 462
streamlining: of architecture, 6, 266–267, 281, 312–313, 323, 412–413, 436–437; of buses, 266–267, 407; of commercial streets, 289–291, 339–341; of images, 66, 71, 102–103, 228–229, 266–267, 277, 434–435; as metaphor, 413; of railway interior, 264–265
street scenes: Chinese American, 188–193; commercial, 7, 21, 32–33, 308–313, 335–349, 450; Mexican American, 182–185; residential, 29
Stryker, Roy, 70–71
studium, 78–79
"stunners," 63, 79

subjects, of postcards. See specific subjects
sublime, the: Burke's definition of, 281; domesticated, 123; electrical, 281, 285, 300–301, 310–313, 316–317, 346–347, 352–353, 380–381; geometrical, 281; at Hoover Dam, 253, 257, 259; in landscape painting, 73, 85, 91; Luminism's avoidance of, 99; in postcard images, 90–91, 100–101, 214–215; technological, 205, 233, 238–239, 281, 320–321
sunsets: desert, 134–135, 140–141; rural, 76, 214–215; urban, 3, 242–243; over water, 94–95, 112–113, 272–273, 386–387
Super Chief train, 62–68, 261, 265
Superior, AZ, 340–341
Superman, 311
surrealism, 357
Swift & Company, 217

Taft, Lorado, 371
Tagg, John, 445–446
Tamiani Trail, FL, 203
Tate Gallery, London, UK, 59
Teague, Walter Dorwin, 159
technology: celebrated, 6, 68, 86, 258–259, 320–321; Native Americans juxtaposed with, 204–205; threat of, 259
Teich, Alfred, 18, 19
Teich, Anna Niether, 32
Teich, Christian, 16–17
Teich, Curt, & Company: branding of, 19, 34, 37, 113, 313; categories of postcards of, 151, 155; and Century of Progress International Exposition, 403, 405; clients, negotiations with, 54, 101, 221, 251, 421, 431 489n52; clients of, referred to, 93, 125, 131, 133, 207, 309, 317, 435, 429, 475n3; color chart of, 47–48, 49; comic cards of, 151, 196–197; competitors of, 67, 311, 425; dating of serial numbers of, 469n2; demise of, 55, 66–67, 133; economics of, 57–58; ethnicity represented by, 172–205; expansion of, 28–34; gendered images of, 206–209; gendered labor at, 51–52, 55; generic approach of, 289–290; generic series of, 76–77, 115, 175, 177, 179, 181, 219; Geographical Index of, 11, 474n6; immigrant employees of, 173; incorporated, 19; introduced, 2, 5; job files of, 8; and landscape photographers, 6; and Leighton, 28–29, 31, 32, 179; letterhead of, 61–62; linen postcards developed by, 36–41, 70; mechanization of printing by, 29–31; and Miami Beach hotels, 426–427; and a national imaginary, 35–37, 70–72, 79–80, 463; and offset lithography, 29–32; production process of, 50–58; production volume of, 151, 253, 465n4 (chap. 1); profiled by American Business, 42–43; and progressive reform, 290; race represented by, 172–205;

sales agents of, 41–50, 60–66, 75, 91; sales volume, by region, 113, 121; Teich, Max, as client of, 423; and Woolworth, 32–33, 435; during World War II, 456. *See also* Teich art department

Teich, Curt Otto: biography of, 5, 13, 16–20, 28–34, 60, 67; on halftone-lithography, 31; interviewed, 275; and linen postcards, 36–41; and lithography, 24; and a national imaginary, 36–37, 79–80, 463; and offset lithography, 31; and Pitchford, 47, 60; on popular subjects, 103, 143, 329, 363

Teich, Curt Otto, Jr., 51, 60, 67, 456

Teich, Elise, 16

Teich, Frederick, 32

Teich, Friedrich, 16, 18

Teich, Max, 16–17, 19, 423

Teich, Ralph D., 11, 44, 55, 58, 60, 67, 391

Teich art department: and Buettner, 28; clients' instructions to, 47, 109, 133; day and night paired views by, 396–397; exaggeration of images by, 156–157, 214–215; generic approaches by, 50, 66, 432–433; inspired by Century of Progress International Exposition, 370–371; interior decorating samples used by, 48, 286; legibility of images of, 96–97, 126–127, 238–239, 344–345, 398–399, 418–419; and Leighton contract, 29; location of, in plant, 32; misrepresentation by, 326–327; non-photo-based views by, 10, 312–313, 412–413, 426–427; Pitchford's complaints to, 221, 251, 253, 353; Pitchford's instructions to, on colorizing, 48, 65–66, 95, 121, 207, 257, 349, 351; Pitchford's instructions to, on photo collage, 353; Pitchford's instructions to, on representing race, 193, 197; Pitchford's instructions to, on retouching, 48, 65–66, 141, 239, 255, 303, 349, 351, 373, 435; reflections in water rendered by, 90–91, 110–111, 362–363; retouching, precision of, by, 138–139; retouching failure by, 215; retouching of artificial structures by, 248–249, 268–269, 364–365, 376–377; retouching of city views by, 185, 243, 273, 301, 341, 379; retouching of faces by, 165, 212–213, 226–227, 265, 384–385, 390–391; retouching of natural scenes by, 90–93; sales agents' instructions to (other than Pitchford), 205, 247, 331, 411, 431; streamlining of images by, 109, 229, 265, 267, 290–291, 341, 435; stylistic influence of, 159; work process of, 50–56. *See also* images: recycling of

Teich Postcard Archives, 11–12, 35, 456

Telephone Building, Bangor, ME, 332–333

terminals, transportation, 194–195, 204–205, 262–263, 266–271

Terminal Tower, Cleveland, OH, 304–305

Texas, 45, 219. *See also specific cities and places*

Texas Gulf Sulphur Company, 225

textile mills, 25–27, 116–117, 232–233

Thackeray, William, 62

theaters, 326–329, 378–381

Third Avenue, Seattle, WA, 338–339

"This Land Is Your Land" (Guthrie), 69–70, 71, 275

Thoreau, Henry David, 145

Tichnor Brothers: colorizing by, 55, 161; image of, pirated by Teich, 249; Los Angeles branch of, 381; as Metrocraft competitor, 225; piracy of Teich images by, 89, 207, 397; retouching by, 305; as Teich competitor, 5, 55, 67, 329

Tijuana, Mexico, 186–187

Times Square, New York, NY, 9, 310–313, 317, 353

Times Square/Broadway Composition (Evans), 353

Title Guarantee Building, Los Angeles, CA, 360–361

To Have and Have Not (film), 442

tourism: cost of, 265; on factory tours, 217, 233; at Grand Canyon National Park, 124–127; at Hoover Dam, 253, 259; images of, 126–127, 150, 196–197; at Long Beach, CA, oil field, 219; at New Orleans docks, 229; at Pan American Airways terminal, 271; postcards related to, 137–169; Seminoles and, 203. *See also* messages, postcard: about tourist sites

tourist attractions, 160–163, 194–195

tourist camps, 152–153

tourist courts, 154–157

tourists, 110–111, 122–123, 126–127, 150–151, 182–183, 194–197

trailer camping, 150–153

Tramor Cafeteria, St. Petersburg, FL, 432–433

travel: conditions of, 89, 123; postcards related to, 137–169. *See also* messages, postcard: about travel conditions

Tribune Building, Chicago, IL, 18–19

Trylon and Perisphere, New York World's Fair of 1939, New York, NY, 410–411

Tuck, Raphael, & Sons, 177

Tucson, AZ, 13, 125, 140–141, 221

Tulsa, OK, 420–421

tunnels, 248–249

Turner, J. M. W., 129, 280

Twenty-Nine Palms Oasis, CA, 132–133

Two Harbors, MN, 230–231

Uncle Tom's Cabin (Stowe), 177

Underhill, Irving, 321

Underwood & Underwood, 74

Union Pacific Railroad, 131, 263

Union Station, Omaha, NE, 262–263

unique versus generic: in messages on postcards, 454; in postcard images, 5, 77–80, 84, 288–291, 365

United States of America: Farm Security Admin-istration, 70–71; Federal Art Project, 276; Federal Writers' Project, 70, 71; U.S. Post Of-fice, 13, 14, 15; Works Progress Administra-tion, 70
universities, 368–369, 450
University of Texas tower, Austin, TX, 9
Untitled [Penny Arcade Portrait of Lauren Ba-call] (Cornell), 442–444
Urban, Joseph, 61
U.S. Capitol Building, Washington, DC, 362–363
U.S. Naval Training Center, Great Lakes, IL, 208–209
U.S. Post Office, 13, 14, 15
U.S. Steel Corporation, 235
utopia: and Chrysler Building image, 319; reflect-ed in postcard images, 4, 59; world's fairs as projections of, 277, 296, 403, 409

Vanderbilt, Paul, 78
Vanity Fair (Thackeray), 62
Verkamp's curio shop, Grand Canyon National Park, AZ, 125
Vine Street, Hollywood, CA, 348–349
volcanoes, 94–97, 100–101
voyeurism, 455, 461–462

Walden (Thoreau), 145
Walmer, J. P., 117
Walters, Ray, 151
Walter Scott Company, 31
Warren, OH, 235
Washington, DC, 103, 263, 362–363, 430–431, 476n8
Washington, George, 75, 76
Washington Post, 431
Watchtower, Desert View, Grand Canyon Nation-al Park, AZ, 124–127
watercolor inks, 37–38, 40–41
waterfalls, 102–103, 116–117, 410–411
Waterville, ME, 25–27
Watkins, Carleton E., 74
Weegee, 286, 319
Wenrich, John C., 411
Werther, Mark, 35, 63, 79
West, the, 113, 121, 288
Western Publishing & Novelty Company, 44, 63, 379, 389, 435
Weston, Edward, 79
White, John, 72
White City. *See* World's Columbian Exposition
White House, Washington, DC, 103, 363, 476n8
whiteness, 6, 208–209, 227. *See also* Anglo-Americans

Whitman, Walt, 70
Wildwood-by-the-Sea, NJ, 391
Willard, Stephen, 133
Williamsport, PA, 48–50
Willis, J. R., 125, 197
Winter, Ezra, 327
Wisconsin Dells, WI, 44, 108–109
Wisdom, Rockefeller Center, New York, NY, 322–323
Wiseman Bridge, Lewiston, ME, 232–233
Wizard of Oz, The (film), 62
Wolfe, Tom, 353
women, images of: African American, 178–179; as central figures, 122–123, 332–333; Chinese American, 189; in comics, 150–151; Mexican American, 182–185; Native American, 194–197, 200–201; white, 122–123, 156, 172–173, 206–207, 209
Woolworth, F. W., Company, 32–33, 47
Woolworth lunch counter, Los Angeles, CA, 434–435
Works Progress Administration, 70, 149, 153, 165, 243, 276
World's Columbian Exposition, Chicago, IL, 13–14, 16–17, 277, 296, 373
world's fairs, 6, 61, 296, 401–413. *See also specific fairs*
World War II: impact of, on FSA documentary photography, 70; impact of, on railroads, 261, 263; impact of, on Teich & Co., 456; and linen postcards, 3, 437; postcard images of, 208–209, 433; postcard messages concern-ing, 456–461; sales of postcards during, 50; war games preceding, 425
WPA. *See* Works Progress Administration
WPA guidebooks. *See* American Guide Series
Wrightsville Beach, NC, 207
Wrigley Company, 313
Wrigley sign, New York, NY, 312–313, 317
Wurts, Richard, 327
Wurts Brothers, 327, 329

Yellowstone National Park, WY, 24, 44, 73, 103, 142–147
Yosemite National Park, CA, 233, 450–451
Youngstown, OH, 234–235
Youngstown News Agency, 235
Youngstown Sheet & Tube Company, 235
Yucca Flat, NV, 259
Yuma, AZ, 48, 250–251

Zaid, Barry, 445, 446
Zenith-Interstate News Company, 43–44